Studies in Corpus Linguistics (SCL)

ISSN 1388-0373

SCL focuses on the use of corpora throughout language study, the development of a quantitative approach to linguistics, the design and use of new tools for processing language texts, and the theoretical implications of a data-rich discipline.

For an overview of all books published in this series, please see
benjamins.com/catalog/scl

General Editor

Ute Römer
Georgia State University

Founding Editor

Elena Tognini-Bonelli
The Tuscan Word Centre/University of Siena

Advisory Board

Laurence Anthony
Waseda University

Antti Arppe
University of Alberta

Michael Barlow
University of Auckland

Monika Bednarek
University of Sydney

Tony Berber Sardinha
Catholic University of São Paulo

Douglas Biber
Northern Arizona University

Marina Bondi
University of Modena and Reggio Emilia

Jonathan Culpeper
Lancaster University

Sylviane Granger
University of Louvain

Stefan Th. Gries
University of California, Santa Barbara

Susan Hunston
University of Birmingham

Michaela Mahlberg
University of Birmingham

Anna Mauranen
University of Helsinki

Andrea Sand
University of Trier

Benedikt Szmrecsanyi
Catholic University of Leuven

Elena Tognini-Bonelli
The Tuscan Word Centre/University of Siena

Yukio Tono
Tokyo University of Foreign Studies

Martin Warren
The Hong Kong Polytechnic University

Stefanie Wulff
University of Florida

Volume 111

Exploring Language and Society with Big Data
Parliamentary discourse across time and space
Edited by Minna Korhonen, Haidee Kotze and Jukka Tyrkkö

Exploring Language and Society with Big Data

Exploring Language and Society with Big Data

Parliamentary discourse across time and space

Edited by

Minna Korhonen

The Australian National University / Macquarie University

Haidee Kotze

Utrecht University / North-West University

Jukka Tyrkkö

Linnaeus University

John Benjamins Publishing Company

Amsterdam / Philadelphia

The paper used in this publication meets the minimum requirements of the American National Standard for Information Sciences – Permanence of Paper for Printed Library Materials, ANSI z39.48-1984.

Cover design: Françoise Berserik
Cover illustration from original painting *Random Order*
by Lorenzo Pezzatini, Florence, 1996.

DOI 10.1075/scl.111

Cataloging-in-Publication Data available from Library of Congress:
LCCN 2023028212 (PRINT) / 2023028213 (E-BOOK)

ISBN 978 90 272 1406 5 (HB)
ISBN 978 90 272 4951 7 (E-BOOK)

© 2023 – John Benjamins B.V.
No part of this book may be reproduced in any form, by print, photoprint, microfilm, or any other means, without written permission from the publisher.

John Benjamins Publishing Company · https://benjamins.com

Table of contents

Perspectives on parliamentary discourse: From corpus linguistics
to cultural analytics   **1**
Jukka Tyrkkö & Haidee Kotze

CHAPTER 1. Speech in the British Hansard   **17**
Marc Alexander

CHAPTER 2. Salient differences between Australian oral parliamentary
discourse and its official written records: A comparison of 'close'
and 'distant' analysis methods   **54**
Haidee Kotze, Minna Korhonen, Adam Smith & Bertus van Rooy

CHAPTER 3. Hansard at Huddersfield: Streamlined corpus methods
and interactive visualisations to pursue research aims
beyond corpus linguistics   **89**
*Lesley Jeffries, Fransina Stradling, Alex von Lünen
& Hugo Sanjurjo González*

CHAPTER 4. Empire, migration and race in the British parliament
(1803–2005)   **118**
Christian Mair

CHAPTER 5. Leaving the EU out of the ingroup: A diachronic analysis
of the use of *we* and *us* in British parliamentary debates (1973–2015)   **142**
Jenni Räikkönen

CHAPTER 6. From *masters* and *servants* to *employers* and *employees*:
Exploring democratisation with big data   **166**
Turo Vartiainen & Minna Palander-Collin

CHAPTER 7. From criminal lunacy to mental disorder: The changing lexis
of mental health in the British parliament   **194**
Minna Nevala & Jukka Tyrkkö

CHAPTER 8. "The job requires considerable expertise": Tracking EXPERTS
and EXPERT KNOWLEDGE in the British parliamentary record (1800–2005)   **227**
Turo Hiltunen

CHAPTER 9. Processing and prescriptivism as constraints on language variation and change: Relative clauses in British and Australian English parliamentary debates   250
Sofie Labat, Haidee Kotze & Benedikt Szmrecsanyi

CHAPTER 10. Language variation in parliamentary speech in Suriname   277
Robert Borges & Margot van den Berg

CHAPTER 11. Morphosyntactic and pragmatic variation in conditional constructions in English and Spanish parliamentary discourse   308
Cristina Lastres-López

CHAPTER 12. Colloquialisation, compression and democratisation in British parliamentary debates   336
Gerold Schneider & Maud Reveilhac

Index   373

Perspectives on parliamentary discourse
From corpus linguistics to cultural analytics

Jukka Tyrkkö[1] & Haidee Kotze[2,3]
[1] Linnaeus University | [2] Utrecht University | [3] North-West University

1. Introduction

Over the last few decades, several important developments have taken place in the way linguistics as a discipline positions itself in relation to both language and society. The scope of linguistic enquiry has extended far beyond the sentence level, come to embrace non-standard varieties and multilingual language use, and started paying increasing attention to language use in specific contexts. Linguists have been increasingly interested in exploring register and genre variation, as well as specialised languages, such as those of medicine, sports, and politics. Many of these developments are reflections of the importance of inclusiveness and representation in society, as well as of the significant contribution that linguistic perspectives can bring to understanding the world around us.

The chapters in this volume, taken together, provide a collective case study that illustrates both of these developments and the synergies between them. They derive principally from a workshop entitled "Big data and the study of language and culture: Parliamentary discourse across time and space", organised by the editors at the ICAME 40 conference on 1 June 2019, in Neuchâtel, Switzerland. As the title suggests, the unifying theme of the workshop was how large corpora of parliamentary discourse could be used to study both the specialised language of parliamentary speech and the societies that the parliaments in question represent and govern.

As the legislative bodies of democratic nations, parliaments play a fundamental role in society, and consequently the linguistic practices observed in parliamentary discourse are of importance to everyone. In more recent times, parliamentary language practices have become available for observation almost in real time via televised sessions and recordings thereof, but in most cases parliamentary records go back decades, if not centuries, in the form of transcripts and both official and unofficial reports. These extensive archives thus provide access to discourses that are of great interest from linguistic, legal, political, and societal perspectives.

https://doi.org/10.1075/scl.111.intro
© 2023 John Benjamins Publishing Company

However, there are many challenges when we go from having access to potential data to actually making well-argued use of it, and thus the other important strand of the workshop concerned the various issues and challenges involved in compiling and using parliamentary archives as linguistic corpora.

Over many decades now, corpus linguistics has become one of the fundamental research methodologies in empirical linguistics, and as the number and size of available corpora have increased, we have witnessed an evolution that is in many ways analogous to the developments alluded to earlier. Corpora have diversified from so-called generic corpora into sometimes extremely specialised datasets, offering recognition and attention to even very specific registers, topics and genres, while at the same time, the increasing size of corpora has broadened representativeness, moving from samples of language to full archival datasets. Parliamentary archives turned corpora are a prime example of datasets that make possible both rigorous linguistic analyses of various kinds, as well as register-specific studies of discourse and society. The interest in parliamentary corpora as a resource for research on language, history, politics, society, and more is evident in the growing range of corpora available. Within the CLARIN ERIC infrastructure, there are currently 31 parliamentary corpora, predominantly from European parliaments.[1] These corpora are highly diverse in their scope and construction. Some are single-language corpora, while others are multilingual or parallel aligned corpora. Some corpora are constructed as multilingual comparable corpora, such as the ParlaMint corpus.[2] Some cover long periods of time and include transcripts of all debates, while others cover much shorter periods and may focus on only select topics or only include transcriptions of specific speakers' turns.

When corpus linguistics was first envisioned and later operationalised as a methodology for studying language in use, plenty of emphasis was afforded to the principles of compiling linguistic corpora. The consensus view tended to be that a corpus should be compiled based on extra-linguistic criteria, consist of authentic language only, and be stratified according to a clearly laid-out structure (Sinclair 2004). Representativeness and balance were to be observed when compiling a corpus (see Biber 1993; Egbert, Biber & Gray 2022). In the early decades, corpora tended to be manually keyed-in from texts selected by the compilers, and both the manual labour involved and the limited power of contemporary computers kept the sizes of corpora down to magnitudes that still allowed the compiler and the user to be familiar with all texts in the corpus, if they felt it necessary. However, as computational power increased, both the methods of compiling corpora

---

1. See <https://www.clarin.eu/resource-families/parliamentary-corpora> for corpora available within the CLARIN ERIC infrastructure, as well as a list of other parliamentary corpora.

2. See <https://www.clarin.eu/parlamint>

and methods used for querying them underwent fundamental changes. Not only were textual and audiovisual data increasingly produced and stored in digital format (giving rise to terms like *born-digital data*), but data that had originally been recorded in print, as photographs, or on audio and video tapes were digitised and converted into formats that are easy to store and read using computers. Thus, from the late 1990s onward, it became increasingly feasible to compile corpora of a size that is far beyond what any single person could hope to read in a lifetime, let alone study in intimate detail (e.g. Renouf 2019). Not only is this a challenge in terms of limiting the amount of close verification of corpus results that can be done, but the very design principles of corpora started changing, with the sheer amount of data forcing corpus compilers to pay less attention to many of the traditional sampling and design principles (e.g. Davies 2019).

As the amount of searchable data increased exponentially, researchers' relationships with primary data changed (see Cukier & Mayer-Schoenberg 2013; Schöch 2013). The creation of massive digital collections of heritage data such as Google Books, HathiTrust Digital Libraries, Project Gutenberg, and the Internet Archive has given rise to entirely new paradigms of cultural and historical research (e.g. Fridlund, Oiva & Paju 2020). The most well-known initiative in the field of *cultural analytics* is probably the Culturomics Project (Michel et al. 2011), in which the then already massive Google Books dataset was exploited for the data-driven study of cultural trends. The central claim of culturomics is that sufficiently large and encompassing collections of books (and other published texts) can be studied as a reasonably reliable window into the culture that produced them. Culturally important topics, individuals, organisations, places, and other entities of interest will show up in the data, and the prevailing views toward them as well as their associations with other concepts and entities can likewise be queried in ways that could never be done before (see e.g. Dechesne & Bandt-Law 2019; Tyrkkö 2020). At the same time, scholars have raised many questions concerning both the quality and reliability of massive datasets that cannot be closely inspected and for which metadata is either limited or altogether unavailable, and the methodologies used for searching and analysing such data (e.g. Koplenig 2017; Pechenick, Danforth & Dodds 2015; Winters 2017).

For corpus linguists, increasingly large collections of texts offer entirely new opportunities for studying language variation and change – but also pose many challenges that smaller purpose-built corpora are less susceptible to (e.g. Laitinen & Säily 2018). An important difference between many of the cultural-analytics approaches and corpus linguistics is that while the former rely almost exclusively on digital humanities methods often described as *distant reading* (Moretti 2005; see also Oberhelman 2015), corpus linguists generally emphasise the importance of mixed-methods research designs, where quantitative findings are verified through selective *close reading* and, quite often, at least semi-manual pruning and classification of data. A compromise thus needs to be struck between the undisputed benefits of massive datasets and the limitations that such magnitudes of data impose on the researcher's ability to engage closely with the data, and to pursue the insights that may emerge from an interplay between quantitative and qualitative analysis, and distant and close reading. Furthermore, while megacorpora of the staggering size now increasingly commonly available can provide evidence of the existence and use of even the rarest words or constructions, the often limited and not infrequently erroneous metadata that very large text archives suffer from can render the usefulness of such resources surprisingly narrow. For purposes of linguistic research at least, the ideal megacorpus would not only be massive in size, but also accurately digitised or transcribed, appended with carefully curated and rich metadata, and linguistically annotated. From this perspective, archives that have been systematically collected by recognised entities such as libraries, research institutes, and parliaments are likely to be superior to the results of automatic crawls of online data or collections based on crowd-sourcing and the work of untrained volunteers.

2.   Parliamentary language and corpus linguistics

Parliamentary language has been a topic of great interest for scholars from a wide variety of disciplines. In practical terms, we define parliamentary language as the language used during sessions of a national parliament, thus excluding the language that members of that parliament may use, for example, in interviews, informal discussions outside of sessions, at political events outside the parliament, or in their private lives. In short, our interest here is in how language is used in parliamentary debates and speeches, or in parliamentary records, which may or may not always be transcriptions of spoken debates and speeches.

As such, parliamentary language can be thought of as a specialised register with a variety of unusual and unique constraints and characteristics. Parliaments are typically formal spaces with rules of conduct and traditions that may date back far into history, both affecting the language and discourse in ways we do not observe in everyday spoken language. Prepared speeches may or may not be allowed, and speakers may be asked to follow specific phraseologies and formulations, to address one another in specific terms, and to avoid using specific expressions. Within the parliament itself, many participants in the discourse, such as the Speaker or the Prime Minister, have specific roles that are associated with prescribed linguistic practices and speech acts.

Over the centuries, the demographics of national parliaments have changed in many ways, which from the linguistic perspective means diachronic changes in the sociolinguistic characteristics of the speakers. In most countries, members of parliament (MPs) today are likely to represent a much broader sample of the demographic than was the situation even a few decades ago. The number of female parliamentarians has increased, the MPs come from all walks of life, and changes in regional representation within the country may have taken place over time. Likewise, new political parties may have emerged and others disappeared, the political views of parties are likely to have undergone changes, and the parties' relative proportional representation in parliament is potentially different after every election cycle. The party or parties that form the government also have a different discursive role from those in the opposition (see also van Rooy & Kotze 2022). Some legislative bodies are divided into two houses or chambers, which may be considerably different in terms of both the sociolinguistic distribution of their respective members, and the discourses that each house or chamber hears.

From the corpus-linguistic perspective, the inclusion or exclusion of the aforementioned sociolinguistic background variables will naturally depend on the available metadata, and the amount of work that is possible to put into further curation of the primary data. Depending on the research question, some of the variables may be of more value than others. In corpus-aided discourse-analytical studies, party affiliations or gender may be of primary importance, while studies of morphosyntactic variation may benefit much more from data on the individual members' regional backgrounds or social classes, however the concept might be defined in a diachronic corpus.

Parliamentary discourses are naturally a reflection of the legislative work carried out in parliament, which means that the topics of discussion have their own diachronic patterns both within a year and across decades and centuries. Parliaments discuss topics that are of importance in contemporary society, and those discussions are usually tightly constrained to specific debates that take place within a limited time period. It can thus be crucial for interpreting linguistic or discourse-analytical observations to know when in the year, or at what point during an election cycle, something was said. In the corpus metadata, individual speeches may or may not be linked to the specific debates to which they belong.

Given the central role that parliamentary debates have in politics and society, there is little surprise in the fact that many of the linguistic studies carried out on parliamentary data around the world have focused on topics such as gender, representation, otherness, discursive strategies, and specific terms and concepts (e.g. Alexander & Struan 2017; Alkenäs 2022; Archer 2017; Berrocal 2017; Garcés García & Filardo Llama 2011; Hidalgo Tenorio 2011; Ilie 2013, 2018; Sunderland 2020; Tyrkkö 2016, 2019). As a specific example, several recent studies have used parliamentary data from both the UK and the EU to study parliamentary discourse leading up to and following Brexit, showing how changing attitudes and differences between political parties can be identified using corpus-assisted methods (e.g. Räikkönen 2020; Wenzl 2019). And, while the special nature of parliamentary data lends itself exceptionally well to discourse-analytical studies, parliamentary data can naturally also be used in the study of language without adopting a political perspective. For example, several recent studies have investigated the processes of colloqualisation in parliamentary language (e.g. Hiltunen, Räikkönen & Tyrkkö 2020; Kotze & van Rooy 2020; Kruger & Smith 2018; Kruger, van Rooy & Smith 2019).

Parliamentary data are also increasingly used to trace processes of linguistic variation and change in particularly postcolonial Englishes (see e.g. Kotze & van Rooy 2020; Kruger, van Rooy & Smith 2019; Smith et al. 2021; Smith & Korhonen 2022; van Rooy & Kotze 2022). In such contexts, parliaments become a microcosm of the competition between the linguistic usage and norms of the colonial centre and the newly evolving norms developing in the (post-)colonial context. This accounts for the recent interest in English parliamentary language beyond the British parliament: studying how language usage varies and changes in parliaments that have their origins in the transplantation of not only a language, but also an entire institutional tradition, provides unique insights into the evolution of new varieties of English and differences in parliamentary discourse in different parts of the world. While the focus has been on English, there is significant scope to extend this also to other pluricentric languages to explore the evolving tensions between a distant 'central' linguistic norm and various local usage norms, over time. Parliamentary language is exceptionally well suited to this type of research, since it is a domain where issues of normativity are particularly salient; the legislative domain is "an especially sensitive barometer of a language's status" (Evans 2014: 480). Moreover, since parliamentary transcripts are edited representations of speech, the editorial practices involved in its production provide a unique window on the processes by means of which a shift from the external, colonial norm to a new local norm takes place.

In this view, the fact that parliamentary records are usually transcribed and edited representations of speeches and debates becomes an *opportunity* to capture changing linguistic norms – and not only a "hazard" (Mollin 2007) to linguistic research. Nevertheless, it is undeniable that the intermediate step of transcription naturally introduces a variety of potential interferences between the words originally spoken and those that we find in the records, and these issues are potentially magnified if the transcription comes from someone other than the linguist studying the text (see e.g. Cribb & Rochford 2018; Mollin 2007; Slembrouck 1992). Several chapters in this volume address the relation between the spoken reality and the written record of parliamentary data in detail, exploring the potential pitfalls and boons.

The focus of the present collection of studies is on parliamentary records as corpora and the various ways in which such data may be studied using corpus-linguistic methods. Whilst the studies in this volume focus primarily on parliamentary language in the English-speaking world, the methods and approaches discussed by the authors should find applications in the study of linguistic practices in parliamentary settings regardless of the languages involved. Notably, a number of recent studies have also explored multilingualism in various parliaments around the world (e.g. Dzahene-Quarshie 2011; Selzer 2010; Stephens & Monk 2012; Szabó 2021), and multilingualism (and language mediation practices) in the European parliament is also well researched (see e.g. Kajzer-Wietrzny et al. 2022). Matters of multilingualism and language mediation are obviously also particularly relevant to parliaments in (post-)colonial settings, where the languages spoken in parliament (and the way in which these are captured and reflected in parliamentary records) change significantly over time. In these contexts, the informal and formalised use of practices like codeswitching, translation, and interpreting has evolved in complex ways, and in these settings, parliaments can therefore also be seen as microcosms of language contact, variation, and change shaped by the ever-changing intersections between language, politics and power. This dimension of parliamentary language has hardly been researched (see e.g. recent work by van Rooy & Kotze 2022 on South Africa).

3. The studies in this volume

The first two chapters in the volume focus on speech representation in parliamentary records, and analyse how the practices of record-keeping, reporting and editing have influenced the language of parliamentary records over time. These questions are pertinent to all researchers who use parliamentary records as sources of data, irrespective of whether their interest is directed more to matters of linguistic interest, or to social questions. Chapter 1, by Marc Alexander, sketches a detailed textual and linguistic history of the British Hansard from 1803 to the present, and discusses the overall development of language in the British Hansard. As the Principal Investigator of the Samuels project, which compiled the British Hansard Corpus at the University of Glasgow, Alexander has an extensive and in-depth understanding of the history and working practices of the Hansard and how these practices have shaped the linguistic material in the Hansard. He shows how commercial, political, editorial and practical factors have combined to influence speech representation in the Hansard, and – importantly – reflects on the implications for research from linguistics specifically, and the social sciences more generally, that relies on data from parliamentary records.

In Chapter 2, Haidee Kotze, Minna Korhonen, Adam Smith and Bertus van Rooy turn their attention to the matter of editorial practices in more detail. As already outlined in Section 2, cautions about the "hazards" (Mollin 2007) of parliamentary records as a source of linguistic data abound. However, existing research on the differences between oral parliamentary discourse and official records tends to be mostly synchronic, and relies on manual comparison of small samples of spoken and written data. In this chapter, the authors use a parallel corpus of transcribed audio recordings from the Australian parliament, and the corresponding Australian records from the period of 1946 to 2015, and explore the differences between oral and written parliamentary discourse over time, by comparing 'close' and 'distant' analytical approaches. While their 'close-reading' analysis reiterates findings from previous studies (such as the reduction of spoken-language features and informality, and greater conservatism), their 'distant-reading' analysis, adapting the multidimensional method of Biber (1988) also shows that, viewed functionally, the overall register shift from the spoken discourse to the written record is less pronounced than might be anticipated (cautioning against overstating differences based on the analysis of individual features). Moreover, these differences also decrease over time. Apart from tracing the effects of editorial intervention on the Australian Hansard record over time (and raising questions about the nature of such intervention in the production of parliamentary records in other parts of the world), this chapter also places front and centre the matter of method, by asking: What are the relative advantages and disadvantages of distant- and close-reading methods in the analysis of parliamentary data? How can these two methods be leveraged to complement one another?

Chapter 3, by Lesley Jeffries, Fransina Stradling, Alex von Lünen and Hugo Sanjurjo-González, counterbalances the two opening chapters and their focus on the constraints and caveats associated with parliamentary records and data, by focusing on the rich potential of such data, if accompanied by streamlined corpus tools and visualisations. It introduces the Hansard at Huddersfield online corpus tool and discusses the important task of making large societally important datasets like the Hansard available to the general public as well as to linguists and other researchers. The authors discuss the design of the user interface and the importance of interactive visualisations that make it easy to interpret trends in large data and then drill in deeper, when necessary.

While the first three chapters focus on corpora as resources, the next five chapters turn the attention to what corpora can tell us about society. In Chapter 4, Christian Mair uses the British Hansard Corpus to study how discourses around the topics of the British Empire, migration and race change over the 200-year time span of British parliamentary discourse. The study, situated at the interface of historical linguistics, colonial history and cultural studies illustrates, methodologically, the interplay between quantitative and qualitative, and distant-reading and close-reading methods already alluded to above (and also exemplified in Chapter 2). While the British Empire is a notable topic from the mid-nineteenth century, it becomes increasingly less important after World War II. Migration is an important topic in the nineteenth and twentieth centuries, but in the nineteenth century emigration is most topical, while in the twentieth century immigration becomes increasingly prominent. Race is invoked in two different types of discourses too: an older classificatory discourse, and a more recent discourse of identity politics.

Jenni Räikkönen, in Chapter 5, also focuses on British parliamentary debates, but in a narrower timeframe of 1973–2015 – the decades leading up to Brexit. She asks the question how diachronic changes in the use of the personal pronouns *us* and *we* reflect changing attitudes of the British parliament toward the EU. Like Mair, she uses a mixed-methods approach that makes use of both frequency trends over time and close reading of discursively revealing debates, investigating when, how and why the EU is included, and when excluded from the ingroup in British parliamentary debates in the House of Commons.

Chapter 6, by Turo Vartiainen and Minna Palander-Collin, places the concept of democratisation in the spotlight, focusing on the sociocultural dimension of this process. It uses the British Hansard corpus, and a strategic selection of concepts used to describe the relationship between employer and employee, to investigate how the gradual democratisation of society is reflected in the shifting terminology used to describe this relationship over time. This chapter is a clear example of a study that attempts to demonstrate how societal democratisation can be studied using linguistic big data by examining the most frequent terms used for different kinds of workers and employers, with particular attention to the terms *master* and *servant*. Vartiainen and Palander-Collin show that social democratisation is clearly evident in the shifting usage of such terms: employees are increasingly often discussed separately from their employers, reflecting a shift away from a construal of the relationship as one of interdependency, to one defined by the rights and duties of the two parties viewed independently. While their study relies on a similar combination of quantitative and qualitative methods as the previous two chapters, they highlight another important methodological point: the fact that in quantitative studies, not only regularities but also exceptions and outliers can be especially revealing of the impact of particular social events.

In Chapter 7, Minna Nevala and Jukka Tyrkkö analyse the changing landscape of mental health in Britain by tracking lexical changes in mental health terminology over two centuries. Using the *Historical Thesaurus of English* as a starting point for the lexical repertoire used to refer to mentally ill people, mental institutions and mental health in general, they show how mental health terminology as used in the British parliamentary record 1800–2020 is associated with key legislative moments in history and how a major terminological shift takes place around World War II.

Chapter 8, by Turo Hiltunen, is the last of this set of five chapters focusing on the use of parliamentary records for tracing processes of sociocultural change. The study is framed by contemporary concerns about how the authority of science and expertise is presented, represented, and challenged in public forums. Hiltunen tracks how experts and expert knowledge are referred to in the British Hansard 1800–2005, and explores the ways in which different types of expertise are invoked in debates, linking these diachronic changes to historical events and changes in the cultural and intellectual landscape over time. As in the other chapters in this section, a combination of quantification and detailed qualitative analysis is used. Hiltunen concludes that while overall trends and detailed insights can be gained from this combination of methods, the considerable variation evident in the usage of individual terms in different discourse contexts cautions against oversimplified inferences of cultural explanations for patterns observed in corpus data.

The last four chapters in the volume share an interest in the use of parliamentary data to understand processes of linguistic variation and change, and thus shift the focus from parliamentary discourse as a reflection of society, to parliamentary discourse as *language use*. In Chapter 9, Sofie Labat, Haidee Kotze and Benedikt Szmrecsanyi showcase how parliamentary records in two varieties of English (British and Australian), spanning approximately a century, can be used to investigate the interplay between processing-related and prescriptivism-related constraints on variation and change in English. They focus on the choice between relative markers *which* and *that* in restrictive relative clauses in subject position – a choice that is conditioned by internal factors related to cognitive processing constraints, but which has also been the target of prescriptive advice. This chapter builds on prior work demonstrating that the relativiser *that* is on the rise in varieties of English (at the cost of *which*), and shows how this ongoing change proceeds in significantly different ways in the two varieties of English – with the British parliamentary records more progressive than the Australian in shifting to *that*. They also show how the adaptation of editorial guidelines for the Australian Hansard, based on broader prescriptive advice, plays a role in the change, together with other factors like a more verbatim approach to reporting. Ultimately, however, their findings suggest that factors other than prescription play the more influential role in the change – or, that prescriptivism acts in consort with other factors.

Chapter 10 is the first study in the volume to focus on a language other than English, and also the only study based on a corpus derived directly from spoken data (rather than using official written parliamentary records). Robert Borges and Margot van den Berg demonstrate how automatic speech-to-text software can be used to construct a corpus of spoken-language data: in this way, they compile a corpus reflecting nearly 37 hours of debates in the Surinamese parliament, *De Nationale Assemblée* 'The National Assembly'. They use this dataset to explore variation between Surinamese and Netherlandic Dutch, focusing on constructions with the particle *er* 'there', word order, and non-standard imperfective constructions. Like Chapter 9, this chapter focuses on linguistic variation in different varieties of the same language, suggesting intriguing possibilities for extending research on the development of local norms in postcolonial varieties of English to other pluricentric languages such as Dutch, Spanish and French. In these contexts, colonialism has played a significant role in transplanting the metropolitan variety (or varieties) to new contexts, in which new varieties (and languages) have developed shaped by these unique sociolinguistic contexts.

Chapter 11, by Cristina Lastres-López, is the second of the two studies in the volume that makes use of parliamentary data from outside the Anglophone world. Focusing on morphosyntactic and pragmatic variation in conditional constructions, the author carries out a contrastive analysis that draws on parliamentary data from the British and Spanish parliaments. Her analysis demonstrates not only how the pragmatic features of parliamentary discourse may vary across languages, but also highlights the importance of considering the specialised nature of parliamentary discourse. She shows how, in addition to their prototypical use in expressing cause–consequence relations, conditionals also assume interpersonal and textual functions in parliamentary discourse, particularly in Spanish.

In Chapter 12, Gerold Schneider and Maud Reveilhac return to the topic of democratisation introduced in Chapter 6, but this time it is considered from a linguistic perspective, in relation to two trends that have been identified as characteristic of language change in English: colloquialisation and compression. Their study aims to draw a link between social democratisation processes, and the ways in which these are reflected in linguistic patterning. With a sampler of the Hansard archive spanning 1803–2005 as their dataset, they consider the relationship between changes in linguistic patterns, and the content of debates, over time. Their approach relies on computational, distant-reading methods only, and suggests how such methods can be used to build a bridge between studies using parliamentary data to investigate social change, and those using it as a data source to understand linguistic variation and change. As such, it is a fitting conclusion to the volume.

4. A look into the future

One volume of studies cannot begin to exhaust a topic as rich and varied as parliamentary discourse, and we hope that this collection will make a positive contribution in attracting more researchers in linguistics and other disciplines to making use of existing parliamentary corpora – and to develop new corpora suited to answering the many research questions that still remain unanswered (and even unasked). The studies in this volume demonstrate how rich and fascinating parliamentary language is as an object of study; the breadth of the studies included ranges from a focus on explicitly linguistic phenomena to topics that contribute to our understanding of language and society. In each case, the value of corpus-linguistic methods rings loud and clear, while simultaneously serving as a reminder of the flexibility and variability of modern corpus-linguistic methodology.

The individual studies collected in this volume make use of both quantitative and qualitative methods, in many cases combining the two. Likewise the studies illustrate many different approaches to dealing with the big data that a parliamentary corpus is, ranging from using the entire corpus to utilising samples that allow for closer examination. This, too, is a fundamental part of the 'big data' perspective that we set off to explore in the workshop in 2019. Some research questions lend themselves to distant-reading methods while others are better addressed by using corpus tools as part of a more comprehensive, multi-phase analytical workflow. We were pleased to see the wide range of different approaches, software, and methods of data visualisation used by the authors, and we hope that the reader will find something in this volume that will provide solutions or inspire new research ideas.

A thread running through all the chapters, and highlighted specifically in a considerable number, is the importance of gaining an understanding of the primary data in terms of the parliament itself as a historical body, the parliamentary record as an archive, and the corpus as the immediate object of study. The importance of reliable metadata and trustworthy transcription practices (or an adequate account of the transcription practices used and the implications of these) is a recurrent point too. The linguist's wish list includes more than merely the text, and irrespective of whether their research interest is more weighted to language, or to society, the irreducible interwovenness of language, its social context, and the people who use it, needs to be given due consideration. In other words, 'big data' is always a means to an end – the end of understanding the complexity of human communication.

In the near future, more and more heritage collections and digital archives will become available for linguistic study around the world. As demonstrated by the studies here, such data will find many eager users among linguists (and researchers from many other disciplines besides), who recognise the rich opportunities afforded by big linguistic datasets.

5. Postscript

Much of the work for this volume was accomplished during the unprecedented COVID-19 pandemic, which negatively affected all of our lives in a variety of ways, regardless of where we live and work. We, the editors, are grateful to all the contributors for their hard work and for persevering through a process that took far longer than we had anticipated. We hope you are as pleased with the final product as we are.

We likewise extend our gratitude to all the external referees for their insightful feedback on all the chapters, to the Series Editor for accepting the volume into the series and for all the help along the way, and to all staff members at John Benjamins who were involved at various stages of the project.

This volume is dedicated to the memory of Jukka's parents, both of whom passed away during the time we were working on it.

References

Alexander, Marc & Struan, Andrew. 2017. Digital Hansard: Politics and the uncivil. In Proceedings of Digital Humanities 2017, Montreal QC, Canada, 8–11 August 2017, 378–380.

Alkenäs, Pauline. 2022. "Men in Grey Suits": Androcentric Language in the House of Commons. A Corpus-Assisted Feminist Critical Discourse Analysis. Master's thesis, Linnaeus University. <https://www.diva-portal.org/smash/record.jsf?pid=diva2%3A1674094&dswid=5890> (28 November 2022).

Archer, Dawn. 2017. Mapping Hansard impression management strategies through time and space. *Studia Neophilologica* 89(1): 5–20.

Berrocal, Martina. 2017. "Victim playing" as a form of verbal aggression in the Czech parliament. *Journal of Language Aggression and Conflict* 5(1): 84–110.

Biber, Douglas. 1988. *Variation across Speech and Writing.* Cambridge: CUP.

Biber, Douglas. 1993. Representativeness in corpus design. *Literary and Linguistic Computing* 8(4): 243–257.

Cribb, V. Michael & Rochford, Shivani. 2018. The transcription and representation of spoken political discourse in the UK House of Commons. *International Journal of English Linguistics* 8(2): 1–14.

Cukier, Kenneth Neil & Mayer-Schoenberg, Victor. 2013. The rise of big data: How it's changing the way we think about the world. *Foreign Affairs* 92(3): 28–40.

Davies, Mark. 2019. Corpus-based studies of lexical and semantic variation: The importance of both corpus size and corpus design. In *From Data to Evidence in English Language Research*, Carla Suhr, Terttu Nevalainen & Irma Taavitsainen (eds), 66–87. Leiden: Brill.

Dechesne, Mark & Bandt-Law, Bryn. 2019. Terror in time: Extending culturomics to address basic terror management mechanisms. *Cognition and Emotion* 33(3): 492–511.

Dzahene-Quarshie, Josephine. 2011. Language policy, language choice and language use in the Tanzanian Parliament. *Legon Journal of the Humanities* 22: 27–69.

Egbert, Jesse, Biber, Douglas & Gray, Bethany. 2022. *Designing and Evaluating Language Corpora: A Practical Framework for Corpus Representativeness*. Cambridge: CUP.

Evans, Stephen. 2014. The decline and fall of English in Hong Kong's Legislative Council. *Journal of Multilingual and Multicultural Development* 35(5): 479–496.

Fridlund, Mats, Oiva, Mila & Paju, Petri (eds). 2020. *Digital Histories: Emergent Approaches within the New Digital History*. Helsinki: Helsinki University Press.

Garcés García, Pilar & Filardo Llama, Laura. 2011. Do lords think in male? Gender and language in parliamentary speech. *Pragmalingüística* 12: 45–54.

Hidalgo Tenorio, Encarnacion. 2011. Politics and language: The representation of some 'Others' in the Spanish parliament. In *Lesbian Realities/Lesbian Fictions in Contemporary Spain*, Jacky Collins & Nancy Vosburg (eds), 119–149. Lewisburg PA: Bucknell University Press.

Hiltunen, Turo, Räikkönen, Jenni & Tyrkkö, Jukka. 2020. Investigating colloquialization in the British parliamentary record in the late 19th and early 20th century. *Language Sciences* 79: 101270.

Ilie, Cornelia. 2013. Gendering confrontational rhetoric: Discursive disorder in the British and Swedish parliaments. *Democratization* 20(3): 501–521.

Ilie, Cornelia. 2018. "Behave yourself, woman!" Patterns of gender discrimination and sexist stereotyping in parliamentary interaction. *Journal of Language and Politics* 17(5): 594–616.

Kajzer-Wietrzny, Marta, Ferraresi, Adriano, Ivaska, Ilmari & Bernardini, Silvia (eds). 2022. *Mediated Discourse at the European Parliament: Empirical Investigations*. Berlin: Language Science Press.

Koplenig, Alexander. 2017. The impact of lacking metadata for the measurement of cultural and linguistic change using the Google Ngram data sets – Reconstructing the composition of the German corpus in time of WWII. *Digital Scholarship in the Humanities* 32(1): 169–188.

Kotze, Haidee & van Rooy, Bertus. 2020. Democratisation in the South African parliamentary Hansard? A study of change in modal auxiliaries. *Language Sciences* 79: 101264.

Kruger, Haidee & Smith, Adam. 2018. Colloquialization versus densification in Australian English: A multidimensional analysis of the Australian Diachronic Hansard Corpus (ADHC). *Australian Journal of Linguistics* 38(3): 293–328.

Kruger, Haidee, van Rooy, Bertus & Smith, Adam. 2019. Register change in the British and Australian Hansard (1901–2015). *Journal of English Linguistics* 47(3): 183–220.

Laitinen, Mikko & Säily, Tanja. 2018. Google Books: A shortcut to studying language variability? In *Patterns of Change in 18th-century English: A Sociolinguistic Approach* [Advances in Historical Sociolinguistics 8], Terttu Nevalainen, Minna Palander-Collin & Tanja Säily (eds), 223–233. Amsterdam: John Benjamins.

Michel, Jean-Baptiste, Shen, Yuan Kui, Aiden, Aviva P., Veres, Adrian, Gray, Matthew K. The Google Books Team, Pickett, Joseph P., Hoiberg, Dale, Clancy, Dan, Norvig, Peter, Orwant, Jon, Pinker, Steven, Nowak, Martin A. & Lieberman Aiden, Erez. 2011. Quantitative analysis of culture using millions of digitized books. *Science* 331(6014): 176–182.

Mollin, Sandra. 2007. The Hansard hazard: Gauging the accuracy of British parliamentary transcripts. *Corpora* 2(2): 187–210.

Moretti, Franco. 2005. *Graphs, Maps, Trees: Abstract Models for a Literary History*. London: Verso.

Oberhelman, David D. 2015. Distant reading, computational stylistics, and corpus linguistics: The critical theory of Digital Humanities for literature subject librarians. In *Digital Humanities in the Library: Challenges and Opportunities for Subject Specialists*, Arianne Hartsell-Gundy, Laura Braunstein, Liorah Golomb (eds), 53–66. Chicago IL: Association of College, Research Libraries. <https://shareok.org/handle/11244/33193> (28 November 2022).

Pechenick, Eitan Adam, Danforth, Christopher M. & Dodds, Peter Sheridan. 2015. Characterizing the Google Books corpus: Strong limits to inferences of socio-cultural and linguistic evolution. *PloS ONE* 10(10): e0137041.

Räikkönen, Jenni. 2020. Metaphors separating the United Kingdom from the EU in British parliamentary debates from 2000 to 2016. In *Metaphor in Political Conflict: Populism and Discourse*, Ruth Breeze & Carmen Llamas (eds), 27–54. Pamplona: EUNSA.

Renouf, Antoinette. 2019. Big data: Opportunities and challenges for English corpus linguistics. In *From Data to Evidence in English Language Research*, Carla Suhr, Terttu Nevalainen & Irma Taavitsainen (eds), 27–65. Leiden: Brill.

Schöch, Christof. 2013. Big? Smart? Clean? Messy? Data in the Humanities. *Journal of Digital Humanities* 2(3): 2–13.

Selzer, Marsanne. 2010. South African Sign Language used in Parliament: Is There a Need for Standardisation? Master's thesis, Stellenbosch University. <https://core.ac.uk/download /pdf/37323874.pdf> (28 November 2022).

Sinclair, John. 2004. Corpus and text: Basic principles. In *Developing Linguistic Corpora: A Guide to Good Practice*, Martin Wynne (ed.). <https://users.ox.ac.uk/~martinw/dlc /chapter1.htm> (28 November 2022).

Slembrouck, Stef. 1992. The parliamentary Hansard 'verbatim' report: The written construction of spoken discourse. *Language and Literature: International Journal of Stylistics* 1: 101–119.

Smith, Adam, Korhonen, Minna, Kotze, Haidee & van Rooy, Bertus. 2021. Modal and semi-midal verbs of obligation in the Australian, New Zealand and British Hansards: 1901–2015. In *Exploring the Ecologies of World Englishes: Language, Society and Culture*, Pam Peters & Kate Burridge (eds), 301–323. Edinburgh: Edinburgh University Press.

Smith, Adam & Korhonen, Minna. 2022. Parliamentary Hansard records and epicentral influence in Australia, New Zealand and Papua New Guinea. *World Englishes* 41: 475–490.

Stephens, Mamari & Monk, Phoebe. 2012. The language of buying biscuits? Māori as a civic language in the modern New Zealand parliament. *Australian Indigenous Law Review* 16(2): 70–80.

Sunderland, Jane. 2020. Gender, language and prejudice: Implicit sexism in the discourse of Boris Johnson. *Open Linguistics* 6: 323–333.

Szabó, Péter K. 2021. Babel Debates: An Ethnographic Language Policy Study of EU Multilingualism in the European Parliament. PhD thesis, Tilburg University. <https://research.tilburguniversity.edu/en/publications/babel-debates-an-ethnographic-language-policy-study-of-eu-multili> (28 November 2022).

Tyrkkö, Jukka. 2016. Looking for rhetorical thresholds: Pronoun frequencies in political speeches. In *The Pragmatics and Stylistics of Identity Construction and Characterisation*, Minna Nevala, Gabrielle Mazzon, Carla Suhr & Ursula Lutzky (eds). Helsinki: Varieng. <http://www.helsinki.fi/varieng/series/volumes/17/tyrkko/> (28 November 2022).

Tyrkkö, Jukka. 2019. Kinship references in the British Parliament, 1800–2005. In *Reference and Identity in Public Discourses* [Pragmatics & Beyond New Series 306], Ursula Lutzky & Minna Nevala (eds), 97–124. Amsterdam: John Benjamins.

Tyrkkö, Jukka. 2020. The war years: Distant reading British parliamentary debates. In *Doing Digital Humanities: Concepts, Approaches, Cases*, Joacim Hansson & Jonas Svensson (eds), 169–199. Växjö: Linnaeus University Press.

van Rooy, Bertus & Kotze, Haidee. 2022. Contrast, contact, convergence? Afrikaans and English modal auxiliaries in South African parliamentary discourse (1925–1985). *Contrastive Pragmatics* 3(2): 159–193.

Wenzl, Nora. 2019. "This is about the kind of Britain we are": National identities as constructed in parliamentary debates about EU membership. In *Discourses of Brexit*, Veronika Koller, Susanne Kopf & Marlene Miglbauer (eds), 32–48. London: Routledge.

Winters, Jane. 2017. Tackling complexity in humanities big data: From parliamentary proceedings to the archived web. In *Big and Rich Data in English Corpus Linguistics: Methods and Explorations*, Turo Hiltunen, Joe McVeigh & Tanja Säily (eds). Helsinki: Varieng. <http://www.helsinki.fi/varieng/series/volumes/19/winters/> (18 November 2022).

CHAPTER 1

Speech in the British Hansard

Marc Alexander
University of Glasgow

This chapter provides a detailed textual and linguistic history of Hansard, the records of debates of the British parliament from 1803 to the present, on which the Hansard Corpus is based. It analyses how parliamentary speech is recorded and presented across that period, examining the changes in direct and indirect speech types arising from commercial factors, pressure from parliament, editorial practice, and the availability and quality of source material. The chapter concludes with a breakdown, for each period of Hansard's history, of what the data for that period does and does not represent.

Keywords: speech reporting, history of Hansard, direct and indirect speech, editorial practice

1. Introduction

[The student of politics] must be on [their] guard against the old words, for the words persist when the reality which lay behind them has changed.

(Bevan 1952: 13)

The richness of the records of proceedings and debates in the UK parliament is profound – historically, politically and linguistically. However, the existence of these records under a single name – Hansard – may give a false sense of consistency. The span of Hansard is instead united only by its persistent discussion of topics of political importance, and only two features of the language of Hansard are consistent: its reports of debates are not verbatim (and always have been clearly signalled as such), and they are written in formal English. Other than its two-column layout, no other consistent features are evident.

The richness of content of Hansard is profoundly exciting to linguists, and is why some time ago colleagues and I created the Hansard Corpus (originally spanning 1803 to 2003, its composition date, then expanded to 2005, and now to the present day). The corpus is an excellent example of humanities 'big data' – but

https://doi.org/10.1075/scl.111.01ale
© 2023 John Benjamins Publishing Company

again the single term 'big data' is not used consistently by researchers. At 1.6 billion words (consisting of 7.6 million 'contributions' such as speeches or interruptions) in its 2005 edition, the corpus is fairly big when considered as raw text; but big data in the humanities is, as Hughes (forthcoming, 2023) has pointed out, a function of *mass*, to which not only size but also density contributes. Complex, dense data has sufficient mass to require 'big data' analytic techniques irrespective of its raw size, and Hansard has not only a large volume of data, and a large ongoing velocity of new material for input, but also a huge complexity of style, content and internal textual variation contained within its virtual and physical covers. In addition to this complexity, the tagged Hansard Corpus contains several layers of semantic annotation, to allow for meaning-related searches of considerable delicacy, in addition to the usual grammatical, multi-word, and lemma annotations. Such density – highly complex data with multiple layers of annotation – requires big data techniques just as much as those resources which are 'big' solely in terms of their size.

Corpus linguists can be simultaneously enticed and frustrated by Hansard. The scope of records it represents – collecting words, thoughts and topics of both great and middling social and political import across two centuries – is attractive for many types of study, and its size, which would take well over a decade of incessant silent reading to get through, makes it intractable for manual methods of analysis and ideal for corpus linguistics. However, its long history and internal complexity mean that it is challenging to understand precisely what it records, and this can be dispiriting in terms of making sure that an analyst is certain what Hansard is telling them.

To use Hansard well, we therefore must understand better how Hansard reports the speech of parliamentarians. This chapter therefore addresses for the first time the linguistic history of speech in Hansard, and by extension the Hansard Corpus. It describes the language of the corpus and the evolution of Hansard across time in order to build a comprehensive picture of Hansard's representation of political speech in English over the last 200 years. Such work allows us to understand what the resource can and cannot tell us about language in use over that period. While below I focus on linguistic points, the conclusions are equally significant for any investigations into the corpus in the Social Sciences and Humanities.

The next two sections review the state of parliamentary reporting before 1803 and introduce Hansard and the Hansard Corpus, while Section 4 discusses the issue of what 'verbatim' means in the context of records of parliamentary speech. Sections 5 to 7 then proceed chronologically through the evolution of Hansard's representation of speech, using Leech and Short's (2007 [1981]) model of speech representation (described in Section 4). The chapter concludes, in Section 8, with a breakdown, for each period of Hansard's history, of what the textual data for that period can and cannot tell researchers.

2. "Tolerably well": Reporting before Hansard

> The history of parliamentary debates is similar to the description given of the history of a newspaper. The first day it is read with eagerness, the next day it is thrown away; after the lapse of some years it is worth its weight in gold.
>
> (Proposed wording by T. P. O'Connor for Parliament 1888a: xi)

Parliamentary reporting in Great Britain and the UK has a complex and tense history. For a significant period of time, parliament considered the reporting of its debates to be a breach of its privilege, "partly because what was said in Parliament was felt to be unfit for public consumption, and partly to protect Members from the wrath of the monarch" (Vice & Farrell 2017: 3). This manifested itself in prohibitions such as a House of Commons resolution in 1722 ordering "That no Printer or Publisher of any printed News Papers do presume to insert in any such Papers any Debates or any other Proceedings of this House or any Committee thereof" (MacDonagh n.d.: 109). Newspapers and monthly magazines continued to test this resolve, with publishers being prosecuted and imprisoned for publishing debates while experimenting with various camouflage (most notably the *London Magazine* and the *Gentleman's Magazine*'s habit of reporting parliamentary debates as if they were fiction from Ancient Rome or in the invented country of Magna Lilliputia, with personal names extremely thinly disguised). Regardless, such records were based either on "memory and hearsay" (as Thomas 1959: ix describes them) or were entirely invented. To underscore that last point, Arthur Murphy's 1792 *Essay* on Samuel Johnson, a sometime parliamentary reporter better known for his lexicography, describes a dinner where a speaker praises a speech by Pitt the Elder, to which Johnson declares he wrote that speech himself in his garret:

> I never had been in the gallery of the House of Commons but once. Cave [publisher of the *Gentleman's Magazine*] had interest with the door-keepers. He, and the persons employed under him, gained admittance: they brought away the subject of discussion, the names of the speakers, the side they took, and the order in which they rose, together with notes of the arguments advanced in the course of the debate. The whole was afterwards communicated to me, and I composed the speeches in the form which they now have in the Parliamentary debates.
>
> (Murphy 1792: 44–45)

Instead of the assembled guests being frustrated by the linguistic or literal inaccuracy of the report of the speech, Murphy (1794: 45) reports they "bestowed lavish encomiums on Johnson", including on his impartiality. Johnson replied that this was not quite true, rather, "I saved appearances tolerably well; but I took care that the WHIG DOGS should not have the best of it" (ibid.).

This is the environment which gave birth to Hansard. The legal prohibition on reporting any proceedings at all, let alone accurate transcripts, meant that accuracy of language was not a concern; generally following the argument in the report and being able to state what speaker spoke at what point was a sufficient advance. The history of the changes in attitudes to reporting is vividly described in Vice and Farrell (2017). In brief: a rapid breakdown in enforcement of parliamentary privilege saw an increasing volume of reports being printed in the time leading up to 1803. This development was partly due to a blind eye being turned to the reports by members of parliament (MPs) who found them advantageous (even when not written by Samuel Johnson), and also due to the continuing ascendance of newspapers, which reported on parliamentary debates in increasing numbers. Although more reports were published, note-taking in the public gallery was still forbidden and so reports were still "pieced together from conversation, gossip, recollections of listeners, comments from Members, reports in rival newspapers, and the memory of reporters in the gallery" (McBath 1970: 28). Some reporters were said to have a prodigious memory, but even then few would argue for linguistic accuracy on the part of these reports other than in key phrases and topic words.

3.   Thomas Curson Hansard, Hansard, and the Hansard Corpus

The volumes of debates that became Hansard began as *Cobbett's Parliamentary Debates* in 1804, although for two years before that date debates were reported as a supplement to *Cobbett's Annual Political Register*. William Cobbett (1763–1835) had a zeal for providing the public with political information, and the new *Debates* were described by him in the *Register* as "the *only* compilation at all likely to be regarded as an authentic record of the Legislative Proceedings of the present time" (Cobbett 1804: 863). The word 'compilation' here is essential: Cobbett employed no reporters but relied on a range of newspaper reports supplemented by various information, including corrections and speech texts sent by MPs who wanted to correct ephemeral newspaper accounts in the firmer record of the handsomely bound volumes of *Debates*. Cobbett soon sold *Parliamentary Debates* to its publisher, Thomas Curson (T.C.) Hansard, whose name and that of his son and successor (also Thomas Curson Hansard) became the commonly used metonymic short title for the publication. In 1892, at the end of the family's involvement with the publication – father and son between them editing the debates for some 86 years – the name 'Hansard' was removed from the title of the *Debates* where it had been since 1829, but in 1943 the Speaker of the House of Commons instructed that the word 'Hansard' would once again be printed on the title page (HC Deb, 4 August 1943, c2303).

Hansard's volumes are arranged into series, with each series containing numbered volumes. Inside each volume, reference is made not to pages but instead to columns (as *Cobbett's Annual Political Register* also reckoned its entries). While 'Hansard' is the overarching term almost universally used, the First to Fourth Series are formally titled some variation on the words 'Parliamentary Debates', and the parliament-produced Fifth and Sixth Series are often referred to as the *Official Report* (split into the Houses of Commons and Lords, each report run by its own department), although those series also have *Parliamentary Debates* on their title page.

The First Series runs from first publication in 1804 to February 1820.[1] The Second Series, at the time known as the 'new series', begun following the accession of a new king, George IV, in January 1820. It spans April 1820 to July 1830, and the Third Series, October 1830 to August 1891, started with the accession to the throne of William IV in June 1830. The Third Series did not cease in 1837 with the beginning of Victoria's reign but instead its end was due not to a change of monarch but to a change of publisher: with Thomas Curson Hansard senior having died in 1833 and Thomas junior retiring in 1888 (later dying in 1891), the business was at that point sold.

From this point until 1899, the work of producing the *Parliamentary Debates* would go through five different owners in eleven years – the business was subsidised by parliament during this period to varying extents, but it was still near-impossible to run at a profit. The sixth owner during this period enjoyed a stretch of relative stability lasting nine further years until the end of the Fourth Series. Increasing dissatisfaction with the subsidised commercial reports built in parliament over a long period, culminating with the establishment of the in-house *Official Report*, which inaugurated the Fifth Series in 1909 (with the House of Commons beginning a Sixth Series in 1981 after the thousandth volume in its Fifth Series; the separately produced Lords Hansard instead continues with the Fifth Series).

---

1. The first volume from 1804 covered 22 November 1803 to 29 March 1804, and so contained material from debates in 1803. The year 1803 is therefore used as the 'start' date of the contents of Hansard, while its publication dates begin in 1804.

No comprehensive survey of Hansard publication yet exists, but the key facts about each series are summarised in Table 1.1, and the size of each year's contributions in words in the 1803–2005 corpus is shown in Figure 1.1.

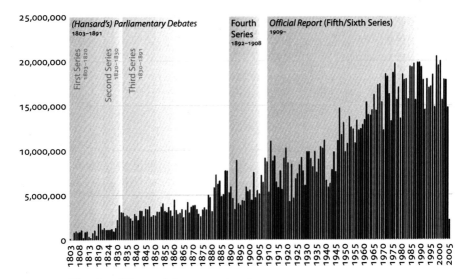

Figure 1.1 The size of Hansard, by year and series

The transition between the Fourth and Fifth Series – a private business pre-1909 and two departments of the houses of parliament thereafter – is the key separation of the text into two major phases. More fine-grained divisions can be distinguished by a careful examination of the publishing history of the debates and their linguistic characteristics, and the following sections undertake this. Note that as the distinction between the first three series relates simply to the regnal years of the parliaments concerned, in later figures I have combined them for simplicity.

A near-full set of all series was digitised in the mid-2000s (with a few minor omissions, some of which are now corrected online). The scanning and optical character recognition (OCR) of the more than three million pages of Hansard then available was funded by parliament itself, and this dataset was made available through a website which was an open-access public beta using free and open-source software (including a public discussion group and issues log), in what was an unusual move both for the time and for parliament. This availability led to a few experimental corpora being created at the University of Glasgow, following the presence of samples of Hansard material in other corpora such as the Lancaster-Oslo-Bergen (LOB) corpus. Funds from the UK Jisc resulted in the 2011 *Parliamentary Discourse* project to create a tagged corpus of the full digitised 'Historic Hansard' (1803–2005; data beyond 2005 was available, but we set the end

Speech in the British Hansard   23

Table 1.1 The series of Hansard, with publishers, personnel, and titles

Series	Title	Starting volume	End volume	Notes
First Series	*Cobbett's Parliamentary Debates*	Vol. 1 (November 1803)	Vol. 22 (March 1812)	Edited by William Cobbett, published by T.C. Hansard (senior). Note that the most commonly available copies from this period are the 1812 reprint series as *The Parliamentary Debates* under T.C. Hansard (senior).
	The Parliamentary Debates	Vol. 23 (May 1812)	Vol. 41 (February 1820)	Edited and published by T.C. Hansard (senior).
Second Series	*The Parliamentary Debates*	Vol. 1 (April 1820)	Vol. 20 (February 1829)	Edited and published by T.C. Hansard (senior).
	Hansard's Parliamentary Debates	Vol. 21 (March 1829)	Vol. 25 (July 1830)	Edited and published by T.C. Hansard (senior).
Third Series	*Hansard's Parliamentary Debates*	Vol. 1 (October 1830)	Vol. 356 (August 1891)	Edited by T.C. Hansard senior until his death in 1833 (vol. 21), then T.C. Hansard junior (no distinction made on title page) until 1888, then editor unspecified. Published by the Hansards, then from 1845 "Printed and published for Mr Hansard by G Woodfall and Son" until 1850, then printing undertaken by Cornelius Buck (later Cornelius Buck and Son) "at the office for Hansard's Parliamentary Debates" from 1850 to 1888, then 1889 onwards, "The Hansard Publishing Union" ("printers, publishers, and proprietors of 'Hansard's Parliamentary Debates' under contract with H.M. Government").
Fourth Series	*The Parliamentary Debates, Authorised Edition*	Vol. 1 (February 1892)	Vol. 199 (December 1908)	Produced by varying firms: Vols. 1–7 (until August 1892) Reuter's; Vols. 8–29 (until August 1894) Eyre and Spottiswoode; Vols. 30–52 (until August 1897) Waterlow and Sons Ltd; Vols. 53–70 (until May 1899) Economic Printing and Publishing Company/F. Moir Bussy; Vols. 71–199 (until December 1908) George Walpole/Wyman and Sons Limited.

Table 1.1 *(continued)*

Series	Title	Starting volume	End volume	Notes
Fifth Series	*Parliamentary Debates (Official Report)*	House of Commons: Vol. 1 (Jan 1909)	House of Commons: Vol. 1,000 (March 1981)	Produced by the Hansard reporters of both Houses. Printers: H. M. Stationery Office.
		House of Lords: Vol. 1 (Jan 1909)	House of Lords: (Ongoing)	
Sixth Series	*Parliamentary Debates (Official Report)*	House of Commons: Vol. 1 (March 1981)	House of Commons: (Ongoing)	Produced by the Hansard reporters of the House of Commons. Note that the House of Lords continues to the present day with the Fifth Series.

date at the UK general election in 2005 to give a clear end date to the corpus). The many gigabytes of text collected were processed to produce one XML file per speech contribution. The metadata were cleaned and made suitable for corpus use, and then the text was tagged twice: once by the UCREL team at Lancaster (led by Paul Rayson), with CLAWS grammatical annotation (see Leech, Garside & Bryant 1994) and USAS semantic annotation (Rayson et al. 2004), and once by the GATE NLP team at Sheffield (Cunningham et al. 2013). The Jisc funding was used to create an annotated offline corpus, although it was also loaded into Glasgow's experimental ENROLLER high-performance computing platform (Anderson 2013). The troubles of distributing the corpus were substantial (primarily involving asking people to post external hard drives to Glasgow, where data would be copied over and posted back).

When planning the SAMUELS project (2014–2015), funded under a specialised 'big data' call, the Hansard Corpus was an ideal large test case ready to use for that project's semantic annotation system, and consequently SAMUELS put the semantically tagged Hansard Corpus online for a wider user base (as Alexander & Davies 2015). Each word in the corpus files is therefore tagged across six dimensions (lemma, CLAWS part of speech tag, USAS semantic tag, a multiword-expression marker, and two levels of SAMUELS semantic tags, each with up to three tags; see Piao et al. 2017 for more on SAMUELS tagging). At Huddersfield, a daughter project to SAMUELS to update the time span of the corpus and make it much friendlier for non-academic users has also been recently completed (see Jeffries et al., this volume), as well as other projects among members of the SAMUELS consortium and other contributors to the corpus.[2]

In addition to the Hansard Corpus as I describe it here (used either offline with the tagged files or online via a range of websites), there are also other corpora of Hansard. These have increased in recent years due to the wide availability of the original files alongside modern tools to obtain large amounts of online text and prepare it for corpus use. While there is therefore a large volume of rich research which involves the creation of Hansard corpora designed for particular purposes, I am not aware of another Hansard corpus intended for general or broad re-use. The range of available versions of Hansard as corpora demonstrates its wide applicability for a range of research questions; this means that a deeper understanding of what Hansard contains, and how each stage of its development represents parliamentary speech, is essential to use its data well. The following sections provide an overview of these key questions for the time span of 1803 to the present.

4. "Fidelity is the first and indispensable requisite"

For researchers using these reports, a key aspect of linguistic interest is the extent to which Hansard at various points provides a verbatim transcript of speech. Historical linguists are now used to asking the question which Culpeper and Kytö (2010: 3) frame as "why are written texts representing spoken face-to-face interaction as they are?"; sources from the history of English always approximate speech to various degrees, and Hansard is no different. Many users of the resource, however, are not historical linguists, and so may not be accustomed to having to trace the relationship of the text to the speech it tries to represent. Beyond this, the issue of how 'verbatim' Hansard is – that is, how directly its text maps to the spoken acts in the Chamber – can be more complex than it first appears. This section discusses this issue in more detail, and introduces the Leech and Short (2007 [1981]) model of speech representation used in the following sections.

Hansard, at heart, is a written account, in the written mode, created as a written text, intended to be read as a written text, but ultimately based on speech. This means the text exists at a distance from the speech it records, as Hansard exists

---

2. See, for example, Alexander et al. (2015), Alexander & Struan (2013, 2022), Archer (2017), Coole, Rayson & Mariani (2020), Piao et al. (2017) and Wattam et al. (2014). Colleagues who worked alongside me on the Hansard Corpus include Jean Anderson, Brian Aitken, Dawn Archer, Alistair Baron, Fraser Dallachy, Mark Davies, Jane Demmen, Lesley Jeffries, Christian Kay, Bethan Malory, Scott Piao, Paul Rayson, Andrew Struan, Brian Walker and Stephen Wattam.

primarily as a legal record and a statement of the content of debates for posterity. In that context, it is clear it could never be 'verbatim' – any beginning student of linguistics knows how wholly unreadable linguistic transcripts are if one is interested just in their sense – and beyond this, the term 'verbatim' is a flawed one in this context. While the term can be literally glossed as 'word for word', it is more generally used to mean something like 'representing what was actually said'. This can encompass a broad cline of meanings, such as:

- a segmented phonetic spectrograph, which is perhaps the most 'accurate' non-spoken representation of speech and the least intervened-with by a transcriber, although it will still involve intervention for ambiguous segments;
- a phonemic transcript where it is acceptable to edit fine phonetic detail, such as reducing allophones to a phoneme, or making choices of phonemic theory and application;
- a linguistic transcript for various purposes – and where, depending on those purposes, it is acceptable to edit out features of low interest, such as hesitation phenomena or phonemic detail, but generally not to alter (for example) syntactic structure;
- a 'readable' transcript, where it is necessary to edit out features which hinder readability, given the different processing demands of speech and text);
- a 'publisher's-standard' transcript, where it is acceptable not only to make a transcript highly readable but also to conform it to explicit and implicit rules of consistency and house style;
- and even more nebulous interpretations of 'verbatim' beyond this, depending on the use case underlying the work.

In the case of Hansard across time, beyond a 'publisher's-standard' transcript there is what we might call a transcript 'for the ages'. Here intervention for readability and consistency is undertaken, but due to the nature of the text as a record of fact there has to be some limited intervention beyond reporting what was said in order to render clear and uncontroversial some instances of what in the full context of speech was understood but not necessarily articulated. This last is the fluid space within which Hansard operates.

Terms such as 'verbatim' only highlight the scale of intervention which lies behind the purpose of a transcript, and in the practice of linguistics are often useless. Linguists interested in the act of speech naturally want transcripts to map as closely as possible to the spoken act, but unless we are the ones paying for them we cannot reasonably expect any given transcript to conform to whatever point of the cline above we would personally prefer. Hansard is entirely accurate as a record of Hansard, and is not entirely accurate as a record of the linguistic acts performed in the houses of parliament. A preferable term, from the perspective of the report, would be 'faithful': is Hansard faithful to the words spoken, given how the spoken act is tightly bound with the context of the speaker and the nature of the institution?

This issue was brought up by John Campbell, a parliamentary reporter in the early nineteenth century who later became Lord High Chancellor (and so is one of the few people who both frequently reported on speeches and then had his own reported on). When reflecting on his time as a reporter he wrote that:

> ... there probably never was a parliamentary debater in whose language there was not some inaccuracy, and who did not fall into occasional repetitions. These are hardly perceived in the rapid stream of extemporaneous eloquence, and are corrected and remedied by the voice, the eye, the action of him to whom we listen; but blazoned on a printed page which we are deliberately to peruse, they would offend and perplex us. [...] Fidelity is the first and indispensable requisite, but this does not demand an exposure of inaccuracies and repetitions.
>
> (Campbell 1881: 106–107)

This is a highly lucid expression of a key linguistic point: Hansard's fidelity, across its long history, does not relate to the linguistic reproduction of syntactic constructions or hesitation phenomena, but to a 'faithful' rendering of what ideally would have taken place were humans able to clearly and consistently speak in coherent prose. Therefore, to use Hansard effectively we must know from its history and text what Hansard consists of, rather than arbitrarily define a moving target of 'accuracy'.

There are two simultaneous phenomena which must be taken into account to understand the language of Hansard and the Hansard Corpus across its two centuries: firstly, the changing relationship of the report's fidelity to the language of its source speech, and secondly, the formal and informal language practices which surround the report across time, set by its various publishers and editors. In short, who was publishing what language, for whom, and with what constraints? In what follows, these two factors are discussed with regard to the three primary linguistic 'phases' of Hansard production they engender.

Throughout the following sections, terms from the Leech and Short (2007 [1981]: 256ff) and the later Semino and Short (2004) stylistic model of speech representation are used. Here, a cline of 'interference' in a speech report is distinguished, based on quotation phenomena, syntactic dependence, pronoun type, tense, deictics, and the presence of reporting verbs. This relies on the presence of a narrator, which is different from a reporter in Hansard terms: a narrator has a distinct voice separate from the author, while a parliamentary reporter is closer to an author, narratologically speaking. Table 1.2 illustrates these different types as they apply to Hansard (with some modifications to what is presented in Semino and

Table 1.2 Types of speech reporting

Type	Characteristics	Example
NRSA Narrative Report of Speech Acts	Narrator in maximal control of report, no claim to quotation, speech described 'at a distance' rather than through any aspect of what was said, third-person pronouns.	Johnson looked at his friends and accepted their compliments on his impartiality.
IS Indirect Speech	Narrator in some control of report but content based on the speech act, no claim to quotation as the narrator uses their own words to represent that content, third-person pronouns.	Johnson looked at his friends and told them he had tried to be impartial and succeeded fairly well.
FIS Free Indirect Speech	Narrator in some control of report, narrator's voice merged partly with the speaker's, no speech attributions, third-person pronouns.	Johnson looked around at his friends. He had certainly saved appearances tolerably well!
DS Direct Speech	Narrator only has partial control of report outside quoted sections, speech attributions (such as quotation marks) often present, third person outside quotes and first person inside quotes.	Johnson looked at his friends. "I saved appearances tolerably well," he said, modestly.
FDS Free Direct Speech	Narrator has no apparent control over speech (or is not distinctly present), intermediary reporting phenomena like quotation marks and reporting verbs removed.	I saved appearances tolerably well.

Short 2004: 10), using examples based on the Samuel Johnson anecdote reported above.

In Hansard's case, a 'pure' and wholly faithful transcription without the presence of an intermediary would be FDS, with a neutral intervention to mark speaker name but without any narratorial 'presence'. Reports which summarise but without any claim to represent the actual words of a speaker all exist in a space occupied by NRSA, IS and FIS. Here a reporter acts as narrator, summarising the words of a speaker in the third person either as NRSA, where the content is unimportant or heavily summarised, or as IS, where the speech is covered in more detail, and where relevant including flashes of FIS, for example to represent notable turns of phrase. Illustrations of each of these are given in the subsequent sections.

We now turn to the major 'phases' of Hansard and what the language used in each can be said to represent.

5. "Bound for the bona fides": The Hansards and the *Parliamentary Debates*, 1803–1888

As already discussed, early Hansard is a 'compilation' of already-published reports supplemented by speech notes and other information supplied by Members. At this time, its principal benefit – as well as being a well-printed volume dedicated to producing reports – was its lack of speed. *The Times*, on its foundation as the *Daily Universal Register*, advertised itself as providing faster reports of the previous night's parliamentary business than any other newspaper; Hansard, therefore, could not compete on speed but could on detail.

The First Series of 1803–1820 was particularly small by comparison to later volumes, as Figure 1.1 shows. The junior T.C. Hansard himself referred to this feature in a note on "Origin and Progress" appended to an advertisement found at the end of some volumes in the 1840s. He says, for the First Series:

> ... owing to the rarity of long Debates and in the then imperfect state of Parliamentary reporting, the proceedings of each Session are reduced into a very small compass [...] being, for the most part, either the careful report of some Speech, (very frequently taken by a friendly Member in his place), or the draft itself of the Speech, or a report supplied by the Member or corrected by him; the materials derived from the gallery of the House are few, but very important, as being a digest of discussions on points of form and privilege by politically interested observers. (T.C. Hansard 1843: 2)

T.C. Hansard here does not refer to the material taken from other publications, perhaps natural in an advertisement, and is clear that he does not employ his own reporters in the gallery. As such, the two options he presents are a "careful report" (NRSA), a speech draft (FDS), or a report corrected by the member (which as a merger of NRSA and DS seems to occupy the FIS space, produced by the merger of narrator and speaker).

Examination of the early volumes themselves supports this analysis. One detailed example will illustrate the varieties present, taken arbitrarily from the House of Commons on 2 June 1819:[3]

> *Sir G. Warrender* rose to move the Navy Estimates. Upon this subject the hon. Baronet said he should think it unnecessary, if not presumptuous on his part, to make any speech, or to enter into any detail, as the question had already been so amply discussed, while all the details connected with it were so perspicuously stated, in the report of the finance committee; therefore, he felt that it rather became him to wait for any observations which might be made on the other side of the House, and to which he would endeavour to submit a satisfactory reply.
> *Mr. Calcraft* expressed his surprise at the course pursued by the hon. Baronet, particularly in referring to, and wholly relying upon, the statements of the finance committee. Was it, from the observation of the hon. Baronet, to be taken for granted that he adopted the recommendation of the finance committee?
> (HC Deb, 2 June 1819, c823–824)

The opening sentence is a clean NRSA/IS statement, although it is impossible to tell if it is one or the other without being certain if Warrender said "I stand to move the Navy Estimates" or something else. Erring on the side of caution, it is best considered NRSA. The remainder of Warrender's speech and the beginning of Calcraft's is likewise NRSA/IS, the third-person pronouns and reporting verbs keeping it at that end of the scale developed by Leech, Semino and Short (see Table 1.2). The final sentence of the excerpt of Calcraft's contribution here (the speech goes on to take up three full columns) poses some other issues. The use of the rhetorical question is a hallmark of FIS in fiction, and a favourite device of many authors; NRSA and IS would be more likely to specify via a reporting verb something like "He asked if it were to be taken for granted...". It can therefore be labelled as FIS, although we should be careful to avoid the implied literariness of that term.

As the junior T.C. Hansard indicates, there are also stretches of *Parliamentary Debates* from the first series onwards in FDS. For example, in Volume 5 of the First Series, a complex debate on a minor loan scandal involving William Pitt the Younger (*HL Deb* 14 June 1805, c385ff) begins with a long speech in FDS, introduced only by the name of the speaker and a long dash. The next speaker in this debate is introduced by "The Chancellor of the Exchequer rose and spoke to the following effect: – Sir, I do not think it necessary to endeavour to follow the hon. Gent...". Here, the speech is introduced by a reporting phrase "spoke to

---

3. 'Arbitrarily' here means that many examples here were taken from debates which occurred on or around an anniversary of the date of the workshop from which some chapters in this volume derive, as a rough means of avoiding systematic selection bias. (Due to weekends and other days parliament does not sit, often this means the nearest date to that anniversary.)

the following effect", which might be thought to introduce NRSA but instead goes to a more direct first-person report. The third speech in the debate returns to clear NRSA: "Mr Henry Lascelles commenced his speech with observing, that it would ill become him, after what the house had heard...". The remainder of the debate continues in NRSA, including contributions by the two speakers whose long introductory speeches were in direct speech. NRSA continues to be the default throughout these first three series, with only occasional interspersed moments in direct speech.

The example just cited is a good example of Hansard's report likely printing a speech from the speaker's notes, as at this time such a long excerpt would be unlikely to be recorded in shorthand. (It would be useful to separate any extemporaneous FDS actually obtained from shorthand from the faux-FDS obtained from prepared notes, although in the historical Hansard context this is likely to be an impossible endeavour.) On the question of shorthand at this time, John Campbell, the one-time reporter quoted in Section 4, commented that "I knew nothing, and did not desire to know anything, of short-hand. Short-hand writers are very useful in taking-down evidence as given in a court of justice, but they are wholly incompetent to report a good speech" (Campbell 1881: 105).

With NRSA and occasional direct speech (of some form) the norm throughout the First to Third Series, the question of how extensive the direct speech is, and how it was obtained, becomes significant. Figure 1.2 reproduces Figure 1.1 but overlays the frequency of *I* per million words. Setting aside the Fourth Series for now (discussed in the following section), the contrast between the *Hansard's Parliamentary Debates* period and the first-person post-1909 *Official Report* is stark. Bearing in mind the small size of the First and Second Series, which accounts for the rather wild changes per million words in that period, the First to Third Series have on average slightly less than one third of the rate of occurrence of *I* as the Official Report does. Approximately a quarter to a third of this period consists of first-person content (with significant year-by-year variation), although the significant length of individual speeches in the first person compared to the NRSA reports means that topics in the first person are substantially overrepresented compared to the third-person material. Similarly, Figure 1.3 shows the decline in the reporting verb *said* – by no means the only reporting verb used in Hansard, but indicative of how the first three series compare to the *Official Report* in terms of markers of NRSA. It should be noted that *I* and *said* are not unique markers of first person and third person wholly in their own right – *I* can be used in a quote in a third-person piece of text, and *said* can be used in first-person text (*as I said earlier* or *as the Government said*). *Said*, however, is heavily used in Hansard's style pre-1909 to introduce third-person speeches, along with close synonyms, and in the corpus the subjects of the verb form of *said* are almost all noun

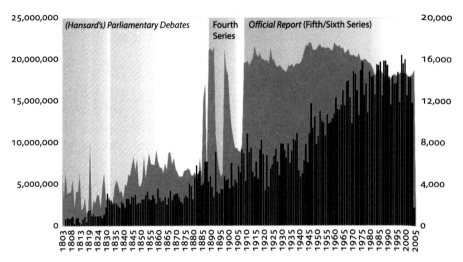

Figure 1.2 Normalised frequency of *I* per million words in the Hansard Corpus, alongside the number of words contained per year, and major Series markers

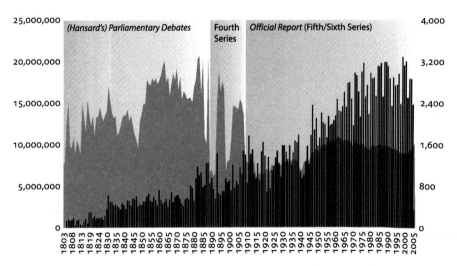

Figure 1.3 Normalised frequency of *said* per million words in the Hansard Corpus alongside the number of words contained per year, and major Series markers

forms representing people. The two words are good proxies, in aggregate, of the two major modes of speech representation with which we are concerned.

What gets to be represented as direct speech? T.C. Hansard's "Origin and Progress" note in his advertisement continues on to discuss the Third Series, and says that:

Peers and Hon. Members, of all parties, of the highest influence and importance, in and out of office, deeply interest themselves in the completeness of the Work – and that IN THE COURSE OF SESSION 1842, UPWARDS OF **Seven Hundred**, and in 1843 **Six Hundred-and-fifty**, SPEECHES WERE REVISED BY THE DIFFERENT SPEAKERS – now, when it is considered that very few speeches but those of length and importance are thus cared for, that much of the volumes is occupied by Minutes of Proceedings, Lists of Division, and minor Debates, it will be evident that HANSARD presents a mass of Reports of the most valuable and authentic character.

(Hansard 1843: 2, formatting in the original)

In 1843, the Hansard Corpus records 2,855,357 words across 4,257 contributions in Commons, and 728,551 words across 1,108 contributions in Lords, so while 650 revised speeches may seem quantitatively small in that context, these 650 will qualitatively represent longer and more major proceedings. (A significant number of the other contributions are very short, too, representing brief questions, interjections, or clarifications rather than the stereotypical and lengthy content-driven speech.) Such correction continued for some time, prompting one member to comment in a debate in 1877:

> I am bound to say that no one recognizes more than I do the able way in which Mr. Hansard has conducted his difficult work during this long number of years [...] Unfortunately, however, this system gives rise to a great deal of inconvenience. Members have to spend a considerable amount of time in correcting their speeches. I am told that several hon. Members are occupied for a very long time in correcting their contribution to the debates. Indeed, I am told that one right hon. Gentleman, who has occupied a very prominent position in this House, has actually been put to the trouble of spending two solid hours in correcting an hour's speech.   (Hon. Charles Hanbury-Tracy, *HC Deb* 20 April 1877, c1552)

For a period from 1889 to the early twentieth century, speeches corrected by a speaker bore a useful asterisk noting the report had been so revised (from 1850–1889 the asterisk meant the speech was taken from a pamphlet or other authorised speech report). With regard to the bulk of speeches not revised in this way or otherwise reported in the first person, some minor elements are either omitted or poorly recorded.

The state of clarity of the debates overall during this period is shown by the frankness of the *Times*, perhaps the foremost newspaper of record of the time, about the limitations of its 'parliamentary intelligence'. For example, on 4 June 1847 Lord Campbell rose to discuss bills of Scottish property law and the *Times* report on parliament on that day stated only that "[t]he noble and learned lord shortly explained the objects of these bills, but the details were inaudible in the gallery". Hansard decides to simply list the bills as being presented, mentioning

Campbell's name in a list, presumably due to a lack of available evidence or considering the speech too minor to investigate any further. As a further example, on 29 April 1836 Hansard neglects to mention either the Earl of Haddington's observations on the Irish Constabulary, which the *Times* reports in some detail, or the response by Viscount Duncannon, on which the *Times* reporter – although able to hear Haddington with some thoroughness – has to report simply that he "said a few words in reply, which were wholly inaudible in the gallery". Where the sources are silent and the speech unimportant, the limitations of Hansard's NRSA sources and the need to ensure what went into the reports was what had been substantiated, meant that silence would often fall over some reports.

This leaves direct speech from a source other than the speaker. Hansard does not wholly recast existing reports but instead copies extremely freely – to modern eyes, rather too freely – from other reports such as the four major London newspapers the *Times*, the *Morning Post*, the *Morning Chronicle*, and the *Morning Herald*. The time lag of Hansard compared to newspapers perhaps excuses this copying on the grounds that *Times* subscribers, for example, were paying for a first look at proceedings, and Hansard reprinting these some weeks later for a different purpose would bring little financial harm to the newspaper. This is why, during these first three Series, the idea of a particular editorial direction in Hansard is very hard to discern; the editorial matter in a direct speech is often unchanged from the source. This can be easily seen through what Vice and Farrell (2017: 21) memorably call "asides and stage directions" – where these are present in the source, Hansard will allow them through unchanged. An example from the corpus is when Sir Robert Peel, on 9 February 1843, rouses the Commons into a frenzy:

> ... I will exhibit to you, in the course of ten months more, that same Governorgeneral at the head of 40,000 men, having effected the evacuation of the kingdom in which we suffered such reverses – having, on the scene of every former disaster, retrieved our honours – [the remainder of the sentence was rendered wholly inaudible by an enthusiastic burst of applause from all parts of the House]. I will show you these dispirited sepoys converted into an army, excited by enthusiasm...
> (*HC Deb*, 9 February 1843, c372)

This speech, and the rest of the debate, is taken directly from the *Times* of the next morning, right down to the phrasing of the interruption. Hansard cannot be easily described as having a clear linguistic style here, given that other than switching round brackets for square ones it absorbs interjections and other editorial matters from its sources.

Alongside the *Times*, the *Morning Chronicle*, and other newspapers, a new competitor to Hansard throughout the first quarter of its Third Series (from January 1828 until October 1841) was the *Mirror of Parliament*. This was founded and edited by John Henry Barrow, now better known as Charles Dickens' uncle. Vice (2018) effectively makes a case for how important Dickens' time working for the *Mirror* was for Dickens' later life, but otherwise the *Mirror* itself has escaped much scholarly attention. Aside from some brief mentions in the histories of Hansard (including Vice & Farrell 2015 and Jordan 1931), the *Mirror* is cited only occasionally by modern scholars working within the narrow period of its existence, a fact not helped by the lack of an easily accessible digital version. These main secondary sources are Everett S. Brown's 1955 article and brief discussions in McBath (1970: 29–30) and in Jupp (1998: 203–205). This is regrettable as the *Mirror* is for much of its existence a superior source to Hansard for a range of purposes: speeches are often – but not always – reported in more detail; it is consistently FDS; it is much more willing to give stage directions, including indicating laughter and exclamation marks; and Jupp (1998: 204) suggests the length of speeches in the *Mirror* match contemporaneous speech timings at a normal speaking pace. In the same debate quoted above, where Hanbury-Tracy mentions the length of time members spent correcting Hansard's record of speeches, the former and future Prime Minister William Ewart Gladstone commented:

> At the time when the curiosity and eagerness of the public about Parliamentary debates was at high-water mark [...] an attempt was boldly made by a gentleman named Barrow, to produce a verbal report of the proceedings of Parliament. He succeeded and carried it on for several years; and, for those years, do not hesitate to say, that Barrow's *Mirror of Parliament* is the primary record, and not *Hansard's Debates*, because of the greater fulness which Barrow aimed at and obtained. It is within my own recollection – in the year 1833 or 1834 – just after the Reform Bill, that Gentlemen, who wanted to correct their speeches, did it for Barrow's *Mirror of Parliament*. I grant that after, I should think, five or six years, it was found impossible to carry it on. Private enterprize would not sustain reporting so carried on; and, after the lapse of that time, there was a decline in the appetite of the public for it. (*HC Deb* 20 April 1877, c1576–77)

As Gladstone states, the cost of producing a report of the quality and length of the *Mirror* was a significant financial challenge, and after some drawn-out troubles the *Mirror* ceased publication in 1841.

The establishment of the *Mirror* in the late 1820s led to some mudslinging between Barrow and T.C. Hansard, giving us some rare public discussions of policy and practice. The first volume of the *Mirror* began with a Prospectus setting out the aims of the work, which dismissed Hansard as "a mere abstract of the reports contained in the daily papers" (which had already been called "decidedly ineffective") and was "excessively abridged" (Barrow 1828: 1–2). This led T.C. Hansard to issue an advertisement in the *Gentleman's Magazine* on 25 April 1828, announcing more frequent publication schedules of his own work and addressing some of the claims of the *Mirror*'s Prospectus.[4] These include criticising the *Mirror*'s fuller reporting, as it spends much space on "trite, temporary matters" and seems to think "*length* is, upon all occasions, to be preferred before *strength*" (Hansard 1828:5). Relevant here is that T.C. Hansard (1828:7) insists, "Hitherto, the practice of giving parliamentary speeches in the first person has been reserved for great occasions" rather than the standard practice for which Barrow aimed. There is even an accusation that Barrow simply borrowed from newspapers (as both Hansards did) and then "changes them, by turning them from the third into the first person, and so disfigures them [...] by repetition, circumlocution, and amplification" (ibid.). The existence of Barrow's ruinously expensive shorthand reporters (including his nephew Dickens) contradicts this claim, although it is an interesting accusation, and it is certainly likely that Barrow did not have enough reporters for the completely full report the *Mirror* produces (Jordan 1931:438).

During this first phase we also have more insight into the editorial practice of Hansard from discussions of subsidy. The issue of subsidising the reports was first raised in 1877, after a period of dissatisfaction with what was recorded in parliament. The fundamental issue was that Hansard's primary sources at that point were newspapers, and newspapers had two main problems when it came to the debates: they only wished to pay to report and print material likely to be of interest to their readers, and they had daily printing deadlines to meet (so when parliament met late into the night, later material went unrecorded while the reporters left to file what they had by the deadline). Consequently the junior T.C. Hansard was granted money in that year by the Exchequer to employ his own shorthand writers in order to record what was neglected by newspapers (discussions after midnight and unpopular but important work such as committees or private bills); the remainder of his material was still collated from newspapers. In evidence to a Select Committee in 1862, he stated "The reports of the Debates are collected from a great number of sources; it is a compilation very carefully and very laboriously edited," but was later drawn to admit "I use the *Times* frequently" (Parliament 1862:41). When asked about accuracy and detail at that Committee, he replied simply, "I hold myself bound for the *bona fides* of the reports, not for their literal accuracy" (Parliament 1862:39). In another Select Committee in 1888, he was asked from where he took his sources for collation:

> I obtain them from the London newspapers, the country newspapers, and from the reports supplied by the Press Association. They are then passed into the hands of the collators, who collate all those sources together; they take the public documents that relate to the subject, and, in fact, compile and edit the whole.
>
> (Parliament 1888a:9)

---

4. I am indebted to John Vice for this reference.

The "country newspapers" were those who would pay extra for reporters to take shorthand notes of speeches by their local MPs, who were often underserved by the metropolitan newspapers.

To illustrate this range of sources for Hansard, we can look at a speech made on 27 March 1840, where Viscount Palmerston, at the time Foreign Secretary, was asked to discuss a minor crisis between Constantinople and Egypt. One section of his speech's report from the *Times* reads:

> His hon. friend seemed to be under the impression that the British Government and Lord Ponsonby stimulated the Sultan to renew hostilities against the Pacha of Egypt. In this his hon. Friend was much mistaken. The Pacha was the aggressor. In the first instance he declared his determination to throw off his allegiance to the Sultan, and make himself the independent sovereign of the province which he was appointed to govern. (*Times*, 28 March 1840: 4)

The *Morning Chronicle*, another major newspaper source of debates, has for the same part of the debate:

> His honourable friend thought that the British government and Lord Ponsonby, the British Ambassador at Constantinople, has stimulated the Sultan to renew hostilities against the Pacha of Egypt. He (Lord Palmerston) could assure him that he was entirely mistaken. In the first place, it was the Pacha who was the aggressor, and not the Sultan, inasmuch as it was the Pacha who in the first instance, publicly declared his determination to throw off his allegiance, and make himself the independent sovereign of the provinces over which he was appointed to govern. (*Morning Chronicle*, 28 March 1840: 4)

Published a few weeks later, Hansard copies the *Morning Chronicle* word for word, although with some changes for house style, as follows:

> His hon. Friend thought that the British Government and Lord Ponsonby, the British Ambassador at Constantinople, had stimulated the Sultan to renew hostilities against the Pacha of Egypt. He (Lord Palmerston) could assure him that he was entirely mistaken. In the first place, it was the Pacha who was the aggressor, and not the Sultan, inasmuch as it was the Pacha who, in the first instance, publicly declared his determination to throw off his allegiance, and make himself the independent sovereign of the provinces over which he was appointed to govern.
> (*HC Deb* 27 March 1840, c193)

Finally, the same section in the *Mirror of Parliament* is:

> My honourable Friend thinks that the British Government and Lord Ponsonby, the British Ambassador at Constantinople, stimulated the Sultan to renew hostilities against the Pacha of Egypt. I can assure him that he is entirely mistaken. In

> the first place, my opinion is, that the Pacha is the aggressor, and not the Sultan; inasmuch as the Pacha, in the first instance, publicly declared his determination to throw off his allegiance, and make himself the independent sovereign of the provinces of which he was appointed the governor.
>
> (*Mirror of Parliament*, 27 March 1840, p2042)

With regard to other newspapers, the *Morning Post* gives only a brief third-person summary of this exchange and the *Standard*'s report is identical to the *Times*. It is notable that the *Morning Chronicle* and the *Mirror of Parliament* match closely but are not identical: as well as the first-person reporting of the *Mirror*, some small changes of phrasing ("over which he was appointed to govern" versus "of which he was appointed the governor", and "In the first place" versus the quasi-hedge in "In the first place, my opinion is") indicate that they were likely independently produced by shorthand writers. By contrast, Hansard simply reprints the *Morning Chronicle* with "hon. Friend" in place of "honourable friend", including the parenthetical "Lord Palmerston" to clarify the reference of the preceding pronoun. As this was part of the *Morning Chronicle*'s editorial decision-making for clarity, it then becomes part of Hansard's. Presumably Palmerston actually said "I", as the *Mirror* records, and so the *Morning Chronicle* decides to render this directly as "he" – but due to the five possible male referents in the passage (admittedly not all referents being equally likely), they decide to insert a clarificatory parenthetical rather than restate Lord Palmerston's name or give his ministerial title again during the actual report of the speech, which does happen elsewhere in Hansard.

Overall, then, in this complex period of Hansard from 1803 to 1888 (the unsubsidised period covered by T.C. Hansard senior and junior), we see the following linguistic characteristics:

- The dominant mode, speech-by-speech, is NRSA, generated by reports in the *Times*, the *Morning Chronicle*, and some others.
    - For much of this period, there is a chance newspaper reports may give more detail than Hansard for NRSA reports of particular days or debates.
    - From 1877 to 1888, subsidy by parliament means that Hansard is more detailed than the newspapers on what T.C. Hansard junior calls the "four points"; "debates upon Private Bills set down by Order; the discussions in Committee upon Public Bills; the discussions in Committee of Supply; and the discussions which take place after midnight or half-past 12" (Parliament 1888a: 6).
    - Sections of NRSA may appear FDS-like. See below for a discussion of NRSA which is adapted from FDS.
    - There are occasional editorial interventions, varying according to the source.

Speech in the British Hansard

- The secondary mode, which is more common proportionally in the text than speech-by-speech, is FDS. This is reproduced where a "great occasion" of a speech occurs (in the judgement of the editor). Hansard may reproduce a period of direct speech (generally FDS) obtained most often by either taking the speech notes of the speaker (which the T.C. Hansards would check against the notes of the speech for veracity), and sometimes by sending a report to the speaker for correction. It is highly unlikely all of a debate will be FDS, and it is most likely only the lengthier opening speeches of a major debate are represented as such, with later contributions (including those by the opening speakers) reverting to NRSA.
  - For 1828 to 1841, the *Mirror of Parliament* also provides comprehensive first-person speeches derived from shorthand of high accuracy.
- Editorial points of style are not easily discernible as being that of Hansard rather than a source.

Therefore, if an individual speech in the corpus from this period is relatively long and has a high frequency of first-person markers such as pronouns and the present tense, it can be processed with a reasonable degree of confidence as a FDS speech. (In considering what is meant by 'relatively long': the average length of a speech in both Houses across the Second and Third Series (excluding the very short First) is approximately 360 words, so anything above 500 could be considered comparatively 'long'.) Given the formal speaking context of the time it should be noted that such speech will be a reading of a highly formal written-to-be-spoken text rather than spoken language *per se*. Hansard's ability to cross-check a speaker's notes with published versions taken from shorthand notes (after the mid-1820s), adds to the likely accuracy of such speeches.

The NRSA material, the majority of the corpus at this period, can be used as a description of major topics discussed – though not necessarily as representative of the language in which it was discussed. Some of what is registered as NRSA will actually be pronoun- and tense-shifted FDS (for an example, see Palmerston's 1840 speech above). With apologies to Leech and Short, I call this 'Narrator's Report of Direct Speech', or NRDS. As this does not present itself as direct speech its editorial standards of accuracy may not be the same as true FDS, and other than length of speech there are few simple linguistic indices to mark this type, so care should be taken in trying to distinguish NRSA from NRDS.

For both modes there should be some wariness attached to frequency counts in the corpus in this period. Content-heavy words in the open grammatical classes will be over-represented in sections of FDS and NRDS and so comparatively under-represented in sections in NRSA. However, the rationale that FDS and NRDS is used for important speeches and speakers means that the effect of this is likely to be mitigated somewhat. Thus a topic of significance, aimed to be measured by corpus frequency, will come up as being high-frequency, and a topic of low frequency will still come up as low-frequency, but relative measures, especially in the middle of the frequency curve, will be distorted compared to a uniform corpus. As very few studies focus on such concepts or lexical items this may not pose a very significant issue – but for large diachronic studies discussing concepts which were important at one time but only of middling importance in another period, it is a consideration which must be taken into account.

6. Hansard without the Hansards: The chaotic *Authorised Edition*, 1889 to 1908

> [...] on certain days if the matters under discussion happen to be dry and do not appear to be interesting, the records of Parliament are practically nil. If the matter is sensational and the subject is one of great interest, then you have a full report, but not otherwise. Now, Sir, I maintain that in this House our records ought to contain not only the sensational but also the dry discussions.
>
> (Hon. Charles Hanbury-Tracy, *HC Deb* 20 April 1877, c1555)

The public, via parliamentary subsidy (as well as subscriptions to the volume from individuals and libraries), would increasingly fund the production of Hansard after the retirement of the junior T.C. Hansard in 1888. The new operators naturally sought a profit from this enterprise; anyone involved in a large and long-term linguistic project could tell them that the great twin complexities of language and discourse are always more expensive and time-consuming than even pessimistic assessments estimate. When the subsidy contracts require a particular turnaround of revisions and publishing, a lack of time can only be compensated by yet more expense.

So it was with the publishers attracted by the idea of putting their name to one of the most prestigious publications of the age: fixing the nation's words of power in time and print by collecting them from reserved seats in the heart of parliament, with the whole soon to be augmented with the title of the "Authorised Edition", in words suggestive of the King James Bible. Even after parliament stepped in with limited subsidy, the cost of producing what parliament both wanted and was willing to pay to subsidise could never match the income from that subsidy plus commercial sales. Members of both Houses continued to be dissatisfied with the report (Port 1990:180), and each successive publisher took different approaches to attempt to satisfy their contract.

The remainder of the Third Series, from 1889 to 1892, was fulfilled by the Hansard Publishing Union, who purchased the rights from T.C. Hansard of the

Hansard name in 1888 and then put in the lowest of 12 bids to a tender from parliament for further subsidy. This subsidy came in return for certain changes to the content of the reports – as the contract of 1888 specified (signed by the immediate predecessor of the Union), "the Contractor shall exercise his own discretion as to the fullness of the Reports given, provided always that in no case shall any speech be reported at less than one-third of its length as delivered" (Parliament 1888b: 2). All speeches were to be recorded equally fully, regardless of the type of debate or Bill or its timing. This transformed Hansard from its pre-1888 form, and is why the 1889 date (rather than the beginning of the Fourth Series in 1892) marks the start of the second linguistic phase of the *Debates*.

The Hansard Publishing Union was short-lived, with its principal handicap being that it was run by a fraudster, who funded generous dividends to its shareholders from a series of large loans. Regardless, by employing dedicated reporters to fulfil its contract it was unlikely to make a profit: McBath (1970: 35) suggests that the Union's investment may have been an error due to confusing the profitable government printing branch of the wider Hansard family (the Luke Hansard side) with the minimally profitable debates branch (the T.C. Hansards). With the Union's collapse at the end of the 1891 session, a Fourth Series was begun in 1892 with the subtitle "Authorised Edition" and no mention of Hansard (all to avoid confusion with the now-disgraced Union; see Vice & Farrell 2017: 25). As outlined in Table 1.1, a series of publishers then followed. Figures 1.2 and 1.3 clearly show the erratic reporting style of this period. Figure 1.4 shows the data from Figure 1.2 and 1.3 within this 1889 to 1908 period in more detail as line graphs, with one year of context from the Third and Fifth Series on either side.

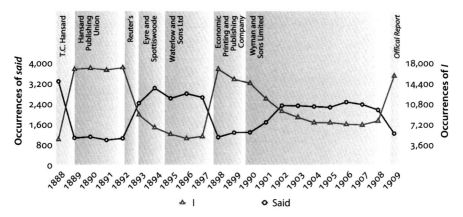

Figure 1.4 *I* per million words and *said* per million words in the Hansard Corpus between 1888 and 1909, with publishers indicated

Taking the ratio of *I* to *said* as an index of first-person speech, there are clear shifts evident in Figure 1.4: first from T.C. Hansard's primarily NRSA accounts to the Hansard Publishing Union's first-person accounts, then Reuter's middling ratio during their brief involvement, and then the next two publishers, including Waterlow and Sons, returning generally to T.C. Hansard's earlier ratio of mainly NRSA. In 1898 the Economic Printing and Publishing Company, then a long period of Wyman and Sons Limited, began a return to more first-person accounts, though these declined over the decade (most likely because of the high costs of accurate shorthand), with a rapid reversal with the start of the *Official Report*. The return to more third-person NRSA reporting during the publishing period of Waterlow and Sons is easily explained:

> One interesting experiment was made in the three years, from 1895 to 1898, when Messrs. Waterlow, the Government printers, were the contractors. The report was furnished by the staff of *The Times*, whose daily record of the proceedings in Parliament formed the chief source from which, under the old arrangements, *Hansard's Debates* were compiled. The reporting staff of *The Times* turned out two separate and distinct reports – one for *The Times* and the other for *The Parliamentary Debates*... (McDonagh [n.d.]: 433)

The *Times* during this period stayed in the third-person NRSA style it generally adopted, and reporting in the third person except for major speeches would save the shorthand writers of the *Times* time in producing the two 'distinct' reports.

The challenges of this period preclude easy generalisations, but its general linguistic characteristics are:

- Each publisher has a broadly different dominant ratio of speech types, but with the exception of the two periods January 1889 to February 1892 and January 1898 to April 1899 the dominant mode is NRSA or NRDS, generated by newspaper reports and other reporters as in the *Hansard's Parliamentary Debates* phase. Occasional speeches are given in FDS following the pattern of the previous phase.
    - From 1895 to 1898 speech notes would be prepared by the same reporters as reported the *Times*.
    - From January 1889 to February 1892, the dominant mode is FDS from shorthand reporters.
    - From January 1898 to April 1899, the dominant mode is FDS from shorthand reporters.

- As required by contract, speech reports could be anywhere between no less than one-third of its length as delivered to full-length as delivered.

- Given the chaotic publication history, editorial points of style are not easily discernible. Stability was only found by Wyman and Sons Limited for their nine-year period as publisher, but Figure 1.4 demonstrates how their style shifted across time as they sought a profitable balance (likely with a higher reliance on newspaper reports).

Any individual speech in this period is hard to categorise, but the characteristics above will apply. The concerns about relative frequencies from the previous section still apply, and could in places be even more erratic. Nonetheless, the same fundamental principle – that the key material, topics, and content words will shine through – also applies.

7.   'Something like literary shape': The *Official Report*, 1909 to present

During the period of the Fourth Series, the House of Commons convened Select Committees on Parliamentary Debates (the Select Committee in 1888 that generated the new system of subsidy was jointly with the House of Lords). The 1893 committee supplied a consensus that there should be a full report "in all cases in the first person" which was "substantially verbatim" and with relatively minimal correction by MPs (Parliament 1893: iv). Parliament being unwilling to dedicate the funds for this, the contractual arrangement continued with minor changes until the next Select Committee report in 1907. This committee criticised the system of putting the reports out for tender, whereby financial incentives existed to lengthen or shorten volumes according to subsidy, whereby the lowest tender was taken up irrespective of a detriment in quality, and which usually still relied on "newspaper cuttings" (Parliament 1907: v). At this point the financial arguments for an in-house report were more substantial than before – while the benefits were greater – and so on 14 May 1908, the reporters employed by Wyman and Sons recorded in the *Parliamentary Debates* the decision to end the contractual outsourcing of reports, beginning in 1909.

The 1893 committee recommended a full Report, "which, though not strictly verbatim, is substantially the verbatim Report, with repetitions and redundancies omitted, and with obvious mistakes corrected; but which, on the other hand, leaves out nothing that adds to the meaning of the speech or illustrates the argument" (Parliament 1893: 2). The 1907 report repeated this word for word (Parliament 1907: iii), and this phrasing remains Hansard's terms of reference to the present day (Vice & Farrell 2017: 25). In the 1908 debate surrounding establishing the *Official Report*, the Financial Secretary who introduced the relevant Select Committee report gave a further gloss:

> Perhaps I might just express to the House what is the meaning of the word 'full,' used in its technical sense. It means a verbatim report, trimmed of all those excrescences and redundancies with which Members are perhaps in the habit of filling up the matter of their speeches. In fact, a 'full' report puts into something like literary shape the efforts with which we endeavour to express our thoughts.
>
> (*HC Deb* 14 May 1908, c1357–8)

Matters of reports being somewhere between a third-to-full-length of the original were therefore dismissed, and the Official Report from the outset was one of first-person full transcripts, transformed and tidied only as the terms of reference permit.

Of the 43 Select Committee on Publications and Debates reports (a Commons committee established from 1909 to 1967) which mention Hansard, almost all are concerned with publication dates and distribution processes (and, during wartime, about reformatting type and binding standards to save paper).[5] Of the 1924 pages of reports in this series, there are only two mentions of matters of language and of the 'trimmed' nature of the reports. The second is the briefest, in a single paragraph in 1944:

> It was brought to the notice of Your Committee that in the official report of Members' speeches the words "shall not" were consistently printed for "shan't", and that similar slight verbal alterations were frequently made, so that emphasis and vividness were sometimes lost. After consideration Your Committee formed the opinion that the Editor of the Official Report should continue to exercise his discretion with regard to minor matters of grammar and spelling in Members' speeches. (Parliament 1944: 3)

No definition is given of "minor", but in the general spirit of the *Official Report* – with which MPs and Lords alike were generally very pleased – the common sense of the editors is left to be the best judge.

An equally brief statement is given in the Committee report in 1930, but with a far more detailed backstory:

> Your Committee considered the question how far alterations and corrections made by Members in the text of the Official Report are admissible, but in view of the statement on this subject made by Mr. Speaker on the 14th November, they consider it unnecessary to make any recommendation with regard to such corrections. (Parliament 1930: iv)

---

5. In addition to this, the most endearing part of these reports is their recurrent dedication to choosing the image for the House of Commons Christmas card.

The statement referred to here was made on 14 November 1929, in a brief debate of significance to the study of the language of Hansard. Hugh O'Neill MP, who was later to serve as Father of the House, disputed a change made by a government minister to Hansard, claiming the minister had openly stated that he "altered what I actually did say into what I ought to have said". O'Neill continued, "Surely, if we are going to have official reports in this House, they should be reports of what is actually spoken in the House [...] The OFFICIAL REPORT ought to be a kind of arbiter whose relentless accuracy is beyond any question" (*HC Deb*, 14 November 1929, c2229). The minister responsible replied that, "Owing to the confusion and noise, an announcement [by this minister] was not heard in the Gallery, and a slip was sent to be filled in" (ibid.). (Such slips are common even now.) A second complaint was then raised by another MP, who objected that they had asked supplementary questions based on the erroneous figures given by the minister, and that as the original statement was corrected, "my supplementary questions looked positively ridiculous in the OFFICIAL REPORT" (ibid.). This, however, was not a complaint about Hansard's practice; instead, the MP continued to say that if only he had been informed about the minister's corrections, "I would willingly have made any arrangement that would have suited the hon. Gentleman, so that both our statements would at any rate have been consistent" (ibid.). The intricacies of the debate reveal on the one hand a desire from some MPs that Hansard should reflect the debate as said in the House, but on the other merely an interest that the key records of state are consistent. The Speaker of the House then proceeded to give an official statement about Hansard and the ability for members to make corrections:

> As regards the first question that he raised, it is, unfortunately, the case that it is not given to all Members to speak with the grammatical precision which is desirable when the spoken word has to be transcribed for the OFFICIAL REPORT. An hon. Member obviously is entitled to correct an error which arises in his speech and to put the speech in grammatical form, but at the same time it is often the case that an hon. Member is imperfectly heard in the Gallery and that a word, perhaps a very important word, is omitted from his speech. Obviously, again, he is entitled to insert that word if it has been spoken in the House and has not been heard in the Gallery. I am ashamed to say that that has happened to myself. [...] if any great difference occurs between what is reported in the OFFICIAL REPORT and what an hon. Member thinks ought to be there, inquiries by the reporters in the Gallery are made, and great care is taken that no untrue report appears in the OFFICIAL REPORT. (*HC Deb*, 14 November 1929, c2231)

This is one of the most explicit statements Hansard records about itself in the era of the *Official Report*. While some MPs were concerned about the literal accuracy of the facts of Hansard (although the known alterations of grammar were not under dispute), some MPs were far less concerned about reflecting what was said and were more concerned with the consistency of the record, and the official position of the House was that errors in fact and grammar were permissible to be corrected, and that when a reporter's evidence failed them or was imperfect, the MP speaking was the arbiter of what was and was not to be recorded. Practically speaking, nothing else could be reasonably counter-proposed, and so this statement by the Speaker of the House, alongside the terms of reference of Hansard, is the firmest public statement available of the contents of the record of debates.

Accounts of the mechanism of creating Hansard in the twentieth and twenty-first century are widely available, and the editors and reporters from both Houses are lucid and enthusiastic communicators of the history, process, and structure of their roles and the place of Hansard – in line with the opening-up of parliament in general to the public in recent years, the public have also been invited to learn more about the *Official Report*. Excellent sources from within include Browne (2017), Hansard Writing Team (2018), Sutherland and Farrell (2013), Sutherland and Vice (2015) and Vice and Farrell (2017).

While the mechanism of creating the *Official Report* has changed with the evolution of technology in the twentieth century, the fundamentals have remained the same. Reporters take 'turns' in the House of five to ten minutes each, then are responsible for producing the report for that timed period (nowadays within 45 minutes of the end of a five-minute turn). From 1909 until the 1970s, this consisted of shorthand notes, then reporters could work instead from audio tapes, and now reporters use digital audio as their source, creating the report directly from them. A brief period of correction or clarification is allowed, with reporters having the ability to pass notes directly to speakers asking for their speech notes or for clarity on particular points.

The view of modern parliamentarians is that Hansard remains

> ... faithful to the Members' words, accurately conveying the nuance of their argument and preserving their speaking style, while also, with the slightest of editorial touches, producing a fluent and readable report that will serve as a working document, a legal record and a historical resource. (Bercow 2017: i)

This objective is also aided by the rapid accessibility of the *Official Report* online, on the same day as the speeches it records.

Some scholars, notably Mollin (2007) and Slembrouck (1992) have analysed modern Hansard in comparison to the audiovisual sources of the Chambers in action, and have discussed what features of spoken speech do not survive the process of producing the 'full' report (notably repetition, hesitation phenomena, the generic *you*, contractions, the *going-to* future; often adverbs and proximal determiners are intensified). In the present volume (Kotze et al., this volume) an analysis of the Australian Hansard between 1946 and 2015 also reveals the effects of editorial practices on the transcription in that parliament. Without retreading the work of these writers, in the course of working on the linguistics of the British Hansard I have been permitted to informally shadow reporters working 'live' on occasion over the past seven years in parliament, and while a fuller analysis is forthcoming there are some initial observations which are relevant for this article.

Firstly, it is interesting from a linguistic perspective that while the audio of the reporter's turn is available digitally, a reporter must still attend the relevant House for the duration of their turn. This is essential for the interpersonal situatedness of the debate (cameras will not necessarily be at an appropriate angle to see to where a speaker gestures or points, for example) as well as to take notes of key words and to hear the opening words of each speaker's turn (as all of the hundreds of microphones in the houses of parliament are not permanently 'live', the process of recognising a speaker who is speaking means that the first few words of their speech, particularly in the House of Lords, is wholly audible in the Chamber and not necessarily audible on a recording). Interventions – only when they merit a response from the current speaker – are included and these are not often picked up by microphones or cameras. Reporters also note key terms in the debate, particularly those which would be worth looking up or requesting clarification on before undertaking the production of the report, such as when a speaker mentions a place, or a report, or (on one occasion) their dog. Members seem to be generous with their speech notes, but reporters refer to them while working with audio rather than unquestioningly copying them.

Producing the report itself involves a significant amount of procedural text, which is the main part of a speaker's words that are reported 'as they should be' rather than as they actually were; if a speaker makes a minor error such as a wrong form of address for a colleague or of parliamentary process (such as saying *this Chamber* instead of *this Committee* or *this House*, or *you* instead of *your Lordships*, or referring to the government in the singular, or producing direct second-person speech), then these are not unnecessarily recorded and exposed but silently altered to fit agreed protocol. Hesitations, false starts, verbal tics, speech errors, stutters and similar phenomena are removed.

Other changes which do not always happen but have been observed include changing *this* to *the* and *among* rather than *amongst*, moving adverbs like *only* elsewhere in a sentence for clarity, removing much otiose repetition (such as *very very*), removing deictics not necessary to the meaning, removing fillers (such as *I mean* or *so*) and removing many sentence adverbs when they are likewise not key to the meaning of the sentence (such as parenthetical *actually* or *really*). Particularly interesting for linguists is the common removal of otiose hedges (such as *I believe* and *I think*) when these do not indicate actual commitment to the sentence – reporters are careful to retain hedges where they are explicit indicators of perception, which often requires careful judgement. For this sort of decision, reporters can spend a fair amount of time working through difficult matters, often consulting colleagues and with the ability to consult more senior editors if necessary.

While there is always the desire from many researchers, discussed above, to have a 'full' transcript including all of these omitted features, it is difficult to criticise any of the changes made. As an item of linguistic anthropology, the more I observed the reporting staff, the more I also came to understand the ways in which effort is taken not to level each speaker's style; stylistic features are still allowed to be present in the record, although with some of the more stylistically explicit markers removed. Reporters discussed instances where a speaker was making a clear point through repetition or redundant phrases – such as when aping overly bureaucratic language – and so such repetition would 'naturally' be kept in. At least twice I asked why a larger change was not made to a speech and the editor responded that such a change would be 'gratuitous'. The phrasing used by John Campbell (1881: 105–107) above, that a reader should not be perplexed, seems to be the principal motivation behind every change, while not permitting errors of fact or the sense of what was said to be altered. (A 'corrections page' is produced in Hansard for any errors of fact to be later corrected; see Parliament 2007.)

The period of the *Official Report* is much simpler to summarise than the previous periods. It is FDS throughout, except where in the first half of the period a formal question is asked by a speaker of a Minister where there is a small section of IS (this is a formulaic section, used when a question is asked with an initial *to*, such as *to ask the Secretary of State for Health whether...*, and rendered as *[speaker name] asked the Secretary...*). On the matter of editorial points, house style has clearly evolved – the modern British Hansard does not edit out split infinitives anymore, for example – and a style guide does exist; future research planned on this area will investigate that particular question in more depth, but editing due to house style generally limits itself to the types of changes listed above. The content nouns, adjectives, and verbs spoken in a debate are very well recorded in the *Official Report*, with the exception of compound verbs of process, such as *give an assurance to* or *be opposed to*, which would generally be changed to *assure* or *oppose*. The post-1909 report is therefore rigorously and semantically full for main content.

8. Conclusion: Hansard for eternity, Hansard for linguists

> Finality is not the language of politics.
> (Benjamin Disraeli, *HC Deb* 28 February 1859, c998)

The preceding discussion has investigated in detail what the language of Hansard over its two-century run represents. The purpose of Hansard is to be a record for the parliament of the day and for the ages, not to be a linguistic corpus, and a modification of that purpose requires a detailed knowledge of the content, which this chapter aims to supply.

The story of Hansard, as we have seen, is one of improvements in quality and reductions in internal heterogeneity. The analyses above give the following outline:

- **1803–1876:** Primarily NRSA/NRDS (NRSA often taken from summaries in the *Times, Morning Chronicle* and other newspapers) with some longer speeches in FDS where the speech is particularly significant (often taken from a speech text, when available). Compared to the speech events in parliament, corpus frequency results from Hansard will be relatively overrepresented in the FDS/NRDS sections which editors considered a 'great occasion'.
- **1877–1888:** As above, but with subsidy generating a) more detail on committee discussions and other areas newspapers do not report for lack of interest and b) more details post-midnight. FDS/NRDS sections are still fairly overrepresented, but a larger volume of NRSA is proportionally present from the subsidised topics.
- **1889–February 1892:** FDS from shorthand. Compression of unimportant speeches is done, and corpus results are likely to be overrepresented for speeches of importance which were reported in more detail.
- **March 1892–1897:** As 1877–1888. FDS/NRDS sections are still relatively overrepresented.
- **1898–April 1899:** FDS from shorthand. Speeches of importance are likely overrepresented, as for 1889–1892.
- **May 1899–1908:** Generally as for 1877–1888 but variable in ratio of NRSA/NRDS to FDS. FDS/NRDS sections are proportionally overrepresented.
- **1909–present:** FDS from shorthand and audiovisual recording; occasional formulaic IS sections decline by 1970s. There is no over-/under-reporting.

In general, those speeches thought to be contemporaneously more significant from 1803 to 1909 will be overrepresented in a corpus, either as an editorial choice (marked in the NRSA-form phases by a shift to FDS and in the FDS-form phases by longer text) or as a source reporter/editor's choice (for NRSA-form through NRDS, for FDS-form by longer text). Debates contemporaneously considered to be less important will be proportionally underrepresented. The presence of topics (through either lexical items or semantic tags) will be well recorded, but their relative frequency in this period is relatively uncertain. Research which focuses on topics of major contemporaneous importance (e.g., war, foreign affairs with major powers, major expenditure) has more solidity in terms of frequency due to the likelihood of results being within the relatively overrepresented category. Frequency results for matters which were not of contemporaneous interest (including much regional matters not affecting London) should be treated with suspicion. Useful qualitative support can be sought from the *Mirror of Parliament* for 1828 to 1841. Useful comparisons can also be gained by contrasting material from 1880 to 1908 with the specific periods of 1889 to February 1892 and 1898 to April 1899 as the nature of reporting and selecting material shifted; a lack of significant change in this period is likely to indicate frequency counts are more robust than otherwise.

In the period 1909 to the present, a 'full report' omits sociolinguistic and conversation-analytic phenomena, elides grammatical variation and information structure, and generates a written-to-be-spoken text from written-to-be-spoken and spontaneous speech alike. It is substantially a highly accurate reflection of spoken semantics, and therefore of content.

Those factors of publishing history, editorial policy, and shifting priorities affect how linguists, humanities scholars, and social scientists should view and use the text of Hansard. It leaves a vast range of research questions still open, and much easily addressable using big data corpus techniques. As well as being the first textual history and linguistic analysis of speech representation in Hansard, it is hoped the present chapter can act as a handbook to the text for future research. The accumulated work of two centuries and many hundreds of hands – T.C. Hansard senior and junior, the army of *Times* and other newspaper shorthand reporters, the early Hansard collators, those reporters employed by the many commercial publishers entrusted with the work, and the careful and judicious staff of the *Official Report* – deserves not only its established pre-eminence in history but also careful curation throughout its growing range of further digital afterlives as an immense quantitative source of information on British culture, language, and society.

Funding

This work was supported primarily by the Leverhulme Trust (grant PLP-2019-341). The Arts and Humanities Research Council in conjunction with the Economic and Social Research Council (grant AH/L010062/1) funded the creation of the annotated Hansard Corpus 1805–2003.

Acknowledgments

This chapter was enriched by the comments of two anonymous reviewers and by generous advice from Jeremy Smith, Andrew Struan and John Vice.

References

Alexander, Marc & Davies, Mark. 2015. The Hansard Corpus 1803–2005. <http://www.english-corpora.org/hansard> (12 June 2022).

Alexander, Marc & Struan, Andrew. 2013. "In countries so unciviliz'd as those?": The language of incivility and the British experience of the world. In *The British Abroad Since the Eighteenth Century, Vol. 2: Experiencing Imperialism*, Martin Farr & Xavier Guégan (eds), 232–249. London: Palgrave Macmillan.

Alexander, Marc & Struan, Andrew. 2022. "In barbarous times and in uncivilized countries": Two centuries of the evolving uncivil in the Hansard Corpus. *International Journal of Corpus Linguistics* 27(4): 480–505.

Alexander, Marc, Dallachy, Fraser, Piao, Scott, Baron, Alistair & Rayson, Paul. 2015. Metaphor, popular science, and semantic tagging: Distant reading with the *Historical Thesaurus of English*. *Digital Scholarship in the Humanities* 30(s1): i16–i27.

Anderson, Jean. 2013. ENROLLER: An experiment in aggregating resources. In *Language in Scotland: Corpus-Based Studies*, Wendy Anderson (ed.), 273–294. Amsterdam: Rodopi.

Archer, Dawn. 2017. Mapping *Hansard* impression management strategies through time and space. *Studia Neophilologica* 89(s1): 5–20.

Barrow, John Henry. 1828. Prospectus. In *The Mirror of Parliament*, Vol. 1, John Henry Barrow (ed.). London: Winchester and Varnham.

Bercow, John. 2017. Foreword. In *The History of Hansard*, John Vice & Stephen Farrell, vii. London: House of Lords Hansard and House of Lords Library.

Bevan, Aneurin. 1952. *In Place of Fear*. Kingswood: Heinemann.

Brown, Everett S. 1955. John Henry Barrow and the *Mirror of Parliament*. *Parliamentary Affairs* 9(3): 311–323.

Browne, Charlie. 2017. Being a *Hansard* reporter: 10 things you thought you knew. *Commons Hansard Blog*, 24 July 2017. <https://commonshansard.blog.parliament.uk/2017/07/24/being-a-hansard-reporter-10-things-you-thought-you-knew/> (1 February 2021).

Campbell, John, 1stBaron Campbell. 1881. *Life of John, Lord Campbell, Lord High Chancellor of Great Britain; Consisting of a Selection from His Autobiography, Diary, and Letters. In Two Volumes. Edited by the Hon. Mrs Hardcastle*, 2nd edn. London: John Murray.

Cobbett, William. 1804. *Cobbett's Weekly Political Register*, Vol. V. London: Cox and Baylis.

Coole, Matthew, Rayson, Paul & Mariani, John. 2020. Unfinished business: Construction and maintenance of a semantically tagged historical parliamentary corpus, UK Hansard from 1803 to the present day. In Proceedings of ParlaCLARIN II Workshop, Marseille, France, 23–27.

Culpeper, Jonathan & Kytö, Merja. 2010. *Early Modern English Dialogues: Spoken Interaction as Writing*. Cambridge: CUP.

Cunningham, Hamish, Tablan, Valentin, Roberts, Angus & Bontcheva, Kalina. 2013. Getting more out of biomedical documents with GATE's Full Lifecycle Open Source Text Analytics. *PLoS Computational Biology* 9(2): e1002854.

Hansard, Thomas Curson (junior). 1828. Hansard's Parliamentary Debates [advertisement]. In *The Gentleman's Magazine and Historical Chronicle*, Vol. XCVII (January–June 1828), Sylvanus Urban (= Edward Cave) (ed.). London: Nichols and Son. [Sections separately numbered; Hansard's advertisement begins approx. 800 pages in.]

Hansard, Thomas Curson (junior). 1843. Hansard's Parliamentary Debates [advertisement appended after the formal end of the debates volume]. In *Hansard's Parliamentary Debates*, Third Series, Vol. LXXI (31 July–24 August 1843), 1–4. London: Thomas Curson Hansard.

Hansard Writing Team. 2018. *The Hansard Story*. London: House of Commons Library.

Hughes, Lorna M. Forthcoming 2023. The ties that bind: Curation and creation in the Digital Humanities. In *The Cambridge Companion to the Digital Humanities*, Andrew Prescott, Lorna M. Hughes, Claudine Moulin & Edward Vanhoutte (eds). Cambridge: CUP.

Jordan, H. Donaldson. 1931. The reports of parliamentary debates, 1803–1908. *Economica* 34: 437–349.

Jupp, Peter. 1998. *British Politics on the Eve of Reform: The Duke of Wellington's Administration, 1828–30*. London: Palgrave Macmillan.

Leech, Geoffrey, Garside, Roger & Bryant, Michael. 1994. CLAWS4: The tagging of the British National Corpus. In Proceedings of the 15th International Conference on Computational Linguistics (COLING 94) Kyoto, Japan, 622–628.

Leech, Geoffrey & Short, Mick. 2007 [1981]. *Style in Fiction*, 2nd edn. London: Routledge. [Reprints certain unaltered chapters from the 1981 first edition.]

MacDonagh, Michael. [n.d., likely 1913]. *The Reporters' Gallery*. London: Hodder and Stoughton.

McBath, James H. 1970. Parliamentary reporting in the nineteenth century. *Communications Monographs* 37(1): 25–35.

Mollin, Sandra. 2007. The *Hansard* hazard: Gauging the accuracy of British parliamentary transcripts. *Corpora* 2(2): 187–210.

Murphy, Arthur. 1792. *An Essay on the Life and Genius of Samuel Johnson LL.D.* London: Longman et al.

Parliament. Select Committee on Parliamentary Proceedings. 1862. *Report*. HC 373. London: Her Majesty's Stationery Office.

Parliament. Joint Select Committee of the House of Lords and House of Commons. 1888a. *The Cost and Method of the Publication of Debates and Proceedings in Parliament*. HC 284. London: Henry Hansard and Son.

Parliament. House of Commons Papers. 1888b. *Copy of Contract Between MacRae, Curtice & Co., Limited, and the Controller of Her Majesty's Stationery Office, for Preparing, Printing, and Publishing Reports of Debates and Other Proceedings in both Houses of Parliament, to Commence from the 1st day of January 1889*. HC 445. London: Henry Hansard and Son.

Parliament. Select Committee on Parliamentary Debates. 1893. *Report*. HC 213. London: His Majesty's Stationery Office.

Parliament. Select Committee on Parliamentary Debates. 1907. *Report*. HC 239. London: His Majesty's Stationery Office.

Parliament. Select Committee on Publications and Debates Reports. 1930. *Report*. HC 164. London: His Majesty's Stationery Office.

Parliament. Select Committee on Publications and Debates Reports. 1944. *Report*. HC 110. London: His Majesty's Stationery Office.

Parliament. House of Commons Procedure Committee. 2007. *Report*. HC 541. London: Her Majesty's Stationery Office.

Piao, Scott, Dallachy, Fraser, Baron, Alistair, Demmen, Jane, Wattam, Stephen, Durkin, Philip, McCracken, James, Rayson, Paul & Alexander, Marc. 2017. A time-sensitive *Historical Thesaurus*-based semantic tagger for deep semantic annotation. *Computer Speech and Language* 46: 113–135.

Port, M.H. 1990. The Official Record. *Parliamentary History* 9: 175–183.

Rayson, Paul, Archer, Dawn, Piao, Scott & McEnery, Tony. 2004. The UCREL semantic analysis system. In Proceedings of the Workshop on Beyond Named Entity Recognition Semantic Labelling for NLP Tasks in Association with 4th International Conference on Language Resources and Evaluation (LREC 2004), Lisbon, Portugal, 7–12.

Semino, Elena & Short, Mick. 2004. *Corpus Stylistics: Speech, Writing and Thought Presentation in a Corpus of English Writing*. London: Routledge.

Slembrouck, Stef. 1992. The parliamentary *Hansard* 'verbatim' report: The written construction of spoken discourse. *Language and Literature* 1(2): 101–119.

Sutherland, Lorraine & Farrell, Stephen. 2013. The History, Workings and Future Challenges of Hansard. UK Parliament Open Lecture, 11 December 2013. <https://www.youtube.com/watch?v=yaLWV9gfiS0> (1 February 2021).

Sutherland, Lorraine & Vice, John. 2015. *Hansard: The Ear of History*. London: House of Lords Library and House of Lords Hansard.

Thomas, P.D.G. 1959. Sources for debates of the House of Commons 1768–1774. *Bulletin of the Institute of Historical Research* (special supplement 4).

Vice, John. 2018. Charles Dickens and Gurney's Shorthand: "That savage stenographic mystery". *Language and History* 61: 77–93.

Vice, John & Farrell, Stephen. 2017. *The History of Hansard*. London: House of Lords Hansard and House of Lords Library.

Wattam, Stephen, Rayson, Paul, Alexander, Marc & Anderson, Jean. 2014. Experiences with parallelisation of an existing NLP Pipeline: Tagging *Hansard*. In Proceedings of the 9th International Conference on Language Resources and Evaluation (LREC '14), Reykjavik, Iceland, 4093–4096.

CHAPTER 2

Salient differences between Australian oral parliamentary discourse and its official written records

A comparison of 'close' and 'distant' analysis methods

Haidee Kotze[1,2] Minna Korhonen[3,4] Adam Smith[4] & Bertus van Rooy[2,5]

[1] Utrecht University | [2] North-West University | [3] The Australian National University | [4] Macquarie University | [5] University of Amsterdam

This chapter addresses the question of editorial practice for the Australian Hansard with the use of an aligned corpus of transcribed audio recordings and the corresponding Hansard records, covering the period 1946–2015. A more traditional, qualitative, bottom-up approach is taken by manually analysing the data to compile a list of differences in the two types of records. In addition, a deductive, quantitative approach is adopted by using the multidimensional analysis method of Biber (1988) to identify significant differences in the frequencies of (clusters of) features between the oral transcripts and written Hansard records and interpret these. Our primary aim is to provide insight into methodological questions associated with working with big linguistic data. Alongside this, we report findings about differences between the written Hansard and the original speeches: reduction of spoken language processing features and informality, greater conservatism, and more density – although these differences decrease over time.

Keywords: Australian Hansard, close reading, distant reading, editorial practice, informality, conservatism, spoken language

https://doi.org/10.1075/scl.111.02kot
© 2023 John Benjamins Publishing Company

1. Introduction

Mollin (2007) coined the phrase "the Hansard hazard" on the basis of her analysis of British parliamentary data, and cautioned linguists against depending uncritically on the official records of parliamentary debates, the Hansard, as representations of spoken language. This caution is based on the fact that the official written record is a written *representation* of the speech of parliamentarians, mediated by various other language users: reporters, transcribers, copyeditors, and proofreaders. While we agree that the Hansard cannot simply be regarded as a transcription of spoken language, we have argued elsewhere (Kruger & Smith 2018; Kruger, van Rooy & Smith 2019) that the hybrid spoken-written nature of the Hansard is, in fact, a unique advantage of the register, allowing an opportunity to gain insight into the norms for the written *representation* of spoken discourse. The long history of the British Hansard, and the fact that colonisation transplanted the same conventions for parliamentary records to many other contexts, opens a window not only on changes in English *usage* over time, and in different contexts, but also on how *norms* for the "institutional practice of discourse representation" (Slembrouck 1992: 107) have changed over time, and in different contexts.

Editorial policy for the Hansard is determined both formally, by style guides, and informally, by a community of practice. While editorial policies generally remain invisible (Edwards 2016: 158), some comments from Hansard reporters and editors over the last century are instructive about the extent of intervention (see also Alexander, this volume). MacDonagh (1913: 32), for example, explains that the (British) Hansard editor's chief task is "so to unwind the verbose skein as to make clear the hidden governing principle, the salient points, of the speaker; to present the vague thought with definiteness, to give the language in which it is expressed consecutiveness and coherency". A century later, Sutherland and Farrell (2013) write that as British Hansard editors they "aim to provide a full, accurate and fluent report... by removing repetition and a good deal of the 'wordiness' of everyday speech patterns. We take out a lot of the verbal scaffolding..." There have been suggestions that editorial practices related to the Hansard are changing, moving from linguistic conservatism towards a greater tolerance for colloquial usage, informality, and a closer verbatim style. While Gravlee (1981) refers to comments from British Hansard reporters (from the 1970s) that they have a particular Hansard style "that we use for certain phrases and we tend to make people speak in that style if we can" (Gravlee 1981: 92), much of the contemporary Australian advice centres on the maxim of "give speakers what they say" (Hansard 2008). Other factors have also bolstered the move towards a more verbatim style over time. The recording and broadcasting of parliamentary business has prompted a less interventionist approach so that the publicly available broadcasts and the official records do not diverge too dramatically. Production mechanisms for the Hansard have changed from shorthand reporting and retyping to recording and respeaking, which favours a more verbatim approach as well.

Despite the awareness of the effects of transcription and editorial intervention on the written representation of parliamentary speeches and debates, there is only limited research on exactly what these differences are – and whether there have been changes in editorial practices over time. The existing research has followed largely the same methodological approach of manually comparing relatively small samples of the British House of Commons Hansard to identify, and sometimes quantify, editorial changes. However, quantitative methods have hardly been used in this area, and it appears that the benefits of 'big data' have not yet been leveraged in identifying the differences between spoken parliamentary discourse and the official written record. Of course, this also raises questions of whether this is the kind of research where "distant reading" (Moretti 2013)[1] methods and the quantitative modelling of textual characteristics using big language data actually yield more robust insights than more traditional methods of 'close reading' analysis. In this chapter, we wish to address this methodological question at the same time as investigating the differences between spoken parliamentary discourse and the written record, and any potential changes in editorial practices in transforming spoken language to writing.

We extracted the Hansard records for archival recordings that we were able to access from 1946 (the year in which radio broadcasts of parliamentary sittings started in Australia) and 1959, as well as selecting from available recordings from 1988–1989, 1995 and 2015. These recordings were transcribed, and used to create a parallel corpus of the original spoken discourse, and the Hansard records that are the direct officially published counterparts of these transcriptions.

---

1. We consciously adopt the term 'distant reading', and its opposite 'close reading' in this chapter, acknowledging that both terms derive from a different domain – literary studies (see also Mair, this volume). We see two advantages in adopting these terms. First, it makes clear the shared (methodological) tensions in both linguistics and literary studies; both areas of research have correlates to these approaches to textual analysis that are foregrounded in debates about the value of computational or digital approaches to textual data in the broader field of the Digital Humanities. Second, we see value in using these terms specifically, rather than other terms that may present themselves, like 'qualitative' versus 'quantitative'. The terms 'close' and 'distant reading' identify, in the first instance, the ways in which researchers engage in the first identification of patterns in data: either manually and through closely reading texts, or digitally, and 'at a distance'. It highlights, also, the involvement of the researcher, in both cases, in the activity of some form of reading. Both close and distant reading can, in our view, be qualitative and quantitative in nature, and, in fact, there is usually a circular movement between quantification and qualitative analysis in both approaches.

The research team followed two different approaches. The first approach, which we term 'close reading', starts with a bottom-up manual close reading of texts to identify and manually annotate changes between the written record and the transcription of the original spoken contributions, culminating in the quantification and interpretation of salient features (executed by Korhonen and Smith, with no knowledge of the findings of the second approach). The second approach, which we term 'distant reading', involves purely automatic annotation of the data by adapting the multidimensional method of Biber (1988), as previously applied by Kruger and Smith (2018) and Kruger, van Rooy and Smith (2019) to Hansard data, followed by quantitative pattern extraction using statistical criteria, before turning to the interpretation of the data (executed by Kotze and van Rooy without knowledge of the findings of the first approach). After completion of the two analyses, the authors convened to compare the findings across the analyses. The aim of combining these analyses is to investigate the convergences and divergences between the two methods, and to determine how their combination might provide insights into editorial practices for the Hansard, and changes in these practices over time.

In the following section we first consider in more detail existing research on the differences between spoken parliamentary discourse and its official transcription in the Hansard record. Based on this, we set out our research questions, focusing on both the substantive dimension (i.e., how the spoken originals are altered in the written representation, and whether editorial practices for this representation change over time) and the methodological dimension (i.e., whether different analytical methods provide convergent or divergent insights in this respect, and whether there are notable advantages and limitations to either method). Subsequent to this we focus on the methods employed in our study. We outline in more detail our corpus, as well as the 'close reading' and 'distant reading' methods we adopted in order to determine the salient differences between the spoken discourse and its written representation over a period of approximately 70 years. This is followed by a presentation of the findings of the two analyses, and reflection on the results these yield.

2.   The 'Hansard hazard'

As far as we are aware, there are only four studies investigating the changes made in transforming parliamentary debates to the written Hansard record. The first three, Slembrouck (1992), Mollin (2007), and Cribb and Rochford (2018), compare transcripts to the official records of the British House of Commons (1987, 2006, and 2012–2014, respectively). The fourth study, by Hibbert (2003) considers the edited and published Hansard alongside the official transcription of the audio record of the South African parliament made by the Hansard production team themselves, together with the audio records as control for the transcriptions. These papers converge on three broad areas of change.

First, there is a shift towards a more formal, 'written' or literate style, which strips out the spoken-language features of the original discourse. Features indexing this tendency listed by Slembrouck (1992), Mollin (2007), and Cribb and Rochford (2018) include the elimination of repetition, incomplete utterances, filled and unfilled pauses, false starts, reformulations, syntactic blends, and disfluencies; and the replacement of contracted verb forms with full forms. This shift also involves the imposition of some hyperconservative or archaic lexical choices and grammatical forms by the Hansard production teams, which leads to a more conservative written record than the original spoken contributions, irrespective of the other transformations to the written style (also noted by Hibbert 2003). Relevant examples of such conservative reformulations include change of the bare infinitive with *help* to *help to*, the *going to* future to *will*, and *will* to *shall*; and more formal lexical choices (e.g. *ensure* instead of *make sure*, *consider* or *examine* instead of *look at*, *must* instead of *have to*).

Second, there is a reduction in the interpersonal (and to some degree, textual) meanings of the discourse, in favour of foregrounding ideational meanings. This is evident, for example, in the reduction in the frequency of amplifiers (*very, really, absolutely, actually, clearly*), the change of generic *you* to impersonal constructions, a reduction in the frequency of hedges (*I think, I guess, I mean*), and a reduction in the frequency of first-person pronouns.

Last, there is a transformation of discourse grounded in the 'here and now' deictic centre of the parliamentary interaction to a more distant, and even "decontextualised report that is also understandable to the distant reader" (Mollin 2007: 208). The most obvious indicators of this tendency are the change of the demonstratives *this* and *these* to *that* and *those*, and increased referential explicitness.

Cribb and Rochford (2018) investigate the same features as in Mollin (2007) to determine whether editorial practices have changed from 2006 to 2012–2014. They do find that "Hansard editors have moved towards a less formal, less conservative representation of spoken language" (Cribb & Rochford 2018: 5), in being more inclined to retain generic *you*, demonstratives, and amplifiers and stance adverbials.

While these papers provide insights into the type of changes typical in the transformation of spoken parliamentary discourse to the written record, they are also methodologically limited, both in respect of the data investigated, and the methods followed. Slembrouck (1992) relies on a discourse-analytical example-based approach drawing on examples from the 1987 budget debate in the British

House of Commons. There is no quantification in this paper. Mollin (2007) makes use of the first four hours of transcription of the sitting in the House of Commons on 13 June 2006, yielding approximately 43,000 words in the transcribed text, and 35,000 in the Hansard. Cribb and Rochford (2018) base their study on a much smaller corpus of approximately 4840 words representing just over 36 minutes of debate, from Prime Minister's Question Time in 2012–2014. Both these papers quantify the frequency of particular changes, identified by Mollin (2007) through manual analysis as changes that occurred more than five times in her corpus. Hibbert (2003), who focuses on South African parliamentary data, uses transcripts and Hansard records of four debates from April to May 1998, in the then National Assembly. She analyses only speeches, by 35 members of the African National Congress (ANC), which amounts to 265 pages of transcribed text and 150 pages of corresponding Hansard (no word counts are given). She follows an iterative, bottom-up discourse-analysis approach to identify changes made during editing.

These four papers are all based on what are essentially 'close reading' methods, manually comparing the transcriptions of audio files to the published record, and noting changes (that are subsequently investigated quantitatively). There is no research that we are aware of that attempts a 'distant reading' approach of quantitatively modelling the textual characteristics of the original oral discourse versus the official record – despite the fact that there has been substantial research in register studies investigating the differences between oral and written styles (e.g. the multidimensional method of Biber 1988). In addition, there is also no research on Hansard editorial practices other than for the British and South African Hansard; in other words, editorial practices in other contexts have hardly been researched (see Kotze 2019; Law 2019; Law & Kotze 2021 for corpus-based investigation of editorial changes in other registers in Australian and South African English). Our study attempts to address these gaps by answering two 'content-related' and two 'methodology-related' questions:

Content
– What are the salient differences between the spoken parliamentary discourse and the written representation of this discourse in the Australian Hansard?
– Have editorial practices shaping written representation changed over time?

Methodology
– Do 'distant reading' and 'close reading' methods converge or diverge in their identification of the differences between spoken parliamentary discourse and the Hansard?
– What are the relative advantages and disadvantages of these methods?

3. Methodology

3.1 Corpus

In building our parallel corpus of transcribed and official records of parliament, it would have been ideal to have access to comparable amounts of recorded data over regular time periods, representing similar types of parliamentary discourse (debates, speeches, presentation of bills, etc.) Unfortunately, while recordings of sittings in the Australian House of Representatives are available online going back until 1988, before that time the archives are quite irregular, and access to recordings is limited. Our first aim was, therefore, to find recordings to cover as broad a period of time as possible, since recording of parliamentary proceedings first started in 1946. Table 2.1 shows the number of words transcribed for each recording collected, alongside the equivalent extract from Hansard.

Table 2.1 Word counts for transcribed recordings and equivalent Hansard record (Number of samples in each year in square brackets. Samples vary between 2,500 and 11,000 words.)

Year	Transcription	Hansard
1946 [2]	8,409	5,885
1959 [3]	13,960	11,212
1988–1989 [4]	37,264	31,992
1995 [4]	34,771	29,686
2015 [4]	34,081	29,093
Total	128,485	107,868

Each of the recordings was transcribed orthographically to provide a verbatim record of the proceedings, including elements excluded from the official Hansard records, such as false starts, repetitions, unsolicited interruptions and, in the case or the earlier recordings, interpolations from commentators (these were excluded from the final wordcount).[2]

We acknowledge that, by the standards of 'big data' our corpus is not large; however, this is an unavoidable limitation of the specialised nature of the dataset. Nevertheless, it is sufficiently substantive to carry out the 'distant reading' analysis in this chapter, particularly because the two sub-corpora are not independent of

---

2. The early recordings in our corpus include commentary from radio presenters, who provided descriptions of what was happening in the chamber, or interpretations of events.

one another, but are 'versions' of each other. Our interest is precisely in the differences between two largely similar datasets; for this purpose, we believe the dataset is large enough, though, of course, it may well be the case that larger datasets reveal more, or other, differences. This is an important avenue for further research.

3.2 'Close reading' methodology

As already noted (Section 2) previous synchronic research in this area has adopted 'close reading' methods to compare the spoken record with the published one. Our research had the aim of investigating whether similar language features and editorial practices would be identified for this diachronic dataset, and whether there were features that might demonstrate editorial changes that went beyond the obviously prescriptive or normative editorial motivation previously identified.

In order to carry out the close reading, we first created a parallel corpus of our transcribed version and the official Hansard, with each spoken utterance side by side with the equivalent sentence in the published version. At points where the proceedings were not reflected in the official Hansard, for instance where the Speaker introduced a member of parliament (MP), a space was left. Table 2.2 illustrates the structure of the parallel corpus.

These parallel texts from each recording were then manually reviewed, and regular edits were noted, to draw up a preliminary list of potential features for investigation, which yielded the following possibilities:

1. performance characteristics (e.g. filled pauses, repetitions, reformulations);
2. parliamentary formulae (e.g. references to turn-taking, uses of titles);
3. contractions presented in full;
4. 'corrections' of grammar (e.g. subject-verb concord, split infinitives);
5. lexical choices (e.g. *about/concerning, like/such as*);
6. use of amplifiers (e.g. *very, really, absolutely, a lot*);
7. use of hedges (e.g. *sort of, quite, I think, I feel*);
8. use of discourse markers (e.g. *well, you know, now, so*);
9. use of demonstratives (e.g. *this, that, these, those*);
10. choice of modals (e.g. *will, shall, be going to*);
11. choice of pronouns (e.g. *I, you, he, myself, himself*).

These categories accord quite closely with those from the previous studies mentioned in Section 2. They reflect a range of potential influences on editorial choices: for example between imposing formal standards (e.g. of parliamentary procedure or prescriptive grammar), or preserving the speakers' choices; and

Table 2.2 Extract from parallel transcription/Hansard corpus (7 October 1946)

Transcription	Hansard
Mr. SPEAKER. – The member for Grey.	
Mr. RUSSELL. – Mr. Speaker, I desire to ask the Minister for Air a question without notice	Mr. RUSSELL. – I ask the Minister for Air
A commentator. – \<overlap\> This is Mr. Russell.	
Mr. RUSSELL. – [unclear] \</overlap\> deciding to close the air training school at Port Pirie would the authorities then consider the converting of some of the huts for suitable homes so as to ease the acute housing shortage of Port Pirie?	whether, in the event of the Department of Air deciding to close the air training school at Port Pirie, the conversion of some of the huts into suitable homes will be considered, so as to ease the acute housing shortage in Port Pirie?
In support of the suggestion I point I wish to point out that electric light and power is laid on together with excellent roads, well-prepared garden space, lawns, water service, deep drainage, swimming pool, recreation grounds, et cetera.	I point out that electric light and power are laid on, and there are excellent roads, a well-prepared garden space, lawns, a water service, deep drainage, a swimming pool, recreation grounds, &c.
Mr. SPEAKER. – The honorable Minister for Air.	

between preserving the messiness of speech through inclusion of performance characteristics and the use of amplifiers and hedges, or cleaning the text up for the written medium. As previous studies have noted the shift to a less formal (Cribb & Rochford 2018) or more colloquial (Kruger & Smith 2018) style, we chose to concentrate on a subset of features that are not necessarily dictated by standardised written norms and have the potential to reveal more subtle attitudinal shifts over time:

1. pronouns (*I, me, you, he, she, one, we, they*);
2. discourse markers (*well, now, you know, I mean, of course, in fact, so*);
3. modals (*will, be going to, would, should, can, may, must, have (got) to, need to*).

In the analysis, we first considered these three features as sets, and then subsequently investigated individual items to identify particular patterns of editorial changes over time.

3.3 'Distant reading' methodology

For the 'distant reading' analysis, we made use of an adaptation of Biber's multidimensional analysis method (for a more detailed discussion, see Kruger & Smith 2018; Kruger, van Rooy & Smith 2019). Biber's (1988) multidimensional analysis method starts with identifying and quantifying a set of 67 linguistic features. The normalised frequency counts of these features are subjected to factor analysis to identify groupings or clusters of dependent variables. These quantitative steps are performed automatically, rather than manually, and we also imposed no initial checks on the accuracy of the automatic annotation. This decision is motivated by the fact that our principal motivation in this chapter is precisely to explore how far an automated 'distant reading' analysis that avoids the manual annotation involved in the 'close reading' analysis can take the analyst – and what the limitations and pitfalls of this approach are. We reflect on this in more detail in Section 4.2.2, where we do implement a post-hoc analysis of the accuracy of the annotation.

The clusters of features identified automatically in the factor analysis are analysed and interpreted to arrive at a characterisation of each factor that reflects the 'shared' variable underlying the feature clusters, a step that does require non-automated engagement by the researchers.

Biber's (1988) analysis identifies six dimensions along which registers vary. While we acknowledge that the interpretation of these dimensions is open to question, we adopt Biber's (1988) characterisations here for the purposes of comparisons with other studies, particularly our own previous work on the Hansard:

1. involved versus informational production;
2. narrative versus non-narrative concerns;
3. explicit versus situation-dependent reference;
4. overt expression of persuasion;
5. abstract versus non-abstract information;
6. on-line information elaboration.

Based on the outline of editorial changes that have been identified by previous researchers (see Section 2), we expect the Hansard to most obviously differ from the original spoken discourse on Dimension 1, 3 and 5.

To perform the multidimensional analysis, we used the Multidimensional Analysis Tagger (MAT) developed by Nini (2014), which implements Biber's (1988) algorithms with a small number of refinements for improved accuracy to extract feature counts, normalise them, and compute dimension scores (a score that reflects where a particular corpus text 'rates' on each dimension, conceived of as a continuum) using the factor loadings of Biber's (1988) original model. The scores are computed automatically by converting the individual variable frequencies to standardised scores (to assign equal weight to all variables, rather than afford much higher weight to more frequent variables) and then adding the standardised frequencies for the variables that load positively on the dimension in question, or subtracting them for the variables that load negatively on the dimension. The standardised frequency of an individual variable is only included in the count for the dimension on which that variable has the highest (absolute) factor loading.

In order to investigate how editorial intervention changes the overall register configuration of parliamentary debates when they are transformed to the Hansard, and whether this intervention changes over time, we first visualise the dimension scores, by period and version. Subsequent to this, we use a paired Wilcoxon test (a non-parametric test for dependent samples) to determine whether the dimension scores are significantly different for the two versions. Devising a statistical method to determine the interaction of period and version (in other words, to statistically determine whether there is a change in the relationship between the transcript and the Hansard over time) is problematised by the dependency structure of the data: the transcripts and Hansard data are not independent of one another, and therefore generalised linear regression modelling cannot be used. We therefore compare, for both the analysis of dimension scores and individual features, only the effect of version, using an appropriate statistical test for dependent samples. In order to assess change over time, we rely on interaction plots. We foresee a more detailed statistical analysis of this interaction of period and version as an avenue for future research.

Subsequently, we investigated each of the 67 individual linguistic features analysed to identify features where there is a significant change in frequency from the parliamentary debates to the official record (again, using a paired Wilcoxon test). Ten features demonstrated a significant difference; we briefly discuss these in relation to existing research, and attempt to identify overall trends in editorial practice regarding these features.

4. Findings

4.1 'Close reading' results

Table 2.3 shows the normalised (per 1,000 words) aggregate frequencies of the three selected groups of features, across the different time periods. A clear pattern of higher frequencies in the transcription corpus than in the official Hansard is evident for pronouns and discourse markers, but not for modals, where the inverse pattern is evident. This is shown in the column reflecting the percentage change from the transcripts to the Hansard. Discourse markers are clearly particularly prone to being removed in the written transcription process.

This is predictable in that discourse markers like *well* or *so* are considered to be a colloquial feature that we might expect editors to tend to remove in the more polished official record, and the changes to pronouns can be accounted for by the fact that there is a parliamentary convention of referring to speakers by title (*the honourable member*, etc.) which may be more rigorously applied in the official record than in spontaneous production. The modals represent a more diverse range of formality and interpersonal functions, so viewing them as a set is unlikely to highlight differences across the corpora.

Table 2.3 Normalised frequencies (per 1,000 words) of selected features in transcriptions vs. Hansard, by time period, with percentage changes in frequency from the spoken discourse to the written record

	Pronouns			Discourse markers			Modals		
	Transcript	Hansard	% change	Transcript	Hansard	% change	Transcript	Hansard	% change
1946	26.5	20.6	−22.6	0.8	0.3	−62.5	14.2	13.8	−2.8
1959	30.2	26.4	−12.6	3.1	1.2	−61.3	12.3	14.4	+17.1
1988–1989	33.6	25.8	−23.2	4.4	1.3	−70.5	15.0	16.8	+12.0
1995	48.4	40.7	−15.9	6.4	1.4	−78.1	16.8	20.3	+20.8
2015	43.8	40.5	−7.5	5.1	1.6	−68.6	10.5	11.7	+11.4

The diachronic tendencies in respect of a closing of the gap between the transcription and Hansard corpora for any of these features (which would reflect the tendency of the Hansard becoming closer to a verbatim record in more recent times; see Section 2) can only be identified tentatively. For pronouns there does seem to be a narrowing of the gap over time, whereas for discourse markers the gap appears to widen. However, there is also much variation from one period to the next. At the same time, it should also be considered that the nature of the 'gap' is not only affected by changes in editorial policies, but also by frequencies of the feature in the spoken discourse. For example, there is a clear increase in frequency of discourse markers over time in the transcripts, with the Hansard reflecting only a small proportion of them in any given period. Editorial approaches thus appear to have remained rather stable, but the norms of formal spoken discourse have changed over time, becoming more colloquial in style.

In the next sections we consider in more detail some of the particular occurrences of pronouns, discourse markers and modals to determine whether they reveal any clear changes in patterns of editorial influence.

4.1.1 *Pronouns*

A few interesting historical shifts can be noted for third-person pronouns (see Table 2.4). Pertinent to the research questions of this chapter is that the formal third-person pronoun *one* declines in frequency in the actual spoken discourse, signalling greater informality, but from 1946 until 1995 it is commonly (and increasingly) added to the Hansard, signalling a move towards a more formal style in the Hansard that actively resists the change in progress in spoken language. The dramatic change between 1995 and 2015 suggests a change in editorial policy in respect of the degree of verbatim-ness of the transcription. The appearance of the feminine pronoun *she*, albeit at very low frequencies, clearly reflects social change in its use to refer to the increasing number of female MPs in parliament, as well as to women in society in general. But this change happens equally across the transcribed and the official records. The frequency of *they* does not show clearly interpretable patterns, whereas the consistently and increasingly lower frequencies of *he* in the Hansard compared to the transcripts reflect the removal of repetition, in some cases, but commonly also a situation where the speaker refers to another member (often from the executive) using a third-person pronoun, whereas the Hansard makes the identity more explicit by inserting the name or title of the person referred to.

Table 2.4 Normalised frequencies (per 1,000 words) of third-person pronouns in transcriptions vs. Hansard, by time period, with percentage changes in frequency from the spoken discourse to the written record

	one			they			she			he		
	Transcript	Hansard	% change	Transcript	Hansard	% change	Transcript	Hansard	% change	Transcript	Hansard	% change
1946	0.2	0.3	+50	2.0	1.2	−40	0.0	0.0		4.6	3.9	−15.2
1959	0.2	0.4	+100	3.8	3.5	−7.9	0.0	0.0		6.1	4.9	−19.7
1988–1989	0.2	0.5	+150	4.5	4.1	−8.9	0.2	0.2	0	4.1	2.9	−29.3
1995	0.1	0.3	+200	7.0	6.0	−14.3	1.0	0.8	−20	4.0	2.8	−30.0
2015	0.05	0.05	0	5.7	5.5	−3.5	0.3	0.3	0	4.6	2.9	−36.9

More salient differences are evident for first- and second-person pronouns, as shown in Table 2.5.

Table 2.5 Normalised frequencies (per 1,000 words) of first- and second-person pronouns in transcriptions vs. Hansard, by time period, with percentage changes in frequency from the spoken discourse to the written record

	we			you			me			I		
	Transcript	Hansard	% change	Transcript	Hansard	% change	Transcript	Hansard	% change	Transcript	Hansard	% change
1946	1.3	0.3	−76.9	0.1	0.0	−100	1.1	1.0	−9.1	17.1	13.8	−19.3
1959	4.9	4.6	−6.1	1.1	0.3	−72.7	1.2	1.3	+8.3	13.0	11.6	−10.8
1988–1989	6.6	6.6	0	5.5	0.7	−87.3	0.7	0.8	+14.2	11.8	9.9	−16.1
1995	12.3	12.6	+2.4	5.8	3.8	−34.5	1.3	1.2	−7.7	17.0	12.6	−25.9
2015	13.4	14.0	+4.5	5.5	4.0	−27.3	0.7	1.0	+42.9	13.6	12.7	−6.6

I and *me* remain relatively constant in their usage over time. The editorial treatment of *me* varies drastically over the time periods, although the low frequencies may well contribute sampling variance to the overall picture, whereas for *I* there is overall a tendency to be reduced in frequency in the Hansard in comparison to the original spoken discourse (in line with the reduction of interpersonal marking outlined in Section 2). *We* shows a dramatic increase in frequency over time in the original spoken parliamentary discourse: a percentage increase of more than 900%. This increase is carried over into the Hansard record, and even slightly reinforced by further additions in the latter part of the timespan under investigation. This signals a clear change in rhetorical strategies in Australian parliamentary discourse, potentially reflecting an emphasis on party politics – where the unified stance of a party is emphasised by the use of *we* – or a direct appeal to the general public as Australians with a common interest (see Examples (1) and (2)).

(1) I acknowledge that some of the projects that this government is building were ideas that *we* shared with the Labor Party when they were last in office.
(Hansard, 3 December 2015)

(2) We simply want to put beyond doubt that our present national flag, of which *we* are proud, cannot be changed without an affirmative vote of the Australian people. (Hansard, 31 August 1989)

The further analysis of this change in rhetorical strategy falls outside the scope of this chapter.

You is hardly used in spoken parliamentary discourse until the late 1950s, signalling close conformance within the chamber of the conventions of parliamentary interaction (where *you* is not to be used unless addressing the Speaker or chair). From the late 1980s onwards, however, there is a clear shift in usage: from the late 1950s to the late 1980s the frequency of *you* in spoken discourse increases by around 400%. Editorial policies until the late 1980s clearly proscribe the use of *you* in the written record, and the 1980s represent a period where there is a particularly strong mismatch between frequent use and strong editorial proscription, with the frequency of *you* reduced by around 87% in the editorial process (see also Example (3)). From the mid-1990s onwards there is clearly more tolerance for a more verbatim rendering of the more informal style taking hold in the Australian parliament, with a narrowing of the gap between the spoken reality and the written record. Parliamentarians continue to adopt the more informal and colloquial *you*, but editors now also transfer it to the written record.

A closer look at the different uses of *you* and the editorial decisions applied is instructive. Table 2.6 shows two different uses of *you*, classified as 'direct address' (Example (3a)) and 'generic' (Example (4a)), and shows the percentage of editorial decisions on whether to retain, change or omit the original usage (note that N/A indicates the whole utterance has been omitted from the Hansard record, not just the pronoun itself).

Table 2.6 Editorial decisions in respect of generic *you* and *you* used as direct address, over time (proportions of decision, with total raw frequency in brackets per year)

	Direct address				Generic			
	N/A	Omitted	Changed	Retained	N/A	Omitted	Changed	Retained
1946 (N=1)	0	0	100	0	0	0	0	0
1959 (N=15)	45	9	27	18	0	0	100	0
1988–1989 (N=206)	15	19	57	10	0	17	67	17
1995 (N=201)	17	37	8	38	0	9	11	80
2015 (N=188)	17	17	3	64	0	6	4	91

There is only one instance of *you* in the transcript for 1946, and this is changed in accordance with the parliamentary convention of addressing the fellow members of the house in the third person, as shown in Example (3).

(3) a. I did notice the paragraph to which *you* refer...   (Transcript)
     b. I noticed the paragraph to which *the honourable member* referred...
                                               (Hansard) (19 July 1946)

This convention has gradually been relaxed over time, so that in the 2015 data there are almost no instances of *you* as a form of direct address being edited out of the record.

There is also a development in the acceptance of the generic *you*, which appears to have happened quite recently. Example (4) shows how the generic *you* was edited out in the Hansard record for 1989.

(4) a. What do *you* do?   (Transcript)
     b. What does *one* do?   (Hansard) (22 December 1989)

Only 5 out of 27 instances of generic *you* were retained in the Hansard record for the period 1988–1989, whereas 61 out of 73 were retained in 1995 and 47 out of 48 in 2015.

The increased usage of *you* as direct address, as well as generic reference, clearly reflects an increasingly informal, personal, interactional and participatory style in Australian parliamentary discourse. This change in the spoken discourse is initially resisted in the formal record, but the increasing editorial acceptance over time also endorses this stylistic shift in the written record.

4.1.2 *Discourse markers*

As noted by Slembrouck (1992: 104), one of the processes involved in Hansard is "filtering out 'spokenness'". Discourse markers most overtly indexing spokenness are often not present in the Hansard at all, and pause fillers such as *um* and *uh* are consistently edited out, alongside other markers of disfluency such as repetitions, incomplete utterances and false starts, as our data clearly show too. These belong to a set of discourse markers that serve to buy the speaker processing time, or otherwise indicate strain on speech production (Biber et al. 1999: 1052–1054).

Table 2.7 shows the normalised frequencies of a further subset of discourse markers in the transcriptions and the Hansard, which are almost consistently edited out whenever they occur. The increasing use of these items in parliamentary discourse until 1995 indicates a process of colloquialisation in the live proceedings that is not reflected in the edited version of the record.

Table 2.8 presents the results for three commonly used discourse markers that are reduced by 50% or more, but not completely deleted (as those in Table 2.7

Table 2.7 Normalised frequencies (per 1,000 words) of discourse markers consistently removed from Hansard, by time period

	I mean		you know		well		now	
	Transcript	Hansard	Transcript	Hansard	Transcript	Hansard	Transcript	Hansard
1946	0.0	0	0.0	0.0	0.2	0.0	0.2	0.0
1959	0.1	0	0.0	0.0	0.2	0.0	1.2	0.1
1988–1989	0.3	0	0.1	0.03	0.4	0.0	1.2	0.03
1995	0.2	0	0.4	0.1	0.6	0.0	1.6	0.0
2015	0.2	0	1.0	0.0	0.2	0.03	1.1	0.0

are). The discourse markers in Table 2.8, as well as *well* (in Table 2.7) often serve the function of discourse organisation, as they are used as means of ordering the presentation of information, combined with a degree of attitudinal signalling. Example (5) shows how *of course* is used to organise the presentation of information, while simultaneously expressing to some degree the speaker's stance. Discourse markers are here used "to signal the pragmatic or discoursal role of the speaker's utterance, dynamically shaping it to the ongoing exchange" (Biber et al. 1999:1046).

(5)   *Of course*, other important measures have been introduced...

(Hansard, 3 June 1988)

Table 2.8 Normalised frequencies (per 1,000 words) of discourse markers retained in reduced amounts in Hansard, by time period, with percentage changes in frequency from the spoken discourse to the written record

	of course			in fact			so		
	Transcript	Hansard	% change	Transcript	Hansard	% change	Transcript	Hansard	% change
1946	0.2	0.0	−100	0.1	0.2	+42	0.0	0.2	
1959	1.4	0.9	−35	0.1	0.2	+29	0.1	0.0	−100
1988–1989	1.3	0.6	−57	0.6	0.3	−53	0.5	0.2	−54
1995	1.5	0.6	−61	0.9	0.2	−72	1.4	0.5	−65
2015	1.0	0.7	−33	0.4	0.3	−11	1.2	0.5	−56

The forms *I mean* and *you know* mainly serve interactive functions, rather than discourse organisational ones (see Biber et al. 1999:1046; also the discussion in Section 2). Their deletion may be attributed to a judgement that they are not necessary to reflect the argument of the speaker in the Hansard. This explanation does not cover *now* and *well*, though. One issue to note with discourse markers in general is that they are unlikely to have been edited systematically. The most recent *Hansard Usage and Editing Guide* that we have access to (Hansard 2008) classifies many of these items as examples of a broad category of spoken language that indicates the speaker may lack confidence, preparation, or experience, or is buying time, and labels them "verbal tics".[3] The guide advises that "editors should exercise caution when editing verbal tics" – that it might be necessary to retain them to "preserve the integrity of meaning of a speech", but that they may need to be deleted if they become too repetitive (Hansard 2008: 45–46). The open-ended nature of the category, and of the advice to editors, allows for a degree of subjective interpretation that makes the apparently quite consistent treatment of these different types of discourse markers over time all the more interesting.

4.1.3 *Modals*

The type of modal forms most commonly occurring in the Hansard records are those that express futurity. Table 2.9 provides the frequencies for *shall*, *will* and the semi-modal *be going to*. These modals illustrate the general pattern of editorial revisions that is in evidence with the other modals too, but at lower frequencies.

In the earlier time periods (1946 and 1959) there is a strong tendency for *shall* to replace *will*, as the more formal option in the Hansard record. The single instance from 1988 is retained, but thereafter *shall* completely disappears, both in the spoken discourse and the Hansard. This is consistent with the general trend for the disappearance of *shall* in English (Leech et al. 2009). Example (6) shows a typical case of the editorial tendency to replace *will* with *shall*.

(6) a. However I *will* have the uh question examined...   (Transcript)
     b. I *shall* have the question examined...   (Hansard) (10 July 1946)

The semi-modal *be going to* first appears in 1959, but only a small proportion of the (low frequency) item is retained in the edited Hansard. It appears at a much higher frequency in the 1988–1989 period, but again most instances are edited out, indicating a conservative approach towards the incoming form. Only in the two most recent periods are the frequencies for the semi-modal form almost equivalent in both the transcribed and the published record, indicating its acceptance

---

3. Of the items identified as discourse markers here, *now, you know, I mean, of course, in fact* and *so* are all specifically identified as examples of "common verbal tics".

Table 2.9 Normalised frequencies (per 1,000 words) of modal markers expressing futurity, by time period, with percentage changes in frequency from the spoken discourse to the written record

	shall			will			be going to		
	Transcript	Hansard	% change	Transcript	Hansard	% change	Transcript	Hansard	% change
1946	1.1	4.1	+281	7.4	7.0	+5	0	0	
1959	0.7	1.4	+99	5.2	5.2	0	0.4	0.2	−58
1988–1989	0.03	0.03	0	4.1	5.2	+26	1.7	0.5	−72
1995	0	0		5.2	6.4	+24	1.0	0.8	−17
2015	0	0		4.1	3.8	−6	0.5	0.4	−10

as a standard option. The editing of modals shows conservatism on the part of the Hansard production team, by retaining or reinserting older forms that are in decline, and by the editing out of innovative new forms in favour of more established forms.

In the next section we discuss the results from the 'distant reading' analysis, to investigate whether this methodology reveals similar or different patterns and relationships between the edited and non-edited versions of the parliamentary data under discussion.

4.2 'Distant reading' results

4.2.1 *Dimension score analysis*

The overall analysis of the difference between the transcription and the Hansard (not taking account of differences in time periods) shows that there is a significant difference in dimension score only for Dimension 2, degree of narrativity ($V=136$, $p<0.05$) – contrary to the expectation we formulated in Section 3.3. However, as we show in Section 4.2.2, this particular significant difference can be explained as a consequence of the automatic data annotation method and not as indicative of an unexpected textual difference. In the remainder of this subsection we briefly discuss each of the dimensions in turn, focusing on the differences between the transcripts and the Hansard, and patterns over time.

Dimension 1 (involved versus informational production) is the dimension that accounts for the overall picture of register variation in the most comprehensive way across different multidimensional studies (Biber 2014:16). Features

Differences between spoken discourse and written records 73

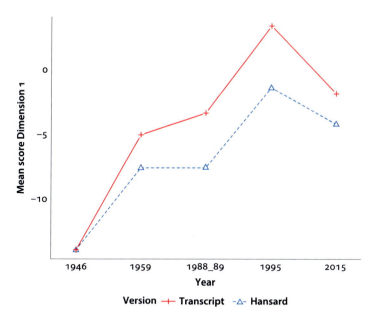

Figure 2.1 Mean scores for Dimension 1 (involved vs. informational production), transcripts vs. Hansard across time periods

that load positively on this dimension characterise informal, interactive, spoken language, while features with negative loadings characterise the opposite pole of informationally dense, typically written, language. Figure 2.1 shows mean scores for Dimension 1 over time, for the transcripts and the Hansard. As anticipated, the Hansard scores consistently slightly lower on this dimension (marking a shift towards more formal and less interactive discourse); however, this difference is not statistically significant. There is also no strong evidence for a dramatic change in editorial practices over time, with the distance between the two versions remaining fairly consistent across the time periods.

Dimension 2 is interpreted by Biber (1988) as reflecting narrative versus non-narrative concerns, or, distinguishing "active, event-oriented discourse and more static, descriptive or expository types of discourse" (Biber 1988: 109). As is shown in Figure 2.2, this is the dimension on which the Hansard (perhaps surprisingly) scores significantly higher, reflecting an adjustment to a more narrative style which appears to occur consistently over time. Three of the six individual linguistic features that load onto this dimension show a consistent pattern where frequency in the Hansard is higher than in the transcriptions of the original speeches across the five sampling periods: past tense verbs, perfect aspect verbs, and present participial clauses, the latter two differences attaining statistical significance. On closer inspection, the two significant differences pertain to very low numbers

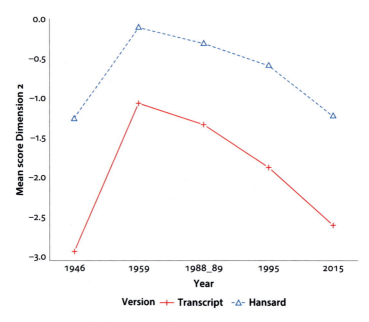

Figure 2.2 Mean scores for Dimension 2 (narrative vs. non-narrative concerns), transcripts vs. Hansard across time periods

and include a considerable proportion of incorrectly tagged forms, especially on the spoken transcriptions (see Section 4.2.2). Thus, in effect, this difference turns out to be relatively unimportant, and can be excluded from consideration.[4]

Dimension 3 captures the distinction between explicit, endophoric, text-dependent reference, and exophoric, situation-dependent reference that relies on the shared context of addresser and addressee for interpretation (Biber 1988: 110). Not surprisingly, the Hansard relies more heavily on endophoric, text-dependent reference, whereas the transcript reflects the shared context of the interlocutors in the chamber (see Figure 2.3). The difference is, however, not significant. There is also no evidence of changes in editorial practices over time.

---

[4]. Methodologically, it is important, whenever an automated analysis is done, to check reliability in the case of each specific study. The reliability of the multidimensional analysis was enhanced with selected post-annotation editing by Biber (1988), while Nini (2014) tried to improve tagging and identification algorithms to improve reliability. In terms of comparing the close and distant reading methodologies in this study, we opt to check for reliability, rather than do manual post-editing, since in large-scale projects, extensive post-editing will not always be feasible. It is a clear limitation of the method, and one of the questions we try to answer in this chapter is precisely how much we gain and how much we lose when adopting an automated data classification strategy.

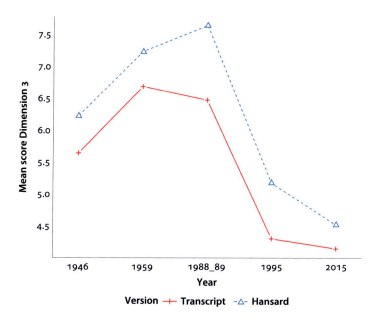

Figure 2.3 Mean scores for Dimension 3 (explicit vs. situation-dependent reference), transcripts vs. Hansard across time periods

Dimension 4 is labelled "Overt expression of persuasion" by Biber (1988: 111), and is particularly relevant to the genre of parliamentary debate, which, by nature, is intended to persuade listeners of a particular viewpoint. As is evident from Figure 2.4, the Hansard follows the transcripts closely in this respect.

Dimension 5 draws a distinction between registers that are "abstract, technical and formal versus other types of discourse" (Biber 1988:113). Figure 2.5 shows that the Hansard, as expected, scores slightly higher on this dimension than the transcripts, although there is evidence of convergence from the 1980s onwards (and, in any case, an overall decline in formality in parliamentary discourse itself, echoed in the Hansard).

Dimension 6 is labelled on-line information elaboration by Biber (1988: 113–114). Positive dimension scores are associated with spoken registers that convey relatively dense information, whereas negative scores are associated with edited, crafted, written registers. The original spoken contributions in parliament are indeed typical of spoken registers with dense information, and the fact that the Hansard also has positive dimension scores suggests that the editorial processes do not alter this characteristic of the data. It is especially clear towards the last two sample years that there is an almost perfect match between the two versions (see Figure 2.6).

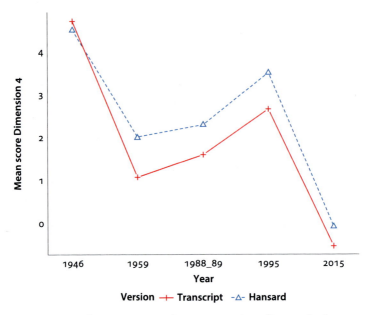

Figure 2.4 Mean scores for Dimension 4 (overt expression of persuasion), transcripts vs. Hansard across time periods

This overall analysis suggests that, once the scope of the analysis is widened to include a large set of features, functionally viewed, the differences between the transcripts and the Hansard appear less dramatic than might be assumed. To some degree, this may be seen as cautioning against a focus on individual features where changes are effected, without taking account of the much larger number of features where changes are not made. However, the inverse of this point may also be argued: a focus on these aggregate dimensions might mask changes in individual features that provide insights into editorial policies, and changes in these.

With this in mind, in the next section we shift the focus of the 'distant' reading to a more fine-grained level. We focus on individual features, but unlike the analysis presented in Section 4.1 we use an inductive method that brings no prior suppositions about editorial changes to determine the individual features that show significant differences between the spoken reality and written record.

4.2.2 Analysis of individual features

Many of the individual features analysed do not show any significant difference in frequency between the original oral discourse and the Hansard. This, in part, is to be expected, but is nevertheless important: the effects of editorial intervention, at the functional level, are less perceptible than one might anticipate based on the caution expressed by previous researchers and succinctly captured in the phrase

Differences between spoken discourse and written records 77

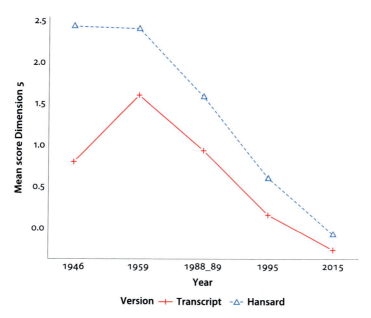

Figure 2.5 Mean scores for Dimension 5 (abstract vs. non-abstract information), transcripts vs. Hansard across time periods

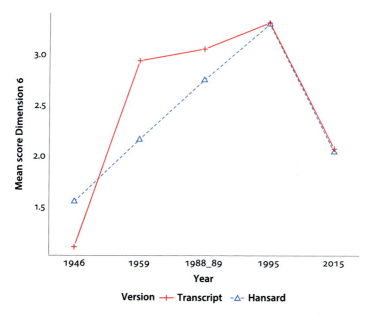

Figure 2.6 Mean scores for Dimension 6 (on-line information elaboration), transcripts vs. Hansard across time periods

"Hansard hazard" by Mollin (2007). Some of the changes made by editors, for instance by changing modals (*shall* instead of *will*, or *will* instead of *be going to*) or altering the vocabulary, represent conservatism, as noted earlier in this chapter, but they elude the multidimensional analysis since they do not lead to a change in the text at the functional or categorial level. In a sense, such conservatism does not alter the nature of the text. A situation of this kind is illustrated by the changes in Example (7), where *assistance* and *troops* in the Hansard replace *system* and *groups* respectively.

(7) a. whether the secretary general of Seato has yet made an approach to the government of the Kingdom of Laos uh with a view to offering them a *system* to repel the uh infiltration from Northern Viet Nam hostile *groups*.
(Transcript)

b. Has the Secretary-General of Seato yet approached the Government of the Kingdom of Laos with a view to offering *assistance* to repel the infiltration of hostile *troops* from North Viet Nam?　　(Hansard) (11 August 1959)

The features that escape this mould are thus of particular interest to us. We focus here only on the ten features that demonstrate a significant difference in frequency using the paired Wilcoxon test.[5] In the case of these features, there is a change to the nature of the text in the conversion from spoken original to written representation, which is the substantive research question of interest. Five of the features relate to shifts from a more oral to a more literate, and a more informal to a more formal style: *that*-deletion, contractions, clausal coordination, type–token ratio and split auxiliaries. Two further features relate to the interpersonal and textual meanings encoded more frequently in spoken and written language respectively: discourse particles and demonstratives. Of these seven features, three (contractions, discourse particles and demonstratives) have been identified by previous studies. We exclude three features from further discussion, because our subsequent manual checking identified them as prone to tagging error and normalisation problems: sentence relatives, perfect-aspect verbs, and present-participial clauses. For instance, in the case of present-participial clauses, the automatic tagging identified 59 cases of this structure across all transcriptions, of which 41 turned out to be valid instances, whereas 88 cases were identified in the written Hansard, of which only 48 turned out to be valid. Excluding these features following manual checking is in line with our methodological strategy of making

---

5. Though the inspection of interaction plots for all features yields evidence of noticeable differences, a strict statistical exclusion criterion was applied. For comments on the limitation of this method, see Section 3.3.

the most of the automated annotation process, while controlling for the possible problems that result from such automated analysis.

Comparisons of the interaction plots for these features suggest three main patterns of changes. First, there is a pattern in which spoken-language features are removed in the editorial process, but, over time, there is a clear change in editorial practice. Features in this category are demonstratives (Figure 2.7), *that*-deletion (Figure 2.8), and the use of clausal *and* (Figure 2.9).[6] In the case of demonstratives, these occur mostly at higher frequencies in the spoken discourse than in the Hansard; however, there is gradual convergence and by 2015 almost complete identity between the two versions in respect of this feature. Example (8) shows an instance of the removal of demonstratives typical of earlier periods.

(8)   a.   I refer to drop these drill halls around uh Hunter and Newcastle divisions.
                                                                    (Transcript)
      b.   I refer to drill halls in the Hunter and Newcastle divisions.
                                                           (Hansard) (10 July 1946)

For clausal *and* a similar trend is evident, though more gradual. For *that*-deletion the change is more sudden, suggesting a change in editorial policy somewhere between 1995 and 2015. Indeed, the 2008 *Hansard Usage and Editing Guide* specifies the following under the entry *I think (that)*: "Hansard once had rules governing the use of 'that' after expressions such as 'I think'. It is no longer necessary to add or delete 'that' after 'I think' or similar expressions. Give speakers what they say." (Hansard 2008: 25).

The second set of features index the categorical removal of markers of informal spoken discourse in the transformation from the spoken reality to the written record. Contracted forms (Figure 2.10) as well as discourse particles (Figure 2.11), such as *well* and *now*, are not used in the Hansard, and this remains largely the case for the period under investigation.

Lastly, two features, combined, index consistent increased complexity in the Hansard: type–token ratio (TTR) (Figure 2.12) and split auxiliaries (Figure 2.13). The Hansard always has a higher TTR than the transcripts do – and, for the 2015 data, this difference appears to be increasing.[7] The higher lexical diversity of the Hansard is, to a large degree, simply the consequence of the removal of the redun-

---

6.   In the analysis of individual features, the basis of normalisation is per 100 words, the default output of MAT (Nini 2014).

7.   TTR was calculated on the first 400 words of each text, and the observed differences in Figure 2.12 are thus not an artefact of differences in text length. This decision was initially made by Biber (1988) and implemented by Nini (2014), with the option to users to change the number, which we did not make use of.

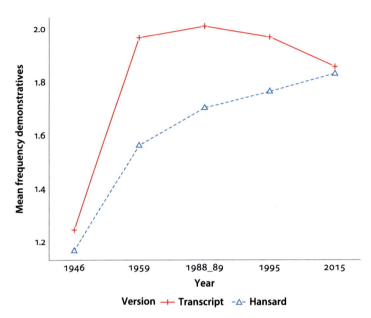

Figure 2.7 Mean normalised frequency (per 100 words) of demonstratives in the transcripts and Hansard, over time

dancy and repetition characteristic of spoken language. Split auxiliaries are significantly more frequent in the Hansard than in the spoken transcripts, which, at face value, seems counterintuitive. However, this difference is also largely the result of the reduction in the number of words: split auxiliaries are generally retained in the transformation from the spoken discourse to the written record; they only occur apparently more frequently because the word count is reduced in the editing process (but split auxiliaries themselves are not removed in this process).

5. Discussion and conclusion

The analyses reported on in this chapter converge on a number of findings in respect of substantive linguistic differences between the oral parliamentary discourse and the written records published in the Hansard. The most prominent difference is the reduction and/or complete deletion of features typical of spoken discourse that have little bearing on the informational content of the parliamentary discourse, confirming the findings of Slembrouck (1992), Mollin (2007) and Cribb and Rochford (2018) on smaller datasets. The finding of no significant differences on Dimension 4 of the multidimensional analysis, the overt expression of

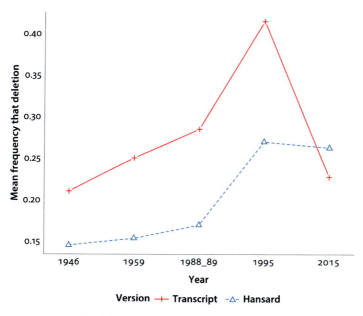

Figure 2.8 Mean normalised frequency of *that*-deletion (per 100 words) in the transcripts and Hansard, over time

persuasion, serves as reinforcement from the distant reading method for a finding that has been established by close reading strategies so far.

False starts and repetitions were not quantified, but from inspection of the texts, are clearly removed completely. Overt indicators of interpersonal interaction, such as discourse markers and non-third-person pronouns, are not deleted altogether, but are very often reduced, and more so in the earlier periods, with closer convergence between the official Hansard version and the original speeches emerging over time. Some forms are removed almost always, such as *well, you know* and *I think*, which are strongly interpersonal and do not contribute much to the hedging or framing of the content. *Now* is almost always omitted when used as a discourse marker, but only occasionally as a time adverb where it serves to organise the discourse. Other forms, like *so, of course* and *in fact* are retained in some cases, but generally about two-thirds are removed. The forms contribute more perceptibly to the organisation of the discourse, and therefore meet the acceptance of the editors more often, as they try to reflect the argumentation of the speakers adequately.

Features of informality that have relatively little impact on the information content of the speeches, such as contractions and the omission of the complementiser *that*, are often changed to their uncontracted and explicit forms respectively during the production of the Hansard. This remains the case throughout

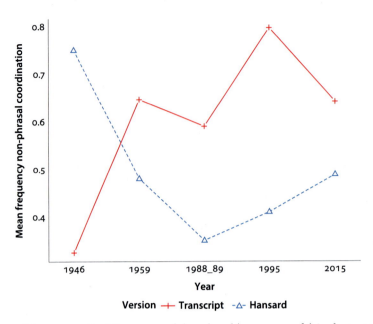

Figure 2.9 Mean normalised frequency of clausal *and* (per 100 words) in the transcripts and Hansard, over time

the entire period under investigation for contractions, but in the case of *that*-omission, there is convergence between the written and spoken versions, such that the omission of *that* by speakers is reflected more closely in the most recent Hansards.

Spoken language is tied to the immediate here and now of the deictic centre more than written language, which is often intended to be read and understood without reliance on the immediacy offered by the deictic orientation. In this respect, the Hansard continues to make an adjustment to lower the frequency of demonstratives in comparison to the original speeches, rendering the written text less reliant on the original spatial context of the parliamentary chamber, as also shown by Mollin (2007). However, gradual convergence takes place, with speeches using fewer and the Hansard retaining a larger proportion of the demonstratives as we come closer to the present. This difference has therefore largely disappeared.

Some of the changes in the data show the imposition of conservative choices by the Hansard editors. Some of these are stylistic choices, which favour the more formal variant, such as the removal of contractions. Another stylistic conservatism is to reflect the institutional convention of not addressing fellow parliamentarians in the second person, but by convention through the speaker as chairperson, leading to a lowering in the frequency of *you* in the Hansard com-

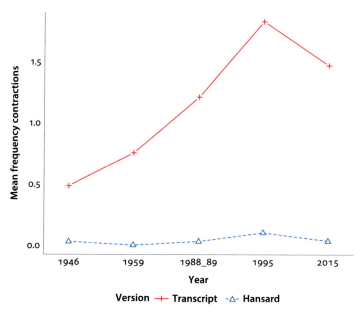

Figure 2.10 Mean normalised frequency of contractions (per 100 words) in the transcripts and Hansard, over time

pared to the original speeches. The continued use of *shall* in the written records, together with the late adoption of *be going to*, points to a different kind of conservatism, by using older forms of the language, and even changing the original speech to conform to the older choices, or failing to admit the incoming form for some time after it already abounds in the spoken language.

Information is presented more densely in the Hansard, which results in differences for some grammatical features associated with density. The TTR of the Hansard is higher than the transcriptions, while the frequency of clausal coordination with *and* is lower. An interesting side-effect of the overall reduction of spoken language features is that the overall density of a feature like split auxiliaries increases, purely because the Hansard texts are shorter, while they do not alter the actual instances of the split auxiliary construction in the input. In part, this is an artefact of calculation, but it does point to an overall densification that is in principle visible for all features in the original spoken presentation that are not targeted for reduction in the process of conversion into the written Hansard.

Two major kinds of changes can be observed in the editorial practices, emanating mainly from the close reading approach. Where incoming variants tended to be accepted later in the Hansard and replaced with more conservative forms in earlier periods, that distance seems to be closing, with the innovative grammatical features of the spoken language being reflected more faithfully in more recent

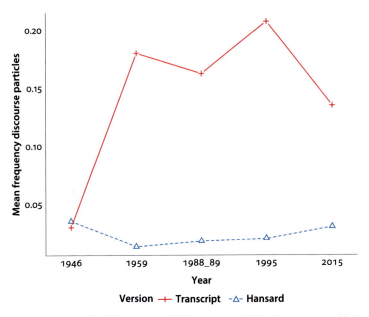

Figure 2.11 Mean normalised frequency of discourse particles (per 100 words) in the transcripts and Hansard, over time

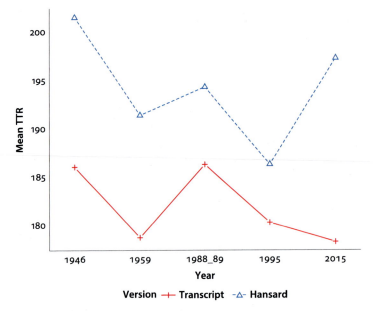

Figure 2.12 Mean TTR in the transcripts and Hansard, over time

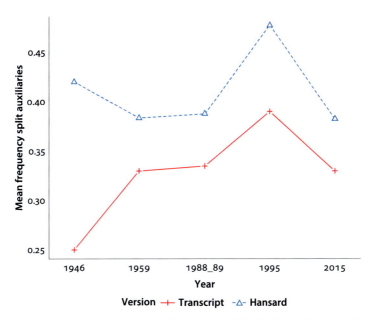

Figure 2.13 Mean normalised frequency (per 100 words) of split auxiliaries in the transcripts and Hansard, over time

Hansard records, as evidenced by modals in particular. Secondly, stylistically, the earlier Hansard records are more different from the spoken language, whereas the Hansard becomes closer to the style of the speeches in recent times, evidenced for example in the increased acceptance of the use of second-person pronouns, as also found by Cribb and Rochford (2018). There is no complete identity though, with false starts, repetitions and filled pauses in particular being removed completely, and some discourse markers also still targeted for removal or reduction in frequency, a revision process that does not seem to be subject to ongoing change.

The two different methods show overall convergence on the types of insight they yield in the data, but there are some differences in terms of the specifics of differences identified, and in the starting points for the interpretation of the differences. The two approaches have complementary strengths, and these can be used to some degree to counter the weaknesses.

The main advantages of the 'close reading' approach include the identification of specific features that are not included in the search strategies of the 'distant reading' models at all, or alternatively, are subsumed with other specific features into larger functional categories that hide differences at more specific levels. It is easier to identify the functional motivations for changes when reading texts closely, since actual instances of changes in the aligned datasets form the starting point for the identification, rather than quantitative differences that require a further step of textual identification when the entry point to the analysis is the 'distant reading' approach.

Disadvantages of the 'close reading' method include that it is time-consuming, and that there is a clear observation bias, both in terms of which features strike the analyst from the inspection of texts, and from the limits of human memory, where identical or similar changes that are several pages apart are not necessary connected in the analyst's memory. A more exhaustive analysis of some of the features excluded from this study (such as hedges and amplifiers), with input from a larger number of investigators would be a way of addressing these limitations.

The 'distant reading' method offers a more holistic view of the data, can yield basic results faster, and may even offer insights beyond the actual intention of the model that guides the quantification, to the extent that outliers and the anomalies in the data can be used as starting points for more in-depth analysis of concordance lines. Another major advantage is that lower-frequency phenomena, not easily visible to the naked eye of the analyst, can more likely be identified by the 'distant reading' method.

Disadvantages of the 'distant reading' method include potentially spurious findings due to tagging errors or limitations in the granularity of the classification scheme, as well as other unavoidable consequences of automatic classification, such as the inability to resolve all ambiguities or polysemous cases in the data, and aggregate scores that mask subtle variation. Close inspection of concordance lines provides some protection against spurious findings, but differences that are missed due to aggregation and clustering of features cannot be recovered using a 'distant reading' method. We have to concede that this is an unavoidable consequence of the automatic classification of data that forms the first step of the method, which we try to show upfront, rather than avoid as part of our comparison of the two methods. A fully automated analysis cannot be adopted without controlling for reliability and finding solutions to improve reliability where necessary, or else putting aside statistical patterns that are based on insufficiently reliable parts of the automated classification.

The quantitative analysis presented in this chapter, from both a 'close reading' and a 'distant reading' perspective, indicates that editorial practices do not lead to as much change from the spoken parliamentary discourse to the written representation in the Hansard as might be anticipated. In other words, the Hansard may not be such a "hazard" (Mollin 2007) for many linguistic features of interest. The overall similarities between the Hansard and the transcriptions of the original speeches on most of the dimensions of the multidimensional analysis strongly cautions against overstating claims of differences. Moreover, convergence between the two versions increases as we come closer to the present. Such precise quantification is a useful antidote to qualitative approaches that are intent on finding differences, and helps to contextualise the differences that are observed against the backdrop of overarching similarity. Insight into parliamentary discourse and its written representation can be refined if future research, based on larger samples than this study, is able to examine speeches, debates and question time as subgenres separate from one another.

References

Biber, Douglas. 1988. *Variation across Speech and Writing*. Cambridge: CUP.

Biber, Douglas. 2014. The ubiquitous oral versus literate dimension: A survey of multidimensional studies. In *Measured Language: Quantitative Studies of Acquisition, Assessment, and Variation*, Jeffrey Connor-Linton & Luke Wander Amoroso (eds), 1–20. Washington DC: Georgetown University Press.

Biber, Douglas, Johansson, Stig, Leech, Geoffrey, Conrad, Susan & Finegan, Edward (eds). 1999. *Longman Grammar of Spoken and Written English*. London: Longman.

Cribb, V. Michael & Rochford, Shivani. 2018. The transcription and representation of spoken political discourse in the UK House of Commons. *International Journal of English Linguistics* 8(2): 1–14.

Edwards, Cecilia. 2016. The political consequences of Hansard editorial policies: The case for greater transparency. *Australasian Parliamentary Review* 31(2): 145–160.

Gravlee, G. Jack. 1981. Reporting proceedings and debates in the British Commons. *Central States Speech Journal* 32(2): 85–99.

Hansard. 2008. *Hansard Usage and Editing Guide*. Canberra: Commonwealth of Australia.

Hibbert, Liesel. 2003. Changing language practices in parliament in South Africa. *Southern African Linguistics and Applied Language Studies* 21(3): 103–117.

Kotze, Haidee. 2019. Does editing matter? Editorial work, endonormativity and convergence in written Englishes in South Africa. In *English in Multilingual South Africa*, Raymond Hickey (ed.), 101–126. Cambridge: CUP.

Kruger, Haidee & Smith, Adam. 2018. Colloquialization and densification in Australian English: A multidimensional analysis of the Australian Diachronic Hansard Corpus. *Australian Journal of Linguistics* 38(3): 293–328.

Kruger, Haidee, van Rooy, Bertus & Smith, Adam. 2019. Register change in the British and Australian Hansard (1901–2015). *Journal of English Linguistics* 47(3): 183–220.

Law, Melanie. 2019. The Role of Editorial Intervention in Ongoing Language Variation and Change in South African and Australian English. PhD dissertation, Macquarie University / North-West University.

Law, Melanie & Kotze, Haidee. 2021. Gender, writing and editing in South African Englishes: Genitive alternation in multifactorial perspective. In *Gender in World Englishes*, Tobias Bernaisch (ed.), 205–232. Cambridge: CUP.

Leech, Geoffrey, Hundt, Marianne, Mair, Christian & Smith, Nicholas. 2009. *Change in Contemporary English: A Grammatical Study*. Cambridge: CUP.

MacDonagh, Michael. 1913. *The Reporters' Gallery*. London: Hodder & Stoughton. <https://archive.org/stream/reportersgalleryoomacdrich/reportersgalleryoomacdrich_djvu.txt> (1 September 2017).

Mollin, Sandra. 2007. The Hansard hazard: Gauging the accuracy of British parliamentary transcripts. *Corpora* 2(2): 187–210.

Moretti, Franco. 2013. *Distant Reading*. London: Verso.

Nini, Andrea. 2014. *Multidimensional analysis tagger 1.1*. <http://sites.google.com/site/multidimensionaltagger> (1 September 2017).

Slembrouck, Stef. 1992. The parliamentary Hansard "verbatim" report: The written construction of spoken discourse. *Language and Literature* 1(2): 101–119.

Sutherland, Lorraine & Farrell, Stephen. 2013. The history, workings and future challenges of Hansard. <https://www.youtube.com/watch?v=yaLWV9gfiSo> (30 November 2019).

CHAPTER 3

Hansard at Huddersfield

Streamlined corpus methods and interactive visualisations to pursue research aims beyond corpus linguistics

Lesley Jeffries,[1] Fransina Stradling,[2] Alexander von Lünen[2] & Hugo Sanjurjo-González[3]

[1] University of Lancaster | [2] University of Huddersfield | [3] University of Deusto

This chapter describes one project's approach to fostering uptake of corpus tools in research beyond corpus linguistics. It introduces the Hansard at Huddersfield web application, a new search tool that combines tried-and-tested corpus tools with interactive visualisations to make Hansard, the official record of the UK parliament (1803–2021), more accessible for in-depth study by non-specialists. The chapter outlines the thinking behind and development of the Hansard at Huddersfield web interface and exemplifies how the site's adapted corpus tools offer non-linguists new entry points for Hansard research through three small sample studies. It further reflects on the process of preparing the large Hansard corpus to allow insights to be gleaned from corpus-style searches by researchers with relatively little training.

Keywords: Hansard, parliamentary debates, corpus applications, data visualisation, impact beyond linguistics

1. Introduction

This chapter introduces a new tool for searching Hansard, the official record of the UK parliament, and argues that such user-friendly versions of corpus-linguistic tools could make significant contributions to research in fields other than linguistics. Our web tool, Hansard at Huddersfield,[1] was designed to use the

---

1. The Hansard at Huddersfield tool was developed as part of the AHRC-funded Hansard at Huddersfield Project, grant reference AH/R007136/1.

https://doi.org/10.1075/scl.111.03jef
© 2023 John Benjamins Publishing Company

tried-and-tested methods of corpus linguistics to provide the kind of searchability that is not normally accessible to those outside the field. We believe that there are many groups of people who would find it enlightening to see the patterns of linguistic usage which corpus linguistics is well adapted to highlight. We anticipated that learning to use the complex standard software of corpus linguistics would be a disincentive for such end-users, so we set about providing a user-friendly searchable version of Hansard, where the results of a range of searches would be presented by means of visualisations providing an entry point to the data whilst always linking back to the data itself. Having previously published the technical details behind the resulting web interface for Hansard (von Lünen et al. 2023), in this chapter, we explain the thinking and operation behind the site and discuss some of the difficulties in its development and our solutions to these. We also raise the issue of how users new to corpus techniques might be assisted in interpreting the results produced in their searches.

2. Hansard's potential for insights into governance

Hansard is the official, substantially verbatim report of UK parliamentary debate. Although edited for repetitions, obvious mistakes, and interjections (Mollin 2007; Slembrouck 1992; see Kotze et al., this volume), it is a verified, accurate and readable record of all that is said in both houses of parliament. Hansard has been produced in printed form since the early 1800s (Ralphs 2009) and remains in print for daily distributions among members of parliament (MPs) today (see Alexander, this volume). While originally compiled from newspaper accounts, in the early twentieth century parliament started employing reporters to produce comprehensive and unbiased records of debates in the Palace of Westminster (Vice & Farrell 2017). In 1997, after an extensive digitisation project, Hansard records dating from 1803 to 2005 were made available online, and more recent records were also made available separately. For several years, Hansard had to be accessed through a range of interfaces of varying quality, but these were finally integrated into one website <hansard.parliament.uk> in 2018.

From its inception, Hansard's central function has been to facilitate public scrutiny of the parliamentary decision-making process. Despite the many ways in which citizens can now access parliamentary debate directly (e.g. via television and social media), Hansard still provides the most comprehensive access to the language of government and parliament. Full machine-readable debate reports between 1803 and today are available online, with draft transcripts of each day's debates uploaded within three hours of finishing. Other forms of access to parliamentary proceedings do not span such a long time period and are not as easily searchable.

Hansard can inform public scrutiny of parliamentary proceedings far beyond a simple account of individual contributions to the day's debate.[2] As a rich source of socio-political and historical information, Hansard can clarify understanding of concurrent or ongoing political response to historical events or topics of societal interest. With help from computational methods, over 200 years of parliamentary proceedings can be searched to establish how societal issues are being discussed in parliament synchronically, or to track the discussion of themes or topics diachronically. It may be also used to track debates on parliamentary bills as they develop, or to understand the involvement of individual parliamentarians in this development. Exploring such issues beyond the visualised results of searches requires an understanding of the discursive construction of the topics under investigation as language usage often reveals the ideas and ideologies held by a speaker (Jeffries 2010).

The nature of Hansard makes it both amenable to and limited in searching for linguistic patterns. Hansard reporters follow a particular reporting style that edits out repetitions, hesitations, interjections, and obvious mistakes to make the report readable, mostly linguistically accurate and factual without changing the meaning of contributions. Lexical and grammatical choices are occasionally altered to fit the Hansard style (Mollin 2007) and/or to suit the sensitivities of the time, though this has changed in recent decades towards a more faithful representation of words and structures (see Kotze et al., this volume). By removing disfluencies and other features of spoken language (Bucholtz 2000:1461), the reporting style makes Hansard easier to scrutinise. However, the mismatch between the spoken contributions of members and the written record has a disproportionate effect on certain kinds of analysis, in particular those concerned with interactional features of face-to-face communication and other features specific to spoken language. Hansard reports are also decontextualised by default, as pragmatic, situational references such as modal constructions and hedges are often left out and interjections not spelled out (Mollin 2007; Slembrouck 1992). On the basis of a comparison between parliamentary video data and Hansard, Shaw (2018) argues that projects focussing on the detail of pragmatic and situational content in parliament should not rely upon Hansard and that all analysts using Hansard should be at the least "critical and reflexive about its use" (Shaw 2018:123).

---

2. Our data is based on the formatting of Hansard and is therefore organised according to each speaker's 'turn', whether that is a short statement, an intervention or a long speech. The generic word we use to refer to these speaker turns is 'contribution'.

There remain good reasons for using Hansard to explore those patterns of language in parliamentary discourse that are not excessively edited and which are relatively amenable to automated searching. These include patterns of lexical usage and some grammatical structures. Our assumption is that lexical patterning is the most likely to be of interest to those concerned with political and democratic debate, though linguists may also find the data useful for charting changes in grammatical usage across time in a uniquely constrained and well-defined context.

Although only quasi-verbatim, no other comprehensive source of parliamentary discourse exists and as such it is a uniquely rich source of data. MPs, peers, journalists and the public use Hansard as an authoritative source to hold parliamentarians to account (Antaki & Leudar 2001) and the data as recorded in Hansard thus holds an official status in the UK's democratic system. Speakers are permitted to question the official record if they think it does not reflect what they said and it may be amended in the House of Commons "if in the opinion of the Editor, they do not alter substantially the meaning of anything that was said in the House"[3] and in the House of Lords "members should not attempt to alter the sense of words spoken by them in debate. Corrections are accepted only when the words that were actually spoken have been incorrectly reported".[4] Whilst no record of amendments is kept, the former editor of Hansard (Lords), John Vice, reports (Vice 2020, personal communication) that most such changes are made because of errors on the part of the reporters, not the speakers themselves. Mishearing *his* as *this* or confusing *viniculture* with *viticulture* are two such examples. There is a system of checking that operates in real time to ensure the accuracy of the record, with clerks delivering paper queries from the Hansard reporters if they are unsure of a word, often a proper name, or do not know the spelling. Once amended and published, the Hansard report is widely agreed to be an accurate representation of both the views of the speaker and the language they are expressed in.

Much of the motivation behind searching for linguistic patterns in parliamentary discourse is likely to concern political topics, themes and their argumentation rather than interactional or spoken language features. Lexical (and some grammatical) features are therefore well-placed to deliver relevant results. The question of how parliamentarians behave interactionally can also throw light on the democratic institutions they inhabit by reflecting the interpersonal and social norms of such institutions. However, these features are much harder to search for in

---

3. See <https://erskinemay.parliament.uk/section/6465/the-commons-official-report/>.

4. See <https://www.parliament.uk/globalassets/documents/publications-records/House-of-Lords-Publications/Rules-guides-for-business/Companion-to-standing-orders/Companion-to-Standing-Orders-2017.pdf>.

the cleaned-up version of speech represented in Hansard.[5] In her treatment of aspects of language that may be trusted in Hansard, Shaw (2018) identifies topics and themes in Hansard as being based on reliable sources in the data. Topics and themes are often found through the analysis of noun phrases (e.g. *abject poverty, fuel poverty*), adjective phrases (e.g. *destitute*) and verb phrases (e.g. *impoverish*), which are reported verbatim in almost every case. Moreover, although Shaw classifies argumentation as "proceed with caution", quantitative patterning may demonstrate patterns of argumentation through the extraction of general themes based on lexical searching. Qualitative analysis of argumentation in individual cases would of course need as much caution as other historical sources.

Though we argue that analysing patterns of lexis and grammar in Hansard could be of interest to non-linguist researchers, Hansard in its current form (i.e., at <hansard.parliament.uk>) does not provide for easy access to such patterning. Official online transcripts are searchable by date, debate, speaker and search term, but the presentation of search results requires the researcher to read every contribution containing the search term to establish whether there are patterns of usage. While users can access raw frequencies of hits for search terms, a new search is required to find the hits on exact dates. Furthermore, results are not presented chronologically and cannot be ordered by speaker. Neither is it possible to delimit a search for date, debate, speaker and search word at the same time.

In this chapter, we propose that methods and software developed by corpus linguists offer an analytical framework that researchers and practitioners in a variety of fields can use to gain a deeper understanding of the patterns of linguistic usage exhibited in Hansard data. Whilst corpus linguists will already be aware of the insights that can be gleaned from reorganising data computationally, many types of end-user of this data may have so far only thought of it in relation to individual contributions, which can be found by existing means. In order to explore how such users might wish to access the data, our project set up a series of end-user meetings with people from museums, libraries, universities (non-linguists), pressure groups, charities and political and historical associations. It was notable how rarely the participants had conceived of looking at data from the point of view of patterns of usage before they encountered our website.

This chapter explores ways in which corpus methods can be adapted to make searching Hansard more straightforward for interested end-users not familiar with techniques of corpus linguistics. We demonstrate how aspects of corpus

---

5. The UK's Parliamentary Data Services is working on options to link Hansard to the online video record of parliamentary business. This is not a straightforward process, but if successful would provide a link between the interactional features and the lexico-grammatical content of the debates.

methods may be simplified to reliably inform research into political proceedings from a variety of disciplines and perspectives, whilst retaining the integrity of the data itself. Finally, we address questions of reliability and the possible pitfalls of the simplified processes that we have included in our web interface with Hansard.

3. The Hansard at Huddersfield website

The Hansard at Huddersfield site provides straightforward exploration of word-based patterns across Hansard data between 1803 and 2021. Having participated in a sub-project working on Hansard for the SAMUELS (Semantic Annotation and Mark-Up for Enhancing Lexical Searches) Project,[6] the Huddersfield team took the opportunity of follow-on funding to develop a more public-facing version of the Hansard data that could be used successfully by those with little or no knowledge of corpus linguistics.

3.1 Aims and challenges

The Hansard at Huddersfield project was designed to respond to a number of challenges encountered during the SAMUELS project in which we attempted to trace the discourse of 'labour relations' through time (see Demmen, Jeffries & Walker 2018). The first challenge was related to the identification of relevant words belonging to the semantic category of labour relations. The hierarchical nature as well as the complexity and sheer number of semantic tags incorporated into the SAMUELS version of Hansard from the *Historical Thesaurus of English* (HTE) meant that 'labour relations' as a topic could be identified only manually as it was found in a total of 82 semantic categories. Furthermore, despite an attested tagging accuracy rate of 94%, the tagger sometimes attributed words related to labour relations to other categories and vice versa, as the tagger was unable to distinguish between relevant and irrelevant uses of a word. For example, the word *labour* itself can refer to childbirth, a political party or work, only the last of which would be relevant to labour relations. Although 94% tagging accuracy for a corpus of this

---

6. This project involved a consortium of Oxford University Press and eight universities, including the University of Glasgow (lead institution), Lancaster University, the University of Huddersfield, the University of Central Lancashire, the University of Strathclyde, Oxford University Press, Brigham Young University (USA), Åbo Akademi University (Finland), and the University of Oulu (Finland). See <http://www.gla.ac.uk/schools/critical/research/funded researchprojects/samuels/>. Grant reference AH/L010062/1; see <http://www.glasgow.ac.uk /samuels>.

size and historical spread is impressive, the amount of manual work needed for our study was considerable and would not be viable for non-linguist researchers. After some attempts to incorporate a slimmed-down version of the SAMUELS tagset into our site, we abandoned this strand of the work because it did not produce reliable or easy-to-interpret results that our target end-users would find helpful.

Another difficulty of this kind of work is that the software for searching corpora is complex and at times difficult to use, even for corpus linguists. The operation of corpus tools is not always self-explanatory, results are not always presented in an easy-to-view format and statistics cannot always be straightforwardly interpreted. Statistical results that are easy to understand, such as frequency, do not necessarily tell us much about the dataset without more complex statistical analysis or contextualisation through qualitative analysis. Those most interested in researching Hansard, for example social or political scientists and historians, are unlikely to have the skills with which to tackle the manipulation of a corpus using available software and may not be motivated or have time to acquire them.

We therefore set about incorporating the Historic Hansard database into a searchable website with some of the same functionality as corpus software, but using visualisations to assist the end-user in exploring what Hansard has to offer. Our aim was to match the ambition of our project to its timescale and produce an effective application of well-known corpus methods to the huge dataset that constitutes Hansard, albeit using fewer of the functions of corpus linguistics than we would like.

3.2 Data preparation

Creating a website that combines a large searchable database with standard visualisations had its challenges. From our involvement in SAMUELS, we had available the tagged Historic Hansard (1803–2005), but this dataset first had to be reformatted to make it compatible with the visualisations we intended to use. Hansard data reflects its print origins in being organised by column and page, but this format proved difficult for searching and linking to visualisations. The dataset also had to be cleaned of corruptions where tag titles had entered the dataset. As the project progressed, we updated our database with the subsequent Hansard data (from 2005) up to 16 December 2021, which saw the last sitting of parliament that year. This dataset needed to be aligned to our database so that despite its long historical timeline, the data is seamless (see von Lünen et al. 2023 for technical details).

The size of the database (over 1.75 billion words) precluded providing fast visualisations of search results online. To speed up the rendering time of the visualisations, we therefore pre-calculated several of the more computationally intensive operations. Given that the underlying data is never altered, analyses like word frequency lists only needed to be computed once.[7] The pre-computed frequency lists are stored in the database and can then be quickly retrieved to produce the visualisations, as memory and storage access times are more advantageous than the computational load on the server's CPU for mathematical-statistical operations on large chunks of data. The advantage to the user of these pre-calculations, however, also limited the type of query made available and the number of visualisations it would be feasible to incorporate into the site.

3.3   A summary of the functions on the website

As mentioned above, the search functions of the site were developed in collaboration with a pool of potential non-linguist end-users of the site. Based on their preferences and our knowledge of corpus methods, we chose two main entry points to the Hansard data: searching by pre-determined search terms (with search boxes) and searching without pre-determining the search terms (with word clouds and bubble charts). Default search box searches can be limited by years and by House (Commons, Lords, or both). An *Advanced Options* button adds the potential to limit a search by debate title, member and individual dates, rather than full years. Users can search using any single word or multi-word phrase.

Searches produce a distribution graph (frequency per million) of the search item across the time period selected. A default search presents the data by calendar year whereas a search with the *Advanced Options* button ticked presents data by year or by month, depending on the length of time period selected. Up to four search terms can be entered for comparison. Selecting a time period on the distribution graph produces all occurrences of the search item within this period in a concordance list which can display either full (document format) or limited (Keyword-in-Context [KWIC] format) co-text. Concordance lists also show the date, speaker, and debate title of the contribution in which the search term appears. Users can download distribution graphs and concordance lists in various formats and they can always click through to the original contribution for closer scrutiny.

To access the Hansard dataset without a pre-determined search term, users can either search by word cloud (based on frequency) or bubble chart (based on keywords). A word cloud visualises the top-500 words occurring within the time period selected in sizes reflecting their relative frequency.[8] Selection of up to four

---

7. Though note that updates to the data require some additional pre-calculation.

8. While the 500 most frequent words are used for the creation of the word cloud, it never actually displays all 500. The cut-off is different for each word cloud, because of the way the system needs to fit in words of differing lengths and sizes into a square.

words from the word cloud can produce a distribution graph and concordance lists for these words. A bubble chart visualises the keywords in one sub-corpus of the data when compared with another. Users can select up to four words from the chart, after which concordance lines of the words within these categories can be accessed.

3.4 Corpus tool inclusion criteria

This section outlines in more detail the rationale for our choice of basic corpus-linguistic methodologies to provide accessible searches and reveal discourse patterns in Hansard that may not be striking enough to be perceived by naked-eye observation, or would be time-consuming to discover manually.

Though some corpus research increasingly attempts to produce sophisticated computational ways of interpreting, as well as organising textual data, our work (see for example Jeffries & Walker 2019) uses established corpus methods to inform qualitative work, rather than pushing the boundaries of algorithmic analysis. We view the practical application of corpus-linguistic methods combined with practices of discourse analysis (Baker 2006; Taylor & Marchi 2018) as the foundation of our work. In this case, we hope that our target end-users can also combine the corpus methods with methodologies from other disciplines, such as History and Politics.

Rather than a sampled dataset representative of a language variety (Leech 1991), Hansard constitutes an entire population of texts of a particular kind (McIntyre & Walker 2019: 112–113) as it contains all UK parliamentary proceedings between 1803 and today. The metadata recorded with each debate contribution (date, speaker and debate title) in Hansard allows comparison of various sub-corpora to be carried out (McEnery & Hardie 2011).

In choosing which corpus tools to provide for studying Hansard, we focussed on well-established tools where the results would be accurate and comprehensible by non-linguist end-users. The frequency list is central to corpus approaches and frequencies are often represented in standard software as raw and/or normalised numbers or visualised by dispersion plots. As Hansard is such a large and complex corpus, simple frequency lists may not be enlightening, so we decided that rather than supplying simple frequency lists we would use normalised frequency statistics to underpin the line graphs across time and to produce word clouds and keyword bubble charts.

In order to identify how search terms construct discourses, concordances provide the user with an easy overview of words in context. We have used this format as our default entry into the data itself, with the option of choosing a KWIC display if helpful. Our view was that historians, political commentators and others interested in parliamentary discourse will always wish to be able to access the full context, and each concordance line can therefore also be expanded to the full contribution of the speaker, whether a short intervention or a long speech. For further investigation of the search term, concordances can be downloaded into a spreadsheet and sorted to reveal patterns of co-occurrence. Computational collocation analysis is more challenging with data of the size and complexity of Hansard, and pre-calculation of all collocations is a vast computational task which we have not yet had the opportunity to carry out. Calculating collocations online would result in extremely long waiting times for users. Future plans for the site therefore include a limited, but user-friendly, version of collocation analysis.

The final corpus approach we chose was keyness, applying the concept of keywords[9] from corpus linguistics: a ranked list of those words which occur relatively more frequently in one corpus or sub-corpus (the target corpus) compared to another (the reference or comparison corpus).[10] As keyword lists highlight saliency, rather than frequency, we considered them potentially more enlightening for our intended end-users. The usual output from a keyword search in corpus-linguistics software is a ranked list, but we used a bubble chart visualisation to make the relative dominance of different keywords more immediately visible. Note that keywords calculated in this way are not necessarily frequent in any absolute sense, but provide a snapshot of how lexical occurrence differs in two corpora. In the case of Hansard, comparing keywords in two sub-corpora allows us to show change over time and gives some indication of the preoccupations of parliamentarians in sub-corpora.

In order to make the response times relatively short, we pre-calculated some sub-corpora to make keyword comparisons easier. These pre-calculated sub-corpora are defined periods matching administrations and service periods of Prime Ministers, according to a demand for these specific periods as articularted during our end-user meetings.

---

9. We are aware that it could be confusing for non-corpus-linguistics users that 'keywords' refer to both the search term in a KWIC concordance layout and also these comparative keywords. However, this confusion is not of our making and we decided we needed to use the commonly recognised term in both ways for those who decide to cross-over into corpus linguistics from other disciplinary backgrounds.

10. See Chapter 5 of McIntyre and Walker (2019) for detailed explanation of the statistics behind keyword analysis.

4. Using Hansard at Huddersfield to pursue research aims

The following three case studies demonstrate how non-linguist researchers might use the website to explore topics of historical and/or contemporary relevance. The case studies serve as cameos to demonstrate that even adapted corpus tools provide the potential to carry out rigorous and transparent research on the Hansard data in pursuit of answers to research questions. These can be deductive, top-down questions (e.g. "What is the frequency of the word *gay* in parliament and when did it change to mean homosexual?"). They can also be inductive, bottom-up questions (e.g. "What topics are discussed more often during the reign of Queen Victoria compared with the reign of Queen Elizabeth?"). The case studies show how the triangulation of various sources of knowledge may be fruitful: socio-political and historical knowledge may both inform and be informed by Hansard searches.

Our first case study demonstrates how a researcher may start from a particular historical event (such as the Peterloo Massacre in Manchester in 1819) and use the search functions of our site to explore its echoes through time and/or discover the connections with other similar examples of public uprisings and their consequences. The second case study focusses on a singularly important word from recent political history, *austerity*, and looks back to see whether its meaning has changed in parliamentary discourse over time. The final case study compares the language of two significant periods in British history, World War I and II, to demonstrate the potential for discovering the differences in ideology and political discourse between two otherwise comparable periods of political upheaval.

4.1 (Un)lawful assembly

This first case study concerns the Peterloo Massacre that took place in Manchester in 1819. It demonstrates how the site can help users track the political reactions to this catastrophic event and see how the symbolism of Peterloo has been employed in political discussion since.

The facts of the attacks on many impoverished and disenfranchised people who had gathered peacefully to hear a speech from Mr Henry Hunt, prominent campaigner for voting rights, are well known. Seeing that Henry Hunt later (1830–1832) became the MP for Preston, one question of interest may be the extent to which he spoke about the events of Peterloo whilst he was an MP. Using the *Advanced Options* button for the default search box to limit the dates to his years in office and choosing Mr Henry Hunt as speaker produces the slightly surprising answer that out of his 738 contributions in the House of Commons,[11] only two explicitly mention *Peterloo* (see Figure 3.1).[12]

▫	Date ▾	Member ♦	Contribution
▫	1832-08-03	Mr Henry Hunt	... d appear that the blood of the people of England had been shed very unnecessarily; and, as was well observed in the newspaper, nothing of the sort had occurred in that county since the bloody transactions of **Peterloo**.... *[o more]*
▫	1832-03-15	Mr Henry Hunt	... er across the thighs with his sabre. He would venture to say, that neither in foreign nor domestic wars, had English soldiers committed acts so disgraceful as those which were perpetrated by the Yeomanry at **Peterloo**. He would ask any man of humanity in that House, whether such disgraceful acts ought to be passed by unnoticed and unpunished, merely because it could be said, that twelve years had elapsed sin... *[o more]*

Figure 3.1 The contributions by Mr Henry Hunt that explicitly mention *Peterloo* in March and August 1832

This concordance display shows some context to understand how *Peterloo* is being referred to by Henry Hunt, but to understand the discursive context it can be instructive to see the wider context in which the reference is made. For example, clicking through to the whole entry for 15 March shows him pleading for a governmental inquiry into the occurrences at the massacre, referring only to these occurrences as *Peterloo* halfway through his speech (Figure 3.2). If closer scrutiny of the context is needed, the whole contribution could also be downloaded.

Since much of Hansard in its early days was extracted from comprehensive news reports, it is often reported in the third person (see Alexander, this volume), though the tone and attitude of the original is nevertheless often evident, as we can see in the paragraph in Figure 3.2 (e.g. "acts so disgraceful").

Using a default search, we can consider both the reactions of others at the time and the continuing influence of Peterloo on the collective memory of parliamentarians. The site can produce a line graph presenting the frequencies of use of the

---

11. However, care should be taken with the statistics produced on data pre-1907 when not every speech in parliament was recorded in Hansard.

12. Typographical and other errors in the examples (e.g. the missing space in "peopleof" here) are reflections of the slight inaccuracies inherent in the electronic (and also probably the printed) version of Hansard.

He would venture to say, that neither in foreign nor domestic wars, had English soldiers committed acts so disgraceful as those which were perpetrated by the Yeomanry at **Peterloo**. He would ask any man of humanity in that House, whether such disgraceful acts ought to be passed by unnoticed and unpunished, merely because it could be said, that twelve years had elapsed since the transaction had taken place? But another excuse that perhaps, might be made was, that the meeting was an illegal one.

Figure 3.2 Concordance display for Henry Hunt's mention of *Peterloo* in the House of Commons Hansard (15 March 1832)

word *Peterloo* in the House of Commons Hansard throughout the whole database (until 2021 at the time of writing; see Figure 3.3).

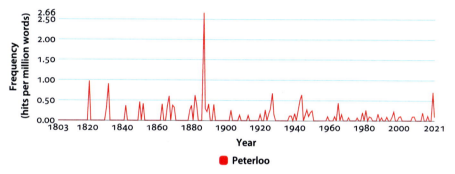

Figure 3.3 Distribution graph of mentions of *Peterloo* in the House of Commons Hansard (1803–2021)

This is an example of the care needed in interpreting the graphs produced by our site due to its normalisation per million words. While a consistent basis of comparison across time works reasonably well for relatively frequent words and/or shorter periods, the graph can be misleading when a search word is relatively infrequent, as is the case with a name like *Peterloo*. The total number of words in Hansard has grown enormously over the years and so the early spikes in this graph represent only one or two occurrences each. The large spike in 1887 represents ten occurrences in that year. Although not a large number, we may wonder why *Peterloo* was discussed more in that year. Clicking through to the data shows that the word occurs in comments comparing the events in Manchester in 1819 and those in Mitchelstown in County Cork, Ireland, on the occasion of another mass meeting resulting in death and injury. This discovery may lead the user to explore the Mitchelstown events in more depth.

Whilst many other searches can be made relating to Peterloo, Mitchelstown and others, there is another direction that may suggest itself from the frequency spike in 1887. This is to explore the topic of 'lawful assembly', in other words the right to meet in public and demonstrate against the government. This freedom is one that is upheld as vital to a functioning democracy, though it was hard-won, as the events of Peterloo show. The site allows for searching the phrase *lawful assembly* and it may also be productive to search for *unlawful assembly*, considering the fact that until 1986 this was a crime in English law, such that the mere suggestion that three or more people meeting in a public space might be planning some kind of sedition could get them arrested. The resulting line graph shows that the topic of *unlawful assembly* has been much more frequent in parliamentary debate than the opposing term, *lawful assembly* (see Figure 3.4).

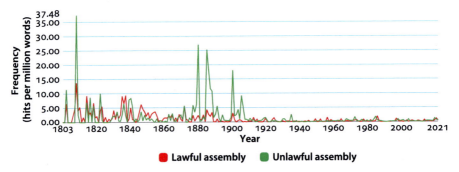

Figure 3.4 Comparing the frequency of *unlawful assembly* and *lawful assembly* in the House of Commons Hansard (1803–2021)

The graph also reflects the fact that much more discussion took place about *unlawful assembly* while it was a crime. This discussion can be explored further by looking at individual contributions qualitatively. Many of these contributions refer to individual cases of *unlawful assembly*, often in relation to a larger point being made about the injustice of attributing this crime to reasonable activities (see Figure 3.5).

This account from 1890, by Mr Clancy,[13] illustrates one of the patterns that can be seen in relation to the 'crime' of *unlawful assembly*, which is that it is discussed in parliament most often in connection with Ireland and with the North of England, always at times of trouble when people are feeling oppressed. In more recent times, during the coal miners' strike of the 1980s when Margaret Thatcher's government sought to close down the coal industry, situations arose

---

13. John Joseph Clancy, Irish Nationalist and MP for North County Dublin 1885–1918.

□	Date ▾	Member ♦	Contribution
□	1890-07-17	Mr John Clancy	... t for freedom. In conclusion, I would give the House one illustration of how justice is administered in Ireland. Last year Mr. John Cullinane was charged before two Justices, including Colonel Caddell, with **unlawful assembly**, and in the judgment then delivered it was stated that the terror resulting from the assembly was not sufficiently great to justify the Magistrates in concluding that the meeting was u... *[1 more]*

Figure 3.5 Full contribution including a mention of *unlawful assembly* by Mr Clancy in the House of Commons Hansard (17 July 1890)

not so different from those of Peterloo and Mitchelstown; workers under pressure reacted to heavy-handed policing. Figure 3.6 shows what Home Secretary Leon Brittan said in 1984.

□	Date ▾	Member ♦	Contribution
□	1984-06-19	Mr Leon Brittan	... cessary to use both mounted officers and officers equipped with shields and helmets. Ninety-three arrests were made. Of those arrested, have since been charged with riot. The remainder have been charged with **unlawful assembly**, assault and public order offences. Twenty-eight police officers suffered injuries. The disorder, during which large numbers of missiles were thrown at police officers, continued until... *[o more]*

Figure 3.6 Contribution including a mention of *unlawful assembly* by Home Secretary Leon Brittan in the House of Commons Hansard (6 June 1984)

This apparently reasonable-sounding reaction to violence against the police finds its echoes amongst the other events in British history which can be investigated alongside each other using the Hansard at Huddersfield website to see how both sides of these arguments play out through the years.

4.2 Austerity[14]

The second case study demonstrates how the site can assist in exploring the changing meaning of a socio-political keyword. Charting the word *austerity* across time in Hansard shows that there is no simple answer to the question of what a word means, but the site can help us find relevant examples and format them as concordance lines to examine how they were used across a selected timeframe.

In recent times, the word *austerity* has been much used in socio-political discourse, not least to distinguish the harsher economic policies of the incoming Conservative-led governments of the Cameron-Clegg coalition of 2005 and the Cameron government of 2010 from the policies of the Labour governments of Blair and Brown that preceded these. One question arising from Cameron's repeated mantra "We're all in this together" (e.g. Cameron 2009) is whether he was invoking the famed solidarity between the citizens of the UK during World War II to persuade the electorate that restricting government spending was (again) necessary. The underlying question is whether *austerity* means the same today as it did during World War II, and if not, what the differences are.

The first kind of search that can help us determine the scope of such a study is using a pre-determined word. A first search for *austerity* across the whole Hansard dataset produces a graph as in Figure 3.7.

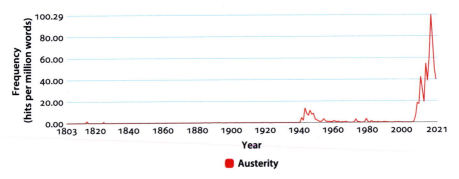

Figure 3.7 The frequency of *austerity* in the House of Commons Hansard (1803–2021)

Figure 3.7 shows that the word was not in frequent use in the House of Commons until the beginning of World War II. The user can confirm that earlier uses are of less interest for this investigation by double-clicking on any year and looking at the word in context. Figure 3.8 shows the single occurrence from 1825, for example, where we see that *austerity* in that period was a description of character or manner, rather than referring to an attitude to fiscal policy.

---

14. This case study is based on Jeffries and Walker (2019).

Hansard at Huddersfield 105

□	Date ▼	Member ♦	Contribution
□	1825-06-23	Mr Charles Ross	… g his residence in Grenada, whence he went to Barbadoes, I can with great truth, testify, that I never knew a more pious or a better man. Possessed of natural cheerfulness of temper, and without any thing of **austerity** or moroseness in his manners, he discharged the duties of his profession with zeal, and as-siduity, and acquired the good-will and esteem of the whole community; and it was to the great regret... *[o more]*

Figure 3.8 Mr Charles Ross using *austerity* in the House of Commons Hansard (23 June 1825)

One option at this stage is to narrow the focus to the relevant years, as shown in Figure 3.9, where a new distribution graph shows occurrences between 1939 and 2021.

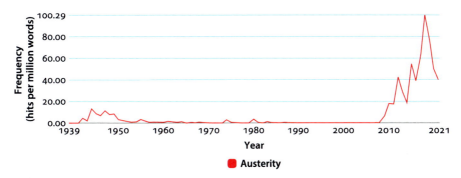

Figure 3.9 The frequency of *austerity* in the House of Commons Hansard (1939–2021)

These graphs are only an indication of where the word is used most, but they provide a helpful entry-point into the large Hansard dataset. A next step could be to investigate the search term in significant years or time periods. For example, collecting all the occurrences from the first peak in 1942 to the drop-off in 1950 produces 393 examples of *austerity* whilst the occurrences between 2008 and 2021 number 3,710. Discounting the huge increase in total number of words spoken in parliament, even the normalised frequency of 13.28 occurrences per 1,000 words in 1944 and 100.29 in 2018 demonstrate a large rise in its use by the second period. The optional KWIC format makes it easy to see what is happening in the co-text (Figure 3.10).

If the co-text is not full enough to understand the sense of the word in context, the user can retrieve the full contribution or download the examples into

	14	1950-06-20	Mrs Barbara Castle	suggest that in a situation of this kind, in which	**austerity**	and sacrifice must still be our watchword and must still
	15	1950-06-20	Flight Lieut Wavell Wakefield	Castle), was, if I understood it aright, that under Socialism,	**austerity**	has to continue indefinitely, and that, m fact, a smokescreen
	16	1950-06-19	Mr Oliver Lyttelton	immoral and that he had better have a pinch of	**austerity**	in a generous action rather than be accused of being
	17	1950-06-15	Mr Cyril Osborne	the government much more than the occasional extravagances of an	**austerity**-ridden	public which is responsiblefor the falling off in savings. The

Figure 3.10 Sample of hits for *austerity* in June 1950

a spreadsheet and reorder the co-text to scan many concordance lines rapidly. Figure 3.11 is one example from the war years which shows the tendency of *austerity* to collocate with everyday items.

1945-03-06	that these short-length socks are just as unpopular as the	**austerity**	suits were? Will he remove this restriction at the earliest
1944-02-15	to point out to the House and the country that	non-**austerity**	suits will not be available in any great quantity for
1944-04-06	help the private trader to get rid of his unsaleable	**austerity**	suits you have to do something about the coupons. The
1944-04-06	be; but I feel that the idea of utilising these	**austerity**	suits, in utility cloth, for clothing the people of the

Figure 3.11 Spreadsheet sample for *austerity* (February 1944 – March 1945)

If we compare this right hand context with examples from a more recent set of data (1973–1981, as displayed in Figure 3.12) where there are two peaks of usage, we can see that there are no longer any "austerity suits" and instead of being a premodifier, *austerity* more often stands alone as a self-explanatory concept, followed by other clause elements such as verbs, or new sentences.

1981-07-14	the House who say that at a time of national	**austerity**	we should play down the coming wedding. I do not
1981-02-18	which my constituents understand. If the hon. Gentleman prefers	**austerity**',	we will stick to that. I am not sure how
1980-07-10	said that we were in for three years of unparalleled	**austerity**.	When does that start? When does it finish? In three
1980-01-24	Secretary? Why are we to face three years of unparalleled	**austerity**	when these are the first three years in British history

Figure 3.12 Spreadsheet sample for *austerity* (January 1980 – July 1981)

In these cases, *austerity* is often itself modified (e.g. *national, unparalleled*) but it is assumed that the reader knows its referent: the restriction of government spending on services and infrastructure. More recently, its mention in the House of Commons is almost universally negative, as we can see in the concordance from the peak of usage in 2018, shown in Figure 3.13.

2018-03-14	Chamber? Does he not think that perhaps the demands that	**austerity**	and Brexit are forcing on our constituencies are having a
2018-03-14	far as I am concerned, if someone wants to end	**austerity**	and to promote social justice, they have to support that
2018-03-13	sense of irony whatsoever, these new regulations remind us that	**austerity**	is far from over. Depriving some of the poorest children
2018-03-13	four years, which goes to show how hard the Government's	**austerity**	programme is hitting families. There has been a huge spike

Figure 3.13 Spreadsheet sample for *austerity* (March 2018)

Similar analysis may be undertaken to find out in which debates *austerity* is discussed and evoked. While the user can search for and display all the debate titles where contributions contain *austerity*, downloading all the examples in a spreadsheet may give a clearer overview and allow the more experienced spreadsheet user to filter options and identify the unique debate titles, which may then be analysed for their topics and themes.

In addition to detailed analysis of the use of a significant word like *austerity*, the site may also be used to compare it with other similar words. The default search box allows users to search for up to four terms and display them as overlapping line graphs. Historical knowledge may feed into this comparative search, leading on to, for example, search on the term *thrift* which is semantically related to *austerity*, but has the tone of a Victorian virtue (Himmelfarb 1995). Comparing *austerity* and *thrift** (with a wildcard to find other forms such as *thrifty* too) shows (see Figure 3.14) that *thrift* has its heyday in the period prior to the rise of *austerity*.

While we cannot assume that the apparent correlation of these patterns is also causal, it may nevertheless be interesting to see how MPs talk about the individual thrifty qualities (or the lack thereof) of citizens and to compare these results with the more government-led policies of austerity. When clicking on the line graph with more than one search term, the site will retrieve occurrences of all the terms, as displayed in Figure 3.15.

The co-text highlights a difference between *thrift* as a personal virtue that the government may wish to foster, whereas *austerity* is a top-down policy of

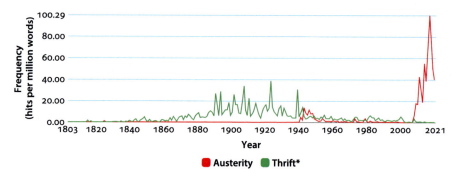

Figure 3.14 Comparison of the frequency of *austerity* and *thrift** in the House of Commons Hansard (1803–2021)

fiscal restraint. Both may save the government money, but there is a difference of emphasis which could be of interest to policy researchers.

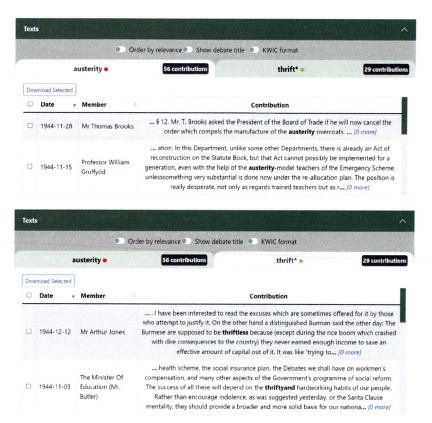

Figure 3.15 Sample comparison concordance lines for *austerity* (top) and *thrift** (bottom) in the House of Commons Hansard (November–December 1944)

Some users may wish to know whether Cameron's later interest in austerity as a government programme was anticipated by previous Prime Ministers. An advanced search limited to Margaret Thatcher[15] during her years of office as MP and Prime Minister (1979–1990), for example, brings up a single example of *austerity* spoken by her in the House of Commons (Figure 3.16).

☐	Date ▾	Member ◆	Contribution
☐	1980-01-24	Mrs Margaret Thatcher	... § The Prime Minister The unparalleled **austerity** came here inbecause the previous Government refused to take the financial steps that they should have taken. We are trying to take those financial steps to reduce public expenditure to a level that the nation can genuinely afford.... *[0 more]*

Figure 3.16 Mrs Margaret Thatcher using *austerity* in the House of Commons Hansard (24 January 1980)

By comparing this single use of the word by Margaret Thatcher with later uses by Cameron and his Chancellor, Osborne, we can see that she is foreshadowing its modern political sense. There is, therefore, scope for using the site both to find patterns that we could not otherwise predict, and also to dig down into the database to find links and echoes that would be difficult to find in other types of search.

4.3 World Wars

The final case study on the topic of the two World Wars of the twentieth century demonstrates how the site may be used to test intuitions about parliamentary interests as documented in Hansard but may also be used to map the topics that arise within a particular period.

There is no doubt that these two wars were significant points in the history of humankind and have ongoing symbolic meaning in the UK, including in parliament. Hansard demonstrates this intuition about the significance of these events in Hansard by a simple search on the word *war* in the complete historic Hansard corpus (see Figure 3.17).

---

15. At the moment users have to make sure they have searched all the versions of a speaker's name. In this case, there are two: Mrs Margaret Thatcher and The Prime Minister Mrs. Margaret Thatcher) – including in the latter case a closing (but not opening) bracket. We (and many others) are working on the lack of consistency in Hansard's naming practices.

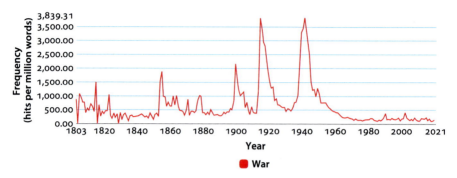

Figure 3.17 The frequency of *war* in the House of Commons Hansard (1803–2021)

The graph confirms the importance of the two wars, evidenced in the spikes in occurrence of *war* in the relevant years. We can also investigate the other peaks, such as in 1854, which corresponds to the Crimean War, or the peak in 1823, which does not correlate with any obvious war the UK was involved in. A note on frequencies is necessary too. If we click on the various peaks, we find that the occurrences of the word *war* in 1815 is just 258 tokens whereas in 1915 it is 7,233 and in 1942 it is 5,915. Because of the difference in sheer quantity of speech between the earlier periods and more recent data, raw numbers are sometimes a better indicator of the amount of discursive content about war than the normalised figures (per million words) represented in the graph.

Searching Hansard on the basis of specific search terms, such as *war*,[16] which can be unambiguously identified, is one way into the data. Users with a wider aim, for example to track key topics in particular periods or compare the language of such periods, can use word clouds or bubble charts instead.

Word clouds shows the most frequently used words in the given time period and differentiates these words by size to reflect their relative frequency. One option is to compare word clouds for two different periods, such as the World Wars, by limiting the word cloud's dates to first 1914–1918 and then 1939–1945. Comparing the two resulting downloaded word clouds (see Figure 3.18), we see the size of the words *whether, think, war, country* and *asked* stays relatively similar, whilst *men* gets smaller and *people* appears for the first time in the later word cloud.

Although the calculations underlying word clouds are rigorous, the interpretation of such visualisations requires caution. It is tempting to conclude from these examples that the war periods were periods of great uncertainty, because of

---

16. It should be noted that even though *war* appears to be unambiguous, it is often used metaphorically in politics and a search on this item will therefore also yield *war on drugs* and *war on terror* in addition to references to conventional wars.

Figure 3.18 Comparison of word clouds for World War I (top, 1914–1918) and World War II (bottom, 1939–1945) in the House of Commons Hansard

the dominance of *whether* and *think*, or that feminism had started to have an effect in the transition from *man/men* to *people*, but such claims need to be backed up with detailed examination of the context. Word clouds are a starting point for detailed exploration; a stimulus to finding patterns that users may otherwise not think to look for. They are based on bald frequencies, so additional insights might be gained from exploring the keywords in the war periods.

Because on our site keywords can only be computed for administrations or entire service periods of Prime Ministers, we cannot compare keywords for all debates that took place during World War I with those during World War II. Both wars saw multiple prime minsters, so for this search we will choose those who served longest during the two war periods: respectively David Lloyd George (1916–1922) and Winston Churchill (1940–1945). If we compare George's service time (target) with Churchill's (comparison), some of the keywords are unsurprisingly linked to the names[17] of the key people of the time, as we can see in Figure 3.19. There are also clear dominant concerns of the period, centred on *Ireland* and the *Irish* as well as preoccupations with the *military, munitions* and, perhaps most significant in this trench-fought war, *men*.

As with word clouds, bubble charts are based on accurate calculations, but their interpretation depends on a more detailed examination of the data itself, as researchers from relevant disciplines would recognise. For this reason, we have ensured that the user can always click through to see the data itself and base their interpretation on the closer analysis of the keywords in their context with the same layout options as with search box searches explained earlier. We can also reverse the sub-corpora, to make Churchill's service period the target in order to see what different keywords this produces (see Figure 3.20). In this case, we see that *Ireland* and *Irish* are no longer the main concern and even *munitions* and *military* have given way to words like *factories, job* and *social*, demonstrating that the focus in parliament appears to have been much more concentrated on the home front than was the case in World War I.

Most searches using word clouds or bubble charts are likely to leave users wanting to dig further into the data, and this is possible by highlighting up to four of the words and clicking through to the original context of their use. Visualisations of the kind used here can only ever be a guide to the user of large complex datasets such as Hansard and for that reason we have made sure that the data is always only a click away. Rather than taking these quantitative patterns at face value, qualitative investigation is almost always needed to confirm the user's interpretation. This is no different from standard corpus-linguistics software which produces simplified pictures of a corpus to help the user navigate the complexities of large datasets such as Hansard.

---

17. Although we excluded grammatical words as far as possible in the bubble charts, it is much harder to exclude names, and some researchers would perhaps not want to lose this aspect of the data. The list of proper names is difficult to define as they are not tagged as such in the database and some names are identical to common nouns (e.g. *Baker/baker*).

Figure 3.19 Keywords from David Lloyd George's service period as Prime Minister (1916–1922) compared to Winston Churchill's service period as Prime Minister (1940–1945)

5. Conclusions

This chapter introduced our attempt to make corpus linguistics more user-friendly for non-linguist researchers who may find corpus methods insightful but have limited time or capacity for learning to use specialist software. Our site shows that even a large corpus such as Hansard can be prepared in such a way that insights from corpus-style searches can be gleaned with relatively little training. It is hoped that end-users from a wide variety of academic disciplines as well as interested parties outside academia will be encouraged to see textual data in a new way, and use our site for discovering patterns of behaviour by parliamentarians that traditional search methods would not allow. As an example, Figure 3.21

Figure 3.20 Keywords from Winston Churchill's service period as Prime Minister (1940–1945) compared with David Lloyd George's service period as Prime Minister (1916–1922)

shows a light-hearted search by a political scientist working in peace and conflict studies who noticed some frequent phrases and wondered if there was a correlation between them.

One of the potential pitfalls of this approach, which such end-users will be aware of, is the danger that a visualisation will be seen as a 'black box' delivering pre-packaged analyses that the interpreter may not understand in any depth or may draw false conclusions from. This is a risk that we have tried to mitigate in the

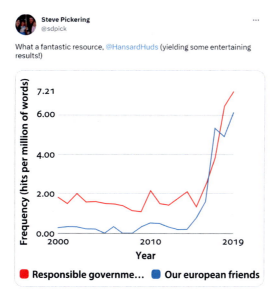

Figure 3.21 Tweet and graph demonstrating a political researcher's use of Hansard at Huddersfield

site by a range of measures, including pop-up help tips, case studies which include warnings about potential misinterpretations, and a user guide which includes warnings about the potential for misunderstanding the results of searches. In all our discussion of the site, we have characterised the searches as entry points to the data, rather than results in themselves, a perspective which will be familiar to corpus linguists already, but may not be so for other users.

The Hansard at Huddersfield site is a tool for analysis which we anticipate will be attractive to many types of end-user interested in democratic processes. What it cannot do is bring the insights of discourse analysis or linguistics more widely to bear upon the results of searches. This is also true of standard corpus software. It is, therefore, incumbent upon the user to remember that the graphs, visualisations and even the concordance lines themselves need to be interpreted through an understanding of how language works, how word meanings change across time and context and how even everyday words can hold great significance in the deliberations of parliament.

Whilst having fulfilled its initial aims, the site is still under development and in a collaboration with Parliamentary Data Services[18] we aim to provide further

---

18. The intention of this collaboration is to develop the site further and explore the potential for incorporating some of our approach to searchability into the official Hansard site in due course.

functionality to improve its usefulness. Some search functions less dependent on corpus methods than on accurate and consistent metadata will be explored in our collaboration. These include the ability to search by party and ensuring that a single speaker's contributions can be identified despite the variation in naming practices in Hansard. In addition, one significant corpus-linguistic feature yet to be exploited is collocation. Though some of the more striking collocates can be found by exporting and sorting concordances by left and right hand context, there are a number of ways in which statistical collocational patterns could feed into the wider study of discursive construction of topics and themes and we plan to explore the potential for incorporating these into the site.

References

Antaki, Charles & Leudar, Ivan. 2001. Recruiting the record: Using opponents' exact words in parliamentary argumentation. *Text* 21(4): 467–488.

Baker, Paul. 2006. *Using Corpora in Discourse Analysis*. London: Continuum.

Bucholtz, Mary. 2000. The politics of transcription. *Journal of Pragmatics* 32(10): 1439–1465.

Cameron, David. 2009. Conservative Party Conference 2009: Full text of David Cameron's speech. *The Guardian*. 8 October. <https://www.theguardian.com/politics/2009/oct/08/david-cameron-speech-in-full> (30 September 2021).

Demmen, Jane, Jeffries, Lesley & Walker, Brian. 2018. Charting the semantics of labour relations in House of Commons debates spanning two hundred years: A study of parliamentary language using corpus linguistic methods and automated semantic tagging. In *Doing Politics: Discursivity, Performativity and Mediation in Political Discourse* [Discourse Approaches to Politics, Society and Culture 80], Michael Kranert & Geraldine Horan (eds), 81–104. Amsterdam: John Benjamins.

Himmelfarb, Gertrude. 1995. *The De-moralization of Society: From Victorian Virtues to Modern Value*. New York NY: Vintage.

Jeffries, Lesley. 2010. *Critical Stylistics: The Power of English*. Basingstoke: Palgrave MacMillan.

Jeffries, Lesley & Walker, Brian. 2019. Austerity in the Commons: A corpus critical analysis of austerity and its surrounding grammatical context in Hansard (1803–2015). In *Discourse Analysis and Austerity: Critical Studies from Economics and Linguistics* [Routledge Frontiers of Political Economy], Kate Power, Tanweer Ali & Eva Lebdušková (eds), 53–79. London: Routledge.

Leech, Geoffrey. 1991. The state of the art in corpus linguistics. In *English Corpus Linguistics: Studies in Honour of Jan Svartvik*, Karin Aijmer & Bengt Altenberg (eds), 8–29. London: Longman.

McEnery, Tony & Hardie, Andrew. 2011. *Corpus Linguistics: Method, Theory and Practice*. Cambridge: CUP.

McIntyre, Dan & Walker, Brian. 2019. *Corpus Stylistics: Theory and Practice*. Edinburgh: EUP.

Mollin, Sandra. 2007. The Hansard hazard: Gauging the accuracy of British parliamentary transcripts. *Corpora* 2(2): 187–210.

Ralphs, Kezia. 2009. Recording parliamentary debates: A brief history with reference to England and New Zealand. *Australasian Parliamentary Review* 24(2): 151–163.

Shaw, Sylvia. 2018. Off the record: The transcription of parliamentary debates for political discourse analysis. In *Doing Politics: Discursivity, Performativity and Mediation in Political Discourse* [Discourse Approaches to Politics, Society and Culture 80], Michael Kranert & Geraldine Horan (eds), 105–126. Amsterdam: John Benjamins.

Slembrouck, Stef. 1992. The parliamentary Hansard "verbatim" report: The written construction of spoken discourse. *Language and Literature* 1(2): 101–120.

Taylor, Charlotte & Marchi, Anna. 2018. Introduction. In *Corpus Approaches to Discourse: A Critical Review*, Charlotte Taylor & Anna Marchi (eds), 1–16. London: Routledge.

Vice, John. 2020. Personal communication: Email to Lesley Jeffries. 30 March.

Vice, John & Farrell, Stephen. 2017. *The History of Hansard.* House of Lords Hansard and the House of Lords Library. <https://www.parliament.uk/documents/lords-library/History-of-Hansard.pdf> (29 October 2019).

von Lünen, Alexander, Jeffries, Lesley, Stradling, Fransina, Sanjurjo González, Hugo & Crossley, Paul. 2023. Hansard at Huddersfield: Adapting corpus linguistic methods for non-specialist use. *International Journal of Humanities and Arts Computing* 17(1): 25–46.

CHAPTER 4

Empire, migration and race in the British parliament (1803–2005)

Christian Mair
University of Freiburg

The chapter studies the intertwined topics of Empire, migration and race in the Hansard Corpus (1803–2005). The British Empire emerges as a prominent topic from the mid-nineteenth century, but rapidly recedes into insignificance in the two decades following World War II. Emigration dominates in the nineteenth century, whereas immigration takes over in the twentieth century. References to *race* remain frequent throughout, though in the context of two contrasting discourses. Older uses show a broad range of adjective + noun combinations classifying the 'human race' on the basis of geographical or physical characteristics (e.g. *English race, Indian race, white/black/brown/yellow race*) or evaluating groups within a colonialist ideology of white supremacy (e.g. *backward/advanced races*). Recent and contemporary use of the term is dominated by high-frequency nominal compounds belonging to the vocabulary of identity politics (e.g. *race relations*). The study situates itself at the interface of historical linguistics, colonial history and cultural studies. Methodologically, it raises the question of the future relationship between corpus linguistics and the Digital Humanities.

Keywords: British Empire, migration, race, discourse, semantic change

1. Introduction

The aim of the present study is to untangle the complex relationships between the topics of Empire, migration and race as they emerge from the Hansard data. The Hansard Corpus (Davies 2015) is particularly appropriate for this purpose because during the period that it covers (1803–2005) the parliament in Westminster provided the single most prominent public stage for the political figures who shaped British colonial policies. Hidden in the mass of 1.6 billion words assembled in the corpus is an anthology of key texts in the history of the British Empire (some of which will be subjected to close reading in Section 5). The mass of text as a whole, by contrast, provides the data needed to study the historical evolution

https://doi.org/10.1075/scl.111.04mai
© 2023 John Benjamins Publishing Company

of the discourses of Empire and race that these individuals contributed to and helped shape. The present study builds on previous research that has used the Hansard Corpus for linguistically informed cultural studies (e.g. Alexander & Struan 2017) and the analysis of political discourse on controversial issues (e.g. Baker, Brezina & McEnery 2017; Mair 2019). It has also benefitted greatly from Mollin (2007) and Sutherland and Farrell (2017), who have described change and evolution in the Hansard tradition of recording parliamentary debates and assessed the potential of the various temporal layers of the data for historical-linguistic analysis (see Alexander, this volume; and Kotze et al., this volume).

Like literary works, parliamentary speeches are easy to identify by external features (in this case, the location in which they are delivered), but they remain internally complex because of considerable heterogeneity in terms of textual structure, register and style. For the corpus linguist who is interested in language history narrowly understood (as the history of sounds, words and grammatical constructions), the Hansard Corpus would not necessarily be the first choice, as the very special discourse setting of parliament introduces numerous complications for analysis. The history of parliamentary language is a history of highly context-specific and ever-evolving traditions of speaking and writing about contested topics, and it is precisely this characteristic which makes the Hansard attractive data for interdisciplinary approaches, "readily accessible for researchers from different disciplines as well as for cross-border and cross-lingual projects", as Fišer and Lenardič (2017: 84) have put it in a survey of parliamentary corpora compiled in the framework of the European CLARIN digital language resources initiative.[1]

What the analysis of changing usage in the Hansard data reveals is that there are collective discourse conventions that act as mostly subconscious constraints on how individual members of parliament (MPs) may express their opinions in a given historical context. For example, differences in the phenotypical appearance of the human species figured as a prominent topic in parliamentary debates during almost the entire period of observation, with hundreds of MPs expressing a wide range of opinions. In that, they were free to speak their minds, but they were not entirely free with regard to the language in which they did so. While the various subdivisions of the one human race were classified according to geographical

---

1. Compare, for example, Dutchparl (Marx & Schuth 2010), a corpus of the parliamentary records of the Netherlands, which would suggest itself for a comparable study on Dutch. The Dutch parliamentary data amount to approximately 800 million words, covering the years from 1814 to 2014, i.e. broadly the same period as the Hansard Corpus. Like Britain, the Netherlands have a history of colonial expansion and colonial and postcolonial migrations. It would be interesting to see how the *Staten-Generaal* have dealt with the issues that are discussed from a Westminster perspective here.

origin (e.g. *British race*), skin colour (e.g. *dark race*) and perceived level of development (*backward* vs. *advanced races*) without hesitation throughout the nineteenth and the first half of the twentieth centuries, this use of the term declined dramatically from the 1950s, and the word has survived mainly in a small number of fossilised fixed expressions (e.g. *race relations*). The gap was filled by new words and categories such as *ethnicity* or *non-white*, for which – on the evidence of the Hansard Corpus – there had been little use before the second half of the twentieth century.

The chapter is structured as follows. Section 2 briefly discusses the data and methods used. Sections 3 and 4 survey changing discourses of migration and race. Section 5 'personalises' and contextualises the analysis by focussing on the language and rhetorical strategies of four high-profile parlamentarians and orators: Benjamin Disraeli, William Ewart Gladstone, Enoch Powell and Anthony Wedgwood Benn. The concluding Section 6 summarises the general findings and suggests directions for further research.

2. Data and methods

The data analysed are from the Hansard Corpus (Davies 2015) of the British parliament, developed by Mark Davies in collaboration with the SAMUELS (Semantic Annotation and Mark-up for Enhancing Lexical Searches) project based at the University of Glasgow (2014–2016) and the UCREL team at Lancaster. The data were obtained by searches for individual items, lexical bundles and lexico-grammatical constructions, relying on the interface's truncation facilities, lemmatisation and part-of-speech tagging. Mutual Information (MI) scores measuring collocational strength were used experimentally, but not systematically, as they did not prove superior to the search strategies adopted in terms of precision and recall (see Footnote 4). Recent corpus-based work on historical/critical discourse analysis has developed innovative and statistically more sophisticated ways of representing the 'peaks' and 'troughs' in usage, for example Usage Fluctuation Analysis (UFA, see e.g. Gabrielatos et al. 2012). In the present study, however, search results were not exported for further statistical processing with other tools. Instead, I opted for a combination of quantitative distant reading (Moretti 2013) and qualitative close reading of specific attestations in their textual and historical contexts.

Moretti's distant reading model was originally developed for the analysis of literary texts, but can be easily extended to the Hansard data (see also Kotze et al., this volume). There is one major contrast between literary works and parliamentary speeches: Only the former are generally fictional. In several other respects, though, there are parallels. The most important one is that both genres are characterised by complex relationships between represented speech in writing and the corresponding oral performances (see also Alexander, this volume). As a resource developed from existing digital data, the Hansard Corpus does not fit the traditional definition of a corpus in linguistics, as a digitally searchable collection of texts compiled by linguists for the purposes of linguistic research. Indeed, Hansard is a corpus that encourages interdisciplinary research by linguists and invites use by scholars outside the corpus-linguistic community (see Jeffries et al., this volume). In other words, it presents an opportunity for corpus linguists to take a more active role in the Digital Humanities movement.

As a corpus linguist, the present writer cannot lay claim to the same level of expertise in the history of the British Empire that he may have in the history of the English language during the nineteenth and twentieth centuries. Some of the generalisations about migration, race and Empire that will be proposed below may be considered as too simplistic by experts in history. To pre-empt potential criticism, I would like to mention some of the historical scholarship that has guided me in the analysis. Hyam (2010) has been an inspiration with regard to the cultural, social and psychological consequences of Empire. With specific regard to the nexus of Empire and race, I have benefitted greatly from Hall's (2012) joint biography of two activists and intellectuals: Zachary Macaulay (1768–1838), fervent evangelical Christian, abolitionist, and for a time head administrator of Sierra Leone, a colony founded to provide a home to liberated slaves; and his son Thomas Babington Macaulay (1800–1859), liberal historian, MP and politician in the service of the Colonial Office, where – through his famous "Minute" of 1835 – he made a lasting contribution to language policy and planning in favour of English in British India. Both men had rich direct experience of colonial encounters, and for both the issue of race was central to their thinking and writing. Particularly with regard to the contested notion of race, the historical literature is complemented by copious research in cultural studies (e.g. Hall 1997; Hall & Morley 2019; Williams 1983)[2] and postcolonial theory (e.g. Ashcroft 2015), which has of course also fed into critical-discourse approaches to race in linguistics (e.g. Alim & Reyes 2011).

As Alim, Rickford and Ball (2016) have recently argued, research on language and race has matured sufficiently in order for it to be consolidated into a coherent research programme, which they call *raciolinguistics* and which they intend to

---

2. Note in this connection that, while not included in the original 1977 edition, both *racial* and *ethnic* were added by Williams for the revised edition of his "vocabulary of culture and society" in 1983. For Hall, *race* is one of the quintessential 'floating signifiers' we need to analyse in order to understand cultural modernity.

promote the academic and societal "conversation on language and race by providing an interdisciplinary space for interaction between sociolinguistics, linguistic anthropology, and educational linguistics" (2016: 6). The findings of the present study, particularly in Sections 4 and 5, show that corpus linguistics can be a natural ally in this enterprise, both for the time-depth it can add to analyses of the present and for the balanced and systematic analysis of large amounts of data which it provides.

3. From the century of emigration to the century of immigration

Figure 4.1 shows the frequency in the Hansard Corpus of references to the British Empire, the topic of emigration, and the topic of immigration.

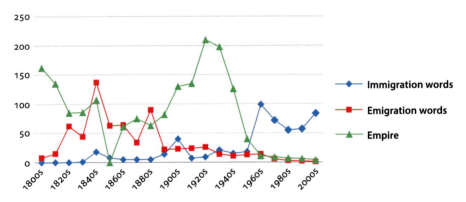

Figure 4.1 References to immigration, emigration and the British Empire in the Hansard Corpus (1803–2005, normalised frequencies per million words)

Immigration and *emigration* words were retrieved by searches for *immigr** and *emigr** (i.e. any word starting with the letter sequences <immigr> or <emigr>). To achieve a tolerable balance between precision and recall in the automatic search, references to the British Empire were collected using the following search string: -Ottoman|Turkish|Roman|German|Russian|Chinese|Soviet|French|Austrian|Austro-Hungarian empire (i.e. empire or Empire preceded by any word except those specified).

This search yielded 100,048 hits. Among the 1,851 different bigrams found in this search, the four most common expressions were *the Empire* (43,746), *British Empire* (18,042), *colonial Empire* (4,390) and *our Empire* (2,318), all of which exclusively or overwhelmingly refer to the British colonial domain. The terms excluded as first elements in the search for *x + Empire* bigrams were identified by going through a list of those 48 bigrams which were attested with a frequency of more than 100. The most commonly mentioned Empires apart from the British were the Turkish (1,854) / Ottoman (1,438) Empire and, interestingly, the Roman Empire (831), which provides confirmation from parliamentary data for the following claim:

> All empires occupy simultaneously two different kinds of space: the world stage – alongside and sometimes in geopolitical competition with other empires – and alien localities over which some degree of rulership is established. They may also occupy a third arena, the historical imagination, as the Roman empire did for the British. (Hyam 2010: 1–2)

Space constraints in the present chapter make it impossible to pursue the matter further, but it should at least be noted that the Hansard material is rife with mentions of classical authorities and quotations from ancient literature, sometimes even in the original languages. The material is definitely sufficient to merit treatment in its own right.[3]

What we learn from Figure 4.1 is that emigration as a topic of discussion is most prominent from the 1820s to the 1880s, with peaks in the 1840s and 1880s. Zooming in on the first peak, we find a generally positive semantic prosody, with *voluntary, free* and *extensive* as the three most common adjectives combining with the noun *emigration*. The three top adjectives for the second peak are *state-aided, voluntary* and *Irish*. *Immigration* shows a slight spike in the first decade of the twentieth century, but does not really become a prominent topic until the 1960s. *Empire* is a fairly common topic in the first two decades of the nineteenth century, then declines somewhat, only to rise again from the 1860s. Peaking in the 1920s and 1930s, it declines to insignificance within the two decades following. It is interesting to note that in the period from the 1890s to the 1950s, when the topic of Empire is very present, debates on any kind of migration are rare. This suggests imperial self-confidence and stability – and a completely different frame of reference in which immigration was dealt with. Today, the word *immigrant* [to Britain] typically denotes a person who migrates to a destination within the UK from outside; emigrants, on the other hand, are people who leave the UK for extended periods or permanently. In the context of the British Empire, major global currents of migration – for example, Irish emigration to Australia or the migration of Indian indentured labourers to the West Indies – did not involve crossing national boundaries and were therefore internal affairs. Similarly,

---

3. As an example consider the following from a eulogy to the Marquis of Wellington: "Talk of an Alexander, a Caesar, and a Hannibal [...]" (Sir Frederick Flood, 1814). Needless to add, the Englishman is said to outshine them all in his glory.

European immigration did not have its present, restricted sense of immigration from the European mainland to the UK, but could refer to emigration from Europe to any part of the Empire. In this situation, an apparently tautological concept such as 'foreign immigrant' made perfect sense. For example, it helped distinguish between European immigrants, such as Jews from Central and Eastern Europe or other Europeans, including those staying in Britain in transit for the US, and Indians in Britain, who – as imperial subjects – were not foreign in this sense. Accordingly, more than half of all attestations (43 out of 64) of *foreign immigrant(s)* are recorded for the high imperial period, the four decades from 1881–1920.

Figure 4.2 shows common terms for the people migrating. The terms *foreigner(s)* and *alien(s)* dominate throughout the nineteenth century, with *alien* producing a further spike caused by the fixed expression *enemy alien(s)* during World War I. The term *immigrant*, on the other hand, is rarely used during this period. It shows a first minor peak in the first decade of the twentieth century and seems to have a distinctly negative semantic prosody from the start, combining with the adjectives *alien* (124), *Indian* (35), *indentured* (29), *Chinese* (25), and *undesirable* (17). While *Indian* and *Chinese* could be understood as neutral geographical descriptions, the context of most examples makes clear that immigration from these regions is considered potentially problematic.

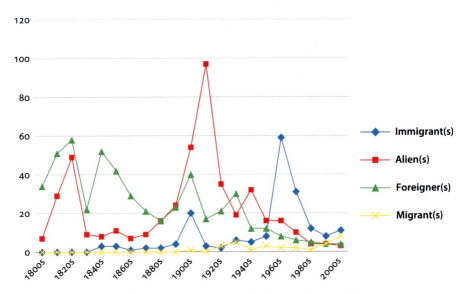

Figure 4.2 Common references to migrants in the Hansard Corpus (1803–2005, normalised frequencies per million words)

In the corpus as a whole, the two most frequent adjectives used with *immigrant(s)* are *illegal* (1,697) and *coloured* (624).[4] In view of the pervasive ideology of white racial superiority, it is somewhat surprising to see that *coloured immigrant* is only attested once before 1950 – in a reference to East Asian immigration to Australia. The decade of its highest frequency is the 1960s, one of two decades in which it even exceeds the frequency of the normally dominant *illegal*. Figure 4.3 presents the trends from 1940 to 2005. In view of a total of 1,514 relevant attestations, the normalised frequencies per million words are very low, so that they have been rescaled to a normalised frequency per 100,000,000.

The decline of *coloured immigrant(s)* from the late 1970s reflects the increasing coyness about references to race in public discourse (see Section 4). As it is the concordance line that "should still be our weapon of first and last resort, the place where quantification and interpretation meet" (Hardie 2017, 57:02ff), it is worth presenting a few examples (Examples (1) to (4)) spanning the period from the 1840s to the 1960s for further illustration.

(1) Under a compulsory system of relief the *immigration of Irish paupers* into England would be increased, because many labourers who are now induced to remain at home in order to support their relatives, would be inclined to come over to England [...] [5]

> (Speaker name not recoverable from database, debate topic: Poor Relief [Ireland] Bill, 1847)

---

4. An anonymous reviewer asked how the adjective + noun combinations yielded by the relatively crude bigram searches for _j* IMMIGRANT compare to those that might have been identified by standard measures of collocational strength. The answer is that the two search strategies tend to corroborate each other, but use of collocational statistics almost always reduces precision without increasing recall. To use the present example, a search for *node: IMMIGRANT/collocate: _j* (3L, 0R)*, ranking the findings by MI score, had *coloured* in third position (10.36) and *illegal* in sixth (9.51), thus confirming their relevance for the present argument. Positions 1 and 2 were occupied by *first-generation* and *second-generation* (MI scores 12.61 and 11.46). However, at frequencies of 26 and 11 (in the entire corpus), these two items are irrelevant to the present argument, and illustrate a well-known weakness of MI, namely that it leads to inflated scores for low-frequency items. The difficulties are exacerbated if one searches sub-corpora rather than the corpus as a whole. The remaining adjectives from the top ten have negative connotations (*would-be, indentured, clandestine, alien*) or are mostly evaluated negatively in the contexts of their use (*Pakistani, Jewish*), which is in line with the observations made above.

5. Except where indicated otherwise, quotations from the Hansard data follow the format of the Hansard Corpus. Some minor changes have been made in the interest of readability. Thus, I have removed spaces before punctuation marks resulting from tokenisation and have re-combined complex forms separated for lemmatisation (e.g. *cannot* < *can not*). Items under discussion are given in italics.

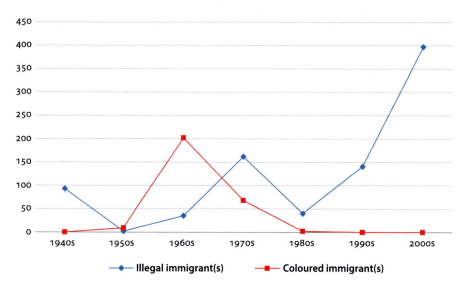

Figure 4.3 *Coloured* and *illegal* immigrants in the Hansard Corpus (1940–2005, normalised frequency per 100 million words)

(2) Other plans had been tried: European colonists had been sent out, but *European immigration* had, to a great extent, failed: *Coolie immigration* had been tried, and that had likewise to a considerable degree failed [...]
(Lord John Russell, 1848, context: post-Abolition West Indies)

(3) [...] they must bear in mind that some of the undoubted evils which had fallen upon portions of the country from an *alien immigration* which was largely *Jewish*, gave those of them who, like the right hon[.] Baronet and himself, condemned nothing more strongly than the manifestation of the anti-Semitic spirit, some reason to fear that this country might be, at however great a distance, in danger of following the evil example set by some other countries [...]
(Arthur Balfour, 1905)

(4) Sir C[.] Osborne asked the Secretary of State for Foreign Affairs whether, in his discussions about Great Britain's entry into the European Common Market, he will make it an absolute condition that the *coloured immigrants* settled here will be entitled freely to live in any of the Common Market countries, no matter how numerous they become in the United Kingdom[.]   (1967)

The fourth term recorded in Figure 4.2, *migrant(s)*, was used at very low frequencies throughout the twentieth century and only sees a definite increase in the final two decades recorded in the Hansard Corpus, which yield 1,340 of the total of 3,414 recorded instances. With 574 occurrences, *economic migrant(s)* is the leading adjective + noun combination (followed by *British migrant(s)*, a distant second with 100 examples, of which 98 are from the period 1921–1960).

4. Colonial and contemporary discourses of race: The evidence from Hansard

As will be shown in the following corpus analyses, in the time window under review here the term *race* has (a) fluctuated in terms of its discourse frequency, (b) profoundly changed in its semantic denotation, and (c) acquired taboo connotations in many of its historically attested uses. As Hall (2012: 13–14) writes:

> The literature of the early modern period, building on medieval discourses of the connections of darkness and evil, blackness and monstrosity, began to encode fundamental divisions between Christians and non-Christians, Europeans and non-Europeans. Race was being made and remade in historically specific times and places, always connected to questions of power and inequality. Neither monogenesis nor the possibility of non-Christians being converted to Christianity appears to have prevented or retarded the construction of hierarchies between peoples. But eighteenth-century notions of race were flexible, mobile and, as a wealth of recent scholarship has demonstrated, embedded in British culture. Racial thinking was sedimented, older conceptions jostled alongside or coexisted, sometimes contradictorily, with newer ideas.

Thomas Macaulay – one of the subjects of Hall's twin biography – served as an MP between 1831 and 1853. He is represented in the Hansard Corpus with 127 speeches. The 35 uses of the term *race* contained in them serve well to indicate the versatility of the notion during the first half of the nineteenth century. Endorsing the planned abolition of slavery, he denounces the institution as a crime against humanity (or, in his own words, the "human race"), as shown in Example (5).

(5) Slavery there [in the West Indies] had been made to do the work of famine, of pestilence, and of war combined: It had accomplished more than they could accomplish, in putting an end to that disposition to increase and multiply which was manifested by the *human race* in every other part of the world [...]
(1833)

Practically all of Macaulay's interventions in his parliamentary speeches are in support of liberal and progressive measures: improving the lot of the British factory worker, supporting Jewish emancipation, or – as exemplified in Example (6) and (7) – establishing the rule of law in India. This humanism does not imply, however, that the subdivisions of the one human race are considered equal.

(6) [...] the most sacred duties which as governors we owe to the governed –; which as a people blessed with far more than an ordinary measure of political liberty and of intellectual light –; we owe to *a race debased* by three thousand years of despotism and priest craft [...]
(1833)

(7) Consider too, Sir, how rapidly the public mind of India is advancing, how much attention is already paid by the higher classes of the natives to those intellectual pursuits on the cultivation of which *the superiority of the European race* to the rest of mankind principally depends: Surely, under such circumstances, from motives of selfish policy, if from no higher motive, we ought to fill the Magistracies of our Eastern Empire with men who may do honour to their country –; with men who may represent the best part of the English nation[.]

(1833)

As Hall (2012: 317) has noted, outside of colonial encounters race often does not denote skin colour as much as "chasms between degrees of whiteness on a civilisational index". This is common in references to *the Jewish* and *Irish races*. There are examples of both in Macaulay's speeches, but a more unusual case is presented by the reference to the 'German race' in Example (8).

(8) I am told that we are in danger of being beaten out of the field by the people of Germany, who work seventeen hours a day, and who are in such a state that the public authorities complain that there is not one among them of stature sufficient to make a soldier: Sir, if ever the English nation is deprived of its commercial prosperity, it will be by *no such race of dwarfs* as these; it will be by some finer people than the English population –; if ever such a people should arise [...]

(1846)

In evaluations involving members of the English race itself, all references to skin colour or degrees of civilisational advancement are suppressed completely, and the only dimension of evaluation that remains is a moral one, as in Macaulay's 1840 reference to a "race of disloyal tories".

The term *race*, attested a total of 69,987 times in the Hansard Corpus in a lemma search (*RACE*), is not easy to disambiguate. Searching for the noun lemma (*RACE_n**) removes irrelevant verbal uses, reduces the number of hits to 56,838, but does not resolve the polysemy between the 'human phenotype' and 'competition' senses. To achieve this with reasonable precision, I went through the 100 most frequent bigrams of the type 'any word + race (noun)' (= * *RACE_n**), eliminating the terms most clearly aligned with the 'competition' sense. The resulting search for -horse|arms|road|motor|armaments|boat|reg|rat|armament|credit|greyhound|dog *RACE_n** reduced the total further to 53,162 hits. As this is about half the number of results obtained in the search for *Empire*, the figure can be taken as quantitative evidence for the importance of the topic of race in parliamentary debates – on Empire but also on many other issues.

Issues of precision and recall were less difficult to handle in the case of references to ethnicity, which were captured by a search for *ethnic** (i.e. *ethnic, ethnicity, ethnical(ly)*). Figure 4.4 shows fluctuation for the frequency of mentions of race throughout the period of observation and a steep increase for ethnicity during the second half of the twentieth century. The rise in mentions of ethnicity is paralleled by the increase of *non-white(s)*, though at lower levels of frequency (see Figure 4.5).

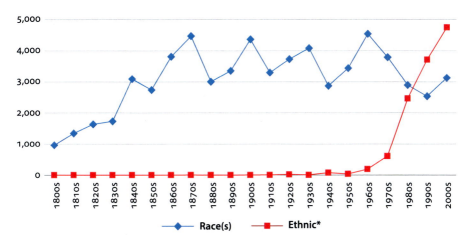

Figure 4.4 Race and ethnicity in the Hansard Corpus (1803–2005, frequencies normalised to 100 million words)

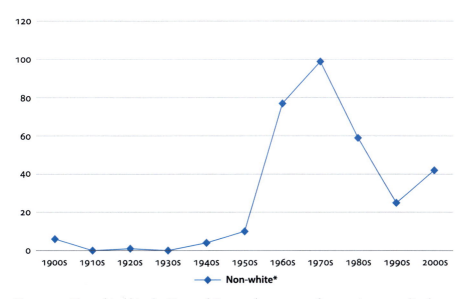

Figure 4.5 *Non-white(s)* in the Hansard Corpus (1900–2005, frequencies normalised to 100 million words)

The gradual rise in prominence of the topic of race during the first half of the nineteenth century is to be expected. It reflects the consolidation of ideologies of cultural superiority and white supremacy during the period of British and European imperial expansion. What the frequency trends do not show, however, are the even more striking changes in the word's meaning and the contexts of its use. There are two different discourses of race: an old or colonial one that dominates throughout the nineteenth and well into the first half of the twentieth century; and a new one that supersedes it from the mid-twentieth century. Central to the older colonial discourse is a desire to classify the human race into sub-groups, which is linguistically reflected in a wide range of adjective + *race* combinations. The most frequent one is *human race* (2,723), followed by *different race(s)* (962), and *native race(s)* (960). Other high-frequency adjectives combining with *race* generally fall into three categories:

–   geographical/historical origin: *Irish, British, Jewish, Anglo-Saxon, English, Celtic, African, German, Scottish*, etc.;
–   phenotype: *coloured, white, black*, etc.;
–   evaluation: *dominant, superior, inferior, backward*, etc.

Metaphorical or extended uses are not uncommon, for example *Christian races* (73) or *English-speaking race* (49).

Needless to say, these usages represent a folk taxonomy which has little factual and scientific substance and no coherent organising principle. What most offends present-day sensibilities is the open expression of the ideology of white supremacy apparent in the division into advanced/backward or superior/inferior races. The most positive thing that can be said about it is that racial categorisation is applied equally to all of humanity. Being white and English is not an unmarked option that does not require mention; the expression *English race* is as ordinary as *African race* or *Celtic race*. This is notably different from present conventions which tend to treat Englishness/whiteness as the unmarked default and ethnicity/race as the marked case requiring its own technical-therapeutic vocabulary (as in the common initialism *BAME* (Black and Asian Minority Ethnic) or in the term *non-white* (Figure 4.5), which lumps together all 'visible' minorities under this dubious heading).

Figure 4.6 presents the evolution of the nineteenth-century colonial discourses of race in parliamentary debates. Evaluation discourse on race is identified by a search for: *dominant|inferior|superior|backward|advanced RACE_n**. Geographical and phenotype-based classifications are identified by the following two searches: *Irish|British|Jewish|African|Celtic|Scottish RACE_n** and *white| coloured|black|brown|yellow RACE_n**.

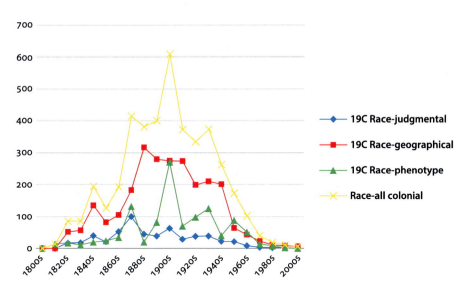

Figure 4.6 Nineteenth-century colonial discourses of race (1803–2005), frequencies normalised to 100 million words

We know that the core ideas of the colonial discourse on race were inherited from the eighteenth century (Hall 2012). What the bell-shaped distribution in Hansard reveals in addition is how popular it became during the nineteenth century (and how rapidly it declined in the latter half of the twentieth). This is a notable finding of the present study revealed by the distant-reading method. Figure 4.6 also shows that the most openly racist sub-type of the colonial discourse (judgmental) was not the dominant one. On the other hand, it should be borne in mind that the outwardly descriptive geographical adjectives also had evaluative connotations in the colonial discourse, so that *native races* or the *Irish race* were not necessarily regarded as being on a par with the *English*, *British* or *Scottish race*.

Figure 4.7 shows the replacement of this traditional colonial discourse on race by the contemporary one. In it, the adjective + noun combinations of the colonial discourse play hardly any role at all. The striking feature of the new discourse is that the continuing high frequency of the word *race* is largely due to the persistent use of just three nominal compounds, namely *race relations*, *race discrimination* and *race equality*.

Noun + noun compounds with *race* as their first element remain rare for the period in which the old colonial discourse is dominant. Not counting obviously irrelevant instances such as *race meeting(s)* and *race horses*, we only find the following attested at frequencies higher than five for the five decades between 1881 and 1930: *race hatred(s)* (18), *race distinction(s)* (10), *race prejudice* (7) and *race animosity/animosities* (6).

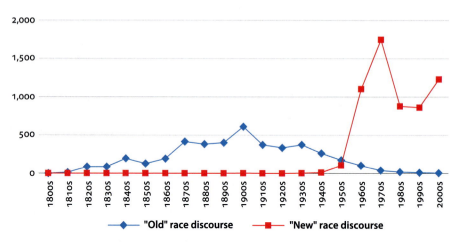

Figure 4.7 Colonial and contemporary discourses of race (1803–2005), frequencies normalised to 100 million words

One of the less common examples is the polemical *race suicide*, attested from 1906 to 1967. The 27 instances show it applied in a wide variety of contexts, not necessarily restricted to racial conflict in the narrow sense. *Race suicide* is also used with reference to a shrinking population, availability of drugs suspected to induce abortion, the assumed debilitating effect of dole payments on the English working classes, the looming threat of nuclear annihilation during the Cold War and – somewhat eccentrically – also in a polemic against the unregulated spread of the motorcar on British roads. It is definitely used in its literal, racist sense in its latest recorded use from 1967, shown in Example (9).

(9) The hon[.] Member for Barnsley (Mr[.] Mason), the Minister of Defence for Equipment, who is grinning at this, should go back to Barnsley and tell his voters that his policy is to have more black people in this country than white and see what they do to him: The Home Office says that by 1985 there will be 3½ million coloured people in this country: It should know more about it than the hon[.] Gentleman does: By doing nothing, the Government are betraying this country and compelling the English [to] *commit race suicide* [Interruption] This is true; it is no good hon[.] Members tut-tutting: For all these reasons I find the Address bitterly disappointing and the Government a cowardly failure […]   (Cyril Osborne, 1967)

To return to the main point: As an abstract pattern, the *race* + noun compound schema is available throughout the entire period of observation, but the distribution changes dramatically. Before about 1950, we find examples in small numbers, but with a wide range of nominal heads. After 1950, frequencies are very high, but this increase is due to just three heads: *race relations* (6,199), *race discrimination*

(317) and *race equality* (183). The bias toward the first one is somewhat levelled if we consider the corresponding adjective + noun compounds, too: *racial discrimination* (2,331), *racial equality* (1,320) and *racial relations* (90).[6] Whereas in the nineteenth century, race was a central epistemic organising category in discourses of human difference, it has become surrounded by taboos of all kinds in the late-twentieth and early twenty-first centuries, surviving mainly in a small number of technical terms in the vocabulary of British identity politics.

One link between the old and new discourses of race is provided by the terms *racism* and *racist(s)*. The OED attests *racism* from 1903. The near synonym *racialism* goes back even further, to 1880.[7] American sources dominate in the early quotations for both. This chronology shows that the terms are critical responses to the nineteenth-century ideology of white supremacy. In the parliamentary debates, they remain extremely rare until after World War II. The first attestations, from 1908 and 1909, refer to South Africa, but not to antagonisms between European immigrants and the indigenous Africans, but rather to the conflict between British and Dutch settlers, as in Example (10).

(10) Briefly the position is this: that you have in the Orange River Colony a dual language established: [...] Some of us pointed out when the Bill was passed that the result –; not intended –; would be that *racialism*, the effects of *racialism*, would ensue: The position now is that in the Orange River Colonies the British children are compelled to learn Dutch: This applies to three subjects –; geometry, geography, and Latin: Just imagine British children being compelled to learn geography, geometry, and Latin in a Dutc[h] language!
(Speaker name not recoverable from database, debate topic: colonial and foreign affairs, 1909)

From the 1950s, *racism* and *racist(s)* emerge as the common choices, showing drastic increases in frequency. The normalised frequencies per million words (combined for all three) are 0.01 for the 1950s, 0.35 for the 1960s, 2.52 for the 1970s, 7.83 for the 1980s, 13.37 for the 1990s and 18.18 for the 2000s.

---

6. The freer combinations familiar from earlier periods, such as *race hate*, *race hatred* or *race riot*, persist into the present, but never reach comparable frequencies.

7. *Racialist* and *racist* follow the corresponding abstract nouns at a few decades' distance, with the adjectival uses being attested after the nominal ones in both cases. The causative verb *racialise* ('impose a racial interpretation on', 'cause to become racist'), attested in the OED from 1917, does not occur in the Hansard data.

5. 'Race': From corpus linguistics to cultural studies

This section links the distant reading of the entire Hansard back to the close reading of selected speeches by four high-profile MPs. Two are from the nineteenth and two from the twentieth century. Each pair represents opposite ends of the political spectrum of their era, but all four were prolific orators who helped shape the conventions of Westminster parliamentary rhetoric. The nineteenth century is represented by Benjamin Disraeli (1804–1881), who brought the Tories back to power after the party's disastrous split over the Corn Laws in 1846, and his Liberal antagonist William Ewart Gladstone (1809–1898). The twentieth century is represented by Enoch Powell (1912–1998), MP for the Conservative and Ulster Unionist parties, and Anthony Wedgwood Benn (1925–2014), a Labour MP on the hard left.

Looking at individual uses of the word *race* by four politicians does more than merely confirm the expected, namely that the politicians necessarily participate to some extent in the prevailing discourses of their time. Thus, both Disraeli and Gladstone routinely refer to the Irish as a race, regardless of the fact that the former vehemently opposes their demands for autonomy while the latter sympathises with them.[8] Similarly, in the twentieth century, both Powell and Benn use the term *race relations* in spite of being on opposite sides of the argument. What is more interesting than this confirmation of the expected, however, is to explore the individual rhetorical creativity displayed by speakers when they strain at some prevailing discourse norm, mock it or even turn it against itself to subvert it.

For Gladstone, who looked at the Empire as a financial liability and an economic risk rather than a source of national pride, the 'Indian Mutiny' of 1857 provides an opportunity for a critique of the colonial project (Example (11)).

(11)   We have before us other questions of a most gigantic character, and, from their accumulation and the unpreparedness of our minds for them, the most overwhelming and appalling that I ever remember as a public man to have had in view: You have to consider the manner in which we are to govern 200,000,000

---

8. Compare the following pronouncement made by Disraeli in 1868: "But for the Irish ostentatiously to declare that they are a conquered *race* is very strange: If they really are a conquered *race*, they are not the people who ought to announce it: It is the conquerors from whom we should learn the fact; for it is not the conquered who should go about the world and announce their shame and humiliation: But I entirely deny that the Irish are a conquered *race* [...]," and an extract from Gladstone's (1889) obituary tribute to John Bright: "The sympathies of Mr[.] Bright were not only strong, but active; they were not sympathies which can answer to the calls made upon them for the moment, but they were the sympathies of a man who sought far and near for objects on which to bestow the inestimable advantage of his eloquence and of his courage: In Ireland in the days when the support of the *Irish race* was rare, in India when the support of the native *race* was rarer still [...]."

of men of another *race*, of another religion; an ancient nation, which you thought you could treat as if they were so many figures of wax, but who have their own institutions, their own ideas, their own history, their own civilization, and with respect to whom we thought we had nothing to do [b]ut to walk into their country and proclaim *the superiority of the Anglo-Saxon race* [...]

(1857)

Gladstone's antagonist Benjamin Disraeli showed similar respect for Indian culture and history, but of course with the opposite political intention, namely to secure Britain's imperial rule in India for the long term. One important gambit in this strategy was to have Queen Victoria (technically, Queen of the United Kingdom of Great Britain and Ireland and its Dependencies) crowned as Empress of India, against considerable Liberal opposition. On 17 February 1876, Disraeli opened the debate on the Royal Titles Bill by reading an extract from the Queen's Speech, shown in Example (12).

(12)   I am deeply thankful for the uninterrupted health which My dear Son, the Prince of Wales, has enjoyed during his journey through India. The hearty affection with which he has been received by *My Indian Subjects, of all classes and races*, assures Me that they are happy under My rule, and loyal to My throne. At the time that the direct government of My Indian Empire was transferred to the Crown, no formal addition was made to the style and titles of the Sovereign. I have deemed the present a fitting opportunity for supplying this omission, and a Bill upon the subject will be presented to you.[9]   (1876)

As shown in Example (13), Disraeli opens his own speech with a profession of his respect for Indian history and culture.

(13)   I remember when I first entered this House, now about 40 years ago, that there were, I believe, even Members of Parliament who looked upon India as a vast country which, generally speaking, was inhabited *by a single and by a subjugated race*. But since then information has been so much diffused among all classes of our countrymen on the subject of India, that even those who have the most ordinary information are now well aware that India is an ancient country of many nations; that it is peopled by various and *varying races, differing in origin, in language, in religion, in manners, and in laws* – some of them highly gifted and highly civilized, and many of them of rare antiquity. And this vast community is governed, under the authority of the Queen, by many Sovereign Princes, some of whom occupy Thrones which were filled by their ancestors when England was a Roman Province.   (1876)

---

9. This long quotation and the following two are given in the style of the official Hansard website: <https://hansard.parliament.uk/>

It is only then that he comes to the point, which is "to introduce a Bill which consists of only one clause, which will enable Her Majesty, by Proclamation, to make that addition to her style and titles which befits the occasion" (1876).

When Enoch Powell entered parliament for the first time in 1950, India and Pakistan were independent nations. His particular version of English nationalism was forged by his experience of World War II and the dissolution of the Empire. Enoch Powell's place in Britain's collective memory is not defined by any of his numerous, sometimes intellectually substantial and always rhetorically well-crafted speeches in parliament, but by his "Rivers of Blood" invective delivered on 20 April 1968 at a meeting in his Wolverhampton-South constituency (Whipple 2009). Both the immediate audience and the general public understood it as an uncompromising call for an end to immigration from the 'non-white' Commonwealth, which earned its author a reputation as a racist. In view of this reputation, the more moderate tone of some of his speeches in parliament comes as a surprise. Powell, it is true, shows himself vehemently opposed to Commonwealth immigration, anti-discrimination legislation and European integration, but his stance on race is complex. He repeatedly emphasises the lack of any kind of scientific basis for traditional folk taxonomies of race and praises the cultural achievements of non-European peoples. In Example (14), from a 1980 speech on the topic of development aid and India, he echoes some of the sentiments voiced by Gladstone.

(14)   After all, if we went back not millennia but only a few centuries and compared this country with the India over which the Great Mogul ruled, we would find that the technical competence and organisation of Mogul India was perhaps superior to ours –; it was greatly admired by the Tudor and Elizabethan travellers –; and we would find that by our measurements, imperfect as they are, the standard of living in Akbar's India was fully comparable with the standard of living in the England of Elizabeth I: What has happened? Why is there this difference, this divergence, this bifurcation? Why are there these masses of people in so contrasted circumstances? I doubt whether the answer to that question is a very simple one: Indeed, I doubt whether a full and satisfactory answer to that question can ever be offered: But I will make a negative assertion: it is not due to any difference in intellectual capacity, human ability or insight: It is *an absurd notion that the European is intellectually superior to vast millions of the human race* in Asia and elsewhere [...]   (1980)

Though reserved for India's past achievements, the genuine appreciation voiced here exonerates the speaker from the charge of blatant old-style nineteenth-century racism. Nevertheless, the argument remains troubling, for what follows the passage quoted is an exercise in rhetorical indirectness, as reflected in Example (15).

(15) In case I be misunderstood, may I say at once that I do not believe that the IQ
produces useful results for this purpose: I doubt whether many of the characteristics which we regard as typically and transcendentally European are
purely intellectual: I think they have in them very much of the moral and very
much of the social: The answer must be that those comparable characteristics
are differently directed, for whatever reasons, and that the scale of values, the
motivation and the whole conception of the world which those populations
entertain is different from that within which the material development we are
so proud of has taken place in Europe or in the West: Yet as we contemplate
the picture of countries in the depths of poverty, whose poverty reacts and
interacts with our own economic objects and ambitions, we are told that what
we should do is to elaborate a system for transferring resources from the developed to the undeveloped [...]   (1980)

Note that excluding the IQ as a relevant measure from the present argument is not
the same as rejecting the assumption that intelligence varies across race and ethnicity. In the end, the argument for European and Western superiority is merely
moved from the biological to the cultural plane ("the scale of values, the motivation
and the whole conception of the world"), with the details remaining distinctly
underspecified – for example the question to what extent aggressive expansionist
policies and economic greed played a role in the colonial project in addition to the
lofty motives usually advanced in parliament during the period of Empire.

In a 1976 debate on anti-discrimination legislation this strategy is carried to
extremes in a lengthy and convoluted word play on colour discrimination, as
shown in Example (16).

(16) [Employers] are to maintain records of colour: Is there to be a Ringelmann
chart against which will be held the complexion of each employee and the
appropriate reading entered? There is a difficulty here: The Ringelmann chart
will not be adequate: Although it will indicate degrees of depth of colouration,
the Ringelmann chart will not indicate tint: Surely it is important that the difference between the same intensity of yellow or brown tint should be registered, since clearly there can be colour discrimination on that ground: When
an employer has finished looking at his employees from the point of view of
colour as he takes them on and has entered their respective colours on the register, he has to enter their *race*: *Race* is something that scientists have found it
extremely difficult satisfactorily to define [...]   (1976)

There is bad faith here. The fact that human skin colour cannot be categorised
systematically ('colour discrimination' in its first sense, irrelevant to the present
argument) does not mean that people are not subjected to discrimination because
of their skin colour on a daily basis ('colour discrimination' in its second sense,

relevant here). As for the second argument, pointing out the absence of a scientific basis for folk notions of race may have a useful effect when the aim is to inform and educate the public, but is not a constructive contribution to the present debate, which is about repairing the social damage wrought by racial prejudice rooted in precisely these folk taxonomies. Again, Enoch Powell distances himself from the cruder forms of racism, such as the belief in a biologically founded superiority of the white race, in order to defend his twentieth-century programme for an English/British nationalism that will accommodate neither immigration from the 'non-white' Commonwealth nor measures for the protection of 'non-whites' already resident in the country.

When Powell argues about European integration, as in Example (17), the frontline on the battlefield changes, but the rhetorical strategies remain the same. What is defended is no longer Britain, Europe and the West against the rest of the world, but England and Britain against the Common Market and the European continent.

(17) [The question] cannot be answered by transposing, as my hon: Friend the Member for Chelmsford did, the phrase "Little England" into "tight isolationist island": In order to answer it, we have to envisage profoundly what we as a nation are: Of course we are a European nation in the sense that we share the common heritage of Europe: We share it in culture, in religion, and in what distinguishes European man from the other branches of the *human race*: In that we are European: We are as European in that sense as any other of the nations of Europe: But it is not in that sense that we are posing this question: For we are talking about economic and political union: We are posing a question about political entity, about nationhood –; the thing for which men, if necessary, fight and, if necessary, die, and to preserve which men think no sacrifice too great [...] (1971)

Starting from the assertion that Britons are Europeans just as Europeans and Britons are part of the human race (a redundant assertion in Westminster, at least, where this would not have been contested by the vast majority of MPs for many centuries), Powell goes on to claim exceptional status for England, Britain and the UK within Europe, by appealing to a concept of 'nationhood' that is elevated to a spiritual or even religious dimension.

Skilful and sometimes reckless use of the whole range of rhetorical strategies of persuasion is a central element of all free parliamentary deliberations, and thus not confined to any one political orientation. This is shown by the extract in Example (18), from a speech by Tony Benn, who goes back to the nineteenth century and slavery days in order to paint a grim picture of the activities of the World Trade Organisation (WTO) at the end of the twentieth century.

Empire, migration and race in Hansard   **139**

(18)   When the Secretary of State drew a comparison with the Luddites, he reminded me of the leading article in The Economist on 26 February 1848 –; a year or two before I entered the House –; in which the slave trade was discussed: The article said: "If in place of entering into Treaties for the suppression of the Slave Trade, we made conventions to ameliorate the conditions of the existing *race* of slaves –; to establish and regulate on unquestionable principles the free emigration of Africans...; we might, with a tenth of the cost, do a great substantial good to the *African Race*": I can imagine Ofslave being set up, with Chris Woodhead in charge, naming and shaming the captains of slave ships on which the sanitary arrangements for slaves are inadequate: For God's sake, surely we must take some account in this debate of the worry of the enormous number of people in the world who have not got rich through free trade: Global capitalism empowers companies to move money freely, but it does not allow workers to move freely: If someone owns a factory in London but the wages are so high that he cannot make a profit, he can close it and open it in Malaysia, where wages are lower: If, however, someone from Malaysia tries to come to London where wages are higher, immigration laws would keep him out: Globalisation has nothing to do with internationalism [...]   (1999)

Ofslave is a satirical neologism, of a type well established in British political-bureaucratic jargon (e.g. *Ofcom*, *Ofsted* and others).[10] In combination with a particularly hypocritical example of the nineteenth-century discourse of race, it makes late twentieth-century WTO practices (which parliament has every right to debate) look bungling, backward, exploitative, inhuman and morally indefensible. The rhetorical display is dazzling; the question of whether the speaker has been 'economical with the truth' remains legitimate.

6.   Conclusion

The present chapter has made the following points on the basis of its analysis of the Hansard Corpus:

- In the nineteenth century Westminster discourse on migration was dominated by the issue of emigration, whereas the focus shifted to immigration in the course of the twentieth century.
- In the era of Empire as well as in our modern period of globalisation the migrant, the person moving from one territory and community into another, has been a topic of discussion which has aroused strong positive or negative

---

10. Ofcom is the UK's regulator and competition authority for communication services; Ofsted is short for Office for Standards in Education, Children's Services and Skills.

emotions and, expectedly, has sparked a lot of lexical-semantic creativity and caused fast turn-over in the lexicon. This has been briefly illustrated on the basis of the formerly very frequent term *alien* and the currently fashionable *immigrant* and *migrant*.

– In the early nineteenth century race emerged as a dominant epistemic category to cope with human difference in Westminster political discourse. Humanity was conceived of as one human race, which was then divided into historically, ethnically or geographically motivated subgroups (e.g. the *British race*, the *Irish race*, the various *native races* from the colonies), into categories based on skin complexion (*black, white, yellow, brown*), but – more controversially – also into hierarchies comprising *superior* and *inferior races*.

– Apart from the compound *race relations* and a number of related words also belonging to the terminology of identity politics (*racism, racist, racialism*), the category *race* receded into the background and was even tabooed in the course of the twentieth century, being superseded by notions such as ethnicity and identity. While it has eliminated the open expression of ideologies of white supremacy from political discourse, the new conventions are not without problems, because they treat whiteness or Englishness as unmarked default norms and only make deviations from this assumed norm lexically explicit.

The Hansard Corpus is a rich, but also a complex and sometimes difficult source of data, and to cope with these complexities an interdisciplinary orientation has proved helpful. The present analysis of changing British parliamentary discourses on Empire, race and migration has combined methods of close and distant reading. It is a corpus-linguistic study on a topic in the history of the English language, but it is also a contribution to corpus-informed cultural studies. Through a diachronic case study, it has explored the "interface between cultures and corpora" (Schneider 2018) and, perhaps, encouraged corpus linguists to take on a more active and visible role in the rapidly expanding Digital Humanities movement.

References

Alexander, Marc & Struan, Andrew. 2017. Digital Hansard: The politics of the uncivil. In *Digital Humanities 2017, Montréal, Conference Abstracts*, 378–380 <https://dh2017.adho .org/abstracts/DH2017-abstracts.pdf> (18 October 2019).

Alim, H. Samy & Reyes, Angela (eds). 2011. Special issue on *Complicating Race: Articulating Race across Multiple Social Dimensions. Discourse and Society* 22(4).

Alim, H. Samy, Rickford, John R. & Ball, Arnetha F. 2016. *Raciolinguistics: How Language Shapes our Ideas about Race.* Oxford: OUP.

Ashcroft, Bill. 2015. Critical histories: Postcolonialism, postmodernism, and race. In *Postmodern Literature and Race*, Len Platt & Sara Upstone (eds), 13–30. Cambridge: CUP.

Baker, Helen, Brezina, Vaclav & McEnery, Tony. 2017. Ireland in British parliamentary debates, 1803–2005. In *Exploring Future Paths for Historical Sociolinguistics* [Advances in Historical Sociolinguistics 7], Tanja Säily, Arja Nurmi, Minna Palander-Collin & Anita Auer (eds), 83–108. Amsterdam: John Benjamins.

Davies, Mark. 2015. Hansard Corpus. <https://www.hansard-corpus.org/> (15 August 2021).

Fišer, Darja & Lenardič, Jakob. 2017. Parliamentary corpora in the CLARIN infrastructure. In *Selected Papers from the CLARIN Annual Conference 2017, Budapest, 18–20 September 2017*, Maciej Piasecki (ed.), 75–85. Linköping: Linköping University Electronic Press. <https://ep.liu.se/ecp/147/007/ecp17147007.pdf> (18 October 2019).

Gabrielatos, Costas, McEnery, Tony, Diggle, Peter & Baker, Paul. 2012. The peaks and troughs of corpus-based contextual analysis. *International Journal of Corpus Linguistics* 17: 151–175.

Hall, Catherine. 2012. *Macaulay and Son: Architects of Imperial Britain*. New Haven CT: Yale University Press.

Hall, Stuart. 1997. *Race: The Floating Signifier* [film, dir. Sut Jhally]. Northampton MA: Media Education Foundation. Preview at <https://shop.mediaed.org/race-the-floating-signifier-p173.aspx> (8 November 2019).

Hall, Stuart & Morley, David. 2019. *Essential Essays, Vol. 2: Identity and Diaspora*. Durham NC: Duke University Press.

Hardie, Andrew. 2017. Exploratory analysis of word frequencies across corpus texts: Towards a critical contrast of approaches. Keynote talk, 2017 Corpus Linguistics (COLING) conference, Birmingham, UK. <https://www.youtube.com/watch?v=ka4yDJLtSSc> (21 July 2021).

Hyam, Ronald. 2010. *Understanding the British Empire*. Cambridge: CUP.

Mair, Christian. 2019. *Brexitiness*: The ebbs and flows of British Eurosceptic rhetoric since 1945. *Open Library of Humanities* 5(1): 50, 1–26.

Marx, Maarten & Schuth, Anne. 2010. DutchParl: A corpus of parliamentary documents in Dutch. In *Proceedings of the 10th Dutch-Belgian Information Retrieval Workshop (DIR 2010)*, 82–83. Nijmegen: Radboud Universiteit Nijmegen, Information Foraging Lab.

Mollin, Sandra. 2007. The Hansard hazard: Gauging the accuracy of British parliamentary transcripts. *Corpora* 2(2): 187–210.

Moretti, Franco. 2013. *Distant Reading*. London: Verso.

Schneider, Edgar. 2018. The interface between cultures and corpora: Tracing reflections and manifestations. *ICAME Journal* 42: 97–132.

Sutherland, Lorraine & Farrell, Stephen. 2017. The history, workings, and future challenges of Hansard. Public lecture, 11 December 2017. <https://www.youtube.com/watch?v=yaLWV9gfiSo> (18 October 2019).

Whipple, Amy. 2009. Revisiting the 'Rivers of Blood' controversy: Letters to Enoch Powell. *Journal of British Studies* 48: 717–735.

Williams, Raymond. 1983. *Keywords: A Vocabulary of Culture and Society*. 2nd ed. Oxford: OUP.

CHAPTER 5

Leaving the EU out of the ingroup

A diachronic analysis of the use of *we* and *us* in British parliamentary debates (1973–2015)

Jenni Räikkönen
Tampere University

In this chapter, I examine what types of diachronic changes the use of first-person plural pronouns signal in the way the EU has been discussed in the British House of Commons. By using methods of corpus-assisted discourse studies, I analyse the use of the pronouns in relation to the EU in parliamentary debates in the time period from 1973 to 2015. I am interested in when and in which contexts the EU is included in and when excluded from the ingroup in the debates. The chapter contributes to linguistic studies on Brexit and is part of a larger research project focusing on diachronic changes in the discursive representation of the EU in British parliamentary debates and press.

Keywords: Brexit, the EU, personal pronouns, corpus-assisted discourse studies, Hansard

1. Introduction

This chapter focuses on diachronic changes in the use of first-person plural pronouns in relation to the EU in the debates of the British House of Commons. The time period analysed stretches from 1973, the year the UK joined the European Economic Community, up to the general election of 2015, in which Brexit was one of the main themes. I am interested in how often and in which situations first-person plural pronouns are used to refer to the whole EU and when to the UK only, excluding the EU. When EU matters are talked about in British parliamentary debates, members of parliament (MPs) make a choice between talking from the national or the EU's perspective. In the former case, MPs focus on what the UK should do in relation to the EU, and in the latter, on what the EU will or should do together. My hypothesis is that in the former case, the EU is seen as an outgroup, while in the latter, the EU is seen as working together as one group.

https://doi.org/10.1075/scl.111.05rai
© 2023 John Benjamins Publishing Company

The study is part of my PhD project focusing on changes in the discursive representation of the EU in British public discourses.[1] In this chapter I examine whether there was a change in the use of the first-person plural pronouns *we* and *us* in the parliamentary debates before the general election of 2015, and whether the pronouns were used increasingly less frequently to refer to the whole EU, increasing the perception in the UK that the EU is somewhere else, but is not 'us'. Pronoun use in the Euro-political context has been studied before, but many previous studies have focused only on a specific topic or one historical context, while diachronic changes over long time periods have not been given much attention. This study aims to fill that gap. The primary data of the study consist of all the debates of the British House of Commons from the time period 1973–2015, not just the debates on the EU, which makes the data more comprehensive than in previous studies.

The questions that I aim to answer are the following:

1. How have the first-person plural pronouns *we* and *us* been used in connection with the EU? What types of groups do they refer to and what kinds of diachronic changes in usage occur?
2. In what kinds of contexts does the pronoun *we* or *us* refer to the UK only and when to the whole EU?

The chapter is divided into five main sections. In the following section I discuss related literature on the use of pronouns in political discourse. In Section 3, I introduce the data and methods used in the study. The findings of the analysis are presented in Section 4, which is followed by concluding remarks.

2. Personal pronouns and the discursive construction of national identities

Pronouns are one of the main rhetorical tools used by politicians and have been considered as deserving of special attention in the field of critical discourse analysis (CDA) (Fairclough 1989:127–128; Íñigo-Mora 2004:36). In CDA, discourse is seen as being socially conditioned and socially constructive (Blommaert & Bulcaen 2000:448). Thus, the ways in which we use language participate in shaping and constituting society (see also Chouliaraki & Fairclough 1999:4). Consequently, discourse is connected to power as it can be strategically used for the

---

1. My PhD dissertation examines the discursive construction of the EU in parliamentary debates and British newspaper articles from 1973 up to 2015. The work is expected to be completed by spring 2024.

benefit of those who have the power to shape public discourses, such as politicians, media and academics (van Dijk 1993). The aim of CDA is to make more visible the choices that may seem 'neutral', but which are consciously made to shape discourses. (Critical) discourse analysis has traditionally utilised qualitative methods such as close reading of a small number of texts, but recently the use of corpus linguistic techniques has become increasingly popular in the field. In corpus-assisted discourse studies (CADS) (Baker et al. 2008; Partington, Duguid & Taylor 2013), qualitative and quantitative methods are combined so that larger datasets can be analysed and typical ways of using language can be detected.

The pronoun *we* has become a topic of interest in the field of CDA partly because of its flexibility. *We* is a complex personal pronoun in that relying only on anaphora does not always reveal what it means and refers to, and the pronoun can even combine a number of different meanings (Mühlhäusler & Harré 1990:168–169). Often, the pronoun refers to a group of people including the speaker, and that group can either include or exclude the addressee(s). Furthermore, pronouns can be used strategically to make a separation between ingroup and outgroup (Wodak 2011), and de Cillia, Reisigl and Wodak (1999:163) state that "the use of the pronoun 'we' [...] appears to be of utmost importance in the discourses about nations and national identities". *We* can be used to signify that there is a group of *others* who do not belong to or are different from *us*, because *we* implies that there is *they*, as much as *here* implies *there* (Billig 2010:99). Consequently, when first-person plural pronouns are used, the text offers definitions of who or what *we* are, what *we* do or what is done to *us*. In person deixis, similarly to other types of deixis such as temporal and spatial deixis, the Self (e.g. *I* and *we*) is the deictic centre, and people position others in their world in relation to themselves (Chilton 2005; Lenz 2003:viii). Typically, the 'distant' entities (namely, the outgroup) are more likely to be assigned negative attributes, and the Self and other 'close' entities (the ingroup) positive attributes (Cap 2018:383; Wodak, de Cillia & Reisigl 2009).

In previous studies on discourses in Euro-political contexts, researchers have been interested in whether there is a 'EUropean' (EU and/or Europe) identity and how, and to what degree, that identity has been put forward by the media and politicians in public discourses where it could enforce the feeling of a collective EUropean identity. Ludlow (2002) has observed that, in British political discourse, Europe, as a place or concept, may or may not include the UK, as *Europe* often refers to continental Europe only, excluding the UK (see also Hardt-Mautner 1995). The use of the pronoun *we* can signify whether speakers position themselves as being part of the European collective or as representing and identifying more with their own country. Krizsán (2011) compared pronoun use in British, Hungarian and Finnish politicians' speeches on the fifth enlargement of the EU, which was completed in 2007, and concluded that, of these three groups, the British representatives had the most speeches about the position of the whole EU, while the Finnish and Hungarian speakers spoke more from the national point of view. Similarly, Cramer (2010) analysed pronouns in speeches by European leaders in a panel on "Europe's purpose" in 2008, where one of the topics was Turkey's accession to the EU. Cramer concluded that the Turkish member of the panel positioned himself in opposition to the European identity and emphasised his Turkish identity by consistently using *we* to refer to Turks only. (See also de Fina 1995; Dekavalla 2010; Íñigo-Mora 2004; Oddo 2011; Petersoo 2007; Proctor & Su 2011.)

3.   Data and methods

The primary data consist of all the debates of the British House of Commons from the start of the UK's membership of the European Community (EC) in January 1973 up to the general election in May 2015, in which leaving the EU was one of the main themes. For the data spanning 1973–2004, I used a full-text Extensible Markup Language (XML) version of the Hansard Corpus (Alexander & Davies 2015),[2] which enabled me to study longer excerpts of text, and even complete speeches if needed, which is not possible with the online version of the corpus. The debates for the period 2005–2015 I collected from the parliament's own website and compiled them into an unannotated corpus for this study. The size of the two corpora combined is circa 450 million words.

As discussed, for instance, in Slembrouck (1992), Mollin (2007) and Hiltunen, Räikkönen and Tyrkkö (2020), using Hansard as data for studying the language spoken in the parliament has its restrictions, as the language in Hansard differs in many ways from the language that is actually used in the parliament (see Alexander, this volume, and Kotze et al., this volume). Reporters of Hansard make changes to the report so that it follows the etiquette of the parliament, for example by removing second-person pronouns if used to refer to another MP (Slembrouck 1992: 114). The editing of Hansard also focuses on some characteristics of spoken language such as hesitations, false starts and inconsistencies. However, the editing should not add anything that was not said or change anything in a way that would change the meaning of the speech. Using first-person plural pronouns is a rhetorical tool and altering the pronouns might change the meaning of the speech, which is why those would typically not be changed in the editing process.

---

2. I would like to thank the SAMUELS project at the University of Glasgow, especially Prof. Marc Alexander and Dr. Fraser Dallachy, for providing me with a local copy of the corpus, and also Prof. Jukka Tyrkkö at Linnaeus University for preparing the copy for my use.

I used methods associated with CADS (Baker 2006; Partington, Duguid & Taylor 2013), focusing on concordance and collocation. I used CasualConc (version 2.0.7; Imao 2008–2018), a concordance program that can read text in XML, to search for excerpts in which the first-person plural pronoun *we* or *us* (henceforth: 1PP) co-occur with *the European Community/-ies* (1973–1993) or *the European Union* (1994–2015) in a span of nine words to the left and right.[3] Clause boundaries were ignored. The span is larger than what is usually used when studying collocation, for instance, but the search was merely the first step in retrieving the relevant contexts for further analysis and was defined so that the amount of data would be manageable for manual analysis.

The search retrieved 11,425 hits in total. Figure 5.1 shows the yearly frequencies. For reference, Figure 5.1 also includes the frequencies of *they* and *them* in a similar context (3,199 in total). The amount of data from the third-person plural pronouns was so small that I decided to focus only on 1PP in this chapter. Some remarks on the use of third-person plural pronouns will be included in Section 4.1.

I chose to use the proper names *the European Community* and *the European Union* as search terms instead of the acronyms *the EC* and *the EU*, because (1) the overall frequency over the entire timeline is higher for the proper names (49,681 for the proper names; 35,678 for acronyms) and (2) based on the list of collocates of the acronyms and the proper names, the usage of these terms is fairly similar. However, a more comprehensive analysis of the use of these terms would be needed to get a better understanding of the differences in their usage in the debates. Nevertheless, as the amount of data from the proper names was already fairly large for manual analysis, I decided to exclude the acronyms from this study.

To give a general impression of the data, Figure 5.2 shows the frequencies of the search terms *the european communit** and *the european union* (case-insensitive) individually in the time period analysed. Until 1981 the frequency of *the European Community/-ies* remains below 50 hits per million words, partly because in the 1970s and 1980s it was common to talk about the Community as "the Common Market" or "the EEC". In 1994, *the European Union* became more frequent than *the European Community/-ies*, at least in the official report of the debates.

---

3. The possessive pronoun *our* was excluded from the analysis, as I wanted to focus on action (where *we* – either the UK or the EU – do something, or something is affecting or done to *us*). However, analysis of the use of *our* in this context could offer further insight into which issues are seen as belonging to the UK only, on the one hand, or as shared issues in the EU, on the other.

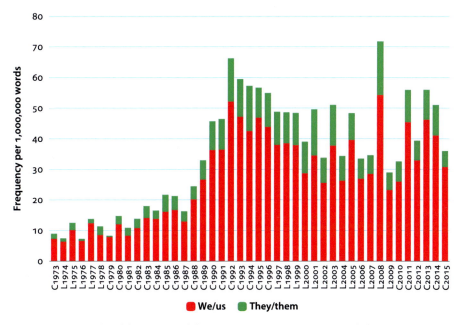

Figure 5.1 Normalised frequency of *the European Community/-ies* and *the European Union* co-occurring with *we/us* or *they/them*. The letters 'C' and 'L' on the x-axis reflect the governing party (Conservative or Labour)

Figure 5.3 shows the frequencies of 1PP in the entire timeline. The frequency of *us* remains between 10 and 13 hits per 10,000 words, while the frequency of *we* has been increasing since 1995.

Instances in which the pronoun occurred in a quote (141/11,425 instances) were excluded from further analysis, as they do not give information on the pronoun use of the speaker. Also, instances in which the search term (*the European Community/-ies* or *the European Union*) was immediately followed by a word such as *Act* or *Bill*, or it was part of some other term, such as *Treaty of the European Union*, were excluded (499 instances). In total, 5.6% of all the instances that were originally retrieved were excluded from the analysis.

After finding the relevant instances, I analysed each of them individually. I identified a referent for each pronoun by either finding a clearly identifiable anaphoric or cataphoric referent or, if there was none, on the basis of any extralinguistic information (exophora). If the referent could not be identified by looking at the concordance line alone, I examined the wider textual context. I used seven categories for the referents: "UK", "EU", "generic", "government", "group", "parliament" and "party". These categories are defined in Table 5.1.

The referent categories were defined heuristically. Some are broader than others (for instance, "group" includes regions, groups of people and groups of

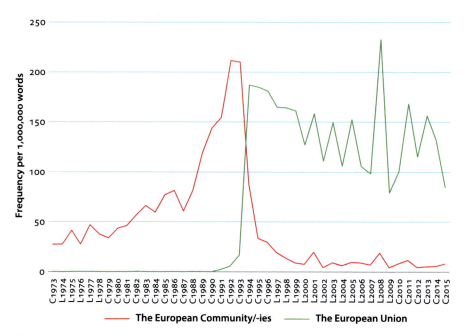

Figure 5.2 Normalised frequency of *the European Community/-ies* and *the European Union* in Hansard. The letters 'C' and 'L' on the x-axis reflect the governing party (Conservative or Labour)

countries), but I did not analyse the instances in these categories further. The categories "UK" and "EU" are the most relevant ones for this study, and the focus will be on those. After identifying the referents for the pronouns, I compared the proportions of each category and examined how they changed in the time period analysed.

I also examined the most common lexical verbs collocating with the pronoun *we* referring either to the UK or the EU. To do this, I compiled two concordance corpora, in which I included the concordance lines that were analysed as containing one or more instances of *we* referring either to the UK or the EU. The concordance lines (approximately 30 words per line) were collected into plain text files, one file containing the concordances from approximately five consecutive years. In those files, I searched for words occurring one, two or three words to the right of the pronoun *we*. In the list of collocates, I then focused on the most frequent lexical verbs (raw frequency), which gave me information on what types of actions were connected to *we* referring to the UK and the EU in each time period.

Figure 5.3 Normalised frequency of *we* and *us* in Hansard in the entire timeline. The letters 'C' and 'L' on the x-axis reflect the governing party (Conservative or Labour)

4. *We* and *us* in relation to the EU in British parliament

In this section I present the findings of the analysis. I start with the referents of 1PP and the overall diachronic changes in their proportions. Then, I discuss some differences in the use of 1PP between the Labour and Conservative parties. This is followed by the analysis of the collocate lists of *we*, focusing on the types of lexical verbs that are connected either to the UK or the EU referred to by the pronoun.

4.1 Referents of 1PP in the context of the EU

Figure 5.4 shows the number of 1PP referring to each referent category in the context of *the European Community/-ies/Union* in the entire timeline (see Table 5.1 for descriptions of the categories). In this section, I focus on the categories "EU" and "UK". However, the second largest referent category is "parliament", whose share has stayed more or less level in the years studied. When the pronoun refers to the parliament, the contribution often includes meta-discourse, as in "*we are talking not about European Communities but about the European Union*" (William Cash, Conservative, 6 February 2008).

Table 5.1 Descriptions of the referent categories for 1PP

Category	Definition	Example
UK	British people, the UK as a nation	We import more cars than *we* export to member states of the European Union... (John Redwood, Conservative, 16 May 1990)
EU	The whole EU (member states and people), the UK included	There is no doubt that within the European Union *we* should extend the benefits of the competitive market to energy and the airline industry. (Ian Taylor, Conservative, 8 March 1995)
generic	People generally or referent could not be identified	In future, *we* will all recognise that one of the European Union's greatest successes is the fact that in all those countries there has been an aspiration for political freedom largely because of the EU's success. (Chirs Bryant, Labour, 20 December 2010)
government	Ministers, government departments	The policy of the Government is to play a strong and positive part in the development of the European Community. *We* shall again present to Parliament... (James Callaghan, Labour, 3 November 1977)
group	A certain group of people or states, or a specific region in the UK (e.g. Wales)	[...] but the fact that we were statistically linked with our colleagues and friends in Devon constituted a barrier preventing *us* from obtaining stand-alone regional status in the European Union and receiving the money. (Candy Atherton, Labour, 12 January 2005)
parliament	The people in the chamber	Will the Foreign Secretary tell *us* what successes the European Community has had in resolving the Arab-Israeli conflict? (Ernie Ross, Conservative, 21 January 1987)
party	The political party to which the speaker belongs	We fundamentally believe that British national interests are best served by playing an active and leading role in the European Union. *We* are also fundamentally a democratic party and one that believes in [...] (Tim Farron, Liberal Democrat, 7 December 2010)

Figure 5.5 shows the diachronic changes in the proportions of the referent categories "UK" and "EU". 1PP clearly refer more often to the UK than to the whole EU, which is not surprising as the data come from the national parliament, where national affairs are often in focus. However, the diachronic changes in the proportions are interesting – especially the changes that have occurred since 1996. Up

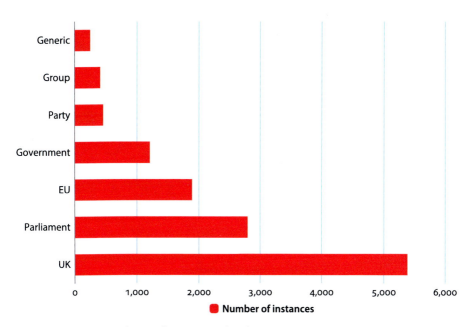

Figure 5.4 Number of 1PP referring to each referent category

until that year, the yearly fluctuations in the proportion of the pronouns referring to the EU are fairly small, if we do not take into account the first years of the membership from which there are not much data. After 1996, the proportion of 1PP with the EU as referent increases, while that with the UK as referent decreases, and in 2002 the two have almost the same proportion – approximately 30% of all 1PP analysed. However, after 2002, the proportion of UK referents increases little by little, while the proportion of EU referents decreases. Between 2011 and 2015 the proportion of the pronouns referring to the EU is at its lowest since 1983, at less than 10%. Thus, it seems that after 2002, the EU became more and more excluded from the ingroup in the British parliament.

Since 2002, there have been at least three major developments in the EU that have probably affected the attitudes towards the EU in the UK, and also the language used about the EU:

1. the introduction of the Euro, which came into existence in 1999 and into public use in 2002 in 12 EU countries, but not the UK;
2. the enlargement of the EU in 2004, which was criticised in the UK, as there was a fear that people from poorer countries would come to the UK in search of work and take advantage of the UK's benefit systems (see e.g. House of Commons debate "EU citizens (Freedom of Movement)", 2 March 2004; also Islentyeva 2018); and

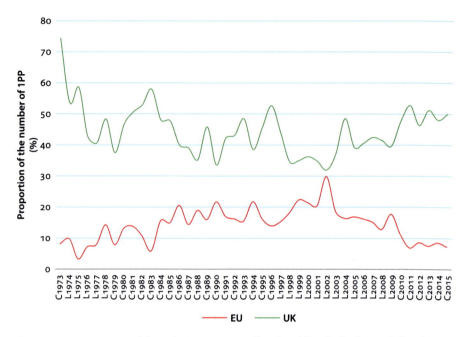

Figure 5.5 Proportions of the referent categories "UK" and "EU". The letters 'C' and 'L' on the x-axis reflect the governing party (Conservative or Labour)

3. the Treaty of Lisbon, which was signed in December 2007 and which increased the power of the European parliament, extending its legislative power to 40 new fields, including agriculture and immigration.

Perhaps these three developments, together with other issues, affected the language use so that the debates became more concerned with how *we* in the UK should act in relation to the EU and how the EU affects *us*, instead of what the EU countries are planning for the future together.[4] Furthermore, the way in which the EU is less often talked about as belonging to *us* has probably affected the public attitude towards the EU.

For reference, Figure 5.6 shows the frequencies of selected, EU-related referents of *they* and *them*. These pronouns rarely refer to the EC or EU, and the largest of the selected referent categories is "non-EU", which represents countries that are not members of the EU. Often these are countries that were about to join the EU. The high frequency of referents of this category, especially before 1995 and 2004, suggests that enlargements of the EU were an important topic in the national parliament. Additionally, the proportion of the referent category for British people

---

4. See also McEnery, Brezina and Baker (2019) on diachronic changes in the usage of *the European Union* in *The Times*.

("people B" in Figure 5.6) is fairly large in 2008 and after that, which suggests that the opinions of the people were increasingly raised when the EU was discussed in the debates.

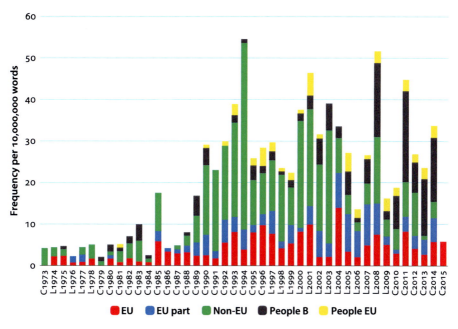

Figure 5.6 Normalised frequency of EU-related referents of *they* and *them* in the context of the EU in Hansard. The letters 'C' and 'L' on the x-axis reflect the governing party (Conservative or Labour)

Next, I consider the differences between the two major parties, Conservative and Labour, in how they have used 1PP in relation to the EU.[5]

4.2 Party differences

In the UK, opinions on the EU have never been split neatly along party-political lines, and there have been both sceptics and supporters of the EU in both of the two major parties. Furthermore, parties as well as individual politicians have changed their stance on the EU over time. For instance, in the 1970s and early 1980s, many members of the Labour party portrayed the EC as an elitist capitalist

---

5. Speeches from Liberal Democratic party were not included in this further analysis because their contributions were infrequent compared to the Conservatives and Labour in debates concerning EU matters.

club, but the development of stronger social policies in the EC in the 1980s and later Blair's pro-EU stance strengthened Labour's support for the EU. Also, Margaret Thatcher is known to have changed her attitude towards the EC during her term as Prime Minister (see e.g. Fontana & Parsons 2015). It should be noted that the findings presented here show the overall differences between the political parties, but do not take into account differences between individual MPs.

Figures 5.7 and 5.8 show the comparison between the proportions of 1PP referring to the UK and the EU in the entire timeline in the speeches of Conservative (Figure 5.7) and Labour (Figure 5.8) parties. As Figure 5.5 already showed, MPs most often speak from the national point of view, and 1PP refer more often to the UK than to the EU. This can also be seen in Figures 5.7 and 5.8. However, it seems that, overall, the Conservatives speak more from the national point of view and include the EU to the ingroup less often than Labour speakers, at least when in government. Between 1990 and 1996, when the Conservatives were in government, the proportion of 1PP referring to the UK in the Conservative contributions is close to or more than 70% (see Figure 5.7). In comparison, when the Labour party were in government between 1997 and 2010, the proportion of UK referents stays below 70% until 2006 (see Figure 5.8). Thus, in Labour MPs' speeches, EU referents' share of the pronouns is proportionally higher than in Conservative contributions. However, after 2006, EU referents' share of the pronouns drops below 30% in Labour's speeches, which suggests that the Labour party also adopted a more national point of view when talking about the EU. After 2010, the proportions of these two referents are quite similar in the speeches of both parties, suggesting that the national perspective became more common in the debates, which can also be seen in Figure 5.5.

General elections seem to have affected the way in which the EU has been talked about, in particular in the speeches of the party that campaigned in the opposition. For instance, there was a general election in 1997, and the Labour party campaigned in the opposition. Consequently, we can see that in Labour's speeches the frequency of 1PP referring to the UK increases in 1995, 1996 and 1997 (frequencies per year: 3.04, 5.52 and 8.93 per million words) while the frequency of 1PP referring to the EU stays almost the same in these three years (1.61, 1.70, 2.09). When the next general election was held in 2001, the figures do not show any notable changes in the contributions of either party. However, before the general election of 2005, when the Conservative party campaigned in the opposition, we can see an increase in the frequency of 1PP referring to the UK in 2003, 2004 and 2005 (3.47, 5.87, 6.36 per million words) and a decrease in those referring to the EU (1.74, 0.98, 0.80) in Conservative contributions. By the general election of 2010, 1PP in Conservative speeches already referred quite rarely to the whole EU, so it is difficult to say how much the elections influenced the pronoun use.

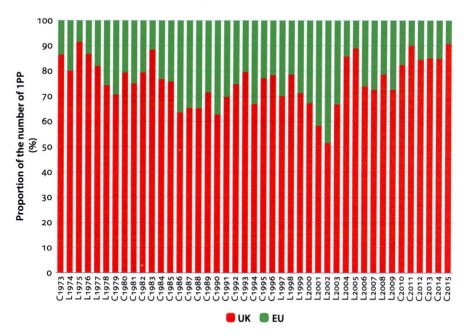

Figure 5.7 Comparison between the proportions of 1PP referring to the UK and the EU in Conservative MPs' speeches. The letters 'C' and 'L' on the x-axis reflect the governing party (Conservative or Labour)

However, these findings seem to suggest that one of the campaigning strategies for the party in the opposition has been that speeches become more nationally centered and focus on what the UK should do in relation to the EU.

4.3 Actions connected to the ingroup

In this section, I examine what types of actions are connected to the UK and the EU when *we* is used to refer to one of them. I am interested in whether the UK and the EU are described as doing similar types of actions, and also, what the verbs associated with *we* in this context tell us about the topics that are common when the EU is included in the ingroup, on the one hand, and when it is excluded from it, on the other. To do this, I analysed collocate lists of the pronoun *we*. In CDA, collocate lists are often examined in order to gain an understanding of whether a word (e.g. *refugee*) is more often surrounded by 'positive' or 'negative' words, because the context in which a word often occurs can affect the way in which the word is understood and, consequently, how people think about the entity referred to by the word (see e.g. Baker et al. 2008). However, in this case, I am not interested in the collocation or the semantic prosody (see e.g. Hunston

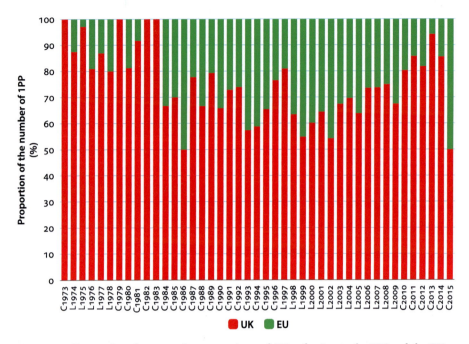

Figure 5.8 Comparison between the proportions of 1PP referring to the UK and the EU in Labour MPs' speeches. The letters 'C' and 'L' on the x-axis reflect the governing party (Conservative or Labour)

2007; Partington 2004; Sinclair 1991, 2004) of the pronoun *we*, but in the differences between the verbs that often occur with the pronoun when referring to the UK or the EU.

I compiled two concordance corpora to use as data in this part of the study: (1) a corpus of the concordances where *we*, co-occurring with *the European Community/-ies/Union*, refers to the UK; and (2) a corpus of the concordances where *we* refers to the EU. I focused on lexical verbs that occurred one, two or three words to the right of the pronoun, so that the verb would reflect what *we*, the UK in the context of the EU or the whole EU, are doing. I only considered raw frequencies, as the corpus was not compiled of complete speeches, but of concordance lines of approximately 30 words including the search term *the European Community/-ies* or *the European Union* and one or more instance of *we*. In the UK corpus, there were 3,901 concordance lines and 4,786 pronouns referring to the UK, and in the EU corpus, 1,490 concordance lines and 1,754 pronouns referring to the EU.[6] The window for collocates (R1–R3) was fairly small, which yields

---

6. The number of concordance lines is smaller than the number of pronouns, because in some cases there was more than one pronoun collocating with the search term.

fewer lexical verbs than there are pronouns. However, I wanted to keep the window small so that the list would not include lexical verbs that did not have the pronoun *we* as their subject.

Table 5.2 shows the list of the most frequent lexical verbs co-occurring with *we* referring to the UK in the said context. The column headings in the table show the timeline, each column representing a period of approximately ten years. The list includes approximately the 20 most frequent lexical verbs in each time period. If there were multiple collocates with the same raw frequency as the 20th in the list, I included those in the table as well. I have grouped the collocates according to the context in which they most often appear and what type of an action they signify. The names of the groups are shown at the top of each group. The raw frequency of the collocates is shown in brackets after each collocate. In the case of semi-modals (such as *need* and *want*), I excluded the instances in which they were used as modal verbs.[7]

I identified three large groups of lexical verbs in the list of collocates. The verbs in the group called "Active UK" signify that the UK is being active and getting things done in the EU. This group of verbs is the most common group in the last three periods. In Examples (1), (2) and (3), the UK is represented as active in the EU and presented as benefitting the whole EU and developing its systems.

(1) I understand the point about the extension of the sanctions, but if we are to be effective, we must also ensure, as the right hon. Member for Devizes said, that *we get other members of the European Union on board.*

(Jack Straw, Labour, 25 June 2002)

(2) The whole tenor of the remarks made by the hon. Member for Stone, who is no longer in his seat, was that it was "they" who were doing this to us, not that we were part of the European Union. We are part of it, and *we must make a big impact within it.* (Mike Gapes, Lab/Co-op, 26 February 2008)

(3) Much of labelling is now in the European Community domain, of course, and *we take a lead* in the Community in ensuring that the public have clear labelling of what is in the products that they buy.

(John Gummer, Conservative, 21 March 1991)

In each of the three examples, the UK is not only described as being an active and effective member, but also as having a significant role in the EU (see Riihimäki 2019). From the point of view of pronoun use, Example (2) is especially interesting: Mr. Gapes points out that the hon. Member for Stone (William Cash,

---

7. I decided not to focus on the use of modal verbs in this chapter, because those alone could not reveal anything about the actual actions of these entities, and thus would constitute a different type of analysis.

Table 5.2 Lexical verbs collocating with *we* referring to the UK

Rank	1973–1984	1985–1994	1995–2004	2005–2015
1	Membership (63)	Active UK (113)	Active UK (147)	Active UK (149)
	join (25)	make (30)	get (31)	get (34)
	enter (14)	take (25)	take (29)	make (24)
	withdraw (9)	play (15)	make (15)	take (18)
	leave (5)	get (15)	play (14)	work (18)
	come (4)	go (13)	work (13)	go (14)
	become (3)	lead (8)	ensure (10)	engage (11)
	remain (3)	ensure (7)	go (10)	play (11)
			use (9)	seek (10)
			seek (8)	trade (9)
			engage (8)	
2	Active UK (41)	Membership (81)	Membership (85)	Membership (103)
	get (11)	join (45)	join (41)	leave (37)
	go (10)	remain (14)	withdraw (16)	remain (27)
	work (4)	enter (10)	remain (14)	join (23)
	seek (4)	come (6)	leave (14)	stay (16)
	develop (3)	leave (6)		
	take (3)			
	trade (3)			
	use (3)			
3	Contribution (11)	Contribution (40)	Contribution (45)	Contribution (68)
	give (7)	contribute (17)	lose (14)	give (24)
	put (4)	pay (12)	give (14)	pay (22)
		give (11)	receive (9)	put (11)
			pay (8)	spend (11)
	Others (16)	**Others (64)**	**Others (48)**	**Others (93)**
	look (6)	need (20)	need (18)	need (42)
	tell (4)	want (11)	want (12)	want (21)
	believe (3)	say (10)	see (10)	say (12)
	need (3)	find (9)	support (8)	find (10)
	face (3)	accept (8)		like (9)
		like (6)		
Total 1 [*]	134	298	325	413
Total 2 [**]	194	547	594	825
% [†]	69	55	55	50

[*] Total raw frequency of the lexical verbs in the list.

[**] Total raw frequency of all the lexical verbs collocating with *we* in this context.

[†] The frequency of the collocates in the list counted against the frequency of all the lexical verbs in this context.

Conservative) had, in his speech, implied that the EU is 'they' who were doing something to 'us'. Mr. Gapes then corrects Mr. Cash and says that "we are part of it", thus putting the EU and the UK in the same group.

The verbs in the group "Membership" were used in contexts where the UK's membership of the EU was being discussed. Of these verbs, *join* is the most or second most frequent one until the last period. Of the 135 cases of *join*, 60 instances are in the context of "since we joined" or "when we joined", where MPs speak about what has changed since the UK joined the EU, or what the situation was before joining the EU compared to what it is now. In Example (4), David Miliband argues that the EU has changed for the better, and in Example (5), Christopher Gill brings up problems in the common fisheries policy that have existed ever since the UK joined the EC.

(4) Labour Members know that our shared planet faces shared problems and needs shared solutions – in the UN, the Commonwealth and the European Union. *When we joined* the EU in the 1970s, there were six members. Now there are 27. Europe has changed for the better.
(David Miliband, Labour, 12 November 2007)

(5) In truth, the problems have not arisen simply in the past 18 years: they have existed ever *since we joined* the European Community.
(Christopher Gill, Conservative, 9 June 1998)

Most of the verbs in this group are either about staying in the EU (*remain, stay*) or leaving it (*leave, come (out of), withdraw*). These verbs are found in the list of top collocates in each of the time periods examined, but in the last period and especially in 2010–2015, these verbs gain more prominence. In 2010–2015, *leave* is the most frequent lexical verb collocating with *we* in this context (29 instances), and *remain* and *stay* are also among the top ten most frequent ones. In this period, 18 of the 29 cases of *leave* occur in *if*-clauses, as in "if we were to leave" and "if we chose to leave". Thus, the consequences of leaving, either good or bad, are contemplated.

In the group called "Contribution" are verbs that are used in contexts where the UK's contribution to the EU and the benefits that the UK receives from the EU are mentioned. This is connected to the common argument against EU membership in the UK, which is that the UK is a 'net contributor' to the EU, paying more than it receives. In Example (6), David Nicholson mentions this argument in his list of matters where the UK loses in the EU.

(6) [...] the facts that the UK has for years run a sizeable deficit on trade with Europe in food and drink, and on wider trade; that *we pay more into the European Union than we get out of it*; and that the UK pays more in than any other country except Germany. (David Nicholson, Conservative, 22 May 1996)

Next, I move on to consider the most frequent lexical verbs that co-occur with *we* referring to the EU. Table 5.3 lists approximately the top 20 collocates, grouped in a similar way as in Table 5.2, by the context in which they most often appear.

Again, I identified three groups in the list of collocates. The group that is the most frequent one in each period is called "Active EU", and it consists of verbs signifying that the EU is developing and 'moving forward',[8] and that the EU works together to achieve its goals. Furthermore, the EU is represented as a global player that can also have influence over countries outside its borders. In Example (7), in a debate about the situation in Ukraine in 2014, William Hague is talking about the actions that the EU is taking against Russia. He stresses that the EU must work together on the issue for the actions to be effective.

(7) [...] but I stressed before that when we take such measures it is important for there to be unity on them, as well as for them to be well judged and well targeted. That means *we must work on them together* in the European Union, and that is what we are doing now.   (William Hague, Conservative, 4 March 2014)

The second most frequent group in each time period is called "Negotiation" and it includes verbs related to negotiations in the EU. These verbs are used when reporting what has been agreed or discussed in meetings at EU level or what is being considered together with other members. Instead of highlighting the disagreements between the member states, these verbs represent the EU as a group that aims for consensus and as a place where everyone has a say. In Example (8), the Secretary of State for Foreign and Commonwealth Affairs, Geoffrey Howe, talks about what the EU is thinking about doing in relation to VAT and other tax increases.

(8) The argument that *we are considering in the European Community* is not, in fact, whether that tax should be increased, but whether the tax revenue to be handed over as own resources should be calculated by reference to a notional increase in the tax.   (Geoffrey Howe, Conservative, 20 July 1983)

In Example (9), Prime Minister John Major is reporting about discussions at the European Council, where many issues that the UK had supported were accepted and agreed on.

(9) Yet again the policies that we have been following in this country were widely accepted to be right across the European Union. *We agreed* that Europe must be more competitive. *We agreed* on the need for more flexible working arrangements for the reduction of labour costs and for better education and training.   (John Major, Conservative, 12 December 1994)

---

8. See Räikkönen (2020) on the use of metaphors in EU debates in British parliament.

The use of *we* and *us* in British parliamentary debates   **161**

Table 5.3 Lexical verbs collocating with *we* referring to the EU

Rank	1973–1984	1985–1994	1995–2004	2005–2015
1	Active EU (9)	Active EU (64)	Active EU (96)	Active EU (56)
	make (4)	make (13)	make (32)	make (13)
	go (3)	achieve (9)	take (13)	take (12)
	travel (1)	get (8)	achieve (8)	reform (8)
	work (1)	move (8)	create (8)	set (6)
		build (6)	get (7)	work (6)
		pursue (6)	reform (7)	get (5)
		work (5)	move (6)	deal (3)
		take (5)	put (6)	move (3)
		approach (4)	go (5)	
			enlarge (5)	
2	Negotiation (9)	Negotiation (22)	Negotiation (36)	Negotiation (22)
	consider (3)	agree (8)	agree (10)	ensure (9)
	accept (2)	ensure (6)	say (8)	agree (7)
	agree (2)	talk (4)	consider (8)	discuss (6)
	discuss (2)	look (4)	ask (5)	
			ensure (5)	
3	Mental (4)	Mental (19)	Mental (25)	Mental (11)
	miss (3)	face (9)	want (11)	face (6)
	hope (1)	want (6)	know (9)	want (5)
		know (4)	believe (5)	
	Others (1)	Others (42)	Others (23)	Others (39)
	fail (1)	need (16)	need (13)	need (28)
		see (13)	extend (5)	see (4)
		find (5)	welcome (5)	end (4)
		allow (4)		show (3)
		give (4)		
Total 1[*]	23	147	180	128
Total 2[**]	23	233	303	169
%[†]	100	63	59	76

* Total raw frequency of the lexical verbs in the list.
** Total raw frequency of all the lexical verbs collocating with *we* in this context.
† The frequency of the collocates in the list counted against the frequency of all the lexical verbs in this context.

As was shown earlier (Section 4.2), the party in government generally speaks more from the EU's perspective than the party in the opposition. One reason for this is that ministers report back to parliament about meetings at EU level which they participated in, as in Examples (8) and (9).

In summary, when *we* refers to the whole EU and the EU is talked about as one group acting together, the topic is often what the EU is planning on doing in the future, and how it should or is going to change how it works. In these passages, the speakers seem optimistic that the EU can be and is being developed, which, at least for the most part, gives a positive image of the EU. When *we* refers to the UK only, the most common topic is what the UK is doing in the EU. However, the other two common topics are the UK's membership of the EU, and how it has affected life in the UK, and the UK's contribution to the EU. Thus, the ingroup, namely the entity to which *we* refers, is usually represented in a positive way both in the case of *we* referring to the whole EU and to the UK only. However, when *we* is used exclusively to refer to the UK, the image of the EU is more negative: the EU is said to cost too much and leaving it is seen as an option for the UK. Thus, the ingroup/outgroup dichotomy does manifest itself in parliamentary debates in relation to the EU. Furthermore, as *we* has decreasingly referred to the whole EU since 2002, the number of positive attributes being ascribed to the EU has probably decreased as well, simply because the EU's common actions have not been raised as often.

5. Conclusion

The findings presented in this chapter have shown that in British parliamentary debates there has, since 2002, been a decrease in the first-person plural pronouns *we* and *us* referring to the whole EU, and an increase in those referring to the UK only. Furthermore, upcoming general elections seemed to cause a change in the language use in that the national perspective became more dominant before the election in the speeches by the party campaigning in opposition. Consequently, as the EU was less often included in the ingroup and referred to by the pronoun *we*, the activities of the EU, in which the UK also participated, came up less often, while the UK's contribution to the EU and the effects of EU membership were more often mentioned. This may have caused a feeling among MPs and the public that the EU is not acting together as one group, but as separate from the UK and, also, that the EU is somewhere outside the UK and is not 'us'. The findings support the claims made by Cap (2018) and Wodak (2011) that personal pronouns can be used as a rhetorical tool to make a separation between ingroup and outgroup, and that the ingroup is often seen in a more positive light than the outgroup. The UK's membership of the EU has been fairly frequently debated in the British parliament, and perhaps the insecurity about the country's future in the EU has affected language use. In a similar way, Cramer (2010) concluded that the Turkish representative separated Turkey from or positioned himself in opposition to the European identity by consistently using *we* to refer to Turkey instead of Europe in a panel where Turkey's possible future membership of the EU was being discussed.

The primary dataset used in this study is exceptional in the sense that it includes all the debates of the House of Commons in the time period between January 1973 and May 2015. Thus, the findings not only describe the pronoun use in relation to a specific topic, but instead show the overall development in a fairly long time period. As already pointed out, it is not surprising that, in the national parliament, the EU has been talked about as if from outside, as MPs tend to focus on national issues, while politicians at the EU level, such as members of the European parliament, focus on the shared concerns of the whole of the EU. However, the finding that the EU has been increasingly excluded from 'us' in the debates is notable. More research is needed to gain an understanding of how common it is for the EU to be referred to as if 'outside' in the national parliaments of EU member states, and whether British politicians became more nationally centered than politicians in other parts of the EU in the period leading up to the Brexit referendum. This could be done, for instance, by using the parliamentary corpora in different languages in the CLARIN infrastructure <https://www.clarin.eu/resource-families/parliamentary-corpora>.

Funding

This work was supported by the Emil Aaltonen Foundation (180218 and 190200), and the Academy of Finland through the research project DEMLANG (295381).

Acknowledgements

I would like to thank two anonymous reviewers for their helpful comments on earlier drafts of the chapter. All remaining errors are my own.

References

Alexander, Marc & Davies, Mark. 2015. The Hansard Corpus 1803–2005. <https://www.english-corpora.org/hansard/> (13 February 2020).

Baker, Paul. 2006. *Using Corpora in Discourse Analysis*. London: Continuum.

Baker, Paul, Gabrielatos, Costas, Khosravinik, Majid, Krzyżanowski, Michał, McEnery, Tony & Wodak, Ruth. 2008. A useful methodological synergy? Combining critical discourse analysis and corpus linguistics to examine discourses of refugees and asylum seekers in the UK press. *Discourse & Society* 19(3): 273–306.

Billig, Michael. 2010. *Banal Nationalism*. London: Sage.

Blommaert, Jan & Bulcaen, Chris. 2000. Critical Discourse Analysis. *Annual Review of Anthropology* 29: 447–466.

Cap, Piotr. 2018. "We don't want any immigrants or terrorists here": The linguistic manufacturing of xenophobia in the post-2015 Poland. *Discourse & Society* 29(4): 380–398.

Chilton, Paul. 2005. Vectors, viewpoint and viewpoint shift: Toward a Discourse Space Theory. *Annual Review of Cognitive Linguistics* 3: 78–116.

Chouliaraki, Lilie & Fairclough, Norman. 1999. *Discourse in Late Modernity: Rethinking Critical Discourse Analysis*. Edinburgh: EUP.

Cramer, Jennifer. 2010. "Do we really want to be like them?": Indexing Europeanness through pronominal use. *Discourse & Society* 21(6): 619–637.

de Cillia, Rudolf, Reisigl, Martin & Wodak, Ruth. 1999. The discursive construction of national identities. *Discourse & Society* 10(2): 149–173.

de Fina, Anna. 1995. Pronominal choice, identity and solidarity in political discourse. *Text: Interdisciplinary Journal for the Study of Discourse* 15(3): 379–410.

Dekavalla, Marina. 2010. Tax, war and waiting lists: The construction of national identity in newspaper coverage of general elections after devolution. *Discourse & Society* 21(6): 638–654.

Fairclough, Norman. 1989. *Language and Power*. New York NY: Longman.

Fontana, Cary & Parsons, Craig. 2015. "One woman's prejudice": Did Margaret Thatcher cause Britain's anti-Europeanism? *Journal of Common Market Studies* 53(1): 89–105.

Hardt-Mautner, Gerlinde. 1995. "Only connect": Critical discourse analysis and corpus linguistics. *UCREL Technical Paper 6*. Lancaster: University of Lancaster.

Hiltunen, Turo, Räikkönen, Jenni & Tyrkkö, Jukka. 2020. Investigating colloquialization in the British parliamentary record in late 19th and early 20th century. *Language Sciences* 79, 101270.

Hunston, Sarah. 2007. Semantic prosody revisited. *International Journal of Corpus Linguistics* 12(2): 249–268.

Imao, Yasu. 2008–2018. *CasualConc* (Version 2.0.7.) [Computer software] <https://sites.google .com/site/casualconc/download> (17 August 2021).

Íñigo-Mora, Isabel. 2004. On the use of the personal pronoun *we* in communities. *Journal of Language and Politics* 3(1): 27–52.

Islentyeva, Anna. 2018. The undesirable migrant in the British press: Creating bias through language. *Neuphilologische Mitteilungen* 119(2): 419–442.

Krizsán, Attila. 2011. *"The EU is Not Them, But Us!" The First Person Plural and the Articulation of Collective Identities in European Political Discourse*. Newcastle upon Tyne: Cambridge Scholars.

Lenz, Friedrich. 2003. Deictic conceptualisation of space, time and person: Introduction. In *Deictic Conceptualisation of Space, Time and Person* [Pragmatics & Beyond New Series 112], Friedrich Lenz (ed.), vi–xiv. Amsterdam: John Benjamins.

Ludlow, Piers. 2002. Us or them? The meaning of Europe in British political discourse. In *The Meaning of Europe*, Mikael af Malmborg & Bo Stråth (eds), 101–124. Oxford: Berg.

McEnery, Tony, Brezina, Vaclav & Baker, Helen. 2019. The UK, Europe and the path to Brexit – the long view: Europe in two centuries of British newspapers. Plenary given at BCICLE 2019: 8th Biennial International Conference on the Linguistics of Contemporary English, 26–28 September 2019. Bamberg, Germany.

Mollin, Sandra. 2007. The Hansard hazard: Gauging the accuracy of British parliamentary transcripts. *Corpora* 2(2): 187–210.

Mühlhäusler, Peter & Harré, Rom. 1990. *Pronouns and People: The Linguistic Construction of Social and Personal Identity*. Oxford: Basil Blackwell.

Oddo, John. 2011. War legitimation discourse: Representing 'us' and 'them' in four US presidential addresses. *Discourse & Society* 22(3): 287–314.

Partington, Alan. 2004. "Utterly content in each other's company": Semantic prosody and semantic preference. *International Journal of Corpus Linguistics* 9(1): 131–156.

Partington, Alan, Duguid, Alison & Taylor, Charlotte. 2013. *Patterns and Meanings in Discourse: Theory and Practice in Corpus-Assisted Discourse Studies (CADS)* [Studies in Corpus Linguistics 55]. Amsterdam: John Benjamins.

Petersoo, Pille. 2007. What does 'we' mean? National deixis in the media. *Journal of Language and Politics* 6(3): 419–436.

Proctor, Katarzyna & Su, Lily I-Wen. 2011. The first person plural in political discourse: American politicians in interviews and in a debate. *Journal of Pragmatics* 43: 3251–3266.

Räikkönen, Jenni. 2020. Metaphors separating the United Kingdom from the EU in British parliamentary debates from 2000 to 2016. In *Metaphor in Political Conflict: Populism and Discourse*, Ruth Breeze & Carmen Llamas (eds), 27–54. Pamplona: EUNSA.

Riihimäki, Jenni. 2019. At the heart and in the margins: Discursive construction of British national identity in relation to the EU in British parliamentary debates from 1973 to 2015. *Discourse & Society* 30(4): 412–431.

Sinclair, John. 1991. *Corpus, Concordance, Collocation*. Oxford: OUP.

Sinclair, John. 2004. *Trust the Text: Language, Corpus and Discourse*. London: Routledge.

Slembrouck, Stef. 1992. The parliamentary Hansard 'verbatim' report: The written construction of spoken discourse. *Language and Literature* 1(2): 101–119.

van Dijk, Teun. 1993. *Elite Discourse and Racism*. Newbury Park CA: Sage.

Wodak, Ruth. 2011. "Us" and "them": Inclusion and exclusion – Discrimination via discourse. In *Identity, Belonging and Migration*, Gerard Delanty, Ruth Wodak & Paul Jones (eds), 54–77. Liverpool: Liverpool University Press.

Wodak, Ruth, de Cillia, Rudolf & Reisigl, Martin. 2009. *The Discursive Construction of National Identities*. Edinburgh: EUP.

CHAPTER 6

From *masters* and *servants* to *employers* and *employees*
Exploring democratisation with big data

Turo Vartiainen & Minna Palander-Collin
University of Helsinki

This chapter explores how societal democratisation can be studied by using linguistic big data. More specifically, we are interested in establishing whether it is possible to see how the gradual democratisation of society affected the employment relationship in nineteenth-century Britain by examining changes in the frequency of constructions where different referential terms for both employers and employees were used in the British parliament. We pay particular attention to the gradual waning of the master–servant institution, whose demise can be directly linked to the increased independence of labourers from their employers. We will also briefly explore how data anomalies or outliers can potentially be used as a heuristic when identifying events of historical interest and importance.

Keywords: democratisation, employment, masters, servants, possessive determiners

1. Introduction

In this chapter, we discuss some aspects of how sociocultural changes in the status of employers and employees are reflected in parliamentary discourse as represented in the Hansard Corpus (Alexander & Davies 2015). Our starting point is a particular kind of relationship between the employer and the employee – that between a *master* and a *servant* – which was described by William Blackstone (1758: I, 24) as one of the private relations on a par with the relationship between a husband and wife or a parent and child. The social and legal roles of master and servant go back at least to medieval times and legislation (see e.g. Atkinson 2013: 3; Hay 2004: 62), and they were gradually renegotiated in nineteenth-century England both in social and legal terms, which makes the Hansard Corpus a particularly interesting resource to study. Moreover, the developments in the master–servant

https://doi.org/10.1075/scl.111.06var
© 2023 John Benjamins Publishing Company

relationship can be linked to and coincide with democratisation processes through which "[l]arge numbers were given significant opportunity for influence over the political process" in the course of the nineteenth century and the first half of the twentieth century (Garrard 2002: 2).

In the nineteenth century, the Early Modern view according to which servants were primarily unmarried men and women, who lived with their masters and over whom the master could exercise significant control, gradually gave way to a more modern view and more general labour laws, according to which all labourers began to be regarded as free and independent actors in the labour market (e.g. Atkinson 2013: 209; Steinfeld 1991: 16). The changing dynamics between masters and servants must also have had repercussions for the ways in which these social roles, and other employment-related roles, were linguistically constructed on the floor of parliament, and this is precisely what we are interested in examining in this chapter.

Our study provides an analysis of the use of *master* and *servant* together with other related terms, including *employer, employee, workman, worker* and *labourer* in the Hansard Corpus, and explores how big data can be used to contextualise language practices and link sociocultural changes to linguistic changes. Our main focus is on how the social roles of *master* and *servant* were constructed in parliament, and how they changed over time, particularly in the nineteenth century. In our linguistic analysis, we pay special attention to adjectival and prepositional modification patterns and to the way in which the interconnectedness of the two roles is expressed by using possessive determiners (e.g. *their masters, his servant*). In this way, we can extend our analysis from the use of individual words to a linguistically well-motivated operationalisation of social roles and relationships. Our results provide a suggestive timeline for the democratisation process, showing that the social changes concerning the increased independence of servants and other labourers were increasingly reflected in the speech of the members of parliament (MPs) throughout the nineteenth century. Furthermore, in parallel with this general process, we see a more specific change in the use of *master* and *servant*, as both terms gradually lost their potential of being used to denote employment relations in the private sphere of life (e.g. masters/servants within the household or in a private company). In sum, our study shows that democratisation processes are embedded in several layers of language, which can best be captured with a triangulation of quantitative and qualitative methods.

The big data approach is invaluable in providing adequate empirical evidence and in revealing patterns that can potentially be linked to specific social changes. However, big data can also behave in unpredictable ways, emphasising some developments while suppressing others, and producing results that may initially seem significant, but which on closer inspection may, at least in part, be due to challenges related to the research design. For instance, in many earlier studies that have attempted to connect sociohistorical developments with shifting patterns of language use, the focus has largely been on the changing frequencies of individual lexical items (see e.g. Michel et al. 2011). This approach not only suffers from problems caused by potential random fluctuations in the data but also from the fact that the confounding effect of polysemy tends to be overlooked. In Greenfield (2013), for example, it is argued that the increased importance of individuality, which is often associated with Western societies, can be traced in corpus data by examining frequency changes of words like *get, obedience* and *choose*. However, this approach does not take into account the fact that a highly polysemous word like *get* is used in many functions that have little or nothing to do with individuality or communality (Hilpert 2020). Indeed, Hilpert (2020) suggests that instead of examining individual words, we should pay attention to the way in which the words are used in specific constructions, and in this way ensure that the words analysed are, in fact, used with the intended meaning.

The present study, based on data from the Hansard Corpus, also highlights the unpredictability of big data. We initially expected the frequencies of different terms and constructions to reflect the debates related to the various employment bills in a rather direct way. However, this expectation was not fully borne out: while we can sometimes see a correlation between text frequencies and the events and laws discussed in parliament, the temporal correspondence may not be entirely exact. For example, according to the literature (see Section 2), the mid-nineteenth century appears to be a watershed in respect of labour laws and related societal movements, but our graphs mapping linguistic changes do not indicate this directly; instead, they show a more even development taking place over the course of the nineteenth century. On the other hand, our data include anomalous peaks which cannot easily be explained within the context of broader social developments. In these cases, we carefully read the debates in their original context and were often able to connect the anomalies to specific events. In other words, what started out as an analytical challenge turned out to be a methodological opportunity for using data anomalies to identify exceptional historical events.

In sum, our study is an attempt to explore how the gradual democratisation of British society is reflected in the way in which employment relations, particularly the relationship between a master and a servant, are constructed in parliamentary discourse. We start in Section 2 by introducing some sociohistorical and legal background concerning the master–servant institution in Britain. This section is intended to provide the necessary backdrop against which we will frame our linguistic case studies. Section 3 introduces the data used in the case studies as well as the constructions studied. Section 4 presents the results of the case studies, and Section 5 concludes the chapter with a discussion of the main findings and some suggestions for future research.

2.   Societal and legal developments and the master–servant institution

Many important societal and legal developments converge in the nineteenth century and influence the development and eventual demise of the master–servant institution. Industrialisation is one of the important nineteenth-century megatrends that changed this relationship, as the nature of work changed. In pre-industrial society, servants were dependent on their masters, and the master–servant relationship was regarded as similar to a husband–wife relationship and parent–child/guardian–ward relationship (Atkinson 2013:208). In households, the master of the family exercised 'domestic rule' over all his dependants, including servants. Pre-industrial work and family relationships were thus tightly interlinked. Hence, *servant* referred to many types of workers dependent on a master – either working and living in the master's household or just working for others, whether they lived in the master's household or not. In addition to referring to service in the master's household, the word *servant* had a broader meaning referring to all those who worked for others, for example, in husbandry as labourers, or as artificers (Atkinson 2013:209; Blackstone 1758:I, 24; Meldrum 2000:25; Steinfeld 1991:18–20).

In the course of the Industrial Revolution, work became increasingly separated from the family, and the master–servant relationship was redefined and eventually abandoned as the way of conceptualising employment relationships. Workers started to be regarded as independent and self-reliant owners of their labour, which they could sell to whomever they liked in the labour market. These developments were not straightforward, and throughout the nineteenth century legal scholars debated whether to situate employees within the private household, as dictated by traditional master–servant relations, or within the market, as commanded by freedom of contract and free labour ideology (Atkinson 2013:214).

In legal terms, the master–servant relationship and the servant's dependent status go back to medieval legislation, such as the Ordinance of Labourers (1349) and the Statute of Labourers (1350). Up to the beginning of the nineteenth century, "imprisonment and whipping and fines" were at the core of English employment laws, as the main purpose of the various labour acts was to control the labourers and prohibit the formation of trade unions (Hay 2004:61). For example, the Master and Servant Act of 1823 made it a criminal offence for a workman to be disobedient. At this point, a servant was defined as someone who entered the service of one master only.

In the 1830s and 1840s, more 'liberal' legislation started to emerge, where the most vulnerable groups, such as small children, were protected against the harsh conditions in factories and mines. The mid-nineteenth century emerges as a kind of turning point in labour laws and labour activity (Frank 2016). The first large-scale expressions of working-class discontent, as well as continued trade union pressure, occurred in the 1840s, and the legal disputes and dissatisfaction over the master and servant acts revolved around the harshness of the laws and the types of workers they should concern (Frank 2004: 412–413). Gradually, the workers' conditions started to improve. For example, the Employers and Workmen Act in 1875 put 'masters' and 'men' on an equal footing regarding breaches of contract. In earlier legislation and legal practice, breaches of contract were typically interpreted in favour of the masters, and the punishments primarily concerned the workers (see Atkinson 2013; Frank 2004; Hay 2004).

In today's parlance, a servant is usually understood narrowly as a domestic servant who in the past worked in a master's household as a maid, valet, butler or cook, for instance. Historically, however, servants also included other workers, who were employed either by private companies (e.g. a servant of the railway company) or by the government or local authorities (e.g. a servant of the Post Office). Nevertheless, domestic servants admittedly formed an important group that persisted until the twentieth century. The decline of the domestic servant institution is usually linked to World War I, although some scholars say that the servant population already reached its peak in the 1871 census (see Higgs 1983: 202). However, census data is difficult to interpret, as *servant* could indicate a variety of relations, including (female) relatives living under the same roof with the head of the household. Furthermore, the practices of counting and classifying people in the census changed over time, which poses additional challenges to the reliability of the estimates (Higgs 1982).

Legislation towards a fairer and more equal labour market has continued after the nineteenth century. For example, during the latter half of the twentieth century, labour laws have focused on topics like gender equality, discrimination based on sexual orientation, parental rights, and human trafficking and slavery (Meek 2021). All these developments can be interpreted in terms of increased democratisation, although the focus has shifted from questions related to the equality between the employer and the employee in the employment relationship to more general questions pertaining to the fair and equal treatment of all citizens.

This discussion has focused on democratisation as a social, political and legal phenomenon, but the term has also been used in linguistic research to describe linguistic trends and tendencies, such as colloquialisation or informalisation processes (for an overview of linguistic democratisation processes, see Farrelly & Seoane 2012). In our study, we understand democratisation primarily as a political concept and a societal process that works in tandem with the linguistic changes observed here. In addition, the changes that we see in the use of *master* and *servant*, as well as in the other terms specifying the roles in the employment relationship, can also be understood in terms of democratisation in the linguistic sense. After all, one of the linguistic outcomes of democratisation is the decreased use of terms that overtly express power asymmetries (Farrelly & Seoane 2012: 393; Leech et al. 2009: 259), which is precisely what we see in our analysis of *master* and *servant*: the changing norms of society are reflected in the language used to refer to employers and employees, and large databases like the Hansard Corpus provide us with direct access to these changes.

3. Data and methods

3.1 The Hansard Corpus as a source for linguistic analysis

Our data come from the Hansard Corpus, which comprises a total of 1.6 billion words of parliamentary discourse from the House of Commons and the House of Lords in the British parliament from 1803 to 2005. In our case studies, we used the corpus in its entirety and accessed it through the online interface at <https:// www.english-corpora.org/hansard/>. As the amount of context available for the results obtained from the Hansard Corpus is relatively small, we also consulted the full texts available at the official website of the Hansard at <https://hansard .parliament.uk/>.

For our purposes, the Hansard Corpus provides plentiful data that enable the exploration of societal and linguistic changes over an extended period of time. While some of the big data corpora have been criticised for being enormous "blobs" of data which cannot be divided into meaningful sections (Davies 2018: 67), the Hansard Corpus provides us with a more controlled setting. We know what kind of genre we are dealing with, and the available metadata provides us with information about, for example, the speaker and the date of the speech. We can thus reconstruct the contexts of the speeches to the extent that is necessary for linking language use to the contemporary discussions and matters debated in parliament at specific points in time. In the case of outliers or anomalies, it is possible to return to the data in order to explore and explain the deviating results in more detail.

In principle, the Hansard represents (relatively formal) speech, but the Official Report produced on the basis of the parliamentary debates has been intentionally edited to omit many performance features, such as incomplete utterances and hesitations (Slembrouck 1992). Furthermore, Hansard editors frequently change lexical and grammatical features that are associated with spoken language in an attempt to gear the texts towards a more conservative and formal style. For example, Mollin (2007: 197–198) observes that multi-word verbs like *make sure* and *look at* are typically replaced by single-word (often Latinate) verbs like *ensure* and *consider* in the Official Report, while degree modifiers (e.g. *very, really*) and epistemic stance markers (e.g. *actually, clearly*) are often omitted altogether (Mollin 2007: 200–201). Consequently, it is vital to take the considerable amount of editing into account in all studies that use the Hansard Corpus as a data source (see also Alexander, this volume, and Kotze et al., this volume).

In addition to issues related to the editing of the texts, there have been substantial changes in the production circumstances of the parliamentary reports (see Alexander, this volume). The earliest texts included in the Hansard Corpus were produced by Thomas Cobbett, who sold his business to Thomas Curson Hansard in 1812. Both Cobbett and Hansard relied on existing press reports in their work (particularly *The Times*), and Thomas Hansard frequently sent parliamentary speeches back to the MPs for correction and revision (Rix 2014: 456–457). The relationship between the press and parliament also had a direct impact on the way in which the debates unfolded. As discussed in Rix (2014: 457–458), MPs used decidedly less eloquent language in sittings of parliament in late July 1833, when all reporters were temporarily banned from following the proceedings. The ban was imposed by Daniel O'Connell, an MP who felt he had not received a fair representation in the press (Macdonagh 1903: 280–282). Although this dispute was settled within two weeks, a more significant change in the reproduction of the parliamentary debates took place in 1909, when selective third-person summaries of the debates were replaced by full (edited) transcripts of the speeches in the first person, marking a significant linguistic change that disrupts the continuity of the genre. Although this occasion has been found to be important from the perspective of colloquialisation (see e.g. Hiltunen, Räikkönen & Tyrkkö 2020), this date does not particularly stand out in our data, as our focus is more on the frequency of individual lexical items and their use in specific constructions instead of features associated with colloquial style, such as *be going to* or the epistemic marker *I think*.

3.2 Constructions studied

The choice of linguistic items studied in this chapter is motivated by two factors. First, based on what we know about the general democratisation of British society, we were interested in seeing how the dissolution of the highly unequal master–servant institution is reflected in parliamentary discourse. In addition to *master* and *servant*, we also decided to study two other general terms that became widely used in the late nineteenth and early twentieth centuries in reference to the two parties in the employment relationship: *employer* and *employee*. These terms were selected based on an initial, unsystematic exploration of the Hansard data. Finally, we supplemented these four terms with three additional terms that are regularly used in the Hansard to refer to employees: *workman, worker* and *labourer.* These terms were selected based on their relatively high rank in the collocational profiles of *masters* and *employers* in the corpus (as far as general terms for employees are concerned), suggesting that they were, at least occasionally, used interchangeably with *employees* and/or *servants.* Both singular and plural forms were extracted from the corpus for further analysis, and in the case of *master* (which could also be used as a verb, 'to master'), we used a POS tag to ensure that the results only included nouns.

As discussed in Section 1, the frequencies of individual lexical items can fluctuate in unpredictable ways in corpus data, and there may be great challenges when trying to link the changing frequencies to sociocultural developments. What would be desirable, then, is to devise an operationalisation that would plausibly connect a cultural process (in our case, democratisation) with a specific linguistic expression (a construction). With this in mind, we decided to focus on a single important aspect in the democratisation process: the increased independence of the workforce. Our hypothesis was that as workers gradually began to be perceived as more independent agents in the labour market, they would also be more often discussed with no reference to their masters/employers. To measure the gradual decrease in the level of reciprocity inherent in the employer/employee relationship, we queried the corpus for possessive noun phrases (e.g. *their masters, his employees*). Here, the head noun refers either to the employer or to the employee, while the possessive determiner refers to the other party. Our hypothesis about the connection between democratisation and the declining use of possessive NPs was informed by a pilot study which we carried out on the witness depositions included in the Old Bailey Corpus (see Huber et al. 2012). In the Old Bailey data, we found a significant decrease in the frequency of *my master* and *your master* in the course of the nineteenth century (Vartiainen et al., 2021), suggesting that the witnesses became increasingly reluctant to portray themselves, or others, as having a master as the century progressed.

In addition to analysing changes in the frequency of the possessive constructions, we also studied *masters* and *servants* from other perspectives. Initial queries of the two terms revealed that it was necessary to study them by using different methods: while *master* is a highly polysemous word, and it is used in the parliamentary debates in a variety of senses, the developments affecting the use of *servant* are somewhat different in nature, mainly concerning the semantic narrowing of the term. Consequently, our analysis of the term *master* focuses on the changing proportions of the different meanings of the word, while the analysis of *servant* is based on the qualitative and quantitative changes related to the adjectival premodifiers and phrasal postmodifiers that are used with *servant* in the corpus. From the perspective of democratisation, our analysis of *master* therefore delves into the question of which word senses continue to be used, and in what proportions, and which have become less frequent or obsolete. Our focus on the modification patterns of *servants*, on the other hand, is motivated by the reduced meaning potential of *servant* and the fact that the word is extremely rarely used without a prenominal adjective in the most recent decades in the corpus. By studying the frequency of postmodifying prepositional phrases, on the other hand, we can examine how often the MPs made a distinction between different kinds of servants, such as *servants of the Crown, servants of the tradesmen* or *servants of the railway company* (all attested in the corpus). We suggest that a high frequency of such structures is indicative of a society where servants are employed in various functions, whereas a low frequency suggests the contrary.

Finally, the constructions chosen for a closer examination are motivated by two additional reasons. First, we could not find any evidence of a prescription against the use of prenominal adjectives, postnominal prepositional phrases or possessive constructions of the kind studied in this chapter, suggesting that the results acquired from the Hansard would be unlikely to be influenced by editorial conventions in these respects. However, Mollin (2007: 202–203) does point out that the frequencies of first- and second-person pronouns (including possessive pronouns) are substantially different in a verbatim transcript of parliamentary debates when compared to the Official Report. From this perspective, the Hansard data (including our own material) provides a somewhat inaccurate representation of pronoun usage in parliament. However, as we do not posit any particular significance to grammatical person in our study, and because Mollin points out that third-person forms remain largely unedited, we are confident that the questions explored in our case studies can be successfully investigated with data from the Hansard Corpus.

Second, we suggest that the constructions studied are unlikely to be used consciously to convey specific, subjective meanings (see also Vartiainen 2017). For instance, if an MP talks about *their employers* (in reference to a group of labourers), it does not seem likely that their purpose is to draw deliberate attention to the dependent nature of the relationship between labourers and employers. Rather, the use of such phrases shows that the issues concerning one group also concern the other. In sum, by focusing on linguistic patterns that are used largely subconsciously, we hope to find examples of language use that have not been targeted by the copyeditors of the Official Report, and which can be considered indicative of the gradual democratisation of the employment relationship in Britain.

4. Exploring the employment relationship in the Hansard Corpus

4.1 General trends

We begin our investigation with a general observation concerning the frequency of the employee-related terms in the Hansard. Figure 6.1 shows the normalised frequency of the five terms studied: *servant(s)*, *labourer(s)*, *workman/-men*, *worker(s)* and *employee(s)*.

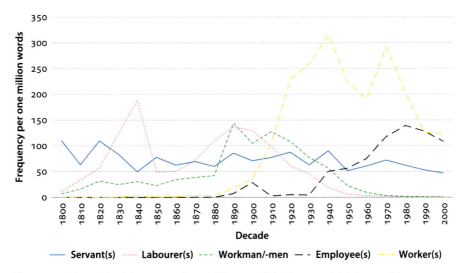

Figure 6.1 Normalised frequency (per million words) of *servant(s)*, *labourer(s)*, *workman/-men*, *employee(s)* and *worker(s)* in the Hansard Corpus

As can be seen in Figure 6.1, some of the terms have largely fallen out of use, while others have gained in popularity. *Labourer* and *workman* are mostly associated with nineteenth-century discourse, while *worker* and *employee* become common in the twentieth century. Interestingly, the frequency of *servant* remains relatively steady throughout the period studied. We return to this observation in Section 4.2.

However, as discussed in Section 1, data on individual lexemes can be relatively unrevealing from a sociohistorical perspective. For example, all we can say based on Figure 6.1 is that some terms that were used to describe the workforce in the nineteenth century have since given way to others. However, we hypothesised that the changing frequencies of specific constructions could yield more interesting results, particularly from the perspective of the increased independence of the workforce. Indeed, we see evidence of this development in our data as the use of possessive determiners with words denoting employers and employees steadily decreases over time, particularly in the nineteenth century. Figure 6.2 shows this trend for the five employee-related terms studied.

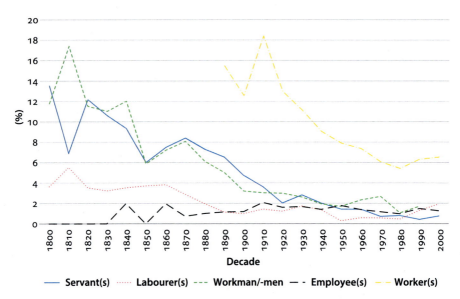

Figure 6.2 The proportion of possessive NPs out of all NPs with *servant(s)*, *labourer(s)*, *workman/-men*, *employee(s)* and *worker(s)* in the Hansard Corpus

The data depicted in Figure 6.2 show that, as far as the three terms that were in common use in the early nineteenth century are concerned (*labourer*, *workman*, *servant*), the interrelatedness of the two parties in the employment relationship was much more often brought to the fore in the early decades of the nineteenth century than in the late nineteenth or the twentieth century. *Worker*, which becomes more common in the early twentieth century, shows a similar decrease in the proportion of possessive NPs as *labourer*, *workman* and *servant*, while *employee* (which is very infrequent in the nineteenth century data) is rarely used in possessive constructions overall.

In the analysis, it is important to bear in mind that the possessive determiner typically functions as a point of reference for the head noun (Langacker 1995), and it therefore expresses given information. In other words, when we find employee terms used as head nouns in a possessive NP, the talk is typically about employers, not employees. In Example (1), for instance, the speaker only mentions *servants* because he is worried about the landowners' right to hunt game on their own grounds. In Example (2), on the other hand, the question is at least as much about the employer as it is about the labourer. Here, the speaker discusses the

From *masters* and *servants* to *employers* and *employees*   177

productivity of cultivation in terms of how much the employer can benefit from his labourers. In both cases, the topic is approached from the employer's perspective, even if the head noun refers to the employee, and it is the employer's rights that have motivated the speakers to introduce the topic in the parliament.

(1)   The right of sporting was now confined chiefly to *persons who had 100£ a year in land*, and they could not employ *their servants* to kill game for their use upon their own estates. (House of Commons, 29 April 1825, Charles Tennyson)

(2)   *The cultivator in Poland* may have a greater abundance of uncultivated or unexhausted land; but this is his grand and primary advantage; I may say, almost his only advantage. For though he pays smaller wages to *his labourer*, yet the labour which he obtains in return, being allied with a much less efficient apparatus of agricultural capital, is far less productive than that of a labourer in England.   (House of Commons, 13 March 1839, George Grote)

These examples contrast with cases like those in Examples (3) and (4), where the terms of reference are used without a possessive determiner.

(3)   What my hon. Friend asked for, and what he is entitled to get, is some indication as to how much of this £18,000 goes to officers of the Household; I mean gentlemen on high salaries; and how much goes to what might without disrespect be called *the servants of the lower order*. I was told that these pensions were going to *domestic servants* performing manual and menial work. It was only at the last moment I saw that the proposal was nothing of the sort, and that the large proportion is going to those who have got large salaries.
(House of Commons, 27 July 1910, George Barnes)

(4)   He was asked how, when dealing with the question of labour, they dealt with the expectation of pensions; and he said it was decided in 1868 that a charge should be added to the salaries of officers and clerks, and to the pay of *the workmen* to represent the eventual charge for pensions, and he actually gave the opinion that 70 per cent would fairly represent the eventual charge.
(House of Commons, 18 July 1887, George Price)

In Example (3), the speaker, George Barnes, first refers to *the servants of the lower order*, and then makes a clarification by speaking of *domestic servants*. This particular debate concerned a pension that was to be paid to the servants of the royal household, and Barnes was concerned that the money might not be given to people who actually worked as servants, but rather to 'decorative officers' of various kinds. Example (4) relates to the pensions of naval officers, clerks and workmen. Again, the focus is strictly on these employee groups. Their relationship with their employer (the Crown) is not relevant to the topic, nor does it receive particular attention.

The increased independence of the workforce can also be clearly seen in the decreased proportion of possessive NPs where *master* or *employer* are used as headwords (see Figure 6.3). The decrease in the use of possessives is particularly striking in the case of *employer(s)*, where 74% of all NPs (28/38) are used with a possessive determiner in the first decade of the nineteenth century, while in the most recent dataset (2000–2005), the corresponding proportion is just 5% (575/12,344). The substantial discrepancy in the absolute frequencies between the two periods cannot be overlooked, of course, but the trend is still convincing. For *master*, the decrease is smaller, but the proportion of possessive NPs nevertheless goes down from its peak at 15% (1820s) to 5% (1900s), after which there is little change in the data.

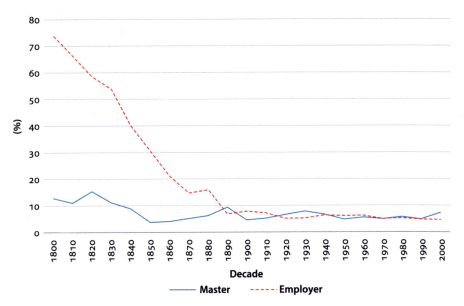

Figure 6.3 The proportion of possessive NPs out of all NPs with *master(s)* and *employer(s)* in the Hansard Corpus

The data depicted in Figures 6.2 and 6.3 emphasise the similarities in the ways in which employers and employees were discussed on the floor of parliament. Indeed, Examples (5) to (7) show that the employers could also function as points of reference for topics that primarily concerned the employees, while also emphasising the interrelated nature of the relationship.

(5) He was surprised the hon. gentleman should say that the operation of this tax was to make the poor pay a greater proportion than they ought. If the labourer paid in the first instance, it was clear that he must be repaid by *his employer*, and that in fact the former only advanced so much in the course of the week to be reimbursed by the latter at the end of it. [The hon. member contended, at considerable length that neither the labourer, the cottager, the agriculturist, nor the manufacturer, felt any inconvenience from this tax.]
(House of Commons, 29 April 1819, Thomas Wallace)

(6) By the influence of that taxation, *the labourers and their employers* were now in a worse condition than ever. (House of Commons, 4 May 1826, Joseph Hume)

(7) It has already been intimated that we conceive it to be no part of our province on this occasion to discuss the justice of the complaints made by *the workmen* against *their employers*: or to decide upon the merits of the dispute existing between them. (House of Commons, 21 February 1843, Thomas Duncombe)

In Example (5), the debate focuses on a proposed salt duty. Here the speaker, Thomas Wallace, spends his entire turn arguing that even poor employees would be able to afford to pay the duty if they were reimbursed by their employers. From the perspective of information structure, the employers are relatively back-grounded as Wallace makes no further mention of them during his turn, and the summarising statement in parentheses makes it clear that he specifically focused on different employee groups in his speech. In Example (6), Joseph Hume argues that the introduction of an excise duty has had serious consequences for the prosperity of both labourers and their employers. In this case, Hume manages to connect the perceived plight of business owners with the suffering of the labourers in a single sentence. It is not entirely clear from the text if the labourers' suffering is perceived to be a consequence of the employers' dwindling profits, but the reciprocal nature of the employer–employee relationship is certainly foregrounded. Finally, in Example (7) we see an instance of the kind of debate where the poor working conditions of the employees were brought to the fore. In such cases, the focus was typically as much on the suffering of the workforce as it was on the employers' responsibility to act in a more responsible manner, again underscoring the interrelated nature of the relationship.

4.2 *Masters* and *servants* in the Hansard Corpus

4.2.1 Masters *in the Hansard Corpus*

Based on the review of the sociohistorical and legal literature presented in Section 2, we would expect to see the text frequency of both *master* and *servant* decrease quite significantly in the corpus over time. This expectation is, however, only borne out in the case of *master*. Figure 6.4 shows that, after some fluctuation in the mid-nineteenth century, the frequency of *master* starts to decrease rapidly from the 1870s onward, and the term becomes increasingly rare in the twentieth-century data. For *servant*, the results are more surprising: despite a slight decrease in the most recent decades, the frequency of *servant* remains relatively stable in the corpus for the entire period studied. Indeed, the frequency of *servant* is as high in the 1990s as in the 1840s dataset.

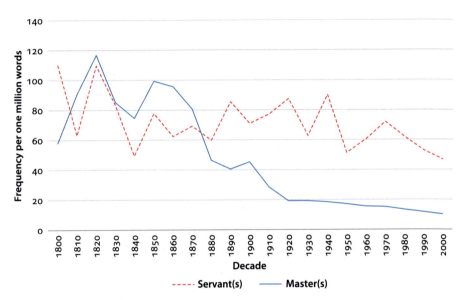

Figure 6.4 Normalised frequency (per million words) of *master(s)* and *servant(s)* in the Hansard Corpus

It is true, of course, that in addition to referring to employers, the term *master* can be used to denote many other things, and therefore the frequency decrease shown in Figure 6.4 should not be taken at face value. In our data, *master* is used to indicate a variety of meanings, which include, for example, a public official, a private employer, a ship's master, a military officer (e.g. a barrack master), a slave's master, a master craftsman, a schoolmaster, a gang leader and a dog's master. While many of these meanings are based on the master–servant institution, it is obvious, of course, that (for example) gang leaders and dog's masters are not relevant to the present discussion.

Nevertheless, even with all the variation, there is a general line of development to be found (see Table 6.1). As expected, private employers are no longer referred to as *masters* in the most recent periods in our data, while the frequency of metaphorical uses, such as in Example (8) and (9), increases. The term also persists in fixed forms of reference, most notably the *Master of the Rolls*, a position that was already established in 1286 (Example (10)), as well as in the names of trade unions, such as the *National Association of Master Bakers* and the *Master Builders Association* (Example (11)). These trade unions were typically founded in the nineteenth or early twentieth centuries, when the term *master* still enjoyed greater currency. In other words, many of the references to *masters* that we find in the most recent decades in the corpus data can be considered historical from this perspective.[1]

(8) A single currency cannot be an objective in itself, except in a limited sense. It must be the servant of the political and economic system that we want, not *its master*.　　　　　(House of Commons, 24 January 1991, Peter Hordern)

(9) Does the Minister agree with the Secretary of State for the Environment that we cannot continue to see the number of motor cars increasing so that life becomes dominated by them? Does he agree also that the car should be our servant and not *our master*?
　　　　　　　　　　　(House of Commons, 21 March 1994, Nick Harvey)

(10) *The Master of the Rolls* has more experience than I of such matters and he may well be right.　　　　(House of Commons, 18 March 1991, Robert Maclennan)

(11) Despite earlier events, I rise to present a petition organised by the Association of *Master Bakers* and presented to me late yesterday by its president.
　　　　　　　(House of Commons, 8 December 1993, Nicholas Winterton)

The overall frequency of *master(s)* is unfortunately too high for a detailed investigation of the diachronic development of the individual senses. Nevertheless, in order to explore general trends, we took a sample of 100 tokens of *master* from each of the five decades (Table 6.1). Based on this sample, we can see that the frequency of individual terms of reference related to public officials like the *Master of the Rolls* remains high even in the 1990s dataset, but in general, the sample reflects the demise of the master–servant institution in interesting ways. For example, the fact that the sample includes references to *dog's masters* and the increase in metaphorical usage in the most recent periods studied can be argued to be a consequence of the decreased frequency of the other senses.[2]

---

1. The *National Association of Master Bakers* was founded in 1887. Interestingly, its members thought that the name had become outdated, and the association was renamed the *Craft Bakers' Association* in 2013 (see Leek 2013).

2. We consulted the *Oxford English Dictionary* (OED Online 2000) when formulating the categories represented in Table 6.1. Ultimately, however, they are based on our close reading of the terms of reference in context. The queries were based on random samples (randomised with the online corpus tool's *Find Sample* function). The token frequency of *master* varies greatly in each decade, and the absolute frequencies from which the samples of 100 tokens were taken are as follows: 1800s: 259, 1850s: 2,965, 1900s: 2,610, 1950s: 1,871, 1990s: 1,898.

Table 6.1 Different senses of *master* in the corpus from the 1800s to the 1990s

Master	1800s	1850s	1900s	1950s	1990s
Public official	35	51	20	29	36
Servant/slave	15	3	2	2	9
Military	13	5	1	0	9
Skill	11	5	7	12	6
Ship's master	8	8	13	8	1
Royalty/ruler	8	7	0	7	1
Guild/manufacturers	2	4	4	14	7
Private company	3	7	5	4	0
Head of family	2	0	1	0	0
Vocative	2	0	0	0	0
One's own master	1	0	4	4	1
School master		8	21	7	7
Academic degree		2	3	1	4
Title			19	3	0
Master plan				5	4
Dog's master				1	3
Metaphorical				3	12
Total	100	100	100	100	100

4.2.2 Servants *in the Hansard Corpus*

As shown in Figure 6.4, the frequency of *servant* remained high in the Hansard Corpus until the early 2000s. The persistence of the term becomes understandable when we examine the developments in the pre- and postmodification patterns of *servants*. For instance, in our most recent dataset from the 2000s, the corpus includes 2,620 tokens of the term *civil servants*, and 389 tokens of *public servants*, which together account for 86% of all instances of *servants*. Indeed, when we examine the data diachronically, it becomes obvious that there is much less variation in the adjective types associated with *servants* in the most recent datasets. For instance, despite the fact that the sub-corpora from the early nineteenth century are much smaller than the sub-corpora from the most recent decades, they typically show much richer variation in the adjective types that modify *servants*. In the 1830s sub-corpus, for instance, we find a total of 79 adjectives used with *servants*, whereas the corresponding number for the 1990s sub-corpus is just 53 – and this is despite the fact that the 1830s sub-corpus only includes 28.1 million words, while the 2000s sub-corpus is over six times as large (177.1 million words).

A closer look at the data reveals that the dominance of *civil servants* and *public servants* in the corpus has emerged gradually as a consequence of the demise of the master–servant institution. Figure 6.5 shows the distribution of ADJ + *servant* patterns in the corpus from the 1830s to the 1990s. The data are classified according to the type of reference (private vs. public employment). Some adjective types occur in the corpus with both kinds of servants, while others could not be assigned to either category with confidence – these are marked as 'ambiguous/both' in Figure 6.5. There were also some recurring formulae (e.g. *your humble servants*), which are classified as 'formulaic' in Figure 6.5.

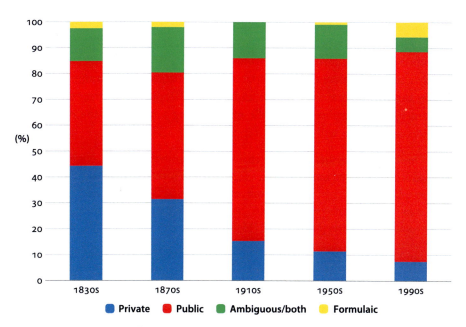

Figure 6.5 Proportional frequency of ADJ + *servants* in the Hansard Corpus classified according to public and private employment (data studied at 40-year intervals from the 1830s to the 1990s)[3]

Figure 6.5 shows that the MPs discussed servants that were privately employed quite regularly in the 1830s and the 1870s, as evidenced by phrases like *domestic servants, menial servants, faithful servants* and *agricultural servants*. However,

---

3. We decided to study the data from the 1830s onwards because of the larger size of the sub-corpus: there are only c. 5 million words of text in the 1800s sub-corpus compared to 28.1 million words in the 1830s sub-corpus.

there is a marked change in the data starting in the 1910s: the proportion of privately employed servants drops from 31% (1870s) to 15% (1910s). This trend continues all the way to the 1990s, where just 11% of all ADJ + *servants* patterns refer to servants in private employment.

Furthermore, although some of the adjectives in the 1990s dataset would seem to be compatible with the description of privately employed servants (e.g. *domestic, good*), on closer inspection it becomes clear that the question is often either about a historical reference or metaphorical usage, as exemplified in Examples (12) to (14). In Example (12), the speaker (Tony Benn) mentions *domestic servants* only because he makes mention of the so-called 'People's Budget' introduced by Lloyd George in 1909. In other words, this usage is similar to the one observed above for *masters*, where *master bakers* and *master builders* continue to occur in the corpus because of the existence of the trade associations that were founded in the nineteenth and early twentieth centuries. Examples (13) and (14) represent metaphorical usage from the 1990s sub-corpus. In Example (13), motor vehicles and alcohol are compared to *servants*, while in Example (14) the speaker describes Abraham Lincoln and Franklin Roosevelt as *great servants of democracy*. The metaphor of a public official being a servant of the people is a common one, and we will return to it in Section 5.

(12)   One could argue that the social chapter began with the Lloyd George Budget, which introduced national insurance. That was seen as a direct threat to employers, and right-wing Conservatives said that they would not stick the stamps on their *domestic servants'* cards because that practice threatened the women who worked for them.   (House of Commons, 23 July 1993, Tony Benn)

(13)   Both the motor vehicle and alcohol, taken separately, may be described as *good servants* and bad masters. Taken together, the combination can be lethal.
(House of Commons, 25 July 1990, Ian Lloyd)

(14)   The fundamental question is how far a democracy is entitled to take measures of an emergency nature to protect democracy itself. That is no new principle. When the state itself was threatened, both Abraham Lincoln and F. D. Roosevelt, who in any democratic society would be respected as *great servants of democracy*, introduced emergency measures to which in normal circumstances they would have objected.
(House of Commons, 11 December 1997, Robert McCartney)

The decreased variation in the use of *servant* can also be seen by examining the frequency of postmodifying prepositional phrases that are used to constrain the reference of the headword, as in Examples (15) and (16).

From *masters* and *servants* to *employers* and *employees*   185

(15) If *the servants of hon. Gentlemen* misconducted themselves, they might be dismissed; but the overseers, who received no reward for their services, were made liable under the Bill to be fined, to be imprisoned, and indicted for misdemeanour.   (House of Commons, 23 May 1834, Sir Samuel Whalley)

(16) The present law was in a most anomalous condition: If a man entered a shop and injured himself by stumbling over a bale of goods, or by falling into a hole, improperly left there by *a servant of the shopkeeper* he had a right of action; but if at a dinner party a basin of soup were thrown over his coat, or, still worse, over the dress of his wife, by a servant, he had no right of action against his host.   (House of Commons, 24 May 1876, William Forsyth)

Our data show that *of* is by far the most common preposition heading the postmodifying prepositional phrase after *servant*. Figure 6.6 shows that the proportion of postmodifying *of*-phrases goes down from its peak in the 1810s, when 53% of all tokens were followed by an *of*-PP, to 7% in the 2000s. This is further evidence of the decreased usage potential of *servant*: as the master–servant institution lost its significance, there was no longer a need to make a distinction between *servants of the Crown* and *servants of the company*, for example. Furthermore, *public servants* and *civil servants* are extremely rarely used with postmodifiers in any case, and this is also reflected in the data.

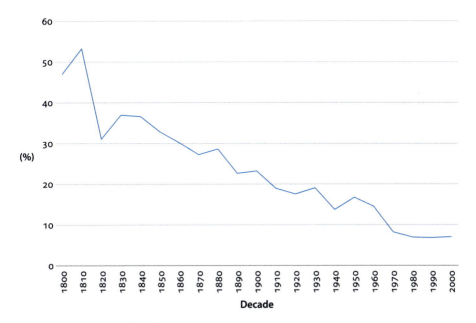

Figure 6.6 Proportion of *of*-PPs following *servant(s)* in the Hansard Corpus

In summary, we have seen in Sections 4.2.1. and 4.2.2. that the changes affecting the use of *masters* and *servants* have proceeded along different paths. In the case of *masters*, the corpus texts can be regarded as rather conservative in the sense that the discussions continue to include references to ancient titles (e.g. *Master of the Rolls*) and historical trade unions (e.g. the *National Association of Master Bakers*). Significantly, in spite of the conservative nature of the corpus, the use of *master* as a term of reference for a private employer falls entirely out of use. *Servant*, on the other hand, has largely become restricted to being used in fixed professional titles for public officials, most notably *civil servants* and *public servants*. This development shows both in the decreased frequency and variation of premodifiers and in the decreased proportion of postmodifying *of*-phrases. In this sense, the remnants of the master–servant institution can largely be seen in the use of *servant*, even though the institution itself has become obsolete. We will return to this point in Section 5.

4.3 Using linguistic outliers to draw attention to historical events

We conclude the empirical part of our chapter with an exploration of how the constructions studied can be used to draw attention to historically extraordinary events. We present two small-scale case studies which are based on data anomalies that were detected in the course of the research project. In both cases, we spotted a surprising peak in the frequency of possessive NPs, which raised the question of whether the data anomaly is caused by random fluctuation or whether an external event could be found to be the underlying cause.

4.3.1 *The Pains and Penalties Bill of 1820*

Our first example concerns an anomaly which we identified in the 1820s data. Figure 6.7 shows that the frequency of *her servant(s)* peaks suddenly, only to decrease immediately in the 1830s.

A closer inspection of the data reveals that the anomaly is due to no fewer than 51 tokens of *her servant(s)* from 1820. The reason for the sudden frequency rise can be explained by the Pains and Penalties Bill, which was introduced in parliament on 5 July 1820. The bill was intended to grant King George IV a divorce from Queen Caroline and to strip Caroline from all her titles and privileges. A trial was subsequently held in the House of Lords, and during the trial the assembled lords heard a number of witnesses questioned by Henry Brougham (Attorney General). Both the Attorney General and the witnesses made frequent reference to the Queen's conduct with her servants (Examples (17) and (18)).

From *masters* and *servants* to *employers* and *employees* 187

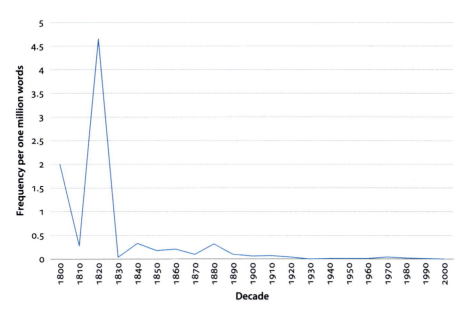

Figure 6.7 Normalised frequency (per million words) of *her servant(s)* in the Hansard Corpus

(17) What manner of conversing with or treating *her servants* had her majesty generally? Uncommon kind, almost to a fault.
(House of Lords, 7 October 1820, Henry Brougham)

(18) But no, my lords, this infatuated attachment had so taken possession of her Majesty's mind, that she actually, in the presence of *her servants*, admits this man, in the garb of a servant, to dine as a companion with her.
(House of Lords, 7 October 1820, Henry Brougham)

The reason why the Queen's relationship with her servants received so much attention in the House of Lords was a rumour that the Queen and her head servant, Bartolomeo Pergami, were lovers, and Example (18) is a direct reference to this rumour. Indeed, King George sought to establish that the Queen was guilty of adultery, which would constitute legal grounds for divorce. The trial of Queen Caroline and the reasons behind it provide an interesting example of how single historical events can affect the frequencies of specific linguistic constructions in corpus data. From another perspective, it shows how the frequency information related to individual constructions can be used to identify historically significant events.

4.3.2 The 1823 slave rebellion in Demerara

Our second example is also from the 1820s. In this case, the data show a conspicuous peak in the use of *his master(s)* and *their master(s)*, as shown in Figure 6.8.

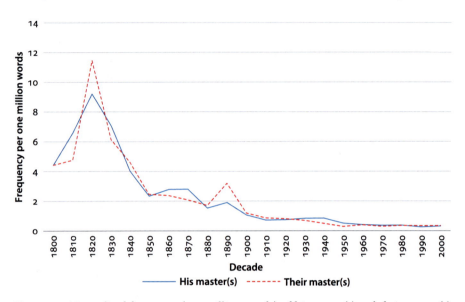

Figure 6.8 Normalised frequency (per million words) of *his master(s)* and *their master(s)* in the Hansard Corpus

The frequency peak can be more precisely located to 1823, and a close reading of the data reveals that the *masters* in question were more specifically slave masters. In this case, the increased frequency of *his/their master(s)* can be explained by a slave rebellion that took place in the colony of Demerara in Guyana. The revolt was brutally crushed by the colonists, and the events attracted much attention in Britain, both in parliament and in the public press. The discussions on the abolition of slavery continued well into the 1830s, which in part explains why the frequency peak in Figure 6.8 goes down relatively gradually. Examples (19) and (20) illustrate the discussions related to the abolition of slavery and the aftermath of the Demerara rebellion in the parliament.

(19) It so happened (and I beg the attention of the House to this), that the principal leaders in this insurrection were high in the confidence of *their masters*; they were trusted, they were well fed, they were well paid, and (if I may be allowed the expression) they were in comparative circumstances of affluence and prosperity. (House of Commons, 1 June 1824, Mary Walrand)

(20) ... liberty, if suddenly given, and, still-more, if violently obtained by men yet unprepared to receive it, would be a curse, and not a blessing; that emancipation must be the work of time, and, above all, must not be wrested forcibly from *their masters*.   (House of Commons, 1 June 1824, Sir Charles Sutton)

In Example (19), the speaker discusses the events in Demerara, arguing that the enslaved people in fact lived in relative prosperity. In Example (20) the speaker engages in the debate concerning the emancipation of enslaved people and argues that it would be irresponsible to release all the slaves in the British colonies at once because they would be ill-prepared to live in freedom. This argument carried much weight in contemporary Britain, and as a consequence, a system of apprenticeship was introduced in some colonies after the Emancipation Act of 1833 was passed. According to the apprentice system, all enslaved people over six years of age would have to serve as apprentices to their former masters for up to eight years before finally gaining their freedom. It is interesting to note that in this short-lived system the slave masters retained their identities as masters. The enslaved people, by contrast, were nominally appointed as apprentices, but in reality, there was little change in their conditions (see e.g. Altink 2001; Holt 1992: 56).

5.   Discussion and conclusions

In this chapter, we have explored how the gradual democratisation of British society is reflected in the discourse pertaining to the participants in the employment relationship in the British parliament. We examined some of the most frequent terms used for different kinds of labourers, as well as two terms used for employers (*master, employer*), with the aim of tracing the democratisation process through time and seeking potential differences between the use of the different terms. We were particularly interested in seeing how *masters* and *servants* were discussed in parliament, as these two roles can be argued to represent a particularly unequal relationship between employers and employees. Our results show that societal democratisation is indeed reflected in the way in which the MPs talked about the different employer and employee groups: the employees start to be increasingly often discussed separately from their employers/masters, which we interpret to be a reflection of the increased independence associated with the status of the labourers. Interestingly, the same trend affected masters/employers, suggesting that the entire concept of employment shifted from a more reciprocal or interdependent relationship to one where the rights and duties of each party are considered and negotiated independently from each other.

From a methodological perspective, our study can be regarded as a corpus-based exploration of democratisation. In this context, it should be pointed out that abstract concepts like 'democratisation' are notoriously difficult to operationalise, and while the constructions that were investigated in this study are intended to capture certain aspects of the democratisation process, they are, of course, open to criticism. We argued, for example, that because possessive noun phrases evoke two referents, they can be used to foreground the dependent nature of the employer/employee relationship. However, it is also true, of course, that the possessive determiner may simply function as a reference point without assuming a particularly interrelated relationship between the referent of the possessive determiner and the referent of the noun. Even so, our data clearly show that the employees were more often discussed together with the employers (and vice versa) in the early Hansard data, and our previous knowledge of the democratisation of British society provides a plausible explanation for this.

When it comes to *masters* and *servants*, our data show a clear decrease in the use of *masters* over time. The term continues to be used with some frequency in parliament due to the longevity of fixed honorary titles (*Master of the Rolls*) as well as names of trade unions, which were established at a time when *master* was still more widely used. However, although parliamentary discourse has retained some traces of nineteenth-century society in this respect, it does reflect the general democratisation affecting the employment relationship in other ways. For instance, private employers are no longer referred to as *masters*, and metaphorical uses (e.g. when an MP speaks mockingly about another MP's 'political masters') increase over time in our data.

The term *servant*, on the other hand, has mainly lived on in two terms: *civil servant* and *public servant*. The reason for this could be that employees in the public sector are no longer truly considered to be servants in the literal sense of the word. In other words, instead of being regarded as socially inferior and dependent workers, *civil servants* and *public servants* are now conceptualised as being metaphorical servants to the public, and this is perceived to be a noble and valuable cause. In addition to observing changes in the use of premodifying adjectives, our results on the use of postmodifying PPs show that the status of servants was changing steadily throughout the nineteenth and the twentieth centuries. Interestingly, this result, as well as our data on the declining frequency of adjectives used to describe servants in private employment, does not agree with the argument that World War I functioned as a cultural watershed after which the servant institution started to crumble: from a linguistic perspective, the development was gradual, and it was already underway in the early 1800s.

Finally, we discussed how data anomalies can be used to draw attention to specific historical events. This would be a rather trivial point if the question was just about single words or lexemes, of course, as the frequency of a particular topic has obvious consequences for the frequency of the associated key terminology. However, we should emphasise that it would not be possible to identify the events discussed in either of our case studies in Section 4.3 by a simple lexeme-based search: the anomalies only become apparent through the study of the possessive construction. Indeed, we suggest that our approach could prove useful in overcoming some of the difficulties that arise when studying the connection between societal developments and language use. By investigating constructions that can plausibly be connected to language-external phenomena, we can gain a clearer perspective on the data and form hypotheses that might explain some of the irregular fluctuations in text frequencies.

Our chapter is a first look at a complex phenomenon that developed over an extended period of time. We consider parliamentary discourse to be a useful starting point for studying the democratisation of the employment relationship, as the labour laws that were passed in parliament directly affected the duties and responsibilities of both employers and employees. However, it is also true that the Hansard data offers just one perspective to this development. For example, while we found support for the results presented in this chapter in a study on witness depositions (the Old Bailey Corpus), our exploration of late nineteenth-century newspaper data yielded different results (see Vartiainen et al. 2021 for both case studies): instead of debates over the rights and working conditions of the workforce, we find a large number of classified ads where people are looking for employment as servants and make frequent mention of their previous masters. In other words, texts in different genres offer different views on society, and it would be a mistake to form strong generalisations based on a single genre.

In the future, a more systematic investigation into the development of work-related terminology could uncover more detailed information about the timeline and specific developments of the democratisation of the employment relationship. Even if we limit the scope of the study to *masters* and *servants*, it is obvious that we are dealing with macro-level roles that conceal a great deal of micro-level variation. Servants, for example, may have been referred to using a more specific description, such as *butler*, *farmhand*, *maid*, *valet*, and so on. In this respect, resources like the *Historical Thesaurus of English* or the *HISCO* database (<https://iisg.amsterdam/en/data/data-websites/history-of-work/>) could prove useful in the identification of all the relevant terminology and serve as the basis for a more comprehensive linguistic account of the employment roles in nineteenth- and twentieth-century Britain.

References

Alexander, Marc & Davies, Mark. 2015. The Hansard Corpus 1803–2005. <https://www.english-corpora.org/hansard/> (1 May 2019).

Altink, Henrice. 2001. Slavery by another name: Apprenticed women in the Jamaican workhouses in the period 1834–1838. *Social History* 26(1): 40–59.

Atkinson, Evelyn. 2013. Out of the household: Master–servant relations and employer liability law. *Yale Journal of Law & the Humanities* 25(2): 205–270.

Blackstone, William. 1758. *An Analysis of the Laws of England* (3rd edn). Oxford: Clarendon Press. <https://heinonline.org/HOL/P?h=hein.beal/anlaengo001&i=1> (1 May 2019).

Davies, Mark. 2018. Corpus-based studies of lexical and semantic variation: The importance of both corpus size and corpus design. In *From Data to Evidence in English Language Research*, Carla Suhr, Terttu Nevalainen & Irma Taavitsainen (eds), 66–87. Leiden: Brill.

Farrelly, Michael & Seoane, Elena. 2012. Democratisation. In *The Oxford Handbook of the History of English*, Terttu Nevalainen & Elizabeth Closs Traugott (eds), 392–401. Oxford: OUP.

Frank, Christopher. 2004. Britain, the defeat of the 1844 Master and Servants Bill. In *Masters, Servants, and Magistrates in Britain and the Empire, 1562–1955*, Douglas Hay & Paul Craven (eds), 402–421. Chapel Hill NC: University of North Carolina Press.

Frank, Christopher. 2016 [2010]. *Master and Servant Law: Chartists, Trade Unions, Radical Lawyers and the Magistracy in England, 1840–1865*. London: Routledge.

Garrard, John. 2002. *Democratisation in Britain: Elites, Civil Society, and Reform since 1800*. Houndmills: Palgrave Macmillan.

Greenfield, Patricia M. 2013. The changing psychology of culture from 1800 through 2000. *Psychological Science* 24(9): 1722–1731.

Hay, Douglas. 2004. England, 1562–1875: The law and its uses. In *Masters, Servants, and Magistrates in Britain and the Empire, 1562–1955*, Douglas Hay & Paul Craven (eds), 59–116. Chapel Hill NC: University of North Carolina Press.

Higgs, Edward. 1982. The tabulation of occupations in the nineteenth-century census, with special reference to domestic servants. *Local Population Studies* 28: 58–66.

Higgs, Edward. 1983. Domestic servants and households in Victorian England. *Social History* 8(2): 201–210.

Hilpert, Martin. 2020. The great temptation: What diachronic corpora do and do not reveal about social change. In *Corpora and the Changing Society. Studies in the Evolution of English* [Studies in Corpus Linguistics 96], Paula Rautionaho, Arja Nurmi & Juhani Klemola (eds), 3–27. Amsterdam: John Benjamins.

Hiltunen, Turo, Räikkönen, Jenni & Tyrkkö, Jukka. 2020. Investigating colloquialization in the British parliamentary record in the late 19th and early 20th century. In *New Perspectives on Democratization: Evidence from English(es)*, Turo Hiltunen & Lucía Loureiro-Porto (eds). Special issue of *Language Sciences* 79: 101270.

Holt, Thomas C. 1992. *The Problem of Freedom: Race, Labor, and Politics in Jamaica and Britain, 1832–1938*. Baltimore MD: Johns Hopkins University Press.

Huber, Magnus, Nissel, Magnus, Maiwald, Patrick & Widlitzki, Bianca. 2012. The Old Bailey Corpus: Spoken English in the 18th and 19th centuries. <www.uni-giessen.de/oldbaileycorpus> (1 May 2019).

Langacker, Ronald W. 1995. Possession and possessive constructions. In *Language and the Cognitive Construal of the World*, John R. Taylor & Robert E. MacLaury (eds), 51–80. Berlin: Walter de Gruyter.

Leech, Geoffrey, Hundt, Marianne, Mair, Christian & Smith, Nicholas. 2009. *Change in Contemporary English: A Grammatical Study*. Cambridge: CUP.

Leek, Martyn. 2013. NAMB to be called Craft Bakers' Association. *British Baker*. <https://bakeryinfo.co.uk/news/namb-to-be-called-craft-bakers-association/617801.article> (7 November 2019).

Macdonagh, Michael. 1903 [1886]. *The Life of Daniel O'Connell*. London: Cassell & Company.

Meek, Fiona. 2021. *History of Employment Law*. Morton Fraser Lawyers. <https://www.morton-fraser.com/knowledge-hub/history-employment> (28 August 2021).

Meldrum, Tim. 2000. *Domestic Service and Gender 1660–1750: Life and Work in the London Household*. Harlow: Longman Pearson Education.

Michel, Jean-Baptiste, Shen, Yuan Kui, Aiden, Aviva Presser, Veres, Adrian, Gray, Matthew K., The Google Books Team, Pickett, Joseph P., Hoiberg, Dale, Clancy, Dan, Norvig, Peter, Orwant, Jon, Pinker, Steven, Nowak, Martin A. & Aiden, Erez Lieberman. 2011. Quantitative analysis of culture using millions of digitized books. *Science* 331(6014): 176–182.

Mollin, Sandra. 2007. The Hansard hazard: Gauging the accuracy of British parliamentary transcripts. *Corpora* 2(2): 187–210.

OED Online. 2000–. *Oxford English Dictionary*. OUP <https://www.oed.com/> (1 May 2019).

Rix, Kathryn. 2014. "Whatever passed in Parliament ought to be communicated to the public": Reporting the proceedings of the Reformed Commons, 1833–1850. *Parliamentary History* 33(3): 453–474.

Slembrouck, Stef. 1992. The parliamentary Hansard 'verbatim' report: The written construction of spoken discourse. *Language and Literature* 1(2): 101–119.

Steinfeld, Robert J. 1991. *The Invention of Free Labor: The Employment Relation in English and American Law and Culture, 1350–1870*. Chapel Hill NC: University of North Carolina Press.

Vartiainen, Turo. 2017. The portrayal of infanticide victims in the Proceedings of the Old Bailey, 1674–1775. *Journal of Historical Sociolinguistics* 3(2): 173–196.

Vartiainen, Turo, Hiltunen, Turo & Palander-Collin, Minna. 2021. Linguistic contexts of social change: Tracing the decline of the master–servant institution in three historical corpora. In *The Role of Context in the Production and Reception of Historical News Discourse*, Nicholas Brownlees (ed.), 129–153. Bern: Peter Lang.

CHAPTER 7

From criminal lunacy to mental disorder
The changing lexis of mental health in the British parliament

Minna Nevala & Jukka Tyrkkö
University of Helsinki | Linnaeus University

This chapter investigates discourses of mental health in the British parliament over two centuries (1800–2020). A pattern-driven approach is used to explore terminology related to mentally ill people, mental institutions, and mental health in general. The study focuses on lexical trends in parliamentary discourse, the extent to which mental health discourse was discussed in general, and the way in which the lexis of modern mental health care has developed. The results show that the major shifts in the entire lexical field have happened in specific time periods, the turning points being in the 1840s, 1930s and 1950s. The general attitude also seems to have shifted, and the data show an increasing concern for legally protecting people with mental illness.

Keywords: mental health, mentally ill people, mental health legislation, lexis, parliamentary discourse, big data

1. Introduction

Democratisation has been one of the enduring processes in Western societies since the early nineteenth century. Defined as a societal movement that widens the visibility of minorities and strives to grant all citizens equal opportunities to participate in public decision-making, democratisation can be observed in language as a growing tendency to adopt linguistic and discursive features and practices that reduce social distance, avoid face-threatening acts, afford agency to all, and take care to adopt referential practices that are inclusive in terms of who are referenced and how reference is made (see e.g. Farrelly & Seoane 2012; McConnell-Ginet 2003). In recent years, mixed-methods approaches characterised by the use of both corpus-aided discourse analysis and socio-pragmatic methods have allowed the tracking of social and cultural developments over long

https://doi.org/10.1075/scl.111.07nev
© 2023 John Benjamins Publishing Company

periods of time from an evidence-based perspective that would have been impossible only a decade ago (see Baker & McEnery 2016; Froehlich 2016; Partington 2013; Tyrkkö 2019).

In the present study, we use the Hansard Corpus as our primary data as we focus on discourses of mental health in the British parliament from 1803 to 2005 (see Arnold 2008; Houston 2000; O'Reilly 2014). Adopting a primarily lexical starting point, we begin by selecting all lexical items used to refer to people with mental illness, to insanity as a condition, and to mental institutions from the relevant categories in the *Historical Thesaurus of English* (hereafter HTE). We then employ a pattern-driven approach to explore the full repertoire of the above-mentioned mental health words, investigating their phraseological and discursive uses both quantitatively and qualitatively.[1] In the quantitative part of the analysis, we are particularly interested in lexical trends in parliamentary discourse; that is, in determining the extent to which mental health discourse was discussed in parliamentary debates, how such topics fluctuated over time, and how the lexis of modern mental health care developed in the parliamentary context. A more qualitative approach is used in the analysis of specific lexical phenomena, focusing in particular on the keyword term *lunatic* and its lexical associations over time. Along the way, we give examples and reflect on what parliamentary discourse reveals about prevalent societal attitudes about mentally ill people as a socially marginalised group (see Froehlich 2016; Hintikka & Nevala 2017; Nevala 2019).

2. Two hundred years of 'mad' society: On British mental health history and legislation

2.1 Social view

Mental illness is one of the most prominent reasons for stigmatisation in all societies. A person perceived to have a mental illness is "dis-qualified from full social acceptance" (Porter 2002: 62): they are commonly believed to be dangerous to themselves and others; to breach moral and social rules, causing discomfort and outrage; and to be incapable of making decisions concerning their own lives. Consequently, societies have sought to implement laws and processes that impose limits on the activities and rights of mentally ill people. Although the procedures of setting the sick apart from the healthy have differed widely throughout the world, the common approach in developed societies has been to rely on medical authority in this enterprise of stigmatisation. When clear lines could be drawn

---

1. For discussion of pattern-driven approaches, see Tyrkkö and Kopaczyk (2018).

between the sane and the crazy, the polarisation also began to legitimise the institutionalising of people with mental illness, which was a common trend from the eighteenth century onwards. The 'mentally ill', a descriptor that covers a wide range of real and supposed conditions from low intelligence and personality disorders to clinically attested psychiatric illnesses, were increasingly sequestered away into asylums and institutions which, especially in the early days, resembled prisons in both theory and practice. Unsurprisingly, it has been commonplace to assert that members of the social margins are all mentally ill to some extent: paupers and beggars, criminals, streetwalkers and vagabonds formed the bulk of the marginalised group, which was seen as not only dangerous and monstrous but also as insane and idiotic (Porter 2002: 92; see O'Reilly 2014 on the stigmatisation of women and immigrants as socially marginal in the Victorian press; also Nevala 2019 on criminals). At times, the notion of 'marginal' has also included women, as already in the early nineteenth century "the symbolic gender of the insane person shifted from male to female" (Long 2015: 133). Madness or hysteria has often been described as a form of sickness characterised by loss of reason, with women being more prone to irrational behaviour than men (see e.g. Froelich 2016 on early modern women). Similarly, the characteristics and behaviours of ethnic and other minorities – homosexual people, transgender people, and many other groups – have been medicalised as mental illnesses.

In Victorian times, mentally ill people were classified as a 'filthy' part of society and the public use of derogatory terms was widely accepted. Although mental illnesses were increasingly recognised as inherently medical issues, those that had them were also seen as deviant and perverse 'monsters' who constituted a threat, and who therefore needed to be locked up and kept away from respectable and proper citizens (Nevala 2019). In Britain, around 5,000 people were held in specialised lunatic asylums before 1800, and it has been estimated that as many mentally ill people occupied various workhouses, bride-wells and jails (Porter 2002: 95; see also Scull, MacKenzie & Hervey 2014). In nineteenth-century England, patient numbers climbed from approximately 10,000 to ten times that number in 1900 (Porter 2002: 112). At the beginning of the nineteenth century, no medical supervision was required in the asylums, and it was not until the 1820s that a series of Acts were passed that mandated medical presence first in public and later in private asylums. This did not, however, mean that psychiatry as we understand it today was the driving medical force behind these institutions from the start. Many mental institutions were known for their cruelty and corruption, and the idea behind the madhouses was to brutally tame 'the wild beasts' by using physical restraint, bloodletting, ice cold baths, purges and vomits (Porter 2002: 100). One of the main purposes of asylums was to prove that, herded together, people with mental illness would be reduced to the lowest common denominator. Still, visiting notorious mental asylums like Bedlam (Bethlem Royal Hospital in London) was considered public entertainment, and the well-to-do flocked in to see the psychotic mad. Victorian pessimists saw asylums not as hospitals for the treatment of insanity, but warehouses for storing incurable lunatics. Gradually over the course of the nineteenth century, practical psychiatry was transformed via asylum experience, and a well-managed asylum was seen as a tool for restoring mentally ill people to health, instead of merely keeping them away from respectable society.

Since the 1900s, mental illness has been discussed more as a personal challenge affecting millions of people than as an anomaly. The World Wars seem to have been a kind of a watershed in many respects. By the 1950s, psychiatry had permanently moved away from thinking of mental illness as something characteristic of socially marginal groups, traditionally perceived as, for example, 'lunatics', criminals or the poor. The 1950s pop culture already created new psychological types like the juvenile delinquent, and in the twenty-first century, new descriptions arise, such as 'emos', referring to teenaged followers of a music trend associated with emotional expression, sensitivity, introversion, depression, self-harm and suicide.

One part of the shift from talking about madness as a disease to discussing mental health in terms of a disorder or personal challenge certainly relates to the notion of patient autonomy. In the nineteenth century, the medical staff both in public and private establishments rarely listened to the patients' requests and barely addressed or treated them as human beings (Scull, MacKenzie & Hervey 2014: 30–31; see also Suzuki 1999).[2] Patients in asylums had no say in what was done to them in terms of treatment even in the early twentieth century: electric shock treatment was introduced to treat shell shock and schizophrenia by force in the 1920s and 1930s. The development of psychiatric medicine in the early 1950s gave mentally ill people a better chance to decide for themselves, since they made it possible for many patients to leave psychiatric hospitals and maintain 'normal' life, under medication. In many present-day societies, the segregation of 'the sane' from 'the mad' is no longer seen as a straightforward norm. Modern psychiatry has come to the conclusion that the greatest proportion of mental disorders can in reality be found not in the asylum but in the community at large, opting for integration instead of segregation.

---

2. The most famous of mentally ill people in Britain, King George III, complained, "I hate all the physicians, but most the Willises; they beat me like a madman" (Porter 1987: 235).

2.2 Legislation and terminology

As a legislative body, the British parliament both makes laws and exercises oversight of the government. Throughout the nineteenth and the twentieth centuries, issues to do with mental health and people with mental illness have been discussed in parliament with some regularity, with changes in the language reflecting the gradual changing of attitudes. Although medical views already carried some weight in the nineteenth-century public debates about mental health, it was not until the twentieth century that psychiatrists and other mental health professionals took on an increasingly prominent role in the public domain, notably both in the courtrooms and in law-making. By the nineteenth century, "lunatics and idiots" (Porter 2002:154) in Britain had long been, under certain circumstances, made wards of the state, and it was accepted that 'the insane', not being responsible for their acts, should be "exempt from punishment for criminal deeds" (ibid.). Distinguishing criminality from insanity was not thought to require medical expertise, and, for example, friends and family were often called in to testify in court. This started changing from the early decades of the nineteenth century onwards, however, when psychiatric experts were increasingly asked to testify in cases where insanity was suspected. They have since been the most prominent sources for the definition of mental illness in law-making.

Legislation in general has been influential for and influenced by public discourse on mental health in Britain. The way mental issues have been perceived and talked about either as indicative of sin, crime, danger, social degradation, illness, symptomaticity or brain electricity is evident in the contents and causes for various laws about mental illness and mentally ill people. Starting from the 1774 Madhouses Act, the parliament required that all *madhouses* be licensed by a committee of the Royal College of Physicians. This license, renewed annually, would permit the holder to maintain a single house for accommodating lunatics. The 1800 Act already used the term *criminal lunatics*. It aimed at placing criminally lunatic people in prison, particularly those who threatened the King. The consequent long-term detention of lunatics in county gaols in turn triggered the 1808 County Asylums Act, the main purpose of which was to remove lunatics from gaols and workhouses to *asylums* where they would be easier to manage. Since members of the lowest social class were considered unable to take care of themselves, the 1834 Poor Law was established to build workhouses for paupers all over England and Wales. Following this act, asylums and other institutions grew in number, resulting in more schools, hospitals, lunatic asylums and aged care homes. As a consequence of the slow progress in moving mentally ill people to asylums of their own, the Lunacy Act 1845 created the Lunacy Commission to focus on legislation. The Lunacy Act's most important result was a change in the status of mentally ill people to *patients*.

Various Lunacy and Idiocy Acts followed in the latter half of the nineteenth century. The Lunacy Act 1890, in particular, was very influential in forming the basis of mental health law in England and Wales from 1890 until 1959. It placed an obligation on local authorities to maintain institutions for people with mental illness, as well as to pay closer attention to those who were not under proper care and control, or who were cruelly treated or neglected. The way in which mentally ill people were discussed changed at the beginning of the twentieth century, when the Mental Deficiency Act was issued in 1913. The Act made provisions for the institutional treatment of people deemed *mentally deficient*, also referred to as *idiots* (unable to guard themselves against common physical dangers), *imbeciles* (incapable of managing themselves or their affairs), *feeble-minded persons* (requiring care, supervision or control, for their protection or for the protection of others) and *moral defectives* (displaying mental weakness with strong vicious or criminal propensities). Further into the century, the Mental Treatment Act 1930 permitted voluntary admission to, and outpatient treatment within, psychiatric hospitals. It replaced the term *asylum* with *mental hospital*.

In the 1950s, legal terminology increasingly changed towards that of mental health. The *Report of the Royal Commission on the Law Relating to Mental Illness and Mental Deficiency* (1954–1957), amongst others, stated that "persons needing care because of mental disorder should be able to receive it as far as possible with no more restriction of liberty or legal formality than is applied to people needing care because of other types of illness, disability or social or economic difficulty" (*Mental Health* 1957: 100). In the years following, mental illness was talked of more and more as a disability, ultimately leading to the 2005 Mental Capacity Act, which aims at protecting people who lack capacity to make particular decisions, but also at maximising their ability to make decisions or to participate in decision-making. Instead of labelling such people as mentally ill, deficient or disabled, the Act refers to *a person without capacity* (Social Care Institute for Excellence 2016 [2006]).

2.3   The Hansard as a record of parliamentary discourse

The present study examines mental health discourse in the British parliament with specific focus on the House of Commons.[3] To do this, we use the Hansard, which is "the edited verbatim report of proceedings of both the House of

---

3. Hansard did not have reporters in the House of Lords before 1889, and as a result the Hansard record is quite unreliable for the House of Lords before that time (see Jordan 1931: 442).

Commons and the House of Lords".[4] As culturally significant databases go, the Hansard is an unusual one because unlike many other archives and collections, it may be described as a *complete dataset*. What we mean by this is that rather than being a sample drawn from a wider population of texts, the Hansard really does comprise all the extant relevant texts, in this case records of all parliamentary debates in the British parliament. Consequently, the Hansard offers an uninterrupted and comprehensive view of how new laws concerning mentally ill and intellectually challenged people were made, the attitudes that members of parliament (MPs) had toward those affected, the development of mental health institutions, and other relevant questions. While it goes without saying that parliamentary debates are only one part of the overall political discourse, they are culturally, socially and politically central in a unique way.

Several chapters in this volume discuss the composition and representativeness of the Hansard corpus as a linguistic resource (see Alexander, this volume), and consequently we will make mention of only a few of the most important caveats. The most consequential of these is the fact that up until 1909, the Hansard was based on reporters' notes rather than consistently produced transcriptions, and thus the early records consist primarily of indirect reported speech, occasionally interspersed with other supporting text types. From 1909 onwards, the parliament employed their own transcribers, or 'reporters' as they are still called for historical reasons. The primary style of the Hansard thus switched to transcribed direct speech, even though the record continues to include written texts as well, such as petitions and written statements. The effects of this text-typological shift are substantial, as demonstrated by Hiltunen, Räikkönen and Tyrkkö (2020) in a large-scale diachronic study of n-gram frequencies, and any study crossing this watershed year ought to pay close attention to how it may have affected the linguistic features they are interested in. In general, studies focusing on lexis and phraseology should be reasonably unaffected, while those focusing on features known to be sensitive to mode of the discourse are likely to be more affected.

The general reliability of the Hansard as a record of spoken language has long been discussed by both parliamentary historians (see Aspinall 1956; Browne 2017; MacDonagh 1913) and linguists (see Mollin 2007), with the consensus view being that the parliament's oft-quoted claim that the Hansard is "a substantially verbatim record of what is said in parliament" is largely accurate (see also Kotze et al., this volume). In addition to inevitable human errors, the scribes also silently correct breaches of parliamentary rules, such as changing instances of direct address by one MP to another into addresses of the Speaker, removing hesitations and false starts, and so on (see Alexander, this volume, and Kotze et al., this volume).

---

4. See <https://hansard.parliament.uk>.

It goes without saying that these revisions will affect some types of research more than others, and in the present case we feel confident that the lexical and discursive dimensions of mental health debates are unlikely to be substantially affected by scribal practices.

3. Data and methods

3.1 The Hansard Corpus

The Hansard Corpus comprises the complete record of all the debates in the British parliament from 1803 to 2005. A dataset of 1.6 billion words and 7.5 million individual debate speeches, the corpus was compiled by the SAMUELS project at the University of Glasgow and released in 2016. At the time this article was written, the Hansard Corpus was available online on two websites: the Brigham Young server <https://www.english-corpora.org/hansard/> and the Hansard at Huddersfield server <https://hansard.hud.ac.uk/> (see also Jeffries et al., this volume). Although providing access to the same underlying dataset, the two corpus tools cater to somewhat different groups of core users and consequently offer slightly different functionalities. However, because the research design of the present study required us to access the corpus at a very detailed level, the study was carried out using a standalone version of the XML-annotated Hansard Corpus and its accompanying metadata files.[5]

Both the overall annual word count and the number of individual debates per year increased significantly well into the first half of the twentieth century, after which point they levelled out. Figure 7.1 illustrates the increase in the total number of words per year.[6]

3.2 Lexis of mental health

The semantic field of mental health covers a wide range of related topics. In the present study, we included words that refer to people with mental illness and those mentally deficient, to insanity as a condition, and to mental institutions. We

---

5. We are grateful to the SAMUELS project and especially to Marc Alexander and Fraser Dallachy for providing us with a copy of the corpus. The data were primarily queried using Python; when other tools were used, they are described in the text.

6. Due to changes in constituency boundaries, the number of MPs has fluctuated over the last two centuries. There were 658 MPs after the Act of Union 1800, 707 after the World War I and the Representation of the People Act, and between 615 and 659 between 1922 and the present day.

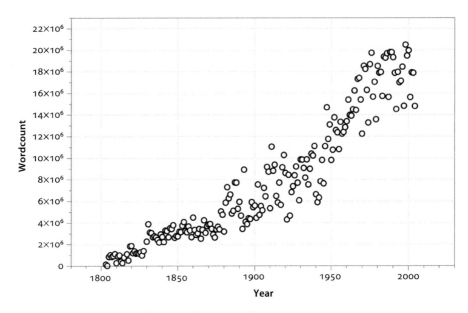

Figure 7.1 Increase in wordcount of the Hansard Corpus over two centuries

did not, as a rule, include specific medical terms, though some of the included words are admittedly borderline cases; *dementia*, for example, is both a medical term referring to a condition of the brain but also a noun used by those outside of the medical profession and in earlier times, especially in reference to mental deficiency. We take as a premise that the terms investigated will be primarily associated with contemporaneous legislative efforts concerning mental health, but rather than trying to predict which terms might be relevant, we approach term selection as broadly as possible.

The first step in the analysis is to establish the inventory of lexical items associated with mental health discourses, relying on the HTE. While only a small fraction of the words in the relevant categories of the HTE appear in the Hansard,[7] it is informative to start with a general overview of the entire lexical field to identify periods of *linguistic trauma*, defined by Alexander (2018) as periods that witness sudden increases in the number of new words within a particular semantic category. Such periods typically signal contemporaneous societal, scientific or technological changes, which create the need for new terms, cause semantic shifts in existing terms, or expose the language community to loanwords through new language contacts. Figure 7.2 shows a timeline of first attestation for the 249

---

7. Although more relaxed today than it was before, parliamentary language is regulated, and colloquial and offensive words are not only deemed unacceptable in speech, but also to be recorded in the Hansard.

lexical items associated with eleven categories in the HTE relevant to mental hospitals, mental deficiency, mentally ill people and the intellectually weak (see Appendix 1), which can be conceptually grouped into three 'macro categories': mental illness, the mentally ill, and institutions of mental care. At this initial stage, we included all items from the Middle English period onward regardless of how widely or for how long each was in use. The first attestations are based on the OED data available through the HTE in October 2019.

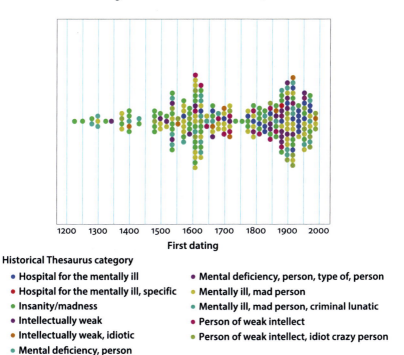

Figure 7.2 Emergence of relevant lexical items in relevant semantic categories of the HTE

The timeline demonstrates that the Elizabethan era and the turn of the nineteenth century were particularly productive periods when it comes to new mental health words (see Figure 7.3). By contrast, it appears that few new words in these semantic fields entered the language during the latter half of the seventeenth century and during the entire eighteenth century. Furthermore, we can see that during the first surge of new terms, the new words mostly referred to *mentally ill people* or to *insanity*, while during the second surge, the emerging institutional context was in evidence in the form of new words referring to *institutional mental care*, such as mental hospitals. The second surge also saw a widening referential range, with an increasing number of words for intellectually challenged people who are not necessarily mentally ill.

A closer look at the centuries relevant to the present study shows that the majority of new words that appeared during this period entered the language between 1870 and 1950, in particular words for mentally ill people, the intellectually weak and psychiatric institutions. Some of the new words in these categories include *crazy, crackpot, looney, deficient, defective, dotty, barmy, natural, nut-house* and *bin*. Appendix 1 shows the higher frequency items in bold.

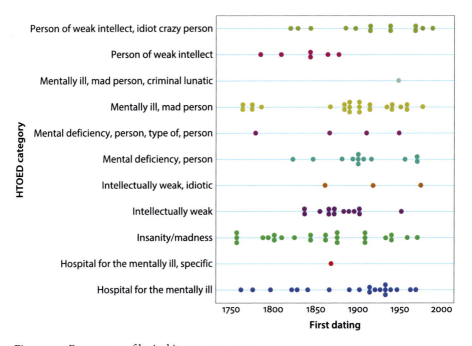

Figure 7.3 Emergence of lexical items, 1750–2000

3.3 Analytical steps

The next step in the analysis was to identify the lexical items that occur in the Hansard at substantial enough frequencies to warrant further quantitative and qualitative analyses. We ran queries for all the items discussed in Section 3.2, with the exception of a selection of polysemous words that occur frequently in a wide variety of contexts and which therefore would have required excessive amounts of manual disambiguation work in order to weed out false positives; these words include *retreat, sick, silly, soft, weak, wanting, natural, unfortunate*, and *fan*. This pruning of the lexical inventory left us with 181 items,[8] which included all the

---

8. As can be seen in Appendix 1, we include multiword units under the definition of *lexical item* in this analytical framework.

higher frequency items. Normalised frequencies (per million words) were calculated for each term on a year-by-year basis using the number of occurrences and total word counts per year and visualised as line charts.[9]

For a more general overview, we also study the agreement of lexical trends over time in the entire lexical repertoire. In order to discern groups of items that follow similar trendlines, we use a dimension reduction method called PROC VARCLUS or *variable clustering*, which can be thought of as a divisive and iterative extension of principal component analysis (see Hiltunen, Räikkönen & Tyrkkö 2020).[10] Primarily used for reducing collinearity in regression models, variable clustering organises the variables into groups based on similarity and for each group identifies a single variable that best represents the group. In the present study, we use the method to identify lexical items with similar diachronic patterns.

Finally, we will briefly discuss the number of individual debates in which the words were used and explore the topics of the debate. This analytical framework allowed us to examine both changes within mental health discourse as well as the use of words related to mental health in other contexts. For reasons of space, we focused on the most frequent mental health term, *lunatic*. We quantified the number of times the term was used by every individual MP to see how uniform or clustered the discourse was, and we carried out collocation analysis on the terms *lunatic* and *lunatics* to explore the changing lexical environments of the terms.

4. Analysis

4.1 Quantitative results: The big picture

The aggregate diachronic trend of all the high-frequency terms reveals a clear historical pattern. The House of Commons discussed mental illnesses, mentally disabled people, and the institutions in which they were held and treated, with considerable interest from the 1860s all the way to World War II, and much less between the beginning of the War and the end of the millennium (see Figure 7.4). The nature of law-making means that the topics that the parliament engages with change from year to year, and this can be seen in the way that the lexical frequency

---

9. We treat the Hansard as a population rather than a sample, that is, we are only interested in what the record shows was said in the House of Commons. Consequently, we are not making inferences based on the observed frequencies but rather reporting the true occurrences.

10. For statistical details, see SAS/STAT User guide, version 15.1, as well as Sanche and Lonergan (2006). The clustering was carried out using the statistical tool JMP 15.

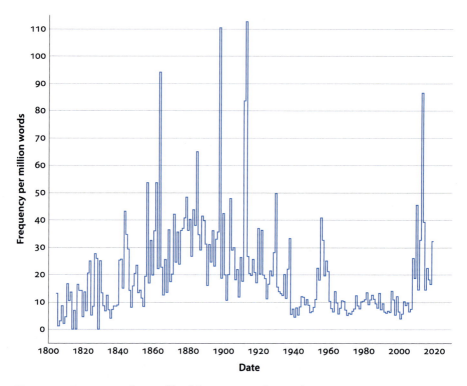

Figure 7.4 Frequency of mental health terms over the timeline (normalised frequency per million words)

curves show much greater peaks and valleys than what we would typically see in a large diachronic corpus.

Breaking the timeline into the three macro categories of illness, person and institution, we see that the parliament has shown more interest in persons and illnesses, rather than institutions (see Figure 7.5).

4.1.1 *References to persons with psychiatric disabilities*

The trendlines of the major terms referring to individuals with psychiatric disabilities reveal at once the overwhelming frequency of the term *lunatic* (see Figure 7.6). Although the term was particularly frequent during the nineteenth century, it did not wane entirely thereafter and in fact appears to have been used all the way through the twentieth century. The terms *idiot* and *imbecile* were in more or less equal use during the nineteenth century; the former more at the beginning of the century and the latter toward the end. Of the two, *idiot* was generally considered the more serious condition. *Madman*, which differs from the

The changing lexis of mental health   207

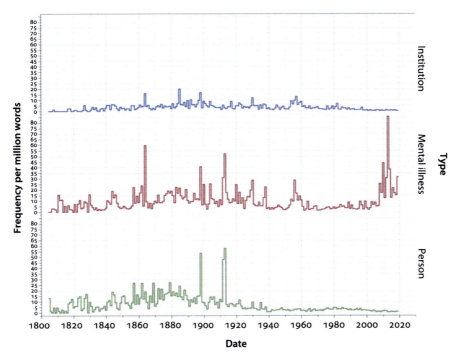

Figure 7.5 References to mental health terms by type over the timeline (normalised frequency per million words)

other terms by not having a medical meaning, was also somewhat frequent during the nineteenth century.

The term *lunatic* was very frequently used in the House of Commons throughout the nineteenth century and indeed all the way to World War II. Contrary to the non-technical and possibly comedic connotations that the term *lunatic* might have today, it was considered a neutral term throughout much of the time period discussed here. Figure 7.7 gives a closer look at the frequency curve of *criminal lunatic* and *pauper lunatic*. The two terms were not highly frequent, but they were persistently used all the way into the twentieth century. Given the limitations of public health services, the relative lack of sophistication in psychiatry and general sentiments toward mentally ill people, it was commonplace to discuss the three intersecting challenges of mental illness, poverty and criminality as a single concept. The figures show that the term *criminal lunatic* came into use at the beginning of the 1860s and remained in use until 1940, while *pauper lunatic* both emerged and withered away twenty years earlier.

One of the common topics debated in parliament was the need for more humane treatment of mentally challenged people, with increasingly loud voices

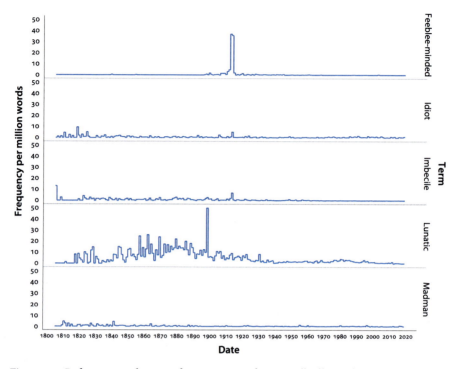

Figure 7.6 References to the most frequent terms for mentally ill people (normalised frequency per million words)

calling for treatment in medical, rather than penal, institutions. Example (1) comes from Mr. Leonard Courtney (10 August 1882).

(1) MR. COURTNEY explained that *pauper lunatic criminals* whose sentences had expired ceased to be *criminals*, and were then simply *pauper lunatics* like any *ordinary pauper lunatic*.

While the technical sense of *lunatic* started to disappear during the first decades of the twentieth century, the term persisted as a colloquial word for someone not fully in control of their mental faculties. References to lunatics were increasingly made as expressions of exasperation over someone else's lack of judgment or inability for rational behaviour, as seen in Example (2), from Mr. Gilbert Mitchison (17 November 1948).

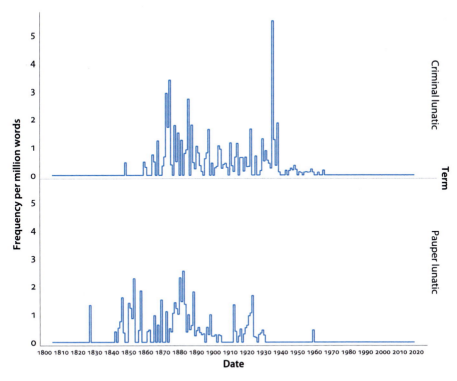

Figure 7.7 References to *criminal lunatic* and *pauper lunatic* over the timeline (normalised frequency per million words)

(2) We want to make ancillary provisions, such as are made in this Bill, for compensation to shareholders, for dealing with labour relations and matters of that sort in the future.
That is quite right and proper. But to attempt to put anything more into it would be to take a step which no private industrialist would ever dream of taking in his own affairs, and which *only a lunatic*, bereft of foresight and any appreciation of what a changing world this is, would attempt for a moment to put into an Act of Parliament.

The semantic shift continued over the rest of the century. In Example (3), Mr. Andrew Bowden comments (on 17 February 1986), on the tactics of animal rights campaigners. It is clear that although Mr. Bowden opposes the activists in the strongest of terms, the word *lunatic* is no longer used in reference to psychiatric illness.

(3) I understand and respect the sincerity of the mobilisation group, but I believe that its tactics are wrong. I totally condemn the extremist groups which go way beyond the mobilisation group and are prepared to use violence. The actions of such groups will, sooner or later, lead to the death of individuals because they are much more concerned with creating anarchy and chaos than helping animals. I hope that everyone in the House will totally disassociate themselves from that *complete lunatic*, extremist and anarchist fringe.

As the high frequency of *lunatic* renders the frequency curves of the other contemporary terms somewhat difficult to read, we also supply the curves separately in Figure 7.8. In addition to *idiot*, *imbecile* and *madman* we also include the term *fanatic*, which was often used to describe a person with extreme passions for a particular cause[11] – there are several examples of MPs describing themselves as fanatics for a particular cause. In many cases the usage suggests enthusiasm bordering on obsession, particularly for religious matters, and we note that especially in the early decades *fanatic* often co-occurs with *bigot*. Notably, the usage of all these terms decreases markedly around World War II. A curious example of another short-lived term is *psychopath*, which first appeared in parliamentary discussion in 1953. Discussing a report on prison reform, Mr. Michael Maitland Stewart argued on 2 March 1953 that a special type of prison should be available for particularly dangerous prisoners (see Example (4)).

(4) There is a reference in our Report to the desirability of a special prison for the type of prisoner known as an aggressive *psychopath*. This was the only constructive recommendation in the section of our Report dealing with discipline, about which there has been so much criticism.

The term *psychopath* remained somewhat popular in parliamentary debates for some ten years, which can be taken as a reflection of the term's general currency in contemporary society.[12]

Perhaps the most curious lexical item in this category is the term *feeble-minded*, which saw a sudden and brief peak during the second decade of the twentieth century mainly due to the Feeble-minded Persons (Control) Bill and the Mental Deficiency Bill, debated in 1912 and 1913, respectively (see Figure 7.9). Although the term *feeble-minded* had already appeared a few times during the previous century, the term appears to have emerged into parliamentary discourse on the heels of the *Report of the Royal Commission on the Feeble-Minded*, published in 1908. The 536-page report provided a formal definition of 'mentally

---

11. It goes without saying that *fanatic* is the source of the later *fan*.

12. The famous thriller *Psycho* by Alfred Hitchcock was released in 1960, and a diagnostic look at the Google n-grams for British books shows a bump around the same period of 1950–1970.

The changing lexis of mental health 211

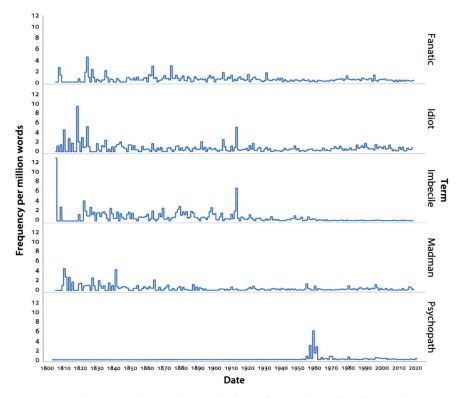

Figure 7.8 References to *fanatic, idiot, imbecile, madman* and *psychopath* over the timeline (normalised frequency per million words)

defective persons', giving nine different categories of mental deficiency.[13] The feeble-minded, one of the categories, are defined as persons who "are capable of earning a living under favourable circumstances", but who cannot compete "on equal terms with their normal fellows" or manage "themselves and their affairs with normal prudence" (1908: 4). Notably, although the title of the report refers to the feeble-minded, the commission used the broader term *mental deficiency* and gave *feeble-mindedness* a more narrow definition. The term *feeble-minded* disappeared from parliamentary debates within a few short years.

---

13. The categories include persons of unsound mind, the mentally infirm, idiots, imbeciles, the feeble-minded, moral imbeciles, epileptics, inebriates, and the deaf and dumb or blind. Notably, the Report does not use the term *lunatic*.

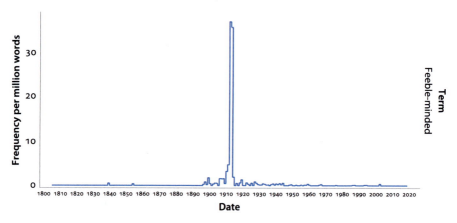

Figure 7.9 References to *feeble-minded* over the timeline (normalised frequency per million words)

4.1.2 *References to psychiatric illnesses*

The second category of mental health terms is words that refer to mental illnesses and deficiencies. Notably, this category covers a wide range of words because the concept of mental illness was understood somewhat differently at different times over the two centuries. The frequency curves of the key terms are given in Figure 7.10.

The periodic nature of mental health terms becomes particularly apparent in Figure 7.10. We see that *derangement, insanity* and *lunacy* are the current terms throughout the nineteenth century; they are replaced by *mental deficiency* from 1910 to 1960, and after that *mental disorder* and *mental illness* begin gaining ground. Some terms, like *neurosis* and *feeble-mindedness*, are used for brief periods of time and then discarded. Perhaps surprisingly, terms like *psychiatric illness* and *psychiatric condition* have never been used in parliamentary language at any substantial frequency, though there is evidence of very occasional use of both since the 1960s.

4.1.3 *References to psychiatric institutions*

Given the prominence of *lunatic* as a term of reference for people with mental illness, it is no surprise that *lunatic asylum* was the common term for the institutions that were charged with housing them. Figure 7.11 gives a very clear overview of the lexical shifts from *lunatic asylum* to *mental hospital* and *mental institution* and finally to *psychiatric hospital*. Less common referents, but ones worth noting, are *bedlam* and *Broadmoor*. *Bedlam*, a common noun for a mental institution, was derived from the name of Bethlem Royal Hospital, previously St Mary Bethlehem. While *bedlam* came to be used as a common noun, the proper noun *Broadmoor*

The changing lexis of mental health 213

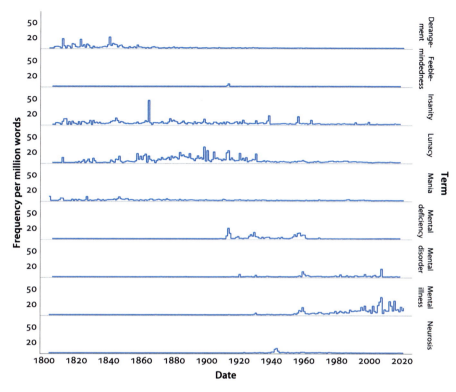

Figure 7.10 References to *derangement, feeble-mindedness, insanity, lunacy, mania, mental deficiency, mental disorder, mental illness* and *neurosis* over the timeline (normalised frequency per million words)

always refers specifically to Broadmoor Hospital, the oldest high-security psychiatric hospital in Britain. Broadmoor was founded in the 1860s, and it features extensively in debates in the House of Commons especially during the 1870s.[14]

The frequent debates concerning *lunatic asylums* ranged in tone, but the general sentiment that comes across concerns the desire to improve the facilities and to make the treatment of psychiatric patients more humane. In the excerpt in Example (5), from 17 July 1863, Mr. John Blake argues that lunatic asylums were at that time more like prisons than hospitals.

---

14. Notably, the other two high-security psychiatric hospitals in Britain, Rampton Secure Hospital and Ashworth Hospital, do not feature in parliamentary discussions as frequently as Broadmoor does. Rampton was established in 1912 as the Rampton Criminal Lunatic Asylum, and Ashworth was originally Moss Side House, established in 1878.

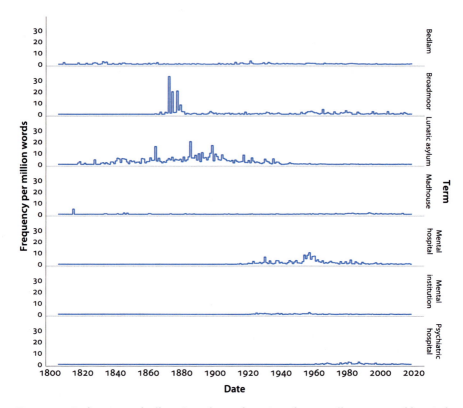

Figure 7.11 References to *bedlam, Broadmoor, lunatic asylum, madhouse, mental hospital, mental institution* and *psychiatric hospital* over the timeline

(5) It cannot be denied, notwithstanding the care and attention which appear generally to be given by the managers and visiting physicians to the patients under their charge, that, on the whole, the lunatic asylums of Ireland wear more the aspect of places merely for the secure detention of lunatics than of curative hospitals for the insane. Probably it is by some considered, that the inmates being poor, the ratepayers should not be called on to provide for them comforts and appliances beyond their position; and something, perhaps, of the idea prevails, that the *lunatic asylum* should not, by the comfort it provides for its inmates, cease to be a test, like the workhouse, for those who seek it as an asylum.

Following the 1930 Mental Treatment Act, the term *lunatic asylum* was gradually phased out and replaced by *mental hospital* and, somewhat later, by *psychiatric hospital*. References to lunatic asylums did not stop entirely, but similarly to *lunatic*, the term acquired a non-technical and often metaphorical meaning to be used in reference to one's political opponents.[15] In Example (6), from 21 November 1963, Mr. Nigel Birch paraphrases Field Marshal Lord Montgomery.

(6) Field Marshal Lord Montgomery certainly made one political pronouncement which I think caught the imagination of people in the country, and one which they approved by their votes. Hon. Gentlemen will remember that at the last Election he said that anyone who voted Labour ought to be sent to a *lunatic asylum*, and obviously the country very generally agreed that he was right. I think, however, that even his greatest admirers must admit that the Field Marshal's other political pronouncements have shown rather less maturity.

The humorous and rhetorical use of old terms for mental hospitals was not limited to *lunatic asylum*. The term *madhouse*, which was never particularly common or consistently used in parliament as an institutional term, became a somewhat popular descriptive term in the latter half of the twentieth century (see Figure 7.12). A few instances of the terms *looney bin, nuthouse* and *lunatic house* also appear during the same period.

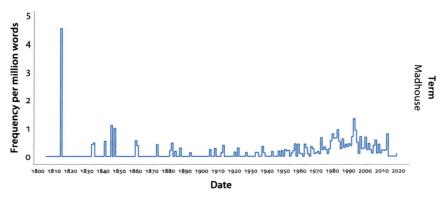

Figure 7.12 References to *madhouse* over the timeline

4.1.4 *Diachronic overview*

The previous sections showed the changing nature of mental health lexis over time in three key areas of mental health discourse. For a more general overview of broader diachronic patterns in the occurrence of the lexical items, we used the variable clustering method (see Section 3.3). The analysis identified eight distinct

---

15. The primary meaning of the word *asylum* also changed during the twentieth century. As the institutional sense receded, the term shifted to meaning political asylum, a term that became particularly frequent in parliament from the 1980s onward.

patterns (see Table 7.1; cluster members listed in Appendix 2), with the overall proportion of variation explained being 0.529.

Table 7.1 Distinct clusters of diachronic patterns identified with variable clustering[16]

Cluster	# of cluster members	Most representative variable	Cluster R^2
1	5	lunatic	0.60
3	5	feeble-mindedness	0.51
2	4	mental hospital	0.57
5	4	mental illness	0.45
7	4	neurosis	0.30
6	3	derangement	0.50
4	2	criminal lunatic	0.77
8	2	madhouse	0.62

Plotting the trendlines of the most representative variables of each cluster using z-scores and organising the plots in a diachronically sensible order reveals the succession and overlapping of these lexical 'waves' (see Figure 7.13). Note that each panel has a slightly different vertical scale; however, our interest here is not in the magnitude of occurrences, but the diachronic patterns.

Examined visually, we can state that there are three distinct periods in the timeline that are associated particularly clearly with lexical shifts. The 1840s begins a period of intense mental health discussion in parliament, as seen in the positive trendlines of Clusters 1 (*lunatic*) and 4 (*criminal lunatic*). We also see that Cluster 6 (*derangement*) begins a decline at the same time. Cluster 3, associated with *feeble-mindedness*, emerges at the turn of the century but does not survive for long. Then, around 1930, we see Clusters 7 (*neurosis*) and 2 (*mental hospital*) beginning to grow, while Clusters 1 (*lunatic*) and 4 (*criminal lunatic*) begin a decline. And finally, around 1950, we see the appearance of Clusters 8 (*madhouse*) and 5 (*mental illness*), heralding in modern mental health terminology. Notably, during this time the term *madhouse* is no longer used in its original meaning as a serious reference to a mental institution, but rather in a more comedic or exasperated sense in reference to a situation that is out of control. We are currently planning a follow-up study in which the changes in parliamentary lexis are compared with contemporary language use in society. All in all, the patterns demonstrate that the topic-specific lexis of parliamentary discourse is ever-evolving.

---

16. Cluster R^2 indicates the proportion of variation explained within each cluster, or in other words how similar the distribution patterns are within each cluster. There are no established threshold values for cluster R^2 in variable clustering, but we can say that the values for Clusters 5 and 7 are relatively low and thus the patterns are less reliable.

The changing lexis of mental health 217

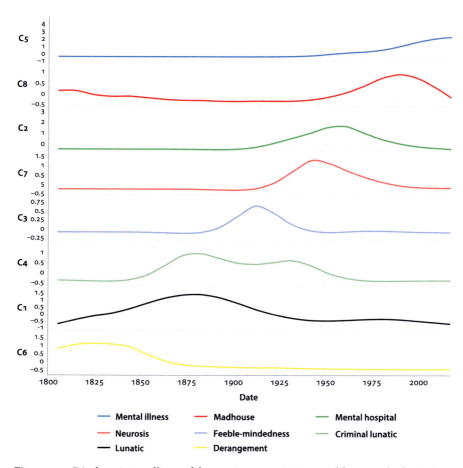

Figure 7.13 Diachronic trendlines of the most representative variables in each cluster

4.2 Case study: The term *lunatic*

To examine the changing nature of mental health discourse in the House of Commons, we focus on the most frequent term for mentally challenged people: *lunatic*. Counting both singular and plural forms, the word appears a total of 7,229 times in 3,954 debates by 2,218 speakers.[17] The term *lunatic* is typically mentioned only a few times in each debate, but there are some exceptions, such as the Non-effective and Charitable Services debate in March 1885, which includes 44 mentions of *lunatic* by 16 different MPs, and the Clause 9 debates in May and June 1898, which include 74 mentions of *lunatic* by 23 different MPs. The overall figures show

---

17. It is worth bearing in mind that individual debates are of considerably different lengths and direct comparisons between debates are therefore somewhat tenuous.

that over the two centuries examined, 95% of the speakers in the Hansard never uttered the word *lunatic* once, and those who did typically did so only once or twice. Only 131 speakers mention lunatics more than ten times during their years in parliament and only six MPs did so more than 50 times. Notably, four out of the six, namely William Corbet, Timothy Healy, Arthur O'Connor and John Dillon, were Irish MPs; the other two were Gerald Balfour and Arthur Balfour, the latter Prime Minister from 1902 to 1905. In general, Irish MPs appear to have participated in debates about mental health with particular vigour around the turn of the century (see Mauger 2017).

The singular and plural forms of the term are used somewhat differently, and to look deeper into the use of both terms, we carried out two collocation analyses and visualised the results with network graphs (see Figures 7.14 and 7.16).[18] The graphs show the strongest collocates of the word *lunatic(s)* within a four-word span in 50-year time periods, with the node sizes reflecting the number of occurrences and the edge weights indicating the association strength (MI);[19] the minimum number of occurrences was ten. Figure 7.14 shows that the term *lunatic* had a much wider range of strong collocates in the nineteenth century than later, and that many of the collocates were shared especially during the earlier periods. The green nodes mark institutional words such as *workhouse*, *reformatory* and *prison*, and they cluster around the period 1860–1900. Notably, the words *asylum* and *asylums* are associated with each of the four time periods, and the word *criminal* is associated with all but the earliest period. The orange nodes indicate various other groups of people, and they, too, are most strongly associated with the latter half of the nineteenth century. Many of these words, such as *patients*, *attendants*, *prisoner* and *inmate* are also related to institutions and to crime.

One interesting example of the later use of *lunatic* is the term *lunatic fringe*, which was first used in parliament in 1943 by Mr. Quintin Hogg and thereafter with some regularity especially in the period 1950–1970 (see Figure 7.15). At this point the term *lunatic* was no longer used as an acceptable term for mentally ill people, but it had shifted to mean eccentricity and fanaticism. In Example (7), from 23 January 1967, Mr. John Peyton describes a political opponent using the term.

---

18. The collocations were obtained using the English Corpora interface to the Hansard Corpus <https://www.english-corpora.org/hansard/> and the network graphs were created using network analysis tool Cytoscape <https://cytoscape.org>.

19. MI stands for Mutual Information, a well-known association strength statistic that measures the effect size of the co-occurrence of two lexical items, i.e. how often the two items tend to co-occur in comparison to them not co-occurring.

The changing lexis of mental health 219

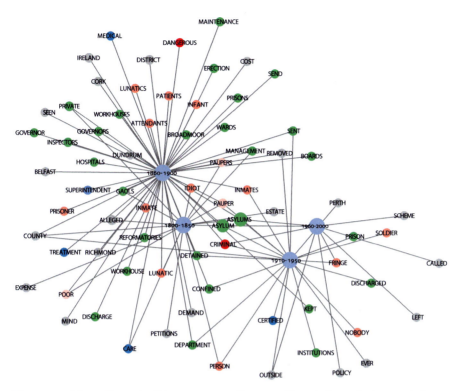

Figure 7.14 Network graph of the strongest collocates of *lunatic* for each time period; colours of nodes denote categories of lexical items

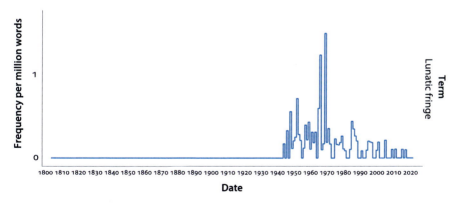

Figure 7.15 References to *lunatic fringe* over the timeline (normalised frequency per million words)

(7) The hon. Gentleman one of these days will learn a little sense, I expect, although it may be highly optimistic to hope for any such thing from one of those who occupy the *lunatic fringe* of his party.

Moving from *lunatic* to *lunatics*, it may be argued that the collocations of the plural form are perhaps even more revealing of the changing tides than those of the singular form (see Figure 7.16). As we can see, the period 1850–1900 shows by far the most collocates. The nodes in green are related to institutions and institutionalisation of lunatics, and as the graph shows, they are by far the most prevalent in the 1860–1900 time period. The associated words include *workhouse, custody, confined* and *asylum*. Likewise, orange nodes, which indicate words associated with other groups, are also found in this time period. Medical terms, in blue, are shared by most of the periods. The red nodes indicate association with crime and criminality. The word *police* and *dangerous* are only associated with the 1860–1900 period, but notably the word *criminals* is shared by all periods except 1800–1850, and the word *criminal* is the only term in the entire network to be shared by all time periods.

The collocations thus confirm the strong and enduring association between mental illness, institutionalisation and crime across the timeline. It goes without saying that parliamentary discourse is primarily concerned with legislation and thus the perspective on any topic will necessarily be focused on the setting up and management of institutions and public services. Although the relative scarcity of associations with medical care may be surprising to us, it is worth noting that by the time medical care assumed centre stage in discourses about mentally ill people, the term *lunatic* was no longer used in that meaning.

5. Discussion and conclusion

If we look at the changes that appear to have occurred in the lexis of mental health in general, major shifts in the entire lexical field have happened in specific time periods, the turning points being in the 1840s, 1930s and 1950s (see Section 4.1.4). Interestingly and by no means surprisingly, these points in time appear alongside particular legal amendments: the Lunacy Act in 1845 resulted in a change in treating mentally ill people as patients; the Mental Treatment Act in 1930 meant voluntary admission to psychiatric hospitals; and the Report on Mental Illness and Mental Deficiency in the 1950s changed the general discussion towards that of mental health instead of mental illness. Generalising further, it may be argued that the period around World War II is revealed to have been a watershed when

The changing lexis of mental health 221

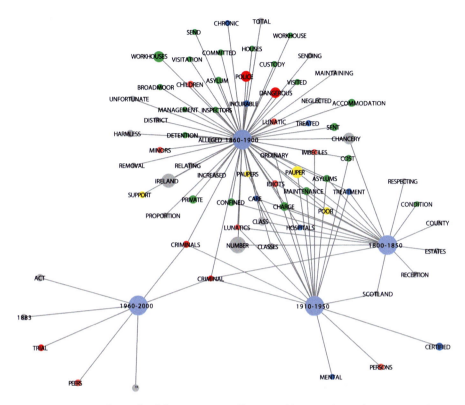

Figure 7.16 Network graph of the strongest collocates of *lunatics* for each time period; colours of nodes denote categories of lexical items

it came to mental health discourse in the parliament.[20] At that time more than before, we witness both a change of terminology, as well a substantial overall decrease in references to mentally ill people. We can also detect further lexical distinctions being made between people with congenital mental disability (*idiot, imbecile*) and those who acquired a mental illness later in life (*insane, maniac*), as well as between colloquial words referring to mental illness and mentally ill people (*crackpot, crazy*) and more medical terminology (*mental health, mental deficiency*). The use of colloquial terms is relatively rare in the parliamentary context, no doubt at least partly due to rules governing the use of unparliamentary language, but nonetheless the data reveal plenty of instances up to and including the present day where political opponents, public figures, heads of state, and others

---

20. For a large-scale quantitative examination of the effects of World War II on parliamentary lexis, see Tyrkkö (2020). In brief, the war years are shown to be associated with a wide-ranging shift in lexis.

are referred to by using terms that only a few decades ago suggested the presence of a mental illness.

The changes go beyond lexis, of course, and what we observe is a change in what might be called the societal mindset. In the nineteenth century those who were mentally ill seemed to be placed in an object position and afforded little or no power, as they were considered a curiosity to be ridiculed or a danger to be locked up and controlled (see Porter 2002). This is clearly seen in lexical choices that highlight the superficial qualities of a mentally ill person's condition (*deranged, criminal lunatic*). In parliamentary discourse, much of the focus is naturally on the institutional perspective, which further highlights the idea of mental health issues as being something to be controlled. The attitudes started shifting later in the century and accordingly the Hansard shows a growing concern both for legal protections for mentally ill people and for their living conditions, whether institutionalised or not. As already discussed in Section 2.1, twentieth-century approaches to mental health no longer automatically robbed a person of agency in their own life, but rather the primary role of health services was seen as helping people with mental illness achieve agency. Modern psychiatry opts for integration instead of segregation, and approbation instead of stigmatisation, which is evident in emergent terms in our data (e.g. *mental health* vs. *mental illness, psychiatric condition* vs. *madness, lunacy*).

Methodologically, this study lends support to the argument that large-scale analyses of culturally important textual datasets have the potential to reveal patterns of change and co-occurrence, which may be difficult to identify from small samples or the close reading of individual texts. Our observations show that while lexical changes and semantic shifts often take place gradually, in specific contexts such as parliamentary discourse it is also possible that a term is used for a brief period of time and then discarded from use, as seen in the case of *feeble-minded*. The brief case study of the word *lunatic* and its changing collocates over time likewise requires sufficient data to allow the drawing of even rudimentary conclusions. In the years to come, the increasing and more varied investigation of complete sets of parliamentary records from linguistic and discursive perspectives will undoubtedly uncover informative, intriguing, and perhaps shocking patterns of language use.

Acknowledgements

We wish to thank the two anonymous referees and the editors for their constructive and helpful comments.

References

Alexander, Marc. 2018. Lexicalization pressure: From frequency to linguistic trauma. Plenary presentation at ICEHL20, Edinburgh, 27–30 August.

Arnold, Catherine. 2008. *Bedlam: London and Its Mad*. New York NY: Simon & Schuster.

Aspinall, A. 1956. The reporting and publishing of the House of Commons' debates 1771–1834. In *Essays Presented to Sir Lewis Namier*, Richard Pares & A.J.P. Taylor (eds), 227–257. London: Macmillan.

Baker, Helen & McEnery, Anthony. 2016. *Corpus Linguistics and 17th-Century Prostitution*. New York NY: Bloomsbury.

Browne, Charlie. 2017. Being a Hansard reporter: 10 things you thought you knew. <https://commonshansard.blog.parliament.uk/2017/07/24/being-a-hansard-reporter-10-things-you-thought-you-knew/> (14 February 2022).

Farrelly, Michael & Seoane, Elena. 2012. Democratization. In *The Oxford Handbook of the History of English*, Terttu Nevalainen & Elizabeth Closs Traugott (eds), 392–401. Oxford: OUP.

Froehlich, Heather. 2016. "Thus to make poor females mad": Finding the 'mad woman' in Early Modern drama. In *The Pragmatics and Stylistics of Construction and Characterisation*, Minna Nevala, Ursula Lutzky, Gabriella Mazzon & Carla Suhr (eds). Helsinki: VARIENG. <http://www.helsinki.fi/varieng/series/volumes/17/froehlich/> (18 February 2022).

Hiltunen, Turo, Räikkönen, Jenni & Tyrkkö, Jukka. 2020. Investigating colloquialization in the British parliamentary record in the late 19th and early 20th century. In *New Perspectives on Democratization: Evidence from English(es)*, Turo Hiltunen & Lucía Loureiro-Porto (eds). Special issue of *Language Sciences* 79: 101270.

Hintikka, Marianna & Nevala, Minna. 2017. Representations of prostitutes and prostitution as a metaphor in nineteenth-century English newspapers. *Journal of Historical Sociolinguistics* 3(2): 219–240.

Houston, Robert Allan. 2000. *Madness and Society in Eighteenth-century Scotland*. London: Clarendon.

Jordan, H. Donaldson. 1931. The reports of parliamentary debates, 1803–1908. *Economica* 34: 437–449.

Long, Vicky. 2015. *Destigmatising Mental Illness? Professional Politics and Public Education in Britain, 1870–1970*. Manchester: Manchester University Press.

MacDonagh, Michael. 1913. *The Reporters' Gallery*. London: Hodder and Stoughton.

Mauger, Alice. 2017. *The Cost of Insanity in Nineteenth-Century Ireland: Public, Voluntary and Private Asylum Care*. London: Palgrave Macmillan.

McConnell-Ginet, Sally. 2003. "What's in a name?" Social labelling and gender practices. In *Handbook of Language and Gender* (Volume 1), Janet Holmes & Miriam Meyerhoff (eds), 69–97. London: Wiley Blackwell.

Mollin, Sandra. 2007. The Hansard hazard: Gauging the accuracy of British parliamentary transcripts. *Corpora* 2(2): 187–210.

Nevala, Minna. 2019. *Two miserable creatures* or *those atrocious criminals*? Evaluative reference in the Mannings murder reporting. In *Reference and Identity in Public Discourses*, Ursula Lutzky & Minna Nevala (eds), 19–41. Amsterdam: John Benjamins.

O'Reilly, Carole. 2014. "Dirt, death and disease": Newspaper discourses on public health in the construction of the modern British city. *Journal of Historical Pragmatics* 15(2): 207–227.

Partington, Alan. 2013. Corpus analysis of political language. In *The Encyclopedia of Applied Linguistics*, Carol Chappelle (ed.). Oxford: Blackwell. <https://onlinelibrary.wiley.com /doi/10.1002/9781405198431.wbeal0250> (14 February 2022).

Porter, Roy. 1987. *Mind-forg'd Manacles: A History of Madness in England from the Restoration to the Regency*. Harvard: Harvard University Press.

Porter, Roy. 2002. *Madness: A Brief History*. Oxford: OUP.

Report of the Royal Commission on the care and control of the feeble-minded, Volume VIII. 1908. London: HMSO.

Sanche, Robert & Lonergan, Kevin. 2006. Variable reduction for predictive modeling with clustering. *Casualty Actuarial Society Forum*, Winter, 89–100.

Scull, Andrew, MacKenzie, Charlotte & Hervey, Nicholas. 2014. *Masters of Bedlam: The Transformation of the Mad-Doctoring Trade*. Princeton: Princeton Legacy Library.

Social Care Institute for Excellence. 2016 [2006]. Mental Capacity Act (MCA). <https://www .scie.org.uk/mca/introduction/mental-capacity-act-2005-at-a-glance#assessment> (8 November 2019).

Suzuki, Akihito. 1999. Framing psychiatric subjectivity: Doctor, patient and record-keeping at Bethlem in the nineteenth century. In *Insanity, Institutions, and Society, 1800–1914: A Social History of Madness in Comparative Perspective*, Bill Forsythe & Joseph Melling (eds), 115–136. London: Routledge.

The Royal Commission on Law Relating to Mental Illness and Mental Deficiency. Some Points from Its Report. 1957. *Mental Health (London)* 16(3): 100–103.

Tyrkkö, Jukka. 2019. Kinship references in the British parliament, 1800–2005. In *Reference and Identity in Public Discourses*, Ursula Lutzky & Minna Nevala (eds), 97–127. Amsterdam: John Benjamins.

Tyrkkö, Jukka. 2020. The war years: Distant reading British parliamentary debates. In *Doing Digital Humanities: Concepts, Approaches, Cases*, Joacim Hansson & Jonas Svensson (eds), 169–199. Växjö: Linnaeus University Press.

Tyrkkö, Jukka & Kopaczyk, Joanna. 2018. Corpus-driven methods: Present applications and future directions. In *Applications of Pattern-driven Methods in Corpus Linguistics*, Joanna Kopaczyk & Jukka Tyrkkö (eds), 1–12. Amsterdam: John Benjamins.

Appendix 1. Mental health words retrieved from the *Historical Thesaurus of English*

Words with a substantial frequency in the Hansard in bold, words not in HTE and supplied by the authors marked with an asterisk

Semantic category	Lexical items
hospital for mentally ill people	asylum, **bedlam**, bedlam-house, bin, booby-hatch, bughouse, Colney Hatch, dull-house, funny farm, idiot asylum, loony bin, **lunatic asylum**, lunatic hospital, lunatic house, madhouse, maison de santé, nut college, nut factory, nut-house, nuttery, rat-house, retreat, silly house, snake-pit, **psychiatric hospital***, **mental hospital***, **mental institution***
hospital for mentally ill people, specific	**Broadmoor**, Rampton*, Moss Side*
intellectually weak	barmy, defective, doddering, doting, dotish, dotty, drippy, **feeble-minded**, half-baked, knock-kneed, lean-minded, lean-witted, sick, silly, soft, tenpence in the shilling, touched, touched in the head, touched in the upper storey, wanting, weak, weak-brained, weak-minded
intellectually weak, idiotic	divvy, fonddial, **idiot**, idiotic, idiotical, idiotish, **imbecile**, imbecilic
mental illness, insanity, madness	madship, woodhede, wood, rage, madhead, madness, madding, frenzy, furiosity, derverye, forcenery, alienation of mind, foursenery, furiousness, demency, unwitness, unwitting, straightness, brainsickness, **lunacy**, insani, distraughtness, straughtedness, cerebrosity, **insanity**, crazedness, bedlam, insanation, distraction, crack, midsummer madness, non compos mentis, doffing, medicineobstetrics, dementation, amenty, disinsanity, vecordy, fanaticness, non-sanity, insaneness, craziness, idiotry, hydrophobia, vecord, vesania, **derangement**, folie, a screw loose, unsoundness, craze, psychosis, crackiness, mental alienation, feyness, dementedness, **dementia**, meshugaas, white ant, crackedness, pottiness, loopiness, wackiness, kink, screwballism, **mental disorder***, **mental illness***, psychiatric illness*, **neurosis***
mental deficiency, person	ament, amentia, auf(e), balmy, changeling, congeon, conjon, Cousin Betty, defective, deficient, fatuity, **feeble-mindedness**, feebleness, fool, idiot, moon-calf, natural, natural fool, idiot, natural born fool, oaf, oligophrenia, retard, retardate, retardee, slimshack, subnormal, underwit, unfortunate, unnaturality, weak-wit, weakling, mentally infirm*

Appendix 1. *(continued)*

Semantic category	Lexical items
mental deficiency, person, type of, person	**cretin**, Mongol, Mongoloid, **moron**
mentally ill, mad person	barm-pot, bedlam, bedlam-beggar, bedlam-man, bedlamer, bedlamite, brainsick, crack, crack-brain, crackpot, craze, crazy, dement, détraqué(e), ding(-)a(-)ling, dingbat, fan, **fanatic**, frantic, frenetic, gelt, insane, Jack o' Bedlam, lakes, Lakes of Killarney, loon(e)y, luny, **lunatic**, lymphatic, mad man, madbrain, madcap, madhead, madling, **madman**, madpash, madwoman, maniac, March hare, mental, meshugener, meshugenah, non compos, non compos mentis, nut, nut-case, nutter, phrenetic, psychopath, psychopathic, shatter-brain, shatterpate, shatterwit, Tom, Tom o' Bedlam, wack, wacko, woodman
mentally ill, mad person, criminal lunatic	Broadmoor patient
person of weak intellect	inane, incapable, insensate, insensible, insipid, insipidity, no conjurer, non-intelligent, opacity, scant-brain, shallow-brains, shallow-pate, underhead, wattle-head
person of weak intellect, idiot, crazy person	ding-a-ling, dingbat, divvydial, drivel, driveller, eejit, feeb, flake, flight-head, gonzo, hare-brain, **idiot, imbecile**, loon, **lunatic**, moonling, nidget, nidiot, poggle, ratbag, shoalbrain, tattie-bogle

Appendix 2. Groups of lexical items based on variable clustering

Cluster	Cluster members
1	**lunatic**, lunacy, lunatic asylum, pauper lunatic, insanity
2	**mental hospital**, psychopath, mental institution, mental disorder
3	**feeble-mindedness**, feeble-minded, mental deficiency, cretin, idiot
4	**criminal lunatic**, Broadmoor
5	**mental illness**, asylum, dementia, bedlam
6	**derangement**, mania, madman
7	**neurosis**, moron, imbecile, fanatic
8	**madhouse**, psychiatric hospital

CHAPTER 8

"The job requires considerable expertise"
Tracking EXPERTS and EXPERT KNOWLEDGE in the British parliamentary record (1800–2005)[*]

Turo Hiltunen
University of Helsinki

While clearly important in decision-making in democratic societies, the authority of science and expertise in public forums is nowadays increasingly challenged by different advocacy groups and crowd-based politics. Using the Hansard Corpus, this chapter explores how experts and expert knowledge are referred to in the British parliamentary record from 1800 to 2005, focusing on how frequently members of parliament (MPs) refer to different kinds of experts and their expertise in parliamentary debates, and whether diachronic changes can be linked to historical events and cultural and intellectual changes. The quantitative analysis is complemented with a qualitative investigation of how experts and expert knowledge are framed in parliamentary debates. The analysis shows that overall the references to experts have increased in the twentieth century and especially after the 1950s. Yet variation among individual terms and discourse contexts is evident, indicating that cultural explanations of corpus data should be approached with caution.

Keywords: expertise, corpus pragmatics, parliamentary debates, Hansard

1. Introduction

Expert knowledge, understood here as societally recognised specialist expertise in a particular domain typically derived from some academic discipline, clearly plays an important role in political decision-making in modern democratic societies (Brown 2009). In many ways, the need for expert knowledge is constantly increasing due to the increasing complexity of issues which policymakers need

---

[*] The quotation is from the Hansard Corpus (Sam Galbraith, House of Commons, 21 June 1988).

https://doi.org/10.1075/scl.111.08hil
© 2023 John Benjamins Publishing Company

to pass judgement on and the expanding use of technology in all areas of life. The nineteenth and especially the twentieth century also demonstrates significant increases in public spending both overall and specifically in the area of education (Brien & Keep 2018), which, coupled with the steady growth in the number of scientific publications (Larsen & von Ins 2010), shows that there is an ever-increasing amount of scientific knowledge available to be used in policymaking. Previous research on policy design suggests that the enthusiasm for research utilisation in policymaking was at its highest during and after World War II until the late 1960s, based on US data (Hird 2005:7). Closer to the present day, modern societies have been confronted with various challenges like crises of financial systems, leading Conway and Gore (2019) to conclude that "government needs experts more than ever". Science and evidence are frequently used to obtain support for policies, as scientific authority and a strong basis in evidence may strengthen the credibility of political claims (Boswell 2009:25; Reyes 2011:786). At the same time recent decades have witnessed a crisis of expertise (Nichols 2017), whereby the authority of science and expertise in public forums has increasingly been challenged by different advocacy groups and crowd-based politics, in which "emotions trump evidence" (Davies 2018:23).

There is a large amount of research on the phenomenon of expertise from various perspectives, mostly carried out in sociology, communication studies, science studies and related fields. Despite some linguistic studies (e.g. Bondi, Cacchiani & Mazzi 2015), conceptualisations of expertise and their textual manifestations outside the traditional domain of science have received much less attention in linguistics. Some previous studies have addressed the concept of expertise when discussing legitimisation in political discourse (e.g. Reyes 2011). However, there are few studies that use large corpora, yet it is precisely such studies that would enable the empirical analysis of how experts and expert knowledge has been invoked over time, and in particular whether societal and cultural changes are linked to specific changes in linguistic usage.

To approach this very question, this chapter uses the Hansard Corpus (Alexander & Davies 2015) to study how frequently, and in what way, members of parliament (MPs) refer to different kinds of experts and their expertise in parliamentary debates, and to explore whether diachronic changes in these references can be linked to cultural and intellectual changes in the last two centuries. Following a corpus-pragmatic approach (e.g. Rühlemann & Aijmer 2015), the chapter considers both quantitative evidence from the changing frequencies of terms related to experts and expert knowledge, and qualitative evidence based on close reading. The analysis shows that while many expertise-related terms increase in frequency over the time period in focus, and especially so in the twentieth century, generalisations about the status of expertise in parliamentary discourse need

2. Background

2.1 Theories of expertise

Experts and the notion of expertise have been discussed and intensely debated in literature on sociology and science studies. Even though the concept is intuitively clear, it is useful to review some of this literature before discussing how it can be applied in the context of corpus linguistics and the analysis of parliamentary discourse. At the same time, it should be emphasised that expertise, as well as the kind of knowledge that is associated with this status, has been conceptualised in different ways. Therefore, rather than attempting to provide a comprehensive review of the concept (which can be found e.g. in Ward et al. 2019), this section highlights those aspects that help us describe how the notion is invoked in the context of parliamentary debates, and considers the reasons for the observed changes in linguistic usage.

In his introduction to the second edition of *The Cambridge Handbook of Expertise and Expert Performance*, Ericsson (2018:3–4) defines the domain of expertise as "[c]haracteristics, skills and knowledge that distinguish experts from novices". One criterion for identifying such characteristics is the ability to achieve superior reproducible performances in tasks that are representative of the domain in question. The status of expert can be bestowed on individuals by other experts. Experts typically have long experience of working within the domain, and they project outward signs of self-confidence.

Further characteristics of experts include mastery of some body of knowledge and techniques of analysis,[1] formal training in their specialist domain, some form of societal recognition (e.g. in the form of professional credentials), and impartiality (not being guided by political agendas, and adherence to some form of professional ethics) (e.g. Väliverronen 2016). The precise form of these criteria may vary depending on the context and the domain in question.

In linguistic studies on expert discourse, expertise is closely linked to the mastery of specific disciplinary discourses, defined in terms of lexis, grammar and discourse conventions as well as genre competence (Tribble 2019:60). For Swales

---

1. For linguists, for example, the ability to use elaborate transcription schemes to produce precise transcriptions of speech situations can be construed as an authoritative expert performance (Jaffe 2007:833–834).

(1990:27), both content and discoursal expertise are prerequisites for membership of an academic discourse community. But expertise also relies on tacit procedural knowledge related to the process of producing academic publications and organising events; in short, academic experts are typically senior researchers who "know the academic ropes of their chosen specialisms" (Swales 2004:56).

Expertise in writing may be highly specific (Bazerman 1994), and claims in expert texts addressed to other experts need to be carefully constructed taking into account both the current state of knowledge and the quality of the new evidence (e.g. Myers 1985). However, more central to this study are situations where experts appear in communicative situations where most or all other participants are non-experts. This is the case when experts are invited to appear in the media, or when policymakers consult them as specialist advisers on some issue, and in such situations their discourse needs to be recontextualised and adapted to meet the requirements of a non-specialist audience. Such recontextualisation may involve different levels of discourse and is manifested in processes like simplification (e.g. omission of technical detail) or elaboration (e.g. illustrating a concept with an example that is relevant to the lay audience) (Bondi, Cacchiani & Mazzi 2015).

2.2 Expertise and technical decision-making

Particularly relevant to the present analysis is the role of experts in technical decision-making (Collins & Evans 2002:36), where the concerns of *science and technology* intersect with the domain of *politics*, because the issues are of relevance to the public. In such situations, policymakers rely on external scientific experts, who in turn may adopt different roles depending on the situation as well as their disposition. Pielke (2007) identifies four idealised roles for scientists in the context of policymaking, which he labels 'pure scientist', 'science arbiter', 'issue advocate', and 'honest broker of policy alternatives'. These roles differ in terms of how the interrelationship of science and democracy is conceptualised. The pure scientist and the science arbiter would focus on accumulating research to be used by policymakers (the former without interacting with policymakers). The issue advocate would openly align with a specific interest group and their agenda. The honest broker of policy alternatives would also collaborate with decision-makers. However, they would not push a specific agenda, but would integrate policymaking and scientific research by clarifying and expanding the options available for decision-makers. On the one hand, for Pielke (2007:18) the choice between these roles should be made based on the degree of consensus as well as the degree of uncertainty among the scientific community. On the other hand, O'Brien (2013) has shown that based on US survey data, the degree of public support for the participation of scientists in policymaking is primarily dependent on whether the scientists are seen as acting with the nation's best interests in mind, whereas scientific consensus, although important, plays a much lesser role in comparison. While in the twenty-first century the public trust in science has been stable, recent years have also seen many high-profile expressions of public criticism levelled at scientific experts in several fields (e.g. climate science, vaccination, nutrition) as well as attempts to control and curtail their freedom of expression (see Väliverronen & Saikkonen 2020).

According to Collins and Evans (2002), technical decision-making gives rise to two problems in democratic societies, namely the *problem of legitimacy* and the *problem of extension*. The former problem concerns the demands that decision-making should not be exclusively based on the pronouncements of elite experts who master some area of knowledge, but that the process should be democratised to allow the participation of a wider groups of citizens. In other words, judgements of experts may lack political legitimacy unless they are subjected to some kind of democratic process. But while few would disagree with these demands, it is not at all clear how far such democratisation should be taken, and this conundrum is what Collins and Evans (2002) refer to as the problem of extension.

In the data under study, references to experts can, for the most part, be seen as taking place in the context of technical decision-making, where the issues being discussed are so complex that their understanding requires specialist expertise in the relevant domain. The necessity of expertise and expert knowledge for making good decisions on difficult issues has become increasingly acute in recent decades (Conway & Gore 2019), which is also recognised in the functions of parliament: the institution has in place mechanisms that enable the appointment and consultation of specialist advisers. A prime example of this is the system of select committees, appointed to consider specific policy sectors and issues assigned by parliament. Select committees have a long history in the UK parliamentary system, but their structure was reformed in the 1960s and 1970s, resulting in the creation of committees for each government department in 1979 (Jones & Norton 2014: 315–316). This being the case, it is not surprising that we observe frequent references to experts in the Hansard to support specific arguments. For instance, in Example (1), the alleged consensus among experts is clearly meant to create an implicature that the policy that was adopted enjoyed their full support.

(1)   I think that every *expert* agrees with us that from the point of view of building schools it was the right policy.

(Henderson Stewart, House of Commons, 21 April 1953)

However, the specific value of such a consensus to political claims is not a given but clearly varies between situations, and MPs can also invoke the problem of legitimacy and the problem of extension to, for example, dismiss specific experts as technocrats (thus questioning their legitimacy) or appeal to common sense and the will of the people ahead of scientific expertise. Examples of these strategies are discussed in Section 4.3.

2.3 Kinds of expertise and expert

A further factor complicating the interpretation of frequency data is the multifaceted nature of expertise. This is particularly clear when we look at the 'Periodic table of expertises' created by British sociologist Collins (2014), which is represented in a simplified form in Table 8.1.

Table 8.1 'Periodic table of expertises' (after Collins 2014)

Ubiquitous expertises					
	Ubiquitous tacit knowledge		*Specialist tacit knowledge*		
Specialist expertises	Beer-mat knowledge	Popular understanding	Primary source knowledge	Interactional expertise	Contributory expertise
	External		*Internal*		
Meta-expertises	Ubiquitous discrimination	Local discrimination	Technical connoisseurship	Downward discrimination	Referred expertise

As space does not permit an exhaustive treatment of this model, I will highlight the key aspects for the present analysis. *Ubiquitous expertise* (the top row in Table 8.1) refers to expertises acquired by virtue of having grown up in a society and are in principle shared by all members. These include the tacit knowledge needed for a large number of functions and activities, including the ability to make political judgments (Collins & Evans 2007: 13). However, more important to the present study are *specialist expertises*, and in particular those aspects found on the right-hand side of the second row, which identify their key characteristics: the ability to do competent research in some (typically narrow) area of the specialist domain (*contributory expertise*) and interact with other experts on questions related to the domain (*interactional expertise*). These expertises are acquired in interaction with other specialist experts as part of formalised training and apprenticeship in higher education institutions.[2]

---

2. The *ubiquitous tacit knowledge* on the left-hand side of the second row, by contrast, can be acquired without interacting with specialist experts, through, for example, extensive reading (Collins 2014: 65).

The type of expertise in the third row of the model, *meta-expertises*, is equally crucial to technical decision-making, as it represents how politicians and other non-experts discriminate between different specialist experts. In the absence of substantive expertise, this discrimination inevitably relies on social criteria, which along with the consideration of basic educational credentials and professional experience typically involves some kind of inside information or local knowledge about specific experts (e.g. their previous track record as scientific advisers). Politicians themselves may also have specialist expertise in some domain which may be transferrable to other domains (*referred expertise*). The analysis of meta-expertises is clearly relevant to the question of how experts are referred to in parliamentary debates. As the social criteria used in the selection of experts, meta-expertises can be invoked to support the arguments being made, but also contested by others.

Along with people to whom the status of *expert* can be ascribed, the present study considers the use of words referring to expert knowledge. Like expertise, expert knowledge is a somewhat elusive notion for which a universal definition does not exist. Following Boswell (2009), it is possible to define expert knowledge as knowledge produced by academic research. What characterises expert knowledge in this sense is that it is produced in institutional settings (typically universities) using appropriate methodologies, and in terms of content and form it matches what the scientific community regards as appropriate knowledge claims in terms of conceptual and theoretical coherence (Boswell 2009: 23–25; see also Tribble 2019). But while this definition captures the most prototypical type of expert knowledge, in practice it is difficult to determine whether specific mentions of terms in parliamentary debates represent purely academic knowledge or rather knowledge produced by other agents like public administrators. For the study of expert knowledge in the Hansard, it is therefore necessary to adopt a somewhat broader conception of expert knowledge, expressed in various types of nouns that represent both individual fields of science and the textual objects into which expert knowledge is encapsulated (e.g. *theory* and *survey*), irrespective of who has produced them.

Like experts, expert knowledge may have a number of different uses in the process of decision-making. Nutley, Walter and Davies (2007: 33) highlight the complexity and the situatedness of the process of applying research evidence in policymaking, resulting in varied and often unpredictable outcomes. Weiss (1979) provides a model of "research utilization", which identifies seven ways that policymaking can be informed by social scientific research. She notes that even though the most common concept is the *problem-solving model*, whereby research is driven by practical policy problems, research evidence is often used strategically and selectively to support existing firmly held positions (*political model*) or merely to try to persuade stakeholders that the adopted views are informed by research (*tactical model*).[3]

To sum up, the above review of theories of expertise provides the necessary background for an empirical analysis of references to experts and expert knowledge in British parliamentary debates. More precisely, it provides the conceptual tools for (1) identifying terms in the conceptual categories EXPERTS and EXPERT KNOWLEDGE in a principled way, (2) determining their frequencies and identifying any patterns of diachronic change, and (3) describing the textual and argumentative contexts in which these terms are used. The precise operationalisation of these notions and the method of analysis is presented in the next section.

3. Material and method

The analysis in this chapter is based on the 1.6-billion-word Hansard Corpus, which contains "nearly every speech given in the parliament from 1803–2005" (Alexander & Davies 2015) and as such is the main source of data for obtaining information about language use in parliament. The corpus has been created by the SAMUELS project[4] based on data from the historic Hansard,[5] and includes different kinds of annotation (tokenisation, lemmatisation, part-of-speech tagging and semantic tagging). While the corpus has been used for many kinds of longitudinal linguistic analyses (see e.g. Archer 2017; Blaxill & Beelen 2016; Hiltunen, Räikkönen & Tyrkkö 2020), it should always be remembered that the records are not fully accurate representations of parliamentary speech, as the early reports were compiled of newspaper accounts (Port 1990), and later, 'verbatim' accounts routinely omit many performance characteristics of spoken language (Mollin 2007); see also Alexander (this volume) and Kotze et al. (this volume). The quantitative analysis represents the entire time period covered by the corpus and comprises all material from both houses of parliament.

The study adopts a corpus-pragmatic framework (e.g. Rühlemann & Aijmer 2015), which integrates exploratory quantitative analysis of frequencies of terms of interest with horizontal analysis of concordance lines, making use of concepts and ideas from previous research on expertise reviewed above. In focus are two sets of terms, those denoting EXPERTS and EXPERT KNOWLEDGE. These categories

---

3. The other models are the *knowledge-driven model* (corresponding to the "linear model" in Pielke 2007), the *interactive model* and the *enlightenment model*.

4. See <https://www.gla.ac.uk/schools/critical/research/fundedresearchprojects/samuels/>.

5. See <https://api.parliament.uk/historic-hansard/index.html>.

are indicated using small caps, and the individual terms representing these two categories are given in italics.

The first stage of the quantitative analysis follows a culturomics-style approach (Michel et al. 2011) in that it focuses on the frequency changes of relevant terms as potential correlates of discursive or cultural change. However, there are well-known methodological problems associated with this method of correlating cultural and linguistic change, most importantly the fact that unigram frequencies in isolation conflate different senses of the word (Jockers 2013: 121).[6] Therefore, qualitative analysis is required to choose the best candidate terms for assessing frequency changes in the conceptual categories in focus, and for linking them to extralinguistic features (Sections 4.1 to 4.2). In addition, qualitative horizontal reading of specific examples in context is used for investigating the rhetorical functions associated with invoking the term *expert*, which can be taken as key term representing the prototypical core of the entire conceptual category (Section 4.3).

The corpus-pragmatic approach thus consists of the following stages, which are described in more detail below:

1. identification of potentially relevant expert words for analysis and their retrieval from the Hansard Corpus;
2. visual exploration of time series of frequencies at ten-year intervals to identify main periods of change;
3. horizontal reading of selected concordances in context to identify some main discursive contexts and rhetorical functions in which these terms appear.

As shown in the previous section, both conceptual categories are broad, and it is difficult to formulate hard-and-fast rules for identifying relevant words in the corpus.[7] For this reason, it is necessary to carefully consider how this category can be operationalised for corpus linguistic study to ensure sufficient construct validity and to attain acceptable levels of recall and precision (Hoffmann 2013: 197–198). For identifying potentially relevant EXPERTS and EXPERTISE terms, I used the semantic categories from the *Historical Thesaurus of English* (HTE), which have been annotated into the corpus. The advantage of this approach is the quick retrieval of a large number of terms, although their analysis is not unproblematic, as will be seen below. The HTE does not include a separate category for experts, so I focus on two categories whose labels best correspond to the definitions of

---

6. Issues with the metadata and poor precision of the OCR process associated specifically with the Google N-gram corpus (Koplenig 2017; McEnery & Baker 2016) are less of an issue with the Hansard Corpus.

7. EXPERTS and EXPERT KNOWLEDGE are not of course exceptional in this sense, as this is true for many conceptually defined categories.

expertise and expert knowledge discussed above. For EXPERTS, the category in focus is AR:36:B:01, which stands for *Learned person, scholar,* and for EXPERT KNOWLEDGE, the relevant category is AR:36:C, labelled *Branch of knowledge.*

After retrieving the frequencies for these terms from the corpus, the lists were critically reviewed to optimise the precision and recall of the quantitative analysis. As for precision, this amounted to making the data less noisy by excluding terms whose main senses do not correspond to EXPERTS or EXPERT KNOWLEDGE. To mitigate the recall problem – the possibility that the chosen semantic categories do not contain all relevant EXPERT terms – the lists were complemented with other potentially relevant terms (*scientist, philosopher, economist* and *consultant*). For each term in focus, time series were extracted and graphically represented as trellis plots to facilitate comparisons.

4. Results

In what follows, I first present the results of the frequency analysis for EXPERTS (Section 4.1) and discuss the procedure of term selection in some detail, including the necessary interpretative caveats, which largely apply to the analysis of EXPERT KNOWLEDGE (Section 4.2). After that, Section 4.3 investigates the rhetorical functions of the term *expert* in the light of Collins's (2014) 'Periodic table of expertises'.

4.1 EXPERTS

The analysis of frequencies of terms for EXPERTS indicates an overall increase across the time period 1800–2005, as can be seen in Figure 8.1, which shows the aggregate of frequencies of all terms corresponding to the semantic category *Learned person, scholar.* Following a period of steady increase in the nineteenth century from 0.04 to 0.08 per 1,000 words (ptw), there is a sharp rise in 1880–1890 up to 0.12 ptw, after which the frequencies remain essentially at the same level with some fluctuation. However, as previously indicated, this figure is problematic because it includes some terms which are not fully compatible with the concept of EXPERT elaborated in Section 2, such as

- terms that clearly do not match the definition of EXPERT (even though they may indicate a degree of learnedness), such as *artist, mistress, gnostic* or *beggar;*[8]

---

8. The raw data also include some apparently erroneously tagged terms such as *cupola,* but these do not have a considerable influence on the analysis due to their low frequencies.

- terms that could reasonably function as legitimate EXPERT terms but due to their polysemy are expected to have poor precision. This is particularly problematic in the case of very frequent terms such as *authority* or *worthy*.[9]

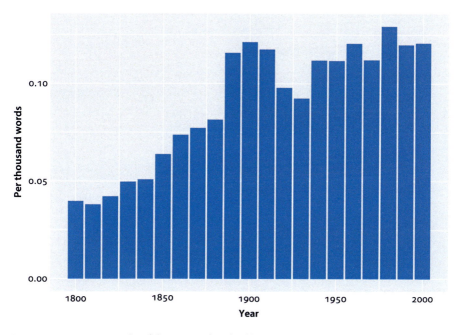

Figure 8.1 Mean normalised frequency (ptw) of *learned person, scholar* (AR:36:B:01)

In addition, aggregate frequencies are less than ideal since they may conflate different patterns of change of individual terms, and at the same time they give little information about the use of infrequent terms, as any changes in their frequencies are neutralised by the patterns of frequently occurring terms. To provide a more accurate approximation of the frequency of use of EXPERTS, a better solution is clearly to focus on (1) more frequent terms which are conceptually closer to the 'prototypical' EXPERT, and (2) their comparison side-by-side. To this end, Figure 8.2 shows the mean normalised frequency per million words (pmw) of five core EXPERT terms (both singular and plural forms): *expert, experts, doctor, doctors,*

---

9. Another possible caveat is the fact that that some terms like *think-tank* and *clerisy* refer to collectives of people rather than individuals, but these are unlikely to present major problems, as they can reasonably be regarded as equivalent to plural forms like *experts*.

scholar, scholars, academic,[10] *academics, specialist* and *specialists*, which together make up 43%[11] of the tokens of this semantic category in the Hansard Corpus.

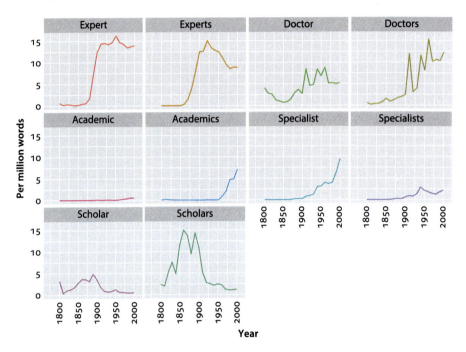

Figure 8.2 Mean normalised frequency (pmw) of selected words referring to EXPERTS

As can be seen in Figure 8.2, most of these core terms increase in frequency over the time period in focus. In particular, we can note that the pattern for *expert* (both singular and plural) follows the well-known S-shaped curve across the nineteenth century and as such largely parallels the pattern attested for aggregated frequencies in Figure 8.1: there is a dramatic increase in the fourth quarter of the nineteenth century followed by a plateau, which suggests a major change in the usage which is likely to be driven by a cultural shift. The two forms diverge in the twentieth century: for the singular form (*expert*), there is moderate fluctuation with a peak in 1950, whereas the frequency of the plural form (*experts*) starts to decrease gradually after a peak in the 1920s.

Like *expert(s)*, *doctor* and *doctors* also exhibit an upward frequency trend in the twentieth century, which is more dramatic for the plural term. *Specialist*

---

10. Tagged as a noun.
11. The percentage is 88% if the tokens of *authority/authorities* are excluded from the aggregate counts.

(singular) and *academics* (plural) have similarly increased, but the sharp rise in their frequencies takes place later, towards the end of the twentieth century. Interestingly, there is no parallel increase for *specialists* (plural) or *academic* (singular). Finally, *scholars* exhibits a distinct pattern with a sharp rise and a peak in the second part of the nineteenth century and a sudden drop at the turn of the century.

As described in Section 3, the problem of recall can be addressed by complementing the list with relevant terms missing from the original list. Indeed, it turns out that the category *Learned person, scholar* excludes many terms denoting individual specialist experts, such as *scientist*[12] and *economist*, which would ideally be considered in a full analysis of EXPERTS. To complement the analysis, Figure 8.3 shows the frequencies of *scientist* and three other terms of potential interest: *economist*, *philosopher* and *consultant*. The use of *philosopher*, like *scholar*, dwindles after the beginning of the twentieth century, whereas both *scientist* and *economist* peak in the middle of the twentieth century. *Consultant* is on the rise throughout the same timeframe.

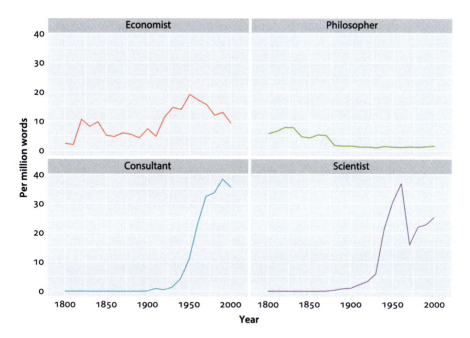

Figure 8.3 Mean normalised frequency (pmw) of complementary terms denoting EXPERTS

---

12. The terms *science* and *scientist* are actually listed in the category *Branch of knowledge*, as well as in *Study of society* (AY:02), where they occur exclusively with the adjectival premodifier *social*.

Looking at Figures 8.2 and 8.3, we can also note that the frequencies of individual terms display rather divergent trajectories, and this is even true for individual wordforms of some lemmas (e.g. *academic*). This finding has two important implications, one related to the analysis of expertise and the other to methodology. The implication for the analysis of expertise is that the linkage between frequency data, and societal and cultural change, is not straightforward, and generalisations are therefore to be made with caution. Some specific links can reasonably be postulated based on frequency data: for example, a steep increase in public spending in the nineteenth century (see e.g. Brien & Keep 2018) coincides with the growth in the mentions of *expert/experts*, and it seems likely that there is also a causal link between the two. Likewise, the decline of these terms roughly coincides with the economic downturn of the 1970s and the general erosion of trust in the power of social sciences to alleviate societal problems (Hird 2005: 11–12), and it could reasonably be hypothesised that these developments are also linked. However, this trajectory seems somewhat specific to *expert(s)*, as the shape of the frequency curve is not fully matched by other curves, so it is clear that a variety of factors are involved in the explanation. In addition, given the polysemy of the terms mentioned above, it is likely that all the curves in Figure 8.2 contain some 'noise' when treated as EXPERT terms, which underlines the necessity of qualitative evidence gleaned from horizontal reading of examples in context. This is the topic of Section 4.3, which focuses specifically on the term *expert*.

The methodological implication is the confirmation of the value of individualised analyses, which in turn means that generalisations about EXPERTS may be difficult to obtain. At the same time, this divergence is not altogether surprising, given that the terms grouped in the same semantic category in HTE are not meant to be fully synonymous.

In addition, previous studies have shown that even distributions of wordforms often vary based on their dominant phraseological behaviours (e.g. Hunston 2003); thus, if *academic* and *academics* were associated with different grammatical environments, then we should not be surprised that their frequencies would also be different. The collocations of the core terms in Figure 8.2 indicate that they are indeed used in divergent ways and not always in reference to the use of experts as part of the political process: for example, *doctor* and *doctors* often refer to medical professionals, and the increasing frequency of the two terms in the Hansard data is likely to be due to there being more discussion about the provision of healthcare, rather than *doctors* being used as scientific experts in policymaking.

In sum, with these caveats in mind, we can conclude that measured as the frequency of use of relevant terms, the overall presence of EXPERTS in parliamentary discourse has increased over time. At the same time, the variation observed in the data underlines the importance of looking into the trajectories of individual terms separately.

4.2 EXPERT KNOWLEDGE

Many of the methodological caveats discussed in the previous section also apply to the analysis of EXPERT KNOWLEDGE. The problem of precision is particularly acute, as the inventory of terms corresponding to the semantic category *Branch of knowledge* in Hansard is varied,[13] which underlines the necessity of pruning the list for quantitative analysis. Figure 8.4 shows the candidate terms selected from the complete list – *theory, science, experiment(s), observation(s), scheme, approach(es), theory/theories, discipline* and *technology*.

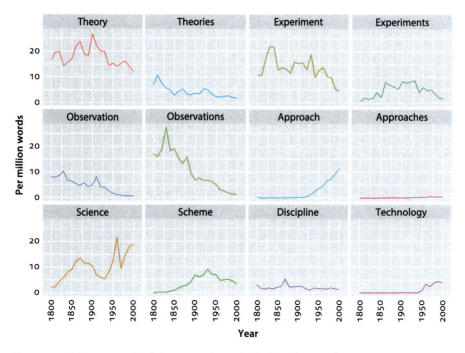

Figure 8.4 Mean normalised frequency (pmw) of selected terms denoting EXPERT KNOWLEDGE

However, it turns out that even these candidate terms are often used in senses not directly related to EXPERT KNOWLEDGE, and the trendlines clearly contain varying degrees of noise as a result. For this reason, even though the downward tra-

---

13. The complete list contains 221 types, and many of them are highly polysemous.

jectories of *observation(s)*, *theories*, and *experiment* resembling inverted S-curves appear interesting at first glance, their decrease cannot be solely attributed to cultural change related to expertise due to their problematic status as EXPERT KNOWLEDGE terms (especially with respect to the narrow definition of Boswell 2009). What further complicates the interpretation is the fact that these terms present a more mixed array of trajectories which cannot be reduced into a simple generalisation. Along with terms that are on the decrease, other terms in the figure (*science*, *approach* and *technology*) show an upward trajectory, similar to that observed for many EXPERT terms in Section 4.1.

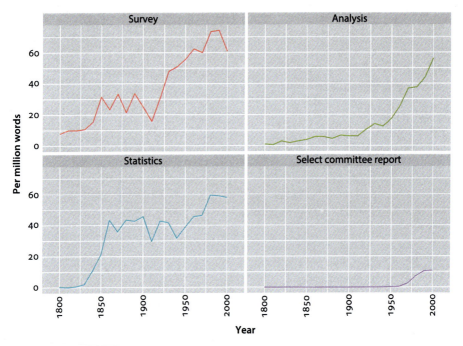

Figure 8.5 Mean normalised frequency (pmw) of complementary terms denoting expert knowledge

To address the recall problem for EXPERT KNOWLEDGE terms, this list was further complemented with four additional terms which were deemed to match the operational definition and for which better precision can be achieved. These complementary terms are *survey*, *analysis*, *statistics* and *select committee report*, and their frequencies are plotted in Figure 8.5. All these terms show an increase especially in the second half of the twentieth century, which suggests that the references to, and possibly reliance on, expert knowledge has indeed been on the increase (see Conway & Gore 2019). Particularly notable is the way in which the reforms of the select committee structure from the 1960s onwards are clearly visible in the steep rise of the term *select committee report* continuing into the twenty-first century (see Example (2)).

(2)   I and my party advocate moving towards funded pensions: Paragraph 12 of the Social Security *Select Committee report* suggests that changing demographic structures will require a substantial increase in national resources devoted to the pension system, unless further cuts were made in pension benefit levels and entitlement.   (John Denham, House of Commons, 11 December 1996)

The increase of *select committee report* is a clear example of a language-external change having a specific impact on linguistic usage, which can be observed in diachronic frequency data. This is in contrast with the other terms, which reflect cultural shifts in a more indirect fashion.

To sum up, even though the semantic category *Branch of knowledge* presents several issues when used as a proxy for EXPERT KNOWLEDGE, the increasing frequencies of selected key terms provide additional support for the increasing presence of expertise in parliamentary debates, matching the findings for EXPERTS discussed in Section 4.1.

4.3   Rhetorical functions of EXPERT terms

The quantitative analysis of both EXPERT and EXPERT KNOWLEDGE has highlighted the importance of qualitative analysis, and for this reason the final section considers how mentions of these terms function in the context of parliamentary debates. The aim of this section is to explore the range of functions that can be identified in the data, and in particular whether specific instantiations of Collins's (2014) 'Periodic table of expertises' can be attested. The discussion focuses exclusively on *expert* (including its derivative forms), which is the most frequently used EXPERT word and semantically a constitutive term of the entire category.

Collins's model identifies *contributory expertise* and *interactional expertise* as key components of specialist expertise, and both can often be attested in actual passages. The notion of contributory expertise is explicitly signalled in Example (3) through the mention that experts have studied the matter in question, and the suggestion that these experts are largely in agreement implies that there is interaction between them. Example (4) does not explicate whether the agreement is based on the experts' own scientific contributions or their *primary source knowledge* (knowledge gleaned from extensive reading of scientific literature); we can assume that the latter is always involved, given the cumulative nature of scientific knowledge and the collaborative nature of scientific work. Both Examples (3) and (4) thus represent the most prototypical function of

EXPERTS in parliamentary discourse: their use as part of a rhetorical strategy whereby expert knowledge legitimises a claim by implying that it is backed by good evidence (see Weiss's (1979) *tactical model* and Reyes's (2011) *legitimation through voices of expertise*).

(3) Many *experts* have studied the problem of restoring prosperity to that sorely tried region: Of course, there is not unanimity among them, but I believe there is a large measure of agreement that prosperity in the Highlands must in great measure depend upon forestry, farming and allied activities of that kind.

(Philip Noel-Baker, House of Commons, 10 September 1941)

(4) Indeed, it is of some urgency that such developments be speeded up because many *experts* agree that there are many areas in which tests on animals are irrelevant to man

(Edward Willis (Lord Willis), House of Lords, 10 December 1973)

In addition to specialist expertises, we can identify cases where specific instances of EXPERT terms make reference to the application of meta-expertise, which in Collins's terminology refers to cases where people discriminate between specialist experts without being experts themselves, with the help of social criteria. This discrimination is implicitly present in Example (3), where the speaker appears to have applied some form of meta-expertise by concluding there to be agreement despite the lack of unanimity, although it is not clear whether this is a case of *ubiquitous* or *local discrimination*. Example (5) is a better example of local discrimination: here the speaker justifies his reliance on advice by a specific expert by adding a statement about his credentials.

(5) All *experts* agree that, given the goodwill, the delay in building a northern bypass need not be more than two to three years: Mr. Brian Parker, *who has been mentioned several times today by various noble Lords and who is a highly qualified independent road engineer*, has advised that a northern route could be in operation within five years...

(Christopher Finch-Hatton (The Earl of Winchilsea and Nottingham), House of Lords, 5 December 1985)

Another form of meta-expertise is *referred expertise*, which is present in instances where the speakers are not experts on the specific matter being discussed but claim to have some relevant expertise due to their expertise in some other area. This can also be attested in Hansard, and is illustrated in Example (6).

(6) I do not pretend to have any *expertise* as regards the armed services but I have *expertise* as regards the police and prison services.

(John Harris (Lord Harris of Greenwich), House of Lords, 24 July 1991)

This example is also interesting in another way: the speaker does not allude to an expert outside the parliament, but himself adopts the role of expert on a specific policy issue. Although the speaker is unlikely to claim to be a 'specialist expert' in Collins's sense, the implication is clearly that this form of referred expertise provides him more authority to opine on the armed services than mere ubiquitous expertise or common sense. Considering concordance lines of *expert*, Example (6) is hardly an isolated case: in fact, MPs routinely comment on their own expertise and the expertise of others, both in positive (Example (7)) and negative terms (Example (8)).

(7) *My hon: Friend*, who is a great *expert* in these matters, says that our railway rates are the highest in the world,...
> (George Lambert, House of Commons, 10 April 1922)

(8) I have great respect for *the hon: Gentleman*, who has considerable *expertise* in these matters, but he is wrong.
> (Nick Raynsford, House of Commons, 4 May 1999)

The final two examples also relate to the rhetorical use of expertise, but in a different way: they represent situations where the MPs' proposals are prefaced with a statement where they acknowledge that they do not have expertise on the matter being discussed, followed by a statement that downplays the importance of such expertise in the specific context. In Example (9), in the absence of precise metrics on the efficiency of Russian shipyards, the speaker legitimises his claim with an allusion to labour practices, which is presented as a sufficient theoretical rationalisation in this context (see van Leeuwen 2007: 103). Example (10) shows an extract related to the MMR vaccine controversy in the UK, where the speaker positions himself as a layperson and as a representative of the concerns of his constituents, to whom he is also accountable through elections.

(9) I am afraid that I am not an *expert* on the time taken by Russian shipyards, but if Russian labour practices are anything to go by, they are considerably slower and less efficient than our own commendable yards.
> (Jonathan Aitken, House of Commons, 12 April 1994)

(10) The measles, mumps and rubella vaccine is a difficult subject, but it is extremely important for my constituents. I do not profess to be an *expert* on the matter but I shall do my best to represent constituents who have presented me with a compelling set of circumstances that I feel obliged to raise on their behalf in this debate. (Norman Baker, House of Commons, 19 November 2003)

This controversy was sparked by a fraudulent research paper published in *Lancet* in 1998 suggesting a link between the MMR vaccine and autism. Although the link has been totally discredited, it led to a public health crisis and mistrust of medicine (see Flaherty 2011). The MMR controversy is a prime example of the range of issues, actors and agendas that emerge in the context of technical decision-making, and it has received a great deal of attention in science and technology studies (e.g. Collins 2004, Chapter 4).

This brief discussion of the data from a qualitative perspective has shown that EXPERT terms are used for a variety of rhetorical functions in Hansard, which can be usefully described with the help of previous sociological research on expertise. At the same time, it has shown that even detailed taxonomies (such as Collins 2014) do not exhaustively capture all instances of terms, which are not only used for introducing expert voices in the argumentation but also appear in contexts where MPs contest someone else's expertise, admit their own lack of knowledge or question the value of expert knowledge altogether. This in turn suggests that the diachronic analysis of expertise from a quantitative perspective would benefit from a more fine-grained breakdown of different phraseological contexts in which the terms are embedded.

5. Conclusion

The advantage of using corpora in the analysis of concepts and discourse is that they can provide empirical validations for theoretical claims and allow us to make generalisations based on a large amount of data. In this study, the corpus-pragmatic analysis of EXPERTS and EXPERT KNOWLEDGE in the Hansard Corpus has shown that many key terms (and notably the term *expert*) clearly increase in frequency across the 200-year time-period covered by the corpus, which matches the expectations based on the increasing complexity of issues on which decisions need to be made. It has also established that semantic categories can be used in the study of expertise in Hansard, provided that some adjustments are made in the selection of terms considering both usage data from concordance lines and the relevant previous work in sociology and science studies, as shown in the discussion of quantitative evidence. These adjustments help to mitigate to some extent the problems associated with the analysis of word frequencies as evidence of cultural change (see e.g. Jockers 2013: 118–122).

At the same time, the qualitative analysis has made it clear that the actual trajectories of change are more complex than what the time series data would imply, due to the polysemy of the search terms as well as the diversity of contexts and rhetorical aims represented in the Hansard data. While this does not prevent generalisations, it strongly suggests that a more nuanced method of analysis, which would be more sensitive to word senses and rhetorical and phrasal contexts, would reduce the amount of noise in the data and increase construct validity. The downside of such an approach is obviously the amount of work needed for a more detailed annotation of the data. Research is also needed to establish whether the two houses of parliament differ in how they refer to experts, or whether there are differences between the representatives of different political parties.

References

Alexander, Marc & Davies, Mark. 2015. The Hansard Corpus 1803–2005. <https://www.english-corpora.org/hansard/> (18 August 2021).

Archer, Dawn. 2017. Mapping Hansard impression management strategies through time and space. *Studia Neophilologica* 89 (Supplement 1): 5–20.

Bazerman, Charles. 1994. *Constructing Experience*. Carbondale: Southern Illinois University Press.

Blaxill, Luke & Beelen, Kaspar. 2016. A feminized language of democracy? The representation of women at Westminster since 1945. *Twentieth Century British History* 27(3): 412–449.

Bondi, Marina, Cacchiani, Silvia & Mazzi, Davide. 2015. Discourse in and through the media: Recontextualizing and reconceptualizing expert discourse. In *Discourse in and through the Media: Recontextualizing and Reconceptualizing Expert Discourse*, Marina Bondi, Silvia Cacchiani & Davide Mazzi (eds), 1–20. Newcastle upon Tyne: Cambridge Scholars.

Boswell, Christina. 2009. *The Political Uses of Expert Knowledge: Immigration Policy and Social Research*. Cambridge: CUP.

Brien, Philip & Keep, Matthew. 2018. The public finances: A historical overview. *House of Commons Library Briefing Paper*, no. 8265.

Brown, Mark B. 2009. *Science in Democracy: Expertise, Institutions, and Representation*. Cambridge, Mass.: MIT Press.

Collins, Harry M. 2014. *Are We All Scientific Experts Now?* Cambridge: Polity.

Collins, Harry M. & Evans, Robert. 2002. The third wave of science studies: Studies of expertise and experience. *Social Studies of Science* 32(2): 235–296.

Collins, Harry M. & Evans, Robert. 2007. *Rethinking Expertise*. Chicago: University of Chicago Press.

Conway, Gareth E. & Gore, Julie. 2019. Framing and translating expertise for government. In *The Oxford Handbook of Expertise*, Paul Ward, Jan Maarten Schraagen, Julie Gore & Emilie M. Roth (eds), 1132–1152. Oxford: OUP.

Davies, William. 2018. *Nervous States: How Feeling Took over the World*. London: Jonathan Cape.

Ericsson, K. Anders. 2018. An introduction to the second edition of the *Cambridge Handbook of Expertise and Expert Performance*: Its development, organization, and content. In *The Cambridge Handbook of Expertise and Expert Performance* (Cambridge Handbooks in Psychology), 2nd ed., K. Anders Ericsson, Robert R. Hoffman, Aaron Kozbelt & A. Williams (eds), 3–20. Cambridge: CUP.

Flaherty, Dennis K. 2011. The vaccine-autism connection: A public health crisis caused by unethical medical practices and fraudulent science. *Annals of Pharmacotherapy* 45(10), 1302–1304.

doi Hiltunen, Turo, Räikkönen, Jenni & Tyrkkö, Jukka. 2020. Investigating colloquialization in the British parliamentary record in the late 19th and early 20th century. In *New Perspectives on Democratization: Evidence from English(es)*, Turo Hiltunen & Lucía Loureiro-Porto (eds). Special issue of *Language Sciences* 79: 101270.

Hird, John A. 2005. *Power, Knowledge, and Politics: Policy Analysis in the States. American Governance and Public Policy*. Washington DC: Georgetown University Press.

doi Hoffmann, Sebastian. 2013. Using tag sequences to retrieve grammatical structures. In *Research Methods in Language Variation and Change*, Manfred Krug & Julia Schlüter (eds), 195–211. Cambridge: CUP.

doi Hunston, Susan. 2003. Lexis, wordform and complementation pattern. *Functions of Language* 10(1): 31–60.

doi Jaffe, Alexandra. 2007. Variability in transcription and the complexities of representation, authority and voice. *Discourse Studies* 9(6): 831–836.

doi Jockers, Matthew Lee. 2013. *Macroanalysis: Digital Methods and Literary History*. Urbana IL: University of Illinois Press.

doi Jones, Bill & Norton, Philip. 2014. *Politics UK*. London: Routledge.

doi Koplenig, Alexander. 2017. The impact of lacking metadata for the measurement of cultural and linguistic change using the Google Ngram data sets: Reconstructing the composition of the German corpus in times of WWII. *Digital Scholarship in the Humanities* 32(1): 169–188.

doi Larsen, Peder Olesen & von Ins, Markus. 2010. The rate of growth in scientific publication and the decline in coverage provided by Science Citation Index. *Scientometrics* 84(3): 575–603.

McEnery, Anthony & Baker, Helen. 2016. *Corpus Linguistics and 17th-Century Prostitution: Computational Linguistics and History*. London: Bloomsbury Academic.

doi Michel, Jean-Baptiste, Shen, Yuan Kui, Aiden, Aviva Presser, Veres, Adrian, Gray, Matthew K., The Google Books Team, Pickett, Joseph P., Hoiberg, Dale, Clancy, Dan, Norvig, Peter, Orwant, Jon, Pinker, Steven, Nowak, Martin A. & Aiden, Erez Lieberman. 2011. Quantitative analysis of culture using millions of digitized books. *Science* 331(6014): 176–182.

doi Mollin, Sandra. 2007. The Hansard hazard: Gauging the accuracy of British parliamentary transcripts. *Corpora* 2(2): 187–210.

doi Myers, Greg. 1985. Texts as knowledge claims: The social construction of two biology articles. *Social Studies of Science* 15(4): 593–630.

Nichols, Tom. 2017. *The Death of Expertise: The Campaign Against Established Knowledge and Why It Matters*. Oxford: OUP.

Nutley, Sandra M., Walter, Isabel & Davies, Huw T.O. 2007. *Using Evidence: How Research Can Inform Public Services*. Bristol: Policy Press.

doi O'Brien, Timothy L. 2013. Scientific authority in policy contexts: Public attitudes about environmental scientists, medical researchers, and economists. *Public Understanding of Science* 22(7): 799–816.

doi Pielke, Roger A. 2007. *The Honest Broker: Making Sense of Science in Policy and Politics*. Cambridge: CUP.

doi Port, M.H. 1990. The official record. *Parliamentary History* 9(1): 175–183.

Reyes, Antonio. 2011. Strategies of legitimization in political discourse: From words to actions. *Discourse & Society* 22(6): 781–807.

Rühlemann, Christoph & Aijmer, Karin. 2015. Corpus pragmatics: Laying the foundations. In *Corpus Pragmatics: A Handbook*, Karin Aijmer & Christoph Rühlemann (eds), 1–26. Cambridge: CUP.

Swales, John M. 1990. *Genre Analysis: English in Academic and Research Settings*. Cambridge: CUP.

Swales, John M. 2004. *Research Genres: Explorations and Applications*. Cambridge: CUP.

Tribble, Christopher. 2019. Expert, native or lingua franca? Paradigm choices in novice academic writer support. In *Novice Writers and Scholarly Publication: Authors, Mentors, Gatekeepers*, Pejman Habibie & Ken Hyland (eds), 53–75. Cham: Springer.

Väliverronen, Esa. 2016. *Julkinen Tiede* (Public Science). Tampere: Vastapaino.

Väliverronen, Esa & Saikkonen, Sampsa. 2020. Freedom of expression challenged: Scientists' perspectives on hidden forms of suppression and self-censorship. *Science, Technology, & Human Values* 46(6): 1172–1200.

van Leeuwen, Theo. 2007. Legitimation in discourse and communication. *Discourse & Communication* 1(1): 91–112.

Ward, Paul, Schraagen, Jan Maarten, Gore, Julie & Roth, Emilie M. 2019. An introduction to the handbook, communities of practice, and definitions of expertise. In *The Oxford Handbook of Expertise*, Paul Ward, Jan Maarten Schraagen, Julie Gore & Emilie M. Roth (eds). Oxford: OUP.

Weiss, Carol H. 1979. The many meanings of research utilization. *Public Administration Review* 39(5): 426–431.

CHAPTER 9

Processing and prescriptivism as constraints on language variation and change

Relative clauses in British and Australian English parliamentary debates[*]

Sofie Labat[1], Haidee Kotze[2,3] & Benedikt Szmrecsanyi[4]
[1] Ghent University | [2] Utrecht University | [3] North-West University | [4] KU Leuven

We investigate the choice between the relative markers *which* and *that* in 8,283 restrictive relative clauses on subject position, with inanimate antecedents, in a written corpus consisting of British and Australian Hansard materials over five sampling years (1901, 1935, 1965, 1995, 2015). Our aim is to determine how processing-related factors and prescriptivism-related factors influence processes of language variation and change across two varieties of English. We analyse how the language-external variables of period and variety (British, Australian) interact with two groups of language-internal variables, namely predictors related to language processing and linguistic predictors associated with prescriptivism. The analysis shows that the relativiser *that* has been on the rise over the past century. The increase is particularly pronounced in the British Hansard, as *which* was comparatively frequent in early twentieth-century British material. As to the relative importance of predictors, we find that language-external predictors are the most important in conditioning the variation in relative markers, followed by processing-related constraints. Prescriptivism-related variables tend to generally be less important in this type of variation.

Keywords: restrictive relative clause, Australian English, British English, real-time study, language processing, prescriptivism

---

[*] This article is based on Labat (2018), and there is thus some overlap between sections of the dissertation and the article.

https://doi.org/10.1075/scl.111.09lab
© 2023 John Benjamins Publishing Company

1. Introduction

The alternation (or, in Labovian parlance, 'variable') we are investigating in this chapter is that between *which* and *that* as relativisers introducing subject restrictive relative clauses after inanimate antecedents, as in Example (1).

(1) a. The mail_antecedent [*that* was sent yesterday]_relative clause has arrived.
     b. The mail_antecedent [*which* was sent yesterday]_relative clause has arrived.

We stress at the outset that the way we define the variable context (which follows the circumscription in e.g. Szmrecsanyi 2019) means that zero relativisers (of the type *the book ___ I bought*), reduced relative clauses (of the type *the book written*), and *wh*-relativisers other than *which* (e.g. *the man who won*) do not come under the remit of this study. In Standard English, zero and reduced relatives only occur in *object* relative clauses, while for example *who* we find only after *animate* antecedents. In short, these are variants that are part of different alternations or variables in Labovian terminology.

Although in Standard English restrictive relative clauses after inanimate antecedents both *that* and *which* are grammatically correct (Biber et al. 2007: 615–616), their distribution differs drastically across registers. This register variation reflects the difference in formality between the two relative markers, as *that* is more frequently used in informal contexts such as conversations and fiction, while *which* is the preferred relativiser in formal, usually written, contexts such as newspaper articles and academic prose (Biber et al. 2007: 610; Sigley 1997). Moreover, Tagliamonte, Smith and Lawrence (2005) explain that the *wh*-relativisers probably entered the English language through formal written registers. According to their data, the *wh*-forms have surprisingly low frequencies in three vernacular varieties of English in Britain, which seems to be a product of "resistance to or general 'distance' from changes taking place in mainstream varieties" (Tagliamonte, Smith & Lawrence 2005: 105).

Variation in relativisation is a well-researched topic in linguistics (see e.g. Collins 2014; D'Arcy & Tagliamonte 2010; Hinrichs, Szmrecsanyi & Bohmann 2015; Leech & Smith 2006, 2009; Leech et al. 2009; Sigley 1997; Tagliamonte, Smith & Lawrence 2005). Most research has focused on American and British English, with some exceptions such as Collins (2014) who investigated Australian English, or Sigley (1997) who used corpora of New Zealand English to determine the role of formality in the choice of relative marker. Some important outputs from this large body of literature are (a) the general increase in *that* at the cost of *which* in written English, (b) the fact that this shift is spearheaded by American English, while British English seems to be more conservative, and (c) arguments that propose an explanation for the shift from *which* to *that*, such as colloquialisation and prescriptivism.

The current study extends previous work on relativisation by drawing on a unique hybrid spoken-written register, the Hansard, the edited written record of parliamentary debates in Commonwealth countries. We sampled British and Australian Hansard material over five sampling years: 1901, 1935, 1965, 1995 and 2015. One of our aims is to examine how the choice between *that* and *which* is probabilistically conditioned over time and across varieties of English. We view the Hansard as produced by the linguistic processing of two sets of users, overlaid on each other: the spoken debates and speeches of parliamentarians, and the transformation of this spoken material into a written record by reporters and editors (Kruger, van Rooy & Smith 2019; see also Kotze et al., this volume). In this respect, it is important to underscore that writing is distinct from speech in several ways. It is not subject to processing pressures under time constraints, and can be carefully crafted and edited to adhere to particular normative and prescriptive constraints (see e.g. Harder 2012). As the distribution of restrictive relative markers changes across registers, channels, and according to the degree of formality involved, our analysis renders some interesting insights on this distribution in the hybrid spoken-written register of the Hansard.

In addition to these language-external factors, we also investigate language-internal predictors and their role in conditioning the alternation between *that* and *which*. One group of language-internal factors is linked to processing effects and constraints. Existing research shows that as the degree of sentence complexity or general processing load increases (which is linked to a similar rise in formality), the relative marker *which* becomes increasingly preferred (see e.g. Sigley 1997). For example, the length of the antecedent and the length of the relative clause are significant predictors in the alternation, and as the length of these constituents increases, the likelihood of *which*, rather than *that*, also rises. The second group of language-internal factors is related to prescriptivism. Hinrichs, Szmrecsanyi and Bohmann (2015) devise an indirect way of determining whether prescription has an influence on the choice of relativiser, by defining a set of predictors related to other prescriptivist advice given in the same style guides (see e.g. Strunk & White 2000) that advocate the so-called *that*-rule. This rule prescribes the use of *that* in restrictive relative clauses, while it aims to restrict the use of *which* to non-restrictive relative clauses. The assumption is that writers are likely to follow prescriptive advice consistently. For example, writers who disregard advice to avoid passive constructions will probably also not comply with the *that*-rule. We investigate the interplay between the language-external (period and variety) and language-internal predictors by means of a multivariate analysis of 8,283 annotated restrictive relative clauses.

Our findings are presented in two parts. First, we consider a number of contingency tables that model the distribution of restrictive relative markers *that* and *which* across time and geography. Our analysis shows that while the relativiser *that* increases in both British and Australian Hansard material, the increase is especially pronounced in the British Hansard between 1965 and 1995, while the shift seems to have happened more gradually in Australian Hansard material. Secondly, a number of random forest models (Breiman 2001) are calculated to compare the relative importance of constraints. In this respect, we find that language-external predictors are the most important constraints on variation in relative markers, followed by processing-related constraints. Prescriptivism-related variables generally tend to be less important, with the exception of the predictor passive-active ratio which is the third most important predictor for both Australian and British English.

The next section provides a concise overview of relevant literature on (a) the relative marker alternation, (b) research on Australian and British English, and (c) prescriptivism and its influence on language variation and change. Section 3 reflects on the methodology that was used to investigate the relative marker alternation in this study. Our hybrid spoken-written corpus is presented in more detail in Section 3.1, whereafter we give a technical description of the variable context of interest in Section 3.2. Section 3.3 introduces the different predictors used in the analysis, and Section 3.4 outlines the analysis methods. In Section 4, we present the findings of the analysis, focusing first on the distribution of the relativisers over time and across varieties, and then on the importance of the different predictors in conditioning the variation. Finally, Section 5 offers some concluding remarks and suggestions for future research.

2. Background

2.1 The relative marker alternation

The literature distinguishes between two types of relative clauses in English, namely restrictive relative clauses (RRCs) and non-restrictive relative clauses (NRRCs), as in Example (2a) and (2b) respectively.

(2) a. In China no consideration is shown to witnesses who are brought up and detained as long as may be thought necessary in the interests of justice, and are tortured if they do not give the evidence [*that* is expected of them]$_{RRC}$. (Australian House of Representatives Hansard, 30 August 1901)

b. This harmless-looking Amendment, [*which* is almost like a drafting Amendment and which has been presented partly as an improvement in drafting]$_{NRRC}$, has considerable implications.

(British House of Commons Hansard, 22 January 1965)

According to Biber et al. (2007:195), "[r]estrictive relative clauses are used to establish the reference of the antecedent, while non-restrictive relatives give additional information which is not required for identification". The restrictive relative clause in Example (2a) identifies the antecedent *evidence*: the clause distinguishes the antecedent *evidence* from other pieces of evidence by adding that this is the evidence *that is expected of them*. In the relative clause in Example (2b), some additional information about the *harmless-looking Amendment* is given, but this information is "not required for identification" (ibid.). In general, relative clauses can be introduced by a range of relativisers: *that, ø,*[1] *what, when, where, which, who, whom* and *whose*. The relativiser *that* can only introduce restrictive relative clauses in Standard English, while *which* is used for both restrictive and non-restrictive relative clauses.

In this chapter, we focus on restrictive relative clauses in subject position; in other words, restrictive relative clauses of which the relativiser introducing the clause is also the subject of the clause. In standard English, such restrictive clauses can be introduced by *that, which* or *who*. Biber et al. (2007) explain that the "relative pronoun *which* rarely occurs with an animate head. Although *which* is attested in conversation as a relative pronoun with animate heads, this occurs so rarely that it might be considered a speech error" (Biber et al. 2007:613). In contrast, the relative marker *who* is exclusively used with animate heads (Biber et al. 2007:612). The relative marker *that*, however, introduces both animate and inanimate antecedents. This is why we restrict our attention to relative clauses with inanimate antecedents, thus excluding the relative marker *who* from the analysis.

As mentioned in Section 1, the distribution of *that* and *which* differs among registers. Whereas *that* is more frequently used in conversations and fiction, *which* is the most popular relativiser in British and American English newspapers and academic prose (Biber et al. 2007:610). In the same vein, Leech et al. (2009) emphasise that "there is a division between the *wh*-relatives, which are more literate in their affinity, and *that* and *zero* relatives, which are more oral" (Leech et al. 2009:227). Sigley (1997) finds that register variation illustrates the underlying difference in formality between the two relativisers. The formal character of *which* can be explained taking a diachronic perspective. In contrast to *that* and *zero*

---

1. In general, *ø* and *zero* are used interchangeably to refer to the 'non-existing' relative marker of relative clauses that start without a relativiser.

relativisers, the first *wh*-relativisers (including *which*) only entered the English language around the twelfth century (Tagliamonte, Smith & Lawrence 2005: 77). Mustanoja (1960) suggested that the *wh*-forms were borrowed from Romance (Tagliamonte, Smith & Lawrence 2005: 93). Nowadays, linguists generally agree on the theory that the *wh*-relativisers entered the English language through formal registers, in other words, complex and prestigious styles. Hence, the entrance of *wh*-relativisers into English can probably be qualified as a Labovian 'change from above', since language users were aware of the implicit prestigious status of these relativisers (ibid.).

Even though there is a difference in formality between *that* and *which*, thus causing variation among these two relativisers, researchers have also demonstrated that the distribution of *that* and *which* is in flux both diachronically and geographically. During the twentieth century, the relativiser *that* has spread as *wh*-relativisers have been declining in frequency (Collins 2014; Hinrichs, Szmrecsanyi & Bohmann 2015; Leech & Smith 2006, 2009; Leech et al. 2009). The shift is much more pronounced in American English than in British English and is "entirely due to one relative pronoun, *which*" (Leech et al. 2009: 230). Collins (2014) claims that in Australian English, the relativiser *that* "overtakes Br[itish] E[nglish] strongly in the second half of the nineteenth century and maintains a lead over [its] British English parent thereafter" (Collins 2014: 367). Collins's research indicates that in the second half of the twentieth century, there was no significant difference between American and Australian English in the *that* vs. *which* alternation. There is, however, a significant difference between Australian and British English for the same period (ibid.). Whereas British English is regarded as the more conservative variety with regard to the relative marker alternation, American English seems to be more progressive in that respect (Biber et al. 2007: 616). The steep increase in the frequency of *that* at the expense of *which* in American English is possibly the result of colloquialisation (Leech & Smith 2006: 195–196; Leech & Smith 2009: 179–181). Moreover, Leech et al. (2009), and Leech and Smith (2009) argue that the sharp decline of *which* in American English might also be the result of a strong prescriptive tradition in the US. The role of prescriptivism and its influence on the alternation is discussed in Section 2.3.

2.2 Australian English

The relationship between Australian and British English is especially interesting from a diachronic perspective, as Australian English has gradually diverged from British English over time. Schneider (2007) describes the linguistic evolution of postcolonial English varieties as a path consisting of five stages: (a) foundation,

(b) exonormative stabilisation, (c) nativisation, (d) endonormative stabilisation, and (e) differentiation. These five stages reflect the gradual loosening of bonds between new varieties of English and British English. Following this framework, the period covered in our Australian Hansard material ranges from the third stage (i.e. nativisation) to the final stage (i.e. differentiation). The exact dates that Schneider (2007) provides for the different phases in Australian English are, however, much debated, suggesting that our corpus potentially also covers the exonormative stabilisation stage. In this respect, Peters (2014) emphasises that the shift from exonormative to endonormative stabilisation is far from self-evident. Although the endonormative codification of new linguistic norms "helps to stabilize the regional variety and contributes to its endonormativity, even settler varieties of English like Canadian, New Zealand and Australian English are affected by internal variation in the changed language habitat" (Leitner 2004, paraphrased in Peters 2014: 582).

Scholarly interest in Australian English developed in the 1960s (see e.g. Mitchell & Delbridge 1965; Ramson 1966) and gained momentum in the 1980s and 1990s (see e.g. Allan 1984; Bryant 1997; Collins & Blair 1989). While there has been considerable research on this variety since, diachronic studies are limited, largely as a result of the unavailability of suitable corpora. This issue has been resolved in recent years with the compilation of more diachronic corpora of Australian English (see e.g. Collins & Yao 2018; Kruger & Smith 2018; Kruger, van Rooy & Smith 2019; Yao & Collins 2019), also to match available diachronic corpora of British and American English to facilitate cross-varietal studies.

2.3 Prescriptivism, varieties of English and language change

Prescriptive grammarians aim to formulate rules that distinguish 'correct' use of language from other, incorrect forms. In an attempt to define prescriptivism, Curzan (2014: 24) introduces four strands of prescriptivism that together cover all of 'prescriptivism's umbrella': (a) standardising prescriptivism, (b) stylistic prescriptivism, (c) restorative prescriptivism, and (d) politically responsive prescriptivism. Prescriptive advice on the *that/which*-alternation is better known as the *that*-rule (see e.g. Strunk & White 2000): usage guides recommend using *that* only in restrictive relative clauses and reserving *which* for use in non-restrictive relative clauses. The rule falls under the second strand of stylistic prescriptivism, as it is not historically or politically motivated and both *that* and *which* are grammatically correct options to introduce restrictive relative clauses. The only motivation for this rule is a quest for more grammatical symmetry: if non-restrictive relative clauses can only be introduced by *which*, then restrictive relative clauses should only be introduced by *that*.

The severity with which this *that*-rule and other prescriptive recommendations are enforced or adhered to is variable over time and across varieties of English. In their survey of post-war American, Australian and British usage books, Peters and Young (1997) investigate eleven variables of grammar and collocational syntax. They find that American usage grammars are in general more likely to accept proscribed forms than their British counterparts which are "more homogenous, cautious and conservative" (Peters & Young 1997: 322). Moreover, the range of advice given in British guides is more restricted than the advice provided in American publications. The *that*-rule is somewhat unusual in this respect, as it has consistently been implemented by American editors (see e.g. Strunk & White 2000), whereas "British and Australian usage guides take a more nuanced approach to the distribution of *that* and *which*" (Peters & Young 1997, paraphrased in Peters 2014: 584).

The influence of prescriptive or usage grammars on language is a controversial topic in modern linguistics. The descriptive linguistic approach that has held sway throughout the twentieth century developed in part in response to prescriptivism, and attempts to approach language "neutrally and scientifically" (Straaijer 2016: 235). Unfortunately, the way in which descriptivism has set itself up in contrast with prescriptivism has been coupled with a general lack of interest in prescriptivism as a topic of (descriptive) linguistic research (Kroch & Small 1978: 45), although there have been exceptions to this.

Prescriptivism is sometimes invoked as a factor in actual language change, but this claim remains speculative. In her book on the influence of nineteenth-century grammar writing on the English verb system, Anderwald (2016) concludes that "both the prescriptive nature and the prescriptive impact of nineteenth-century grammar writing on actual language change have been greatly overestimated by previous scholars" (Anderwald 2016: 245). In their research on future temporal reference in French, Poplack and Dion (2009) discover "a great and growing disconnect between the variable rules governing speech and the normative dictates that underlie the notion of the standard" (Poplack & Dion 2009: 557). In this respect, Woolard and Schieffelin (1994: 69) explain that prescriptive guidelines have little to only pernicious effects on speech, while the same norms might have a less negligible impact on written registers. Similarly, Curzan (2014) acknowledges that at present there is no conclusive evidence for any significant influence of prescriptivism on speech, but she also warns against an easy dismissal of the phenomenon, underscoring that some evidence exists for its influence on written texts. In their study on variation in relative markers in the Brown quartet of corpora, Hinrichs, Szremcsanyi and Bohmann (2015) show that prescriptivism might be one of the factors involved in conditioning the shift from *which* to *that*. Nevertheless, they conclude that prescriptivism alone cannot be seen as having caused the change, since other factors such as colloquialisation are also involved.[2]

3. Methods and data

3.1 The Hansard: A hybrid spoken-written register

As mentioned, this article draws on a unique corpus consisting of British and Australian Hansard records. Traditionally, 'Hansard' was the name given to transcripts of British parliamentary debates, but through the years, other Commonwealth countries (e.g. Australia, Canada, Fiji, New Zealand) began to use the same name for similar reports of their own parliamentary debates. The uniqueness of the Hansard as linguistic data resides in the fact that it is an edited written reconstruction of parliamentary debates and speeches. Consequently, one aspect that has occupied linguists is the extent to which this hybrid spoken-written register is an accurate representation of the original recordings (see e.g. Slembrouck 1992; Mollin 2007). Moreover, how did editorial practices for the Hansard (in different countries) change over time? (See also Kotze et al., this volume.)

While the Australian Hansard adopted a 'verbatim' policy from the beginning of the federal parliament (in 1901), the British Select Committee on Parliamentary Debates only adopted such a policy for the British Hansard in 1907. Before this time, the British Hansard was a mixture of reported and direct speech, with substantial paraphrase (see also Alexander, this volume). The Select Committee defined the notion of the full, verbatim report as one which,

> though not strictly verbatim, is substantially the verbatim report, with repetitions and redundancies omitted and with obvious mistakes corrected, but which on the other hand leaves out nothing that adds to the meaning of the speech or illustrates the argument.
> (Hansard 1907, quoted in House of Commons Information Office 2010: 3)

This is the concept of 'verbatim' that continues to underlie the production of the Hansard to this day.

It is therefore, evidently, not possible to interpret the Hansard as a true verbatim record of spoken production. In a study on British Hansard reports from

---

2. Hinrichs, Szmrecsanyi and Bohmann (2015: 830) also note that while grammar checkers these days do help enforce the *that*-rule, they cannot have set the drift towards *that* in motion, as word processors such as Microsoft Word started implementing grammar checkers only in the 1990s.

March 1987 and their corresponding recordings, Slembrouck (1992) notices "considerable discrepancies between the spoken proceedings and what is reported in direct form" (Slembrouck 1992:117). Instead of interpreting the Hansard as a verbatim record, we regard parliamentary records as reconstructions of speech, and specifically reconstructions in which various agents have participated. Kruger, van Rooy and Smith (2019:187) explain that three groups of language users participate in this "fused production":

> (a) the parliamentarians who produce speeches and participate in debates; (b) Hansard reporters, who transform the speeches and debates into written material; and (c) Hansard (sub-)editors, who polish the written record and apply the house style of the publication.

These groups are, in turn, influenced by three different sets of external mechanisms. Firstly, there is the broader social context in which the parliament itself is also embedded as an institution. The broader social context influences the three groups of language users when, for example, the society becomes less hierarchical and more democratised. Secondly, there are the factors "related to the immediate production context of the Hansard: editorial policy and practice, and production mechanisms" (Kruger, van Rooy & Smith 2019:188). This means that changes in the Hansard style manuals or innovations in the existing reporting techniques (e.g. digital recordings) also have had an impact on the Hansard. The remaining factors deal with "the relationship between the parliamentary debate/Hansard and the context. These are the aim or function of the register and the intended audience" (Kruger, van Rooy & Smith 2019:188). The radio and television broadcasts of parliamentary proceedings caused a change in the nature of the debates, as speeches became increasingly prepared and parliamentarians started realising that they were 'performing' in front of a larger audience. It is precisely these interacting factors which make the Hansard a suitable corpus for a study on the influence of prescriptivism or even colloquialisation, but the same interacting factors will also yield some interesting insights into the overlaid processing mechanisms that lie at the basis of this corpus.

The Hansard texts included in the corpus for this study were initially collected from the publicly accessible digital archives of the Australian House of Representatives and the British House of Commons Hansard, for five sample years: 1901, 1935, 1965, 1995 and 2015 (see Kruger & Smith 2018; Kruger, van Rooy & Smith 2019 for a more detailed description of the two corpora). Our corpus consists of a sample of 50 text files, each containing a single full day's sitting, from these larger corpora. The files were selected in a random fashion for each respective year and dialect, although we ensured that the sittings were distributed over the year, and controlled for the number of tokens to make sure that the ten variational settings contain an approximately similar number of words. In Table 9.1, we give an overview of the distribution of these text files across British and Australian Hansard materials and across the different sampling years. At the end of each row, the total number of texts for that period is indicated between parentheses. Note that the files are not equally distributed across different years. The reason for this is that certain text files contain fewer words than others. The Australian Hansard material of our corpus consists of 1,362,134 words, while its British counterpart contains 1,555,875 words. The corpus shown in Table 1 was part-of-speech (PoS) tagged using the Stanford Tagger.

Table 9.1 Corpus composition

Variety	Year	Token count	Dates of sittings
AusE	1901	203,713	13 December, 27 September, 28 June, 29 November, 30 August, 31 July, 31 May (7)
	1935	271,572	5 December, 10 April, 26 September, 28 November, 29 March, 31 October (6)
	1965	275,682	10 December, 26 May, 29 April, 29 October, 30 March, 30 November (6)
	1995	300,770	26 October, 28 February, 30 August (3)
	2015	314,081	17 September, 22 October, 26 February (3)
BrE	1901	250,015	1 March, 8 August, 18 February, 25 June, 26 April (5)
	1935	350,634	10 December, 24 October, 28 March, 29 April, 31 July (5)
	1965	285,918	22 December, 22 January, 26 February, 29 October, 30 April, 30 July (6)
	1995	324,096	28 April, 28 February, 30 June, 30 November, 31 October (5)
	2015	347,111	26 March, 28 May, 30 November, 30 October (4)

3.2 The variable context and corpus retrieval

Our focus in this study is on restrictive subject relative clauses with inanimate antecedents which can be introduced by either *that* or *which*. In a first step, candidate relativisers were automatically selected by means of a Perl-script, based on the following two conditions. Firstly, the relativiser had to be preceded by a noun. The noun could be either a single or mass noun, a plural noun, a singular proper noun or a plural proper noun. This implies that the relative markers *that* and *which* cannot be preceded by a comma, and thus non-restrictive relative clauses were excluded by this criterion. The Australian *Hansard Style Manual*

(Hansard 2017) adopts the following policy for punctuation with restrictive and non-restrictive relative clauses:

> The insertion or omission of a comma before a relative (...) clause is necessary to inform the reader whether that clause is defining or non-defining. If the relative clause defines – that is, contains information which is an essential part of the meaning of the sentence – it should not be marked off with commas (and should be introduced with "that" or "who").   (Hansard 2017: 82)[3]

The second selection criterion involves the word that occurs after either *that* or *which*. A first constraint is that the word which follows the relativiser cannot be a personal pronoun. If this were the case, we would be dealing with a restrictive relative clause on object position instead of one on subject position. A similar constraint was placed on other word classes, such as possessive pronouns, adjectives, nouns and determiners.

The restrictive relative clauses extracted in this way were manually inspected by the first author. If the clauses were indeed restrictive relative clauses on subject position with inanimate antecedent, they were further manually annotated. If not, they were removed from our dataset. This process yielded a dataframe containing 8,283 observations.

3.3 Predicting relativiser choice

We distinguish between three different types of predictors in this study: (a) language-external, (b) prescriptivism-related, and (c) processing-related predictors.

3.3.1 *Language-external predictors*

We include two language-external predictors, namely **year (of composition)** and **variety of English**. For the latter variable, we compare Australian Hansard material to British Hansard material. As for **year of composition**, we randomly sampled Hansard materials from five distinct points in time, namely 1901, 1935, 1965, 1995, and 2015 (as described in Section 3.1).

---

3. The style manual from which this fragment was taken is available on the Internet. It is, however, not the only circulating manual. Another style manual of the Australian Hansard that was created in 2008 (see Hansard 2008) gives more or less the same advice, but it differs on one striking point: the last part "(and should be introduced with 'that' or 'who')" is left out. In other words, editorial guidelines changed sometime between 2008 and 2017, with the 'that'-rule codified in the later style manual. Such an adaptation in editorial policies may have influenced the relative marker alternation, an important point raised in the discussion of the findings (see Section 4.1).

3.3.2 *Prescriptivism-related predictors*

The analysis in Section 4 includes six prescriptivism-related predictors: **shall-will** ratio, **passives, preposition stranding, split infinitives, presence of** *you*, and **contractions**. The first four predictors are partially replicated from Hinrichs, Szmrecsanyi and Bohmann (2015), who identify these as four variables about which "prescriptivists were propagating fairly consistent advice throughout most of the twentieth century" (Hinrichs, Szmrecsanyi & Bohmann 2015:807). Some usage grammars advise their readers to use *shall* as first-person future marker (see e.g. Strunk & White 2000), with *will* proscribed in this context. Many prescriptivist sources continue to discourage preposition stranding and the use of split infinitives. Strunk and White (2000) emphasise that "the active voice is usually more direct and vigorous than the passive" (Strunk & White 2000:28), and the active voice is therefore regarded as the prescribed form in this study.[4]

The last two predictors are prescriptivism-related predictors particular to the Hansard (Kruger & Smith 2018). In the case of the use of *you*, parliamentary convention dictates that third-person forms of address are to be used when members of parliament refer to one another, except where the Speaker is being addressed. Kruger and Smith (2018) and Kruger, van Rooy and Smith (2019) show that over time, this rule is enforced less strictly in the Australian Hansard, but maintained in the British Hansard. In the case of the use of contracted forms, this particularly spoken-language feature is largely discouraged in the Hansard.

We arbitrarily chose a sufficiently large window of 2,000 words to calculate the frequency of prescriptivism-related variables. This window was placed around the relativiser, so that typically 1,000 words before and after the relative marker are considered. In cases where the relative marker occurred less than 1,000 words from the beginning or end of the file, we simply adapted the location of the window by including all the words from the beginning/end of the file until the relative marker (window size x) and extending the window on the other side of the relativiser (window size $2,000 - x$).

Besides the predictor **presence of** *you*, all other prescriptive predictors are calculated as the number of proscribed forms divided by the number of prescribed forms. A small quotient indicates that many prescribed forms occur in the window, while a larger quotient means an increase in the number of proscribed forms. *Shall-will* ratio was calculated as the number of *will*-tokens divided by the number of *shall*-tokens. The predictor variable **passives** presents the proportion of passive conjugated verbs vis-à-vis active conjugated verbs. **Preposition stranding**

---

4. We hasten to add that usage of the passive may in principle also be considered a predictor related to language processing, as we know that all other things being equal, processing passive sentences is harder than processing active sentences (e.g. Lee & Doherty 2019).

Processing and prescriptivism as constraints on variation **263**

reflects the fraction of stranded prepositions divided by non-stranded prepositions. Values for the variable **split infinitives** equals the number of split infinitives divided by the number of infinitives that are preceded by *to*. The predictor
contractions indicates the frequency of contractions vis-à-vis the frequency of the
corresponding full forms of the words. For the variable **presence of** *you*, we consider the number of times the word *you* occurred in the 2,000-word window.

3.3.3 *Predictors related to language processing*

Language processing refers to the way in which language users choose particular
words or constructions to express their ideas, and to the way in which these communicated words are processed and understood by other language users. In this
respect, writing differs from speech in that it is not influenced by processing pressures related to time constraints. In addition, in contrast to speech, writers also do
not necessarily share the same communicative context as their readers, which has
consequences for the linguistic structures selected. As discussed in Section 3.2, we
view the Hansard as a hybrid spoken-written register produced by an overlay of
the language production of two groups: parliamentarians produce spoken debates
and speeches, after which reporters and editors reconstruct their spoken language
into written texts. Therefore, the hybrid texts from the Hansard may shed light
on the combined linguistic processing of two groups of language users. The seven
processing-related variables included in this study are **persistence, persistence
distance, distance antecedent HN start RC, distance AP start RC, length RC,
distance AP end RC,** and **mean word length.**

–   **Persistence**: It has been found that once language users have chosen for a
    particular construction, they are more likely to repeat the same construction
    further on in the text or speech (Szmrecsanyi 2006). Persistence is a Boolean
    variable that compares the current variant (i.e. *that* or *which*) to the variant
    chosen the last time there was a choice, namely *that*, *which*, or *non-applicable*
    (used in case the current variant is the first relative marker in the file). Con-
    cretely, persistence is 1 if the current and the previous relativiser are identical,
    while it receives a 0 value when this is not the case. Instances for which no
    previous relativiser exists (*non-applicable*) are not considered for this vari-
    able.
–   **Persistence distance**: This variable indicates the distance (in words) between
    the previously used relativiser and the current one in the corpus file. If the
    distance between these two relativisers increases, the odds that language users
    will re-use the previous relativiser are supposed to decrease.
–   **Distance antecedent HN start RC**: This is the number of words that occur
    between the antecedent head noun and the relativiser introducing the relative

clause, including the antecedent head noun. Hinrichs, Szmrecsanyi and Bohmann (2015: 826) observe that "[a]s antecedents and relative clauses become longer, and processing load becomes larger, writers increasingly favour (...) *which*".

- **Distance AP start RC**: This variable is the distance (in words) from the start of the antecedent phrase to the respective relativiser. This predictor is a measure of complexity.
- **Length RC**: Length (in words) of the restrictive relative clause. This predictor is another measure of complexity.
- **Distance AP end RC**: The sum of **distance AP start RC** and **length RC**.
- **Mean word length**: This last predictor measures the lexical complexity of the text surrounding the relativisers. The hypothesis is that the relativiser *which* is favoured in linguistic environments with long and complex words, thanks to its formal character. The variable **mean word length** is computed in the 2,000-word window. In this window, no distinction is made between punctuation marks and words. Since punctuation marks are included in a consistent way, the predictor **mean word length** can be used for the purpose of statistical analysis. Nevertheless, the actual mean length will probably be higher than the values of this predictor.

3.4 Analysis

Our analysis proceeds in two parts. We first consider a number of contingency tables that model the distribution of the restrictive relative markers *that* and *which* across time and varieties of English (see Section 4.1). Subsequently, we assess the relative importance of predictors by carrying out a conditional random forest analysis, as introduced by Breiman (2001) and implemented in the 'party' package in R (Strobl, Malley & Tutz 2009). In this package, random forests are calculated on the basis of numerous conditional inference trees in order to create a ranking of the importance of each individual predictor in the alternation. Szmrecsanyi et al. (2016: 113–114) concisely summarise the principles behind conditional inference trees and conditional random forest analysis as follows:

> [Conditional inference trees] predict outcomes by recursively partitioning the data into smaller and smaller subsets according to those predictors that co-vary most strongly with the outcome. Informally, binary splits in the data are made by trying to maximize the homogeneity or 'purity' of the data partitions with respect to the values of the outcome [...]. The CRF [conditional random forests] approach is based on conditional inference trees; unlike individual inference trees, however, CRF uses ensemble methods in a forest of trees built on randomly sampled data subsets to arrive at an aggregated estimate of a particular outcome's

probability. Additionally, each tree is restricted to a random subset of predictors whose significance is assessed through random permutation tests. By amalgamating the results over the entire forest of trees, we obtain a model that is both highly accurate and robust to predictor multicollinearity and data overfitting [...].

4. Results and discussion

4.1 *Distributional analysis of the relative markers* which *and* that

We begin by inspecting the effect of the language-external predictors on the alternation among subject relative markers *that* and *which*. Three contingency tables were created: Table 9.2 reports the distribution of relativisers in our corpus of Hansard material, Table 9.3 shows the diachronic distribution of the relativisers for the Australian Hansard material, while Table 9.4 shows this distribution for the British English Hansard material. The first line in the cells indicates the raw frequencies, while the second line shows the column percentages. On the basis of the column percentages in Tables 9.3 and 9.4, we constructed two column charts to further visualize the diachronic shift (Figure 9.1 and 9.2).

Table 9.2 The distribution of subject relative markers *that* and *which* across the two Hansard corpora

	Australian Hansard	British Hansard	Row total
that	2,213	1,878	4,091
	52.9%	45.8%	
which	1,967	2,225	4,192
	47.1%	54.2%	
Column total	4,180	4,103	8,283
	50.5%	49.5%	

Pearson's χ2-test: $\chi2 = 42.60$; $df = 1$; $p < 0.001$

Table 9.2 shows that there are more instances of *that* introducing subject relative clauses with inanimate antecedents in the Australian Hansard (52.9%), while in the British Hansard, *which* seems to be the preferred relativiser (54.2%). The preference for the relativiser *that* in the Australian Hansard material might reflect the more permissive nature of the Australian Hansard towards "spoken-language features in writing" (Kruger, van Rooy & Smith 2019: 205). The distribution of the relative markers across the two varieties differs significantly.

Tables 9.3 and 9.4 and Figures 9.1 and 9.2 further indicate that the relative frequency of *that* has increased over time in both varieties. This shift is moderate

Table 9.3 The diachronic distribution of subject relative markers *that* and *which* in the Australian Hansard material

	1901	1935	1965	1995	2015	Row total
that	185	228	486	515	799	2,213
	31.4%	30.6%	52.5%	54.0%	82.7%	
which	404	518	440	438	167	1,967
	68.6%	69.4%	47.5%	46.0%	17.3%	
Column total	589	746	926	953	966	4,180
	14.1%	17.8%	22.2%	22.8%	23.1%	

Pearson's χ2-test: χ2 = 603.77; df = 4; p < 0.001

Table 9.4 The diachronic distribution of subject relative markers *that* and *which* in the British Hansard material

	1901	1935	1965	1995	2015	Row total
that	88	303	110	664	713	1,878
	14.6%	26.2%	15.2%	79.2%	91.1%	
which	513	853	615	174	70	2,225
	85.4%	73.8%	84.8%	20.8%	8.9%	
Column total	589	746	926	953	966	4,180
	14.1%	17.8%	22.2%	22.8%	23.1%	

Pearson's χ2-test: χ2 = 1711.42; df = 4; p < 0.001

in the Australian Hansard: the relativiser *that* increases by 21.9 percentage points and 28.7 percentage points between 1935 and 1965 and 1995 and 2015, respectively. As for the other periods, there are no significant diachronic developments in the alternation. The rise of *that* and the corresponding decline of *which* are, however, particularly pronounced in the British Hansard. In 1965, the relativiser *which* was still the preferred form by far to introduce subject relative clauses with inanimate antecedents. This situation shifted drastically in the next 30 years: by 1995, *that* had increased by 64 percentage points at the cost of *which*. During the next 20 years, the shift continued: in 2015, the relative marker *which* was used in only 8.9% of choice contexts. In sum, while *that* is more frequent in the British Hansard than in its Australian counterpart in the last two sampling years, *that* occurred twice as often in the Australian Hansard material than in its British counterpart at the beginning of the twentieth century.

Some of these results tie in with the general literature on the variation in relative markers. Firstly, a shift from *which* to *that* does indeed occur in both the Australian and the British Hansard material. Moreover, in the beginning of the

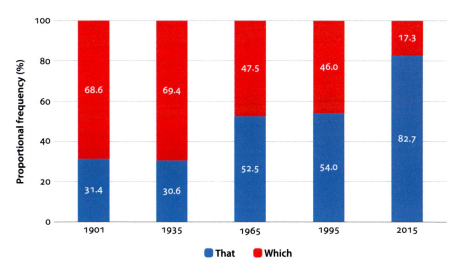

Figure 9.1 The diachronic distribution of subject relative markers *that* and *which* in the Australian Hansard material

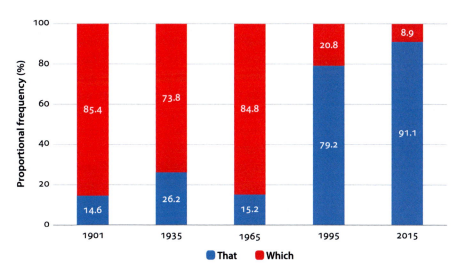

Figure 9.2 The diachronic distribution of subject relative markers *that* and *which* in the British Hansard material

twentieth century, the relativiser *that* is more frequently used in the Australian than in the British Hansard material. That being said, Collins (2014) argues that regarding the use of *that*, Australian English "maintain[s] a lead over [its] Br[itish] E[nglish] parent" (Collins 2014: 367). This claim does not hold for the Hansard, as *that* becomes more frequent in the British Hansard than in the Australian Hansard. Our results are in line, however, with results from research on the Brown family of corpora (Hinrichs, Szmrecsanyi & Bohmann 2015; Leech & Smith 2006, 2009; Leech et al. 2009), in that a shift from *which* to *that* occurs also in the hybrid written-spoken register. Whereas previous research on written standard English has characterised British English as the conservative variety regarding relativisation, our findings suggest that this trend is not supported for the Hansard materials: in the two last sampling years of our corpus, British English proves to actually be more progressive than Australian English in shifting to *that*.

Several factors that are specific to the Hansard register might have contributed to the shift from *which* to *that*. The editorial guidelines of the Australian Hansard changed sometime between 2008 and 2017 (see Hansard 2008, 2017), with the 'that-rule' being codified in the later style manual. Although we do not have access to the precise editorial guidelines that were used in 1995 and 2015, we suspect that the increase of *that* between these years might be the result of such an adaptation of the editorial guidelines underlying the creation of the Australian Hansard. In addition, the production mechanisms of the Hansard drastically changed in this period, due to the gradual shift from shorthand reporting to recordings and voice recognition.

As for the earlier period, the rise of *that* between 1935 and 1965 in the Australian Hansard coincides with the introduction of radio broadcasts of parliamentary proceedings in 1946. The argument is that as broadcasts and recordings started, it became possible to compare the actual spoken records with the written Hansard, which probably led to a more verbatim reporting style. If parliamentarians were using more *that*, as one would expect from speech, it would have been transferred more accurately to the Hansard.

We were unable to find editorial guidelines for the British Hansard. Hence, we can only hypothesise that the strong rise of *that* and corresponding decline of *which* between 1965 and 1995 is the result of some similar changes in editorial style guides. The production mechanisms of the British Hansard only started to change in the early 1980s when, in some contexts, tape recordings were beginning to be used in producing the British House of Commons Hansard (Gravlee 1981: 88). While by 2015, the move to recordings and voice transcriptions would have been made, it remains unclear whether this was already the case in 1995. In Britain, there initially was also considerable resistance against recording parliamentary proceedings, and it was not until 1978 that regular radio broadcasts began (Hendy 2017).

4.2 Probing the importance of constraints on relativiser choice

Based on conditional random forest modelling, Figure 9.3 plots the variable importance ranking for the Australian Hansard material, while Figure 9.4 plots the ranking for the British material. The vertical dotted line in the plots is the absolute value of the least significant variable in conditioning the variation. By convention, this line represents the threshold between significance and insignificance: all predictors to the right of the line play a significant role in the alternation, while all predictors to the left of the line are insignificant. The indices of concordance indicate that the underlying models have a good fit (C-index > 0.85).[5]

The four most important predictors are identical in both varieties: the language-external predictor **year of composition** is the most significant predictor in both British and Australian English, which underlines the massive real time shift towards *that* in both varieties. To get an impression of the role played by the other language-external predictor **variety**, we calculated a supplementary conditional random forest model (C-index = 0.92) (not shown here) based on a combined British-Australian dataset. This random forest ranks **variety** as the third highest ranked predictor, after **year** and **persistence**.

Second, in both varieties, predictors that are related to processing constraints and effects seem to play a more significant role in conditioning the choice between *that* and *which* than prescriptivism-related predictors do. One exception to this general trend is the predictor **passives**, which ranks third in both varieties, although we should remark that this predictor is not entirely unrelated to processing constraints (see Footnote 4). The two most important processing-related predictors are the same in both varieties, namely **persistence** and **distance AP end RC. Distance antecedent HN start RC, mean word length** and **persistence distance** are processing-related predictors that are highly ranked in the random forest for the Australian English parliamentary material, whereas **mean word length, length RC** and **distance antecedent HN** are important in the British English material.

While **passives** is the highest-ranked prescriptivism-related predictor in both varieties, other prescriptivism-related predictors also contribute to a certain, somewhat lower degree in conditioning the variation. **Preposition stranding** and *shall-will* **ratio** are respectively the second and third most influential prescriptivism-related predictors in the Australian English data. The same con-

---

5. The C-index (sometimes also referred to as concordance statistic or C-statistic) is a measure of goodness of fit. It can be used to determine the robustness or performance of classifiers (including random forests). Values over 0.8 indicate that the model is strong, meaning that it is good at predicting our binary outcome variable (i.e. *that* or *which*) by means of the different predictors.

straints are important in the random forest for the British English data: *shall-will ratio* is ranked as sixth most important predictor, while **preposition stranding** is indicated as the ninth most significant predictor.

In other words, prescriptive recommendations might have contributed to the shift from *which* to *that*, but prescriptivism alone cannot account for the change. Moreover, it is hard to evaluate to what extent general style guides have influenced the editorial guidelines of the Hansards, as we only have two (Australian) editorial guides at our disposal (see Section 4.1). Although the more extensive *Hansard Usage and Editing Guide* (Hansard 2008) gives some suggestions[6] on how to deal with preposition stranding, contractions, and split infinitives, it does not deal with *shall/will* or active/passive voice. We suspect, however, that the influence and type of prescriptive advice varies across sampling periods, as the guidelines probably underwent considerable changes during the twentieth century. Nevertheless, we would need more data to make reliable estimations for the different sampling years.

In addition, other processes such as colloquialisation are probably also involved in the shift, with parliamentarians more likely to use *that* in their spoken discourse. Accompanying this, there is a tendency towards a more verbatim rendering in the Hansards, prompted by widespread broadcasting and increasingly synchronised audio/video and written records, as well as change towards production mechanisms that encourage verbatim transcription rather than edited reconstruction. It is likely that these factors act in consort in accounting for the observed changes.

5. Conclusion

In this chapter, we investigated variation between *that* and *which* in restrictive subject relative clauses with inanimate antecedents in British and Australian English Hansard material from the period between 1901 and 2015. Taking the approach of comparative variationist analysis, we investigated relative frequencies and explored the conditioning of variation, distinguishing between three types of predictors: (a) language-external predictors, (b) processing constraints and effects, and (c) prescriptivism-related constraints. Our point of departure was that previous research has shown that the relative marker *that* has been on the rise throughout the twentieth century, at the expense of the relativiser *which* (Collins 2014; Hinrichs, Szmrecsanyi & Bohmann 2015; Leech & Smith 2006,

---

6. These suggestions first refer to some long-standing 'rules' in the prescriptive tradition, but then underscore the importance of "giv[ing] speakers what they say" (Hansard 2008:16); in other words remaining close to the original speech.

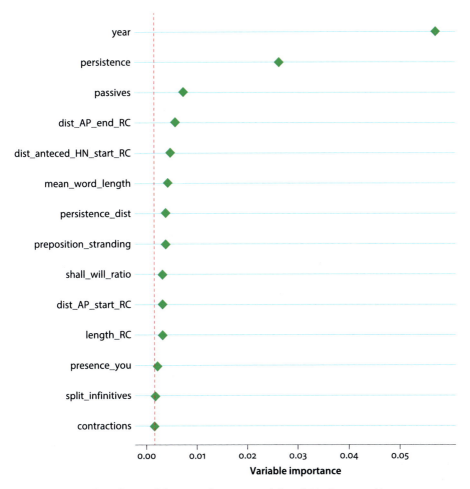

Figure 9.3 Random forest of the Australian Hansard data (*C*-index = 0.90)

2009; Leech et al. 2009). We find evidence that a similar drift is underway in the Hansard material under study here. Whereas the shift is relatively moderate in the Australian material, the rise of *that* at the cost of *which* is particularly pronounced in the British material. Although at the beginning of the twentieth century, *that* occurred twice as often in the Australian Hansard (31.4%) as in the British Hansard (14.6%), the situation had shifted drastically by 2015, as the relative marker *which* occurs only in 8.9% of the British and in 17.3% of the Australian restrictive subject relative clauses.

By means of conditional random forest analysis, we set out to determine which predictors are most influential in conditioning the choice between either *that* or *which*. The analysis shows that the language-external predictor of time-frame is the most important predictor in the relative marker alternation in both

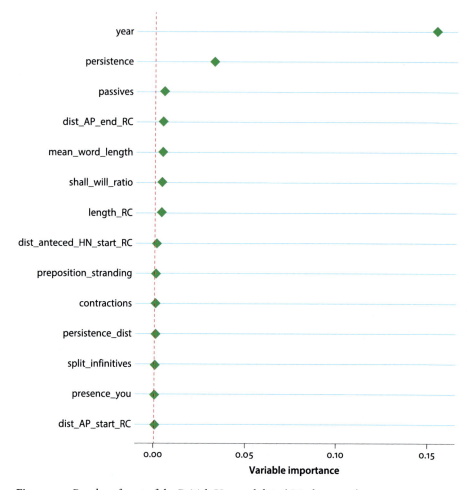

Figure 9.4 Random forest of the British Hansard data (C-index = 0.95)

varieties – and variety itself is an important predictor in an analysis of the full dataset, suggesting real-time differentiated change in the two varieties in question. Language-internal predictors related to language processing play an important role in conditioning the choice, while some individual prescriptivism-related predictors, such as passives, also correlate significantly with the outcome variable. Nevertheless, prescriptivist recommendations alone cannot account for the shift from *which* to *that*.

The findings of the study support the much-highlighted colloquialism of Australian English, in that the more informal *that*-variant is proportionally more frequent in the Australian Hansard from the outset. This informality in all likelihood partially emanates from the speech input of parliamentarians; however, the Australian Hansard editorial guidelines for representing speech are also permissive of reflecting such speech accurately, as evident in the oft-repeated dictum of "give speakers what they say" (Hansard 2008). While starting out from a higher proportional frequency of relativiser *that*, the further increase seems to occur from 1965 onwards, already. While there is some disagreement about the periodisation of endonormative stabilisation of Australian English, Moore (2008) argues that the period from the 1960s to the 1980s was crucial in the "discarding of the external English standard of language" (Moore 2008:xii), and Yao and Collins (2019) find that indeed Australian English experienced substantial (and rapid) grammatical change from 1961 to 1991. Notable is also the publication of the first *Australian Government Style Manual* in 1966 (now in its seventh edition), which marked a clear encoding of Australian grammatical and stylistic standards.

It should be noted, however, that even though the Australian Hansard is more 'progressive' in adopting the more frequent use of the relativiser *that*, by 2015, the British Hansard has overtaken the Australian Hansard in the proportional preference for *that*. The change sets in later (it is only evident from the 1995 data onwards), and it is dramatic – rather than the more gradual change evident in the Australian Hansard. This dramatic change is suggestive of a change in editorial policies (as also argued by Kruger & Smith 2018); in the absence of access to style manuals for the British Hansard, it is not possible to confirm this hypothesis. More focused investigations of, particularly, the influence of the *that*-rule (see Section 1) in Australian and British writing practice is needed; it may also be that this rule, particularly influential in American English, had more general uptake in Australian English than in British English.

When considered against the general assumption that usage tends to win out over prescriptivism (see Section 3.2), the findings of this study prompt us to more careful reflection: In registers that enforce careful editorial control, like the Hansard (but, in fact, all published genres), prescriptive advice no doubt plays a role. However, it evidently acts in consort with other factors, like colloquialisation, and it seems clear that the rise of *that* needs to be understood as a case where usage and prescription acted in mutual reinforcement.

Future research may expand the study of *that* or *which* by including data from other new Englishes (e.g. New Zealand English), performing regression analyses on the data in order to determine whether a predictor prefers either *that* or *which*, and including restrictive relative clauses in object position. More insight in the relationship between prescriptivism and other factors (like colloquialisation) will be gained by also analysing variables where prescriptive advice and usage pull in opposite directions.

Funding

This research received funding from the Flemish Government under the AI Research Program – 174L00121.

Acknowledgements

We would like to thank the anonymous reviewers and the editors of this volume for their constructive feedback and their valuable suggestions for improvements.

References

Allan, Keith. 1984. The component functions of the high rise terminal contour in Australian declarative sentences. *Australian Journal of Linguistics* 4(1): 19–32.

Anderwald, Lieselotte. 2016. *Language between Description and Prescription: Verbs and Verb Categories in Nineteenth-Century Grammars of English*. Oxford: OUP.

Biber, Douglas, Johansson, Stig, Leech, Geoffrey, Conrad, Susan, Finegan, Edward & Quirk, Randolph. 2007. *Longman Grammar of Spoken and Written English*. London: Longman.

Breiman, Leo. 2001. Random forests. *Machine Learning* 45: 5–32.

Bryant, Pauline. 1997. A dialect survey of the lexicon of Australian English. *English World-Wide* 18(2): 211–241.

Collins, Peter. 2014. Relative clauses in Australian English: A cross-varietal diachronic study. In *Selected Papers from the 44th Conference of the Australian Linguistic Society*, Lauren Gawne & Jill Vaughan (eds), 355–371. Melbourne: University of Melbourne.

Collins, Peter & Blair, David. 1989. *Australian English: The Language of a New Society*. Brisbane: University of Queensland Press.

Collins, Peter & Yao, Xinyue. 2018. Colloquialisation and the evolution of Australian English: A cross-varietal and cross-generic study of Australian, British, and American English from 1931 to 2006. *English World-Wide* 39(3): 253–277.

Curzan, Anne. 2014. *Fixing English: Prescriptivism and Language History*. Cambridge: CUP.

D'Arcy, Alexandra & Tagliamonte, Sali. 2010. Prestige, accommodation, and the legacy of relative *who*. *Language in Society* 39(3): 383–410.

Gravlee, G. Jack. 1981. Reporting proceedings and debates in the British Commons. *Central States Speech Journal* 32(2): 85–99.

Hansard. 2008. *Hansard Usage and Editing Guide*. Canberra: Commonwealth of Australia.

Hansard. 2017. *Hansard Style Manual*. Canberra: Office of the Legislative Assembly for the Australian Capital Territory. <https://www.parliament.act.gov.au/__data/assets/pdf_file/0008/1507958/Style-Manual-2017-Accessible-version.pdf> (20 February 2021).

Harder, Peter. 2012. Variation, structure and norms. *Review of Cognitive Linguistics* 10(2): 294–314.

Hendy, David. 2017. History of the BBC: Broadcasting Parliament. <https://www.bbc.com/historyofthebbc/100voices/elections/broadcasting-parliament> (20 February 2021).

Hinrichs, Lars, Szmrecsanyi, Benedikt & Bohmann, Axel. 2015. *Which*-hunting and the Standard English relative clause. *Language* 91(4): 806–836.

House of Commons Information Office. 2010. *Factsheet G17 General Series: The Official Report.* <https://www.parliament.uk/globalassets/documents/commons-information-office/g17.pdf> (27 July 2021).

Kroch, Anthony & Small, Cathy. 1978. Grammatical ideology and its effects on speech. In *Linguistic Variation: Models and Methods*, David Sankoff (ed.), 45–55. New York NY: Academic Press.

Kruger, Haidee & Smith, Adam. 2018. Colloquialization versus densification in Australian English: A multidimensional analysis of the Australian Diachronic Hansard Corpus (ADHC). *Australian Journal of Linguistics* 38(3): 293–328.

Kruger, Haidee, van Rooy, Bertus & Smith, Adam. 2019. Register change in the British and Australian Hansard (1901–2015). *Journal of English Linguistics* 47(3): 183–220.

Labat, Sofie. 2018. Relative Markers in Parliamentary Speech: A Real-time Study of Australian and British English. MA thesis, KU Leuven.

Lee, James F. & Doherty, Stephen. 2019. Native and nonnative processing of active and passive sentences: The effects of processing instruction on the allocation of visual attention. *Studies in Second Language Acquisition* 41(4): 853–879.

Leech, Geoffrey & Smith, Nicholas. 2006. Recent grammatical change in written English 1961–1992: Some preliminary findings of a comparison of American with British English. In *The Changing Face of Corpus Linguistics*, Antoinette Renouf & Andrew Kehoe (eds), 185–204. Amsterdam: Rodopi.

Leech, Geoffrey & Smith, Nicholas. 2009. Change and constancy in linguistic change: How grammatical usage in written English evolved in the period 1931–1991. In *Corpus Linguistics: Refinements and Reassessments*, Antoinette Renouf & Andrew Kehoe (eds), 173–200. Amsterdam: Rodopi.

Leech, Geoffrey, Hundt, Marianne, Mair, Christian & Smith, Nicholas. 2009. *Change in Contemporary English: A Grammatical Study.* Cambridge: CUP.

Leitner, Gerhard. 2004. *Australia's Many Voices: Australian English – The National Language.* Berlin: Mouton de Gruyter.

Mitchell, Alexander George & Delbridge, Arthur. 1965. *The Speech of Australian Adolescents.* Sydney: Angus & Robertson.

Mollin, Sandra. 2007. The Hansard hazard: Gauging the accuracy of British parliamentary transcripts. *Corpora* 2(2): 187–210.

Moore, Bruce. 2008. *Speaking Our Language: The Story of Australian English.* Sydney: OUP.

Mustanoja, Tauno Frans. 1960. *A Middle English Syntax.* Helsinki: Société Néophilologique.

Peters, Pam. 2014. Usage guides and usage trends in Australian and British English. *Australian Journal of Linguistics* 34(4): 581–598.

Peters, Pam & Young, Wendy. 1997. English grammar and the lexicography of usage. *Journal of English Linguistics* 25(4): 315–331.

Poplack, Shana & Dion, Nathalie. 2009. Prescription vs. praxis: The evolution of future temporal reference in French. *Language* 85(3): 557–587.

Ramson, William Stanley. 1966. *Australian English: An Historical Study of the Vocabulary, 1788–1898*. Canberra: Australian National University Press.

Schneider, Edgar W. 2007. *Postcolonial English: Varieties around the World*. Cambridge: CUP.

Sigley, Robert. 1997. The influence of formality and channel on relative pronoun choice in New Zealand English. *English Language and Linguistics* 1(2): 207–232.

Slembrouck, Stef. 1992. The parliamentary Hansard 'verbatim' report: The written construction of spoken discourse. *Language and Literature* 1(2): 101–119.

Straaijer, Robin. 2016. Attitudes to prescriptivism: An introduction. *Journal of Multilingual and Multicultural Development* 37(3): 233–242.

Strobl, Carolin, Malley, James & Tutz, Gerhard. 2009. An introduction to recursive partitioning: Rationale, application, and characteristics of classification and regression trees, bagging, and random forests. *Psychological Methods* 14(4): 323–348.

Strunk, William & White, Elwyn Brooks. 2000. *The Elements of Style*, 4th edn. London: Longman.

Szmrecsanyi, Benedikt. 2006. *Morphosyntactic Persistence in Spoken English: A Corpus Study at the Intersection of Variationist Sociolinguistics, Psycholinguistics, and Discourse Analysis*. Berlin: Mouton de Gruyter.

Szmrecsanyi, Benedikt. 2019. Register in variationist linguistics. *Register Studies* 1(1): 76–99.

Szmrecsanyi, Benedikt, Grafmiller, Jason, Heller, Benedikt & Röthlisberger, Melanie. 2016. Around the world in three alternations: Modeling syntactic variation in varieties of English. *English World-Wide* 37(2): 109–137.

Tagliamonte, Sali, Smith, Jennifer & Lawrence, Helen. 2005. No taming the vernacular! Insights from the relatives in northern Britain. *Language Variation and Change* 17(1): 75–112.

Woolard, Kathryn A. & Schieffelin, Bambi B. 1994. Language ideology. *Annual Review of Anthropology* 23(1): 55–82.

Yao, Xinyue & Collins, Peter. 2019. Developments in Australian, British, and American English grammar from 1931 to 2006: An aggregate, comparative approach to dialectal variation and change. *Journal of English Linguistics* 47(2): 120–149.

CHAPTER 10

Language variation in parliamentary speech in Suriname

Robert Borges & Margot van den Berg
Institute of Slavic Studies, Polish Academy of Sciences | Utrecht University

Surinamese Dutch is widely considered to be distinct from Netherlandic Dutch varieties, but grammatical differences remain understudied. The primary aim of this chapter is to explore some of the claims made in the literature about how the grammar of Surinamese Dutch differs from Netherlandic Dutch, using spoken data from the Surinamese parliament. We also introduce an exploratory method that uses automatic speech-to-text software to efficiently construct a corpus of spoken-language data, avoiding some of the pitfalls associated with working with spoken language data. We explore constructions involving the particle *er* 'there', word order, and non-standard imperfective constructions in the Surinamese Dutch data. Our analyses illustrate that pinpointing characteristic differences between Surinamese and Netherlandic Dutch is extremely nuanced.

Keywords: Dutch, Sranan, Surinamese parliament, speech-to-text, imperfective, word order

1. Introduction

Wan bon/So meni wiwiri/Wan bon. One tree, so many leaves, one tree. These lines are the opening lines from the poem entitled 'Wan bon', which was presented by the Surinamese poet and member of parliament Robin 'Dobru' Raveles in the first meeting of the Surinamese parliament after the declaration of independence in 1975. This performance is generally considered as the first time that Sranantongo (Sranan), a Surinamese creole language, was heard in the domain of government (de Bies 1990). Sranan is generally seen as an ingroup language for the Creole community but it also functions as a lingua franca language for daily communication among the Surinamese population, alongside Dutch.

https://doi.org/10.1075/scl.111.10bor
© 2023 John Benjamins Publishing Company

Even though Suriname is a multilingual and multiethnic nation, Dutch is currently the only official language of Suriname. It has been the main language of parliamentary meetings and other matters of Surinamese government since Suriname became a Dutch colony in 1667, despite the multilingual and multiethnic make-up of its population.[1] However, the hegemony of Dutch in this domain may change, as politicians, scholars, schoolteachers and other stakeholders are currently reviewing the country's language policy. On 2 November 2021, the new Language Board of Suriname was established to facilitate the regulation and organisation of multilingualism in Suriname, and to protect the language rights of all residents of the country.

Since 2011, public meetings of the Surinamese parliament, known in Suriname as *De Nationale Assemblée* (DNA) 'The National Assembly', have been video recorded and published on the body's YouTube channel in order to increase the transparency of the policy-making process. Over 1,000 recordings of their public meetings can be viewed at present. These recordings not only offer an interesting window on the contents and form of parliamentary meetings from political and sociohistorical perspectives, but are also interesting from a linguistic perspective. They can facilitate a better understanding of Dutch as it is spoken in Suriname in a domain that has hardly been studied, but that is of importance for political and historical reasons as well as for sociolinguistic reasons. In general, parliamentary language has high status and carries overt prestige. Parliamentary language can therefore be regarded as an influential force in the linguistic landscape of Suriname. On the one hand, it may drive language variation and change, while on the other hand, it may prevent new variants from spreading due to adherence to linguistic norms that are reinforced in the formal context of parliamentary language use.

Language use in the parliamentary domain is a relatively new field of linguistic enquiry. The emergence of this area of study has benefited from technological advances that facilitate the construction of large digital archival collections ('big data'), resulting in an increased interest in the use of large digitised archives as linguistic primary data for the empirical investigation of language variation and change. Parliamentary language has only recently been considered as material for corpora, for example, within the EU (see Fišer & Lenardic 2018 for an overview). These corpora consist of original audio in transcribed form, so they are particularly well-suited for discourse analysis and sociolinguistic studies of contemporary spoken language (Bayley 2004; Hirst et al. 2014; Rheault et al. 2016).

---

1. Except, of course, for the years 1799–1802 and 1804–1815, when Suriname was under British rule.

In addition to these (transcribed) contemporary spoken language corpora, corpora of parliamentary language have also been constructed from the written records of parliamentary debates, to facilitate the study of parliamentary language from a diachronic perspective. These include the well-known British Hansard Corpus (Alexander & Davies 2015), and comparable corpora of parliamentary records from Australia, Britain, New Zealand, South Africa and the USA (Collins et al. 2021; Kotze & van Rooy 2020; Kruger, van Rooy & Smith 2019; Smith et al. 2021). The British Hansard tradition was transplanted through colonisation to other contexts, where parliamentary language practices were reshaped, giving rise to distinct differences in parliamentary language use in the various regions. Thus, these historical corpora facilitate the study of language and register change resulting from societal shifts and by different contexts, linking linguistic change to societal change (Kruger & Smith 2018).

The aim of this chapter is twofold. First, it reports on the construction of a new corpus of spoken Surinamese parliamentary language by means of automated transcription of DNA recordings on YouTube. Spoken language corpora are often left out of discussions that make use of 'big' archival data due to the bottleneck imposed by the amount of labour required to transcribe audio recordings. In the current age, where the Internet, social media, audio/video recording devices, and digital storage are readily available, exclusive reliance on written texts omits an enormous proportion of available data that could be utilised in research on language variation and change. We relate our experiences with the automatisation process in an instructive manner so that others can learn from it and create their own language corpora from spoken data. Second, this chapter aims to show the workings and the usefulness of the corpus by means of three case studies. Each case study investigates the (non-)occurrence of a language characteristic that is generally regarded as typical of Surinamese Dutch in order to determine the nature of the variety that is spoken in parliament. To what extent does the variety that is spoken in the Surinamese parliament align with existing descriptions of Surinamese Dutch?

In the remainder of this chapter, we will present a brief linguistic history of Suriname (Section 1.1) with a focus on Dutch (Section 1.2), and we will introduce the Surinamese parliament (Section 1.3). Section 2 describes the methods of automatisation of the transcription process and data mining. In Section 3, results are presented from three case studies that investigate language use in the Surinamese parliament with data from the DNA corpus. In the final section we discuss the ramifications of our findings for the debate on the Dutch continuum in Suriname, and the utility of working with parliamentary language corpora.

1.1 A brief linguistic history of Suriname

It is impossible to do the history of Suriname justice here. We will merely highlight some major linguistic events that contributed to the making of Suriname as a multilingual and multicultural society since the middle of the seventeenth century (see Carlin & Arends 2002, and Gobardhan-Rambocus 2001 for more detailed histories).

The original inhabitants of the region that is officially known as the Republic of Suriname were multiple indigenous Amerindian groups, such as Kaliña (Caribs), Lokono (Arawak), Akurio, Trio and Wayana (Carlin & Arends 2002; Rybka 2017). Their territories were invaded by Europeans from a variety of nations, which included English-, Scottish-, French-, Portuguese- and Dutch-speaking colonists, who were often multilingual. From 1667 onwards, the Dutch administered the region as a plantation economy, relying heavily on the Transatlantic slave trade. From the sixteenth to the nineteenth century, enslaved Africans were imported from a huge catchment area on Africa's western coast, spanning from contemporary Senegal to Angola. In this setting, with multiple European and African languages, a Creole language developed (Plantation Sranan or Early Sranan), which is directly linked to the contemporary language known as Sranan or Sranantongo. In addition to contemporary Sranan, Plantation Sranan contributed to the emergence of six Maroon languages in the interior, where Africans who escaped the atrocities of plantation life founded new societies. They are known as the Saramaka, Matawai and Kwinti (central Suriname), and the Ndyuka, Aluku and Paramaka (eastern Suriname and western French Guiana).

Following the abolition of slavery in the late nineteenth century, plantation labour needs were met by the import of indentured workers from East Asia, resulting in the addition of languages from territories that we now know as India, China, and Indonesia, as well as the emergence of new local contact varieties such as Sarnami (Yakpo 2017), Hakka Chinese (Tjon Sie Fat 2015), and Surinamese Javanese (Villerius 2018).

In twentieth-century Suriname, linguistic and population diversity continued to increase with new waves of chain migration from Chinese territories, as well as Portuguese-speaking artisanal gold miners from Brazil, and domestic migrant workers from Haiti, among others. Major events, including independence from the Netherlands (1975) and the civil war (1986–1992) among others, caused significant segments of the Surinamese population to relocate to the Netherlands and elsewhere, but not always permanently. Transmigration occurs regularly, between Suriname and the Netherlands, but also between Suriname and neighbouring French Guiana and other territories. Consequently, ties between the population in Suriname and the Surinamese population in the Netherlands in particular continue to be close, supporting the influence of (Netherlandic) Dutch in Suriname, whereas contacts with French Guyana strengthen the presence of French in Suriname, in particular among the Maroon communities (Migge & Léglise 2013).

This concludes the general overview of linguistic events that contributed to the making of Suriname as a linguistically and culturally diverse nation that consists of a little over 600,000 people.[2] Due to the historical developments outlined above, many people are multilingual, often (but not always) speaking Dutch and Sranantongo, as well as one or more other languages. While almost everybody is multilingual in Suriname, it should be noted that this does not mean that everybody speaks the same combinations of languages. Furthermore, language proficiency may differ greatly between languages as well as people.

Dutch and Sranan are both used as outgroup languages, though situations and contexts calling for one, the other or a mixture of the two differ, and usage indexes social distance and identity, depending on how they are used and by whom (Westmaas 1983). Other local languages are primarily ingroup languages, catering to a particular ethnolinguistic entity and used in informal contexts among people who belong to that particular group and know that particular language. But even in such contexts, borrowing, codeswitching, transfer and other instances of language contact with Dutch and/or Sranan can be observed in these ingroup interactions; see, for example, Villerius (2018) on Surinamese Javanese, and Migge and Léglise (2011) on Eastern Maroon Creole. In general, people use the languages in their repertoire creatively and strategically in accordance with a range of factors such as the communicative situation, the interlocutors (ethnic background, social status, degree of familiarity), their self-positioning, their goals and intentions, and the topic of the conversation.

The language situation of Suriname is difficult to describe in traditional terms such as stable bilingualism and diglossia. Rather, since the last quarter of the twentieth century following the independence of Suriname, the situation can be described as 'leaky' or 'encroaching' diglossia (Dimmendaal 1989; Ferguson 1959), where domains for language use are not strictly adhered to as in the original conceptualisation of diglossia. Leaky diglossia, however, is often viewed as an indicator of language shift. We therefore follow Winford (1985), who proposes that the creole communities of the anglophone Caribbean can be regarded as special cases of diglossia, because they share with defining cases of diglossia "the existence of relatively stable oppositions of linguistic forms proceeding from systematic grammatical differences and reinforced by two conflicting sets of underlying social values" (Winford 1985:355). In the case of Suriname, we need to allow for more than two conflicting sets of underlying social values, because of the multitude of in-

---

2. Note that this is an estimate. The last census was held in 2012.

group languages and two outgroup languages, but other than that, in our view this description fairly accurately captures the relationship between Sranan and Dutch in Suriname. Note that "relatively stable oppositions of linguistic forms" do not exclude language variation and change; Yakpo and Muysken (2014) show that both Dutch and Sranan have changed because of a complex push-and-pull relationship between the languages. The notion of stability refers to the perceived opposition of the languages and the sets of social values that speakers associate with the languages. Dutch is the linguistic means to realise power and formality, while Sranan generally expresses social values such as solidarity, spontaneity and authenticity.

In terms of prestige, Dutch in Suriname can be said to have overt prestige, while the prestige of Sranantongo can be regarded as covert rather than overt. For example, not many people will say that they can speak Sranantongo even when it is clear that they can and that they do. In particular in the 1960s and 1970s speaking Sranantongo in the household in parent-child interactions was discouraged and in some cases even punished. Many believed in those days that multilingualism was detrimental to the child's development of language proficiency in Dutch and further, that proficiency in Dutch was needed in order to increase social mobility. Thus, acquisition of Dutch and Sranantongo can take place in different ways: Dutch may be transmitted from parent to child in those cases where Dutch is a home language, while Sranantongo is transmitted horizontally rather than vertically. Children learn the language from their older siblings and peers rather than their parents. These different modes of language transmission continued and reinforced the differences in language attitudes towards Dutch and Sranantongo that persist to this day.

Because of these language attitudes, results from surveys and questionnaires that focus on language choice and language use across domains, such as Kroon and Yağmur (2012), Léglise and Migge (2015), Algemeen Bureau voor de Statistiek (1999, 2005, 2006) and Rys et al. (2021), need to be critically assessed. The surveys may be more about respondents' attitudes toward languages than about actual language use (see also Léglise & Migge 2015). In general, knowledge and use of other Surinamese languages than Dutch and Sranan correlate fairly well with ethnicity reported in these surveys. But claims about use, knowledge and acquisition of Dutch are often overreported, while claims about use, knowledge and acquisition of Sranantongo are extremely underreported, suggesting that knowledge of Sranan is generally undervalued.[3] Thus, the reported increase in the use of

---

3. Studies with different research methodologies report that Sranantongo is expanding in terms of speaker numbers and functional domains, and that it is already known and used by the

Dutch in various domains in Suriname in the *Staat van het Nederlands* [The state of Dutch] survey of 2021 (Rys et al. 2021) may not necessarily reflect an actual increase in the use of Dutch since 2018, when the survey was held for the first time.

1.2 Dutch in Suriname

Dutch exists in Suriname in a number of varieties, ranging from a formal variety that is very similar to Netherlandic Dutch, via various intermediate varieties to a clearly local variety with features that result from borrowing, codeswitching, transfer and other language contact processes that are typically encountered in settings where multiple languages are in close contact with each other. For example, the *Dictionary of Surinamese Dutch* (de Bies, Martin & Smedts 2009) includes a large number of Sranantongo loans and calques. These varieties are commonly known as *Surinaams-Nederlands* 'Surinamese Dutch' (SD), as well as *Surinaams* 'Surinamese' and/or simply *Nederlands* 'Dutch'.

Many laypeople and linguists (present authors included) consider the Dutch spoken in Suriname to be a distinct variety of Dutch, one that is currently spoken primarily in Suriname, but also in the Netherlands, as a result of the migratory movements discussed above. It is widely recognised as an ethnolect in the Netherlands (see Muysken 2013), and some of its features, such as the bilabial /w/ as well as certain words and phrases, have led to both ethnic stereotypes as well as a platform on which speakers can index a non-Euronormative identity. Descriptions of Surinamese Dutch have been attempted on a number of occasions, in part under the rubric of 'mistakes' of Surinamese children in the Dutch classroom. Charry (1983) is still the most sophisticated study focusing on phonological variation in this variety in the Dutch context, which requires much more investigation. De Kleine (2007) is an extensive morphosyntactic study of SD as spoken in urban Suriname. In Suriname, paradoxically, SD is not an ethnolect but an ethnically neutral national variety. It is, however, a marker of social class and education due to socio-historical developments in the nineteenth century.

The Dutch language served only a marginal role outside of official domains of Surinamese society in the seventeenth and the eighteenth century, partly because Dutch-speaking Europeans did not form the majority among the European population in Suriname until the second half of the nineteenth century (Arends 2002). As a result of the Emancipation Act of 1862, which stated that education had to be supported by the state, the government established schools in Suriname that were modelled on schools in the Netherlands. In 1876, the Dutch colonial government implemented a compulsory education policy, called *leerplicht* 'learning

---

vast majority of the Surinamese population (Charry 1983; Eersel 1983; Essed-Fruin 1983; Léglise & Migge 2015).

duty' in Dutch, whereby most children in the colony were required to attend school (Gobardhan-Ramvocus 2001). Dutch was the main language of instruction and most of the pedagogical methods and instruction materials were developed in the Netherlands for a Netherlandic Dutch audience and context.[4] Thus, the Emancipation Act contributed to the spread of (Netherlandic) Dutch as a language of power and authority in Suriname, and, at the same time, to the further marginalisation of the other languages of Suriname.

After the independence of Suriname in 1975, Dutch remained a language of power and authority. But the position of Sranantongo as the unofficial national lingua franca was enforced via nation-building efforts such as the expansion of the anthem with a verse in Sranantongo and the promotion of independence via popular music in Sranantongo, among others. In 2004, Suriname joined the *Taalunie* (the Dutch Language Union), the official intergovernmental policy organisation that governs Dutch language issues, as an associate member, which could be seen as a strengthening of the position of Dutch in Suriname (den Besten & Hinskens 2005).

Studies by linguists like de Kleine (2002, 2007) and Borges et al. (2017) have effectively pigeon-holed Surinamese Dutch as a variety with a particular set of morphosyntactic characteristics based on analyses of particular datasets (with all their usual limitations). In Section 3, we examine three distinguishing features of Surinamese Dutch, which are identified in Borges et al. (2017), with the DNA data. The features are the Dutch pronominal element *er* 'there', word order and imperfective marking.

1.3 *De Nationale Assemblée*

A rich source of data, which has yet to be explored in terms of sociolinguistics, is produced in the regular meetings of the Surinamese parliament, the DNA. These data form the primary object of the research reported here. As Suriname's main legislative body, the DNA meets frequently (multiple times per week) to conduct its business in public meetings. The DNA is made up of 51 members, representing the country's districts in proportion to population size. DNA members are elected for a five-year period. The previous parliament (2015–2020), from where the data was sourced, represented eight political parties.

A study of language use in the DNA is therefore very practical. First, a large, born-digital dataset is already in existence. Second, the individual participants are public figures and recordings of the meetings are officially released into the pub-

---

4. There were some books and methods developed in Suriname by Surinamese experts, but not many and not all schools used them. See Gobardhan-Rambocus (2001) for overviews.

lic domain, eliminating the most common ethical issues in the study of spoken language use. Finally, given that the DNA records and publishes public meetings itself, there is no researcher interference or role in the creation of data, eliminating the observer's paradox, one of the most well-known problems in sociolinguistic research.

Meetings follow a rather rigid set of rules for conduct (De Nationale Assemblée 1990). For example, all discussions should be addressed to the chairperson; parliamentarians should not address each other directly. There is no mention of language in this *Reglement van Orde* [Rules of Order], but Dutch is the default language of communication. However, we noticed in the recordings that members regularly employ multilingual communication strategies, such as code mixing with Sranantongo, Maroon languages and, to a lesser extent, English, during these meetings. Within such a pluralistic context, the DNA provides an interesting venue for the study of language variation, not least because of the formality of the setting, with its well-established norms of behaviour: any violation of these norms can be viewed as highly performative.

Earlier we stated that Dutch exists in Suriname in a number of varieties, ranging from a formal variety that is very similar to Netherlandic Dutch, to an informal variety that is heavily influenced by multilingualism and language contact in the Surinamese context. Given the formality of the domain, we would therefore expect Surinamese parliamentary language to align more with the formal variety than the informal variety. It would be interesting, however, to find instances of typical SD features in the DNA corpus as their occurrence could be taken as a sign of maturation of Surinamese Dutch.

2.   Corpus construction and analysis

At the time of writing (May 2021), the DNA YouTube channel consisted of more than 1,000 videos, ranging in length from under a minute to more than six hours. For our purposes, a selection of clips was downloaded in original quality, and we automated part of the pre-analytical data handling process that usually consumes much, if not most, of the labour hours needed to analyse spoken-language material. In the remainder of this section, we outline the steps we followed.

1.   **Download data:** Video segments were selected from the DNA YouTube channel. In practice, we selected segments that were most recent at the time when we were beginning to look at the DNA data. The only criterion was that the videos were of regular parliamentary sessions. The selected media segments are listed along with their duration in minutes in Table 10.1. A set of files –

.wav audio and .mp4 video – was downloaded for each selected segment using an online YouTube video download service. This was done manually for each selected video segment.

2. **Create Elan project for each selected segment**: An Elan (Sloetjes & Wittenberg 2008) project was created for the audio and video files associated with each selected segment. The .wav audio file was set as the master media, meaning that actions taken in Steps 3–6 operated on the audio file. The .mp4 video was kept for added analytical support, but is actually unnecessary for the process described here. We developed a basic tier structure to include space for transcription of the spoken language, an indication of who the speaker of a given utterance is, a place to keep a record of code-mixing, and a tier for general notes and observations. After an initial tier structure was established, this step was automated in a shell script.

3. **Recognise utterance chunks**: Before attempting to implement speech recognition, utterance boundaries must be delimited in order to maintain time alignment between audio and text. Conveniently, Elan hosts several built-in recognisers to aid in this process. After some experimentation, the best results were achieved on our dataset with the *Fine Audio Segmentation for Splitting Audio into Utterance Level Segments* recogniser. Running the recogniser generates an additional Elan tier, where each recognised utterance is delimited according to its start and end times. This step was done manually in the Elan Graphical User Interface (GUI).

4. **Chunk audio according to utterances**: With the start and end times of each utterance coded in a tier, a third-party tool, 'elan2split' (Cavar 2016) was used to create individual audio files corresponding to each recognised utterance from the original media. 'elan2split' is a command-line tool that works by reading the start and end time of each annotation in a predetermined tier, in this case that which was created by the recogniser in Step 3, and copying the media between those times to a new file. We automated this step with a shell script.

5. **Speech-recognise utterances**: Using a custom Python script, each utterance audio file generated in the previous step was sent to Google's speech recognition API and the returned text value, the 'transcription', was then inserted at the correct corresponding position in the Elan tier structure. The result of this step is a time-aligned transcription of the original audio. We automated this step with a shell script.

6. **Diarise audio**: Another of Elan's default-installed recognisers *Speaker Analysis Component to Diarise an Unknown Number of Speakers in a Single Audio File* was used in order to identify individual speakers of each utterance. The recogniser generates an additional tier in the Elan project, where the recog-

niser's attempt to identify a speaker is listed as 'Speaker 1', 'Speaker 2', and so on. Given that parameters for a reasonable amount of accuracy differed greatly from file to file, this step was done manually in the Elan GUI, and once speakers had been identified to an acceptable level, we replaced the generic recogniser-generated speaker labels with the speakers' actual names using *Find and Replace* in Elan.

Table 10.1 Media files included in the study. Labels in the 'Video' column reflect the date the media was recorded. In the case when there are multiple files recorded on the same date, video labels are suffixed with '_' and a numerical index

Video	Duration (minutes)	Video	Duration (minutes)
20181113	2	20190411_01	60
20181123_01	85	20190411_02	90
20181123_02	111	20190411_03	24
20181123_03	18	20190411_04	48
20181101	19	20190405_04	101
20181121_01	21	20190405_05	100
20181121_02	87	20190409_01	102
20190405_06	73	20190409_02	30
20190405_07	33	20190405_01	57
20190405_08	1	20190405_02	57
20190101_02	359	20190405_03	43
20190402	384	20190404_02	311
Total	2,216 minutes (36 hours 56 minutes)		

There are some weaknesses and potential threats when using this method, however. Using speech-to-text is fast, but the results are sometimes inaccurate and unverified. We do not have a structured way to provide measurements of accuracy at this point, but we can say that it depends on a number of factors including the individual speaker's language use, voice quality, and speech rate; and background noise. We coped with this by exploring the data with hypotheses in mind, searching targeted features relating to the hypotheses, and then verifying the search results by looking back at the data while listening to the audio for that particular segment.

Concordance searches were done in the Elan GUI, utilising both the *Structured Search Multiple .eaf... Multiple Layer Search* and regular expressions (regexes) on a domain consisting of the entire corpus of .eaf documents. In this way, we spent more time than usual in the analytical phase than would be expected in a corpus-like analysis of written documents or already-verified transcriptions; however our method is still better in terms of a labour/accuracy trade-off than manual transcription and coding of data.

3. Results

3.1 Overview of the dataset

Following the method outlined in Section 2, we compiled a corpus of nearly 37 hours of transcribed spoken parliamentary language using approximately 20 labour hours. Summary statistics are presented in Table 10.2. The benefits of this method are clear: data are handled and transcribed at a fraction of the time/ cost of manual transcription for a dataset of this size (approximately 370 labour hours [= 9+ full time work weeks] using a standard formula to calculate labour time for transcriptions [10 labour hours per hour of audio]). Thus the method allows access to larger datasets in less time and with fewer labour hours. With speech-to-text-generated transcription of spoken data, we were able to begin almost immediately engaging with structured linguistic analysis and application of corpus-based methods. For instance, we are able to generate summary statistics of usage among participants in the parliamentary sessions. In Figure 10.1, we plot the number of tokens produced by each speaker (left panel) and the vocabulary diversity (measured as type–token ratio) for each speaker (right panel).

Table 10.2 Summary statistics of the DNA corpus

Duration transcribed:	36 hours, 56 minutes
Annotations:	21,560
Words:	285,346 total / 15,297 unique
Speakers:	54

One important consideration for interpreting these figures is that the outliers evident in the left panel of Figure 10.1 skew the results shown in the right panel of the figure to the lower end. Similarly, outliers in the right panel of Figure 10.1 represent those speakers who fall in the first quartile of the plot in the left panel of the figure. These issues could be handled by balancing the sample in various ways; however, for the purpose of this chapter Figure 10.1 illustrates the general range of speaker contributions and lexical diversity in the second and third quartiles.

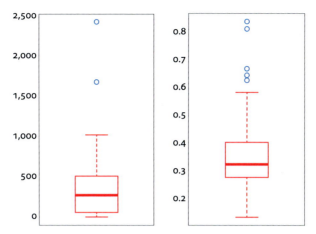

Figure 10.1 Boxplots showing the number of word tokens spoken by each speaker in the DNA meetings represented in the corpus (left panel), and the type–token ratio calculated on each speaker's total contribution to the corpus (right panel)

3.2 The particle *er* 'there'

The Dutch pronominal element *er* 'there' is one of the most frequently mentioned features by Dutch linguists and others when they attempt to describe the differences between Surinamese Dutch and Netherlandic Dutch. The differences in the use of *er* are usually (but incorrectly) explained in terms of difficulty in speaking Dutch and/or failure to acquire Dutch by the Surinamese, as illustrated by the following text from Schoonhoven (1939: 156): "het zo beweeglijke woordje 'er' biedt veel moeilijkheden, zodat het of wegblijft of in de zin verdwaalt" [the dynamic little word 'er' presents many difficulties, so that it is either left out or it gets lost in the sentence]. According to Schoonhoven, *er* is difficult for Surinamese speakers of Dutch because of its variable occurrence, so they either leave it out or they position it in the sentence where it would not occur in Netherlandic Dutch. Our findings on the use of *er* in the variety of Dutch that is used in the Surinamese parliament show that this is not the case, as we will illustrate below.

It is not so much Surinamese speakers of Dutch, but mostly linguists, for whom *er* has been particularly troublesome. It has been labelled (among others) a dummy subject, a dummy adverbial, an expletive, a presentative and an accessibility marker in the literature, depending on the theoretical persuasions of the researcher. For scholars operating within structuralist and generative frameworks, sentence-initial *er* is a dummy subject, while scholars in the functionalist tradition reject this view. Instead, they assign propositional and discursive meanings to *er* (see Grondelaers, Speelman & Geeraerts 2008 for an overview of various views on Netherlandic and Belgian Dutch *er*). According to an earlier version of the *Algemene Nederlandse Spraakkunst* (ANS), the standard reference grammar of Dutch, no strict rules could be given for the presence or absence of *er* (Geerts 1984: 820). However, in the most recent version of the ANS, the third electronic version (e-ANS) that was published online in 2021,[5] a number of factors have been identified that govern the multiple uses and functions of *er* in Netherlandic Dutch and Belgian Dutch, based on the ground-breaking research of Stef Grondelaers and his colleagues, who studied the functions of *er* from a cognitive sociolinguistics perspective by means of the ConDiv-corpus, a written corpus of Dutch and Belgian texts from quality and popular newspapers, and contributions to online newsgroups in the form of email messages. Their research shows that the presence and absence of *er* results from the complex interplay between contextual factors, such as region and register, and more importantly, lexicogrammatical factors such as verbal specificity and adjunct type, in the case of fronted or adjunct-initial presentative sentences. In general, their findings on *er* can be summarised as follows:

- **Region:** *er* is attested more frequently in Belgium than in the Netherlands.
- **Register:** *er* is attested more frequently in informal than in formal registers.
- **Verbal specificity:** *er* is attested less frequently in sentences with a specific main verb.
- **Adjunct type:** *er* is attested more frequently in sentences with a sentence-initial adjunct than in sentences with a locative adjunct.

The following overview of uses of Dutch *er* is a general summary that is far from being exhaustive or complete, but it suffices for the purpose of this case study; that is, to investigate occurrences of *er* in the variety of Dutch that is spoken in parliament in Suriname, in order to find out if the use of *er* in Surinamese parliamentary speech converges or diverges from patterns of use that have been attested for Netherlandic Dutch. In short, *er* can be used in two different manners in Netherlandic Dutch; that is, in a referential manner and a non-referential manner. Examples of its referential use are presented in Examples (1) to (3), taken from van Dijk and Coopmans (2013: 77).

(1) *Locative er (Type 1)*
Jan ging naar de winkel. Hij kocht er een boek.
Jan went to the store he bought ER a book
'Jan went to the store. There, he bought a book.'

Locative *er* refers to a location or a situation. In Example (1), *er* refers to the store where the purchase took place. It can be replaced with the Dutch locative adverbials *hier* 'here' or *daar* 'there'.

---

5. See <https://e-ans.ivdnt.org/>.

Language variation in parliamentary speech in Suriname   **291**

(2) *Prepositional er (Type 2)*
Heb je   van het ongeluk gehoord? Ik heb   er   met   hem over   gesproken.
have you of   the accident hear   I   have ER with him about spoken
'Did you hear about the accident? I've spoken to him about it.'

In Dutch verb–preposition collocations such as *spreken over* 'speak about', *er* attaches to the preposition, but the resulting word complex can be split up, as illustrated in the second utterance in Example (2). Here, *er* refers to the situation mentioned in the previous utterance, that is, the accident. In addition to prepositions in verb–preposition collocations, *er* further combines with words that express quantity. The use of *er* in the utterance of Speaker B in Example (3) refers to the puppets that were mentioned by Speaker A, of which Speaker B bought two. While the adverbs *hier* 'here' and *daar* 'there' can be used to replace *er* in Examples (1) and (2), these adverbs cannot replace quantitative *er* in Example (3).

(3) *Quantitative er (Type 3)*
    A:
    Heb je   die   rode poppen   gevonden.
    have you those red   puppets found

    'Did you find those red puppets?'

    B:
    Ik heb   er gisteren   twee gekocht.
    I   have ER yesterday two bought

    'I bought two of them yesterday.'

Furthermore, *er* can be used in a non-referential manner, as illustrated by the cases in Example (4). Non-referential *er* usually appears in sentence-initial position where it is followed by the verb, as in Example (4a). This type of use of *er* is commonly known as presentative *er*. Fronting causes presentative *er* to move, resulting in a change of position with regard to the verb. It then follows the verb, as shown in Example (4b). When presentative *er* is used in a complement sentence, the verb is usually in sentence-final position; see Example (4c). When presentative *er* is used in a question, the verb and *er* also change positions, as illustrated in Example (4d).

(4) *Non-referential er (Type 4)*
    a. *Er is een hond in de tuin.*
       ER is a   dog   in the garden
       'There is a dog in the garden.'
    b. *In de tuin   is er een hond.*
       in the garden is ER a   dog
       'In the garden there is a dog.'

c. *Ik geloof dat er een hond in de tuin   is.*
I believe that ER a   dog in the garden is
'I believe that there is a dog in the garden.'
d. *Wat gaat er gebeuren met de hond in de tuin?*
what goes ER happen   with the dog in the garden
'What will happen with the dog in the garden?'

While the above already presents a fairly complex picture of the use of *er* in Netherlandic Dutch, we should point out the variable occurrence of *er* in constructions that start with an adjunct, such as Example (4b). Grondelaers, Speelman and Geeraerts (2008) have shown that temporal adjuncts in particular trigger *er* in Netherlandic Dutch, while locative adjuncts typically do not, especially when the sentence features a verb that is more specific in terms of content than the verb *ZIJN* 'be'.

In short, there are many factors involved in the use of *er*. It is one of the features that is generally considered difficult to learn when one learns Dutch as a second language. But Surinamese Dutch is not a learner variety of Dutch, as we discussed in Section 1. Dutch exists in Suriname alongside various other languages. Variation due to language contact is inevitable, partly because so many Surinamese are multilingual and language mixing is common practice. In particular, Sranantongo and Dutch have a complex push-pull relationship, where both languages model language patterns that are sometimes adopted by each other as well as other Surinamese languages (see Section 1.1 and Borges 2013: 215–222).

With regard to *er*, there are some notable differences between Sranantongo and Dutch. Equivalents of prepositional *er* and quantitative *er* do not occur in Sranantongo. There is also no equivalent of locative *er* in Sranantongo. Instead, spatial deictic adverbs are used, such as *dya(so)* 'here', *d(r)ape* 'there' and *yanda* 'over there, yonder' (Bruyn 1995). There are some similarities between Dutch sentence-initial presentative *er* and Sranantongo sentence-initial *na* (positive) and *a no* (negative), as illustrated in Example (5), but there are no word order changes due to fronting, subordination or question formation in Sranantongo.[6,7]

(5) a. *Na wan dagu de na ini a dyari.*
'There is a dog in the garden.'
A no wan dagu de na ini a dyari.
'There is no dog in the garden.'

---

6. For a detailed study on the emergence of this type of construction, see Arends (1989). See also Winford and Plag (2013) for more information on contemporary Sranantongo.

7. Note that the translation for Example (4d) is not included in Example (5), since *na/a no* cannot appear in this type of construction.

b. *Na ini a dyari wan dagu de.*
   'In the garden there is a dog.'
   Na ini a dyari a no wan dagu de.
   'In the garden there is no dog.'
c. *Mi e bribi taki na wan dagu de na ini a dyari.*
   'I believe that there is a dog in the garden.'
   Mi e bribi taki a no wan dagu de na ini a dyari.
   'I believe that there is no dog in the garden.'

Given the intense and prolonged contact between Dutch and Sranantongo, one could hypothesise that, if there are occurrences of *er* in Surinamese parliamentary speech that differ from the uses of *er* in Netherlandic Dutch specified above, they may result from language contact in general and, more particularly, from contact with Sranantongo.

We extracted all instances of *er* from the corpus by using regexes in Elan's *Multiple .eaf Search* function on a domain that covered all transcriptions in the corpus. The regex to find exact matches of *er* was *ber\b*, and to find matches of *er* as preposition(-like) affix (e.g. matching *erbij* 'therewith', *erdoor* 'therethrough') the regex *ber(.*)?\b* was used. This search strategy resulted in some 1,500 occurrences of *er*.

All occurrences in the transcriptions were manually examined and compared with the original recordings by research assistant Fleur Mahieu at Utrecht University from February to April 2020, resulting in a clean corpus of 1,289 instances of *er*. Various types of transcription errors were deleted, ranging from mismatches between sound and text, as well as misplacement of word boundaries. Mahieu further checked the categorisation made by Margot van den Berg, which distinguished between the four types of *er* that were discussed above: locative *er* (Type 1), prepositional *er* (Type 2), quantitative *er* (Type 3) and presentative *er* (Type 4). Furthermore, sentences with *er* that included a question word were also counted and checked. An overview of frequency and percentage of occurrence of *er* per category in the corpus is presented in Table 10.3.

All types of uses of *er* that are encountered in Netherlandic Dutch are also attested in the DNA corpus, but they are not evenly distributed. There is a sizeable difference between presentative *er* and other types of *er*. Presentative *er* occurs most frequently. Of 1,289 occurrences of *er*, 1,144 are instances of presentative *er*.[8] The other types occur less frequently: only 104 occurrences (8.07%) are instances of locative *er*, while prepositional *er* and quantitative *er* number 21 (1.63%) and

---

8. Table 10.3 distinguishes between frequency of occurrence of presentative *er* in utterances with question words (N = 174) and other types of utterances (N = 970). Thus, the total number of instances of presentative *er* is 1,144.

Table 10.3 Instances of *er* in the corpus

	Frequency	Percentage
Locative	104	8.07
Prepositional	21	1.63
Presentative	970	75.25
Quantitative	20	1.55
Question word	174	13.50
Total	1,289	100.00

20 (1.55%) respectively. It may be the case that these low frequencies and percentages suggest a tendency to avoid locative *er*, prepositional *er* and quantitative *er* due to contact with Sranantongo. As far as we know, the distribution of types of *er* in Netherlandic Dutch is unknown. Grondelaers, Speelman and Geeraerts (2008) limited their research to a particular actualisation of presentative *er;* they restricted their research to presentative *er* with sentence-initial locatives or temporal adjuncts. Other instances of *er* are not included in their study. A comparison between the use of all types of *er* in the DNA corpus and the ConDiv corpus is needed to directly compare differences in the distribution of the various types of *er*. Furthermore, follow-up research should investigate the impact of linguistic factors such as verbal specificity and adjunct type to uncover the factors that influence the presence and absence of *er* in Surinamese parliamentary language in general, as well as for individual speakers.

The co-occurrence of cases such as Examples (6a) and (6b) in the corpus is intriguing; do the rules identified by Grondelaers, Speelman and Geeraerts (2008) for Netherlandic Dutch and Belgian Dutch also apply to Surinamese Dutch *er*? Or are new rules needed to explain the use of *er* in Suriname? In future research the DNA corpus can be used to answer these questions in a systematic and data-driven manner.

(6) a. *Wat gebeurt met water etcetera?*
what happens with water etcetera
'What happens with water, etcetera?'   (DNA 20190405)

     b. *Wat gebeurt er dan, is er dan bescherming?*
what happens ER then, is ER then protection
'What happens then, is there protection at that time?' (DNA 20190409)

3.3 Word order

Surinamese Dutch has been hypothesised to have a more rigid word order than Netherlandic Dutch (de Kleine 1999). While word order in Netherlandic Dutch is generally Subject–Verb–Object (SVO) in declarative main clauses (see Examples (7a) and (7b)), there are clauses with different orderings of the constituents that correspond to the roles of S, V and O.[9] For example, when a main clause starts with an adverbial due to topicalisation, the subject of that clause will follow the verb. This is shown in Example (7c) where the subject *zij/ze* 'she' follows the verb in the clauses that start with the time adverb, *gisteren* 'yesterday'.

(7) a. *Ze aaide gisteren de hond.*
         she petted yesterday the dog
     b. *Ze aaide de hond gisteren.*
         she petted the dog yesterday
         'She petted the dog yesterday.'
     c. *Gisteren aaide ze de hond.*
         yesterday petted she the dog
         'Yesterday she petted the dog.'

Furthermore, the subject sometimes follows the verb in direct yes/no questions (see Examples (8a) and (8b)), but it always follows the verb in direct or indirect questions that start with a question word, as in Example (8c).[10]

(8) a. *Aaide ze de hond?*
         petted she the dog
     b. *Ze aaide de hond?*
         she petted the dog
         'Did she pet the dog?'
     c. *Waarom aaide ze de hond?*
         why petted she the dog
         'Why did she pet the dog?'

Variable word order is further encountered in complex clauses. Coordinated clauses have the same SVO word order, but in dependent clauses, word order is

---

9. Note that, while it is true that word order is fairly rigid in standard Netherlandic Dutch, there is considerable variation in the various dialects of Dutch in the case of word-order variation in verb clusters (van Craenenbroeck, van Koppen & van den Bosch 2019). Furthermore, Dutch word order is subject to processes such as scrambling where adverbs and objects can occur in different positions (van Bergen & de Swart 2010).

10. Direct yes/no questions with the subject before the verb can be differentiated from declaratives and other sentence types because of the rising intonation near the end of the clause.

generally SOV. Compare the coordination in Example (9a) with the subordination in Example (9b).[11] Example (9c) further shows that when the subordinated clause is the first clause, the subject not only follows the verb in the subordinated clause, but also in the main clause.

(9) a. *Ze bleef thuis want   ze wilde de hond aaien.*
       she stayed home because[COORD] she wanted the dog pet
   b. *Ze bleef thuis omdat   ze de hond wilde   aaien.*
       she stayed home because[SUBORD] she the dog   wanted pet
       'She stayed home because she wanted to pet the dog.'
   c. *Omdat ze de hond wilde   aaien bleef ze thuis.*
       because she the dog   wanted to.pet stayed she home
       'Because she wanted to pet the dog, she stayed home.'

De Kleine (1999) suggests that word order in Surinamese Dutch is SVO in main and dependent clauses, even if adverbials occur in sentence-initial position in main clauses, due to language contact. Most languages in Suriname have strict SVO word order across clause types (Sranantongo, Maroon creoles, Cantonese, Hakka, Javanese, Portuguese, etc.).

Starting with the corpus as 'bag of words' (list of unique lexemes ranked by the number of times each occurs), we selected those lexemes in the high end of the ranking (occurring more than 10 times) that are conjunctions and adverbs known to typically occur in clause initial position (triggering inversion of S and V) or lexemes that can mark dependent clauses (triggering V in dependent clause-final position and potential reversal of S and V in the main clause). The resulting lexemes provided input to pattern searching across the corpus, using the regex:

> \b(aangezien|al|alhoewel|als|altijd|daarna|dan|dat|doordat|eerst|hoezeer|indien|
> meestal|mits|nadat|nooit|nu|ofschoon|omdat|regelmatig|sedert|sinds|soms|
> tenslotte|tenzij|terwijl|tijdens|toen|vaak|verder|vervolgens|voordat|voorzover|
> wanneer|zelden|zoals|zodat|zodra|zolang)\b

This resulted in 9,152 matches; frequencies are shown in Table 10.4.[12] Note that some annotations contain more than one of the listed lexemes, meaning that the

---

11. For reasons of space we will not discuss word order variation in Netherlandic Dutch in detail here. See Broekhuis and Corver (2016) for more information.

12. It should be noted that some of these lexemes *always* correlate with the phenomena we are interested in (e.g. *omdat* 'because'), some do not necessarily, depending on the intended meaning of the utterance (see Examples (7) to (9)) or due to the lexeme's multiple meanings and functions. For instance, *dat* 'that' co-occurs with subordinate clauses and always with SOV order when it functions as a subordinating conjunction, but the same form can also function as a demonstrative, as in *dat meisje* 'that girl'. In this way, the 9,152 matches should not be interpreted as an exact number of potential non-SVO clauses.

sum of the second column is greater than the total number of annotations; since the regular expression used returns on the first match, there are no duplicate annotations.

Table 10.4 Frequency distribution of lexemes causing S movement in main clauses and V movement in dependent clauses

Dutch	English	N tokens
al	already	6,101
dan	then	3,762
dat	which, that	1,601
wanneer	when	1,549
vaak	often	880
omdat	because	494
nu	now	463
als	as	247
voordat	before	197
verder	further	167
toen	back then	153
zodra	so that	147
terwijl	while	113
eerst	first	109
soms	sometimes	94
altijd	always	93
aangezien	since	86
zoals	like	83
indien	in the event that	58
nooit	never	53
regelmatig	regularly	37
daarna	afterwards	19
sinds	ever since	16
vervolgens	thereafter	16
tenslotte	last but not least	15
zolang	so long	14
nadat	once	14
doordat	because	12
meestal	mostly	12

We manually verified transcriptions and analysed approximately 1,000 randomly selected instances returned from the regex, which produced just a few examples that needed closer inspection, such as Example (10).

(10) *Minister heeft tijdens haar spreekbeurt bij Essent aangegeven er   komt*
      minister has   during her   lecture   at Essent indicated   there come
      wijziging met Nova en   alles.
      changes with Nova and all
      'During her lecture at Essent, the minister has indicated that there will be
      changes with Nova and everything.'   (DNA 20190404)

Example (10) is a complex sentence where the subordinate clause (*er komt... en alles*) follows the main clause (*minister heeft... aangegeven*). The verb should precede the subject, by Netherlandic Dutch standards, but that is not what is heard. However, the brief pause (257 ms) after *aangegeven*, in which it is clear that the speaker inhales, could indicate a change in discourse perspective; the speaker may be quoting the minister directly instead of indirectly. In this reading, the word order of utterance in Example (10) would be perfectly acceptable by Netherlandic Dutch norms. Other examples that caught our attention in the transcription could be interpreted in a similar manner: short pauses or false starts refute the ungrammaticality suggested by the transcription alone.

We found only one case, shown in Example (11), to be ungrammatical by Netherlandic Dutch standards both in transcription and after consulting the recorded audio.

(11) *Voor zwangerschap ben ik nog steeds van mening dat er   was geen reden*
      for pregnancy   am I yet still   of opinion that there was no   reason
      om...
      to...
      'About pregnancy, I'm still of the opinion that there was no reason to...'
                                                       (DNA 20190411)

With a Netherlandic point of reference, we would expect *was* to appear in clause-final position. However, the speaker produces an SVO structure in a dependent clause where SOV order is the expected norm. Cognitive interference is expected among multilinguals in more-or-less monolingual discourse contexts, perhaps as illustrated by Example (11), but our analyses of the data do not support an overwhelming or even minor pattern whereby SD appears to have lost or is losing either V2 or inversion rules. Most complex clauses in the DNA corpus follow the patterns described above for Netherlandic Dutch: the subject follows the verb in certain main clauses (questions, complex sentences with the main clause as the second clause). Word order is generally SOV in subordinate clauses, except for subordinate clauses that reflect direct speech. This is also encountered in Netherlandic Dutch.

3.4   Imperfective marking

The last feature that we will address concerns the marking of aspect by grammatical means. Dutch is a so-called tense language but there are a number of ways in which the internal temporal organisation of events denoted by lexical verbs can be expressed in Dutch (see Broekhuis, Corver & Vos 2015 for an overview). Here, we focus on two constructions that denote that the events are still ongoing at the point of reference, which can be the speech time or another moment in time. The first is the construction *bezig ZIJN (om) te...* 'BE busy to...' (as in Example (12a)). The second is the progressive construction *aan het* + INF ('on the INF'), as shown in Example (12b).

(12)   a.   *Ze is bezig de hond te aaien.*
            she is busy the dog   to pet
            'She is busy petting the dog.'
       b.   *Ze is de hond aan het aaien.*
            she is the dog   on   the to.pet
            'She is petting the dog.'

Borges et al. (2017) claim that Surinamese Dutch speakers overuse these constructions, from a Netherlandic Dutch perspective. Their explanation was that these constructions are based on the model and frequency of usage of the Sranan imperfective marker *e*. Their data was semi-experimental and involved multilingual speakers describing a set of video stimuli in both Dutch and Sranan. While the use of these constructions was intuitively peculiar to the Netherlandic Dutch-speaking co-author (Muysken) and a number of other Netherlandic Dutch speakers consulted, it also occurred in precisely the context where Sranan *e* was used in the Sranan versions of the elicitation. Example (13), from Borges et al. (2017: 334), illustrates the use of Sranantongo and Surinamese Dutch imperfective marking.

(13)   a.   *Een muis   is aan het slapen.*
            a   mouse is on   the to.sleep
       b.   *Moismoisi e   sribi.*
            mouse   IPFV sleep
            'A mouse is sleeping.'

c. *Een muis   was bezig te lezen.*
 a   mouse was busy to read
d. *Moismoisi e   leisi.*
 mouse   IPFV read
 'A mouse was reading.'

As with the previous features, we employed regex searches across the corpus. Searches for *aan het* (\b*aan het*\b) yielded 231 hits. These were manually verified, and the majority (≈74%) of instances were not imperfective marking, rather *aan* as a preposition and *het* as an ordinary NP determiner, as in Example (14). Instances of *aan het* with an imperfective reading could be found in the corpus (see Example (15)); however, these were in the minority of the 231 results, and furthermore, their usage is not unusual from a Netherlandic Dutch perspective.

(14) *Aan het begin   van deze vergadering...*
 at   the beginning of   this meeting...
 'At the beginning of this meeting...'   (DNA 20190404)

(15) a. *En we weten dat Tamarendjo een soort centrum aan het worden   is...*
 and we know that Tamarendjo a   sort centre   on the to.become is...
 'And we know that Tamarendjo is becoming a sort of center...'
                                                            (DNA 20190402)
b. *Ik wil   nog wel   aangeven dat we nog aan het bekijken zijn...*
 I want still really indicate   that we still on the to.look be...
 'I actually want to still indicate that we are looking (investigating)...'
                                                            (DNA 20181123)
c. *In 2016, toen   wij het ontwikkelingsplan aan het behandelen waren in het*
 in 2016 when we the development.plan on   the to.handle   be   in the
 parlement, heeft de vice president gezegd...
 parliament has   the vice president said...
 'In 2016 when we were handling the development plan, the vice president said...'   (DNA 20190404)
d. *Nu al   weten we dat de zeespiegel aan het stijgen is.*
 now already know we that the sea.level on the rising be
 'Now we already know that the sea level is rising.'   (DNA 20190402)

A similar strategy was employed in search of *bezig ZIJN+te* constructions, using the regex search \b*bezig te*\b. This yielded zero matches. The search was broadened to only match instances of *bezig* (\b*bezig*\b), which yielded 123 hits. Some cases are presented in Example (16).

(16) a. *Ik zeg het wederom regering   laat ons zien wat je   doet want   we*
    I say it   again   government let   us   see   what you do   because we
    weten dat je   bezig bent te werken.
    know that you busy   are   to work
    'I say it again, government, let us see what you do, because we know you
    are busy working.'   (DNA 20190405)

     b. *Ik ben echt   bezig om hier hier objectief   de   begroting te behandelen.*
        I am   really busy to   here here objectively the budget   to address
        'I am really busy here to address the budget in a objective manner.'
                                                   (DNA 20190101)

     c. *Hoe zullen we het invoeren?   Wanneer wij al   40 jaar bezig zijn te*
        how shall   we it   implement when   we already 40 year busy be   to
        discussiëren over   een simpele recht en   dat is het moederschapsverlof.
        discuss   about a   simple   right and that is the maternity.leave
        'How can we implement it? When we have been discussing already for
        more than forty years a basic human right, and that is maternity leave.'
                                                    (DNA 20190411)

Note that all instances with *bezig* in the DNA corpus would be acceptable from a Netherlandic Dutch perspective.

While both *aan het* and *bezig* constructions are described in the *Algemene Nederlandse Spraakkunst* (e-ANS) as well as in Broekhuis, Corver and Vos (2015), no information on their distribution, usage or style is offered. Our intuitive impression is that these constructions may be more frequent in domains where a more informal style of speaking is considered appropriate. This is supported by the fact that the constructions discussed here do not seem to occur in Dutch speeches given in the European parliament (142,015 annotations at the time of writing, see further Borges & Gast in preparation). The same search parameters used in this study were used to explore their occurrence in these speeches in the European parliament. A preliminary analysis revealed that *aan het* search results were limited to the preposition + NP type, and only a handful of instances of the word *bezig* are attested. This could be taken as an indication that formality of register may impact occurrence of these constructions. They were abundant in the Borges et al. (2017) dataset, but they are less frequent, by comparison, in the DNA data.

4.   Conclusion

In this chapter, we reported on a study using a novel method to construct a corpus of spoken-language data from the Surinamese parliament. We then used these data to examine claims about Surinamese Dutch, hypothesising that the variety of

Dutch that is spoken in parliamentary meetings would be representative of Surinamese Dutch rather than Netherlandic Dutch. Our findings do not support this view. We examined word order, imperfective marking and the use of the pronominal element *er*, because earlier claims stated that in Surinamese Dutch:

- word order is more strictly SVO than in Netherlandic Dutch;
- the use of *aan het* and *bezig ZIJN + te* constructions with imperfective reading is more frequent than in Netherlandic Dutch; and
- the pronominal element *er* is used in positions in sentences where it would not occur in Netherlandic Dutch, and left out, where it is expected in Netherlandic Dutch.

We found no instances of stricter word order in the DNA corpus. The number of occurrences of *aan het* and *bezig ZIJN + te* constructions with imperfective reading is not particularly high, but note that a more rigorous comparison with a similar corpus of Netherlandic Dutch parliamentary speech is needed to fully understand the significance of these findings. We found no instances of *er* in sentence positions where they could not occur in Netherlandic Dutch, but the relatively high number of instances of presentative *er* and the relatively low number of instances of locative *er*, prepositional *er* and quantitative *er* may indicate that the rules that govern the presence and absence of *er* in Surinamese Dutch may be different from the rules that govern the use of *er* in Netherlandic Dutch (or Belgian Dutch), possibly due to cross-linguistic influence from Sranatongo. Further research on the use of *er* in the DNA corpus is needed to understand the influence of linguistic factors such as verbal specificity and adjunct type, as well as stress and animacy of the referent (in the case that *er* has a referent that is not a location or a situation). Comparative research is needed to determine whether the findings on *er* in Surinamese parliamentary language can be used to draw out the grammatical differences between Surinamese Dutch and Netherlandic Dutch in a more systematic and empirically motivated manner. A multidimensional comparison between uses of *er* and other features in the DNA corpus and (for example) the ConDiv corpus, but preferably a corpus of Netherlandic Dutch parliamentary speech, will lead to a more detailed overview of the differences and similarities in language use in this domain, a better understanding of the complex interaction between Netherlandic Dutch and Surinamese Dutch in Suriname, and more insight in Surinamese Dutch grammar. The latter is particularly important for the emancipation of Surinamese Dutch (Eersel 2007, 2012).

Finally, we would like to emphasise the utility of the methodological approach presented here. It allowed us to generate a fairly sizeable dataset in a relatively short time, with which we could apply basic corpus utilities to test hypotheses about naturalistic, spoken language. The work reported on here served as a pilot for the methodological approach, and a further elaborated version, with improved automation is currently being applied to spoken data from the European parliament in most languages of the European Union (Borges & Gast in preparation; see also Gast & Borges 2023), including original oral addresses and simultaneous interpretations of these addresses (the Multimodal Europarl corpus).

The construction of corpora such as the DNA corpus and the Multimodal Europarl corpus facilitates important advancements in the study of parliamentary language use. Most studies focus on English-language parliamentary corpora (and particularly the Hansard Corpus). More importantly, these corpora are built from written records, the official transcripts of the parliamentary meetings, even though it is known that there are notable differences between the spoken reality and the official written records of those meetings (see also Kotze et al., this volume). The method presented in this chapter shows that it is possible to build parliamentary corpora in languages other than English (see also Lastres-López, this volume for Spanish), as we illustrated here for Dutch in Suriname, and further, that it is possible to build useful corpora from audio video recordings of parliamentary meetings. Comparative studies of these spoken corpora with their written equivalents present exciting new avenues for investigation. For example, it will generate new insights in the norms and conventions of language use in this domain (see Kotze et al., this volume for one such exploration). Comparisons of spoken and written parliamentary corpora from different sociocultural groups, each with their own unique histories and contexts, will greatly advance our understanding of the relationships between linguistic change and societal change, resulting in universals of retention, adaptation and innovation in the domain of parliamentary language on the one hand, while on the other hand, generating more group-specific insights about each sociocultural group.

References

Alexander, Marc & Davies, Mark. 2015. The Hansard Corpus 1803–2005. <https://www.english-corpora.org/hansard/> (5 February 2022).

Algemeen Bureau voor de Statistiek. 1999. *Huishoudens in Suriname. Suriname in cijfers: 181-1999/0*. Paramaribo: Algemeen Bureau voor de Statistiek.

Algemeen Bureau voor de Statistiek. 2005. *Zevende algemene volks- en woningtelling in Suriname, landelijke resultaten, Vol. I: Demografische en sociale karakteristieken* [Suriname in Cijfers 213, 2005/02]. Paramaribo: Algemeen Bureau voor de Statistiek.

Algemeen Bureau voor de Statistiek. 2006. *Zevende algemene volks- en woningtelling in Suriname, Districtsresultaten, Vol. I: Paramaribo* [Suriname in Cijfers 224, 2006/06]. Paramaribo: Algemeen Bureau voor de Statistiek.

Arends, Jacques. 1989. *Syntactic Developments in Sranan: Creolization as a Gradual Process.* Nijmegen: Katholieke Universiteit ti Nijmegen.

Arends, Jacques. 2002. The history of the Surinamese Creoles I: A socio-historical survey. In *Atlas of the Languages of Suriname*, Ethne Carlin & Jacques Arends (eds), 115–130. Leiden: KITLV Press.

Bayley, Paul (ed.). 2004. *Cross-Cultural Perspectives on Parliamentary Discourse* [Discourse Approaches to Politics, Society and Culture 10]. Amsterdam: John Benjamins.

Borges, Robert. 2013. *The Life of Language: Dynamics of Language Contact in Suriname.* Utrecht: LOT.

Borges, Robert & Gast, Volker. In preparation. *A Multi-modal Corpus of European Parliament.*

Borges, Robert, Muysken, Pieter, Villerius, Sophie & Yakpo, Kofi. 2017. The tense-mood-aspect systems of the languages of Suriname. In *Boundaries and Bridges: Language Contact in Multilingual Ecologies*, Kofi Yakpo & Pieter C. Muysken (eds), 311–362. Berlin: De Gruyter.

Broekhuis, Hans & Corver, Norbert. 2016. *Syntax of Dutch: Verbs and Verb Phrases*, Vol. 3. Amsterdam: Amsterdam University Press.

Broekhuis, Hans, Corver, Norbert & Vos, Riet. 2015. *Syntax of Dutch: Verbs and Verb Phrases*, Vol. 1. Amsterdam: Amsterdam University Press.

Bruyn, Adrienne. 1995. *Grammaticalization in Creoles: The Development of Determiners and Relative Clauses in Sranan.* Amsterdam: IFOTT.

Carlin, Eithne & Arends, Jacques. 2002. *Atlas of the Languages of Suriname.* Leiden: KITLV.

Cavar, Damir. 2016. *Elan2split.* <https://bitbucket.org/dcavar/elan2split> (5 February 2022).

Charry, Eddy. 1983. Een sociolinguïstische verkenning van het Surinaams-Nederlands. In *De talen van Suriname: Achtergronden en ontwikkelingen*, Eddy Charry, Geert Koefoed & Pieter Muysken (eds), 138–161. Muiderberg: Coutinho.

Collins, Peter, Korhonen, Minna, Kotze, Haidee, Smith, Adam & Yao, Xinyue. 2021. Diachronic register change: A corpus-based study of Australian English, with comparisons across British and American English. *Register Studies* 3(1): 33–87.

de Bies, Renata. 1990. Taalproblemen in De Nationale Assemblée van Suriname. In *Confli(c)t, ABLA Papers 14: Proceedings of the International Symposium Contact + Confli(c)t, Brussels, 2–4 June 1988*, Peter H. Nelde (ed.), 9–22. Brussels: ABLA.

de Bies, Renata, Martin, Willy & Smedts, Willy. 2009. *Prisma woordenboek Surinaams-Nederlands.* Amsterdam: Prisma.

de Kleine, Christa. 1999. *A Morphosyntactic Analysis of Surinamese Dutch as Spoken by the Creole Population of Paramaribo, Suriname.* New York NY: City University of New York.

de Kleine, Christa. 2002. Surinamese Dutch. In *Atlas of the Languages of Suriname*, Eithne B. Carlin & Jacques Arends (eds), 209–232. Leiden: KITLV.

de Kleine, Christa. 2007. *A Morphosyntactic Analysis of Surinamese Dutch.* München: Lincom.

De Nationale Assemblée. 1990. *Reglement van orde voor De Nationale Assemblée.* Paramaribo: De Nationale Assemblée. <http://www.dna.sr/media/18750/reglement_van_orde_dna.pdf> (5 February 2022).

den Besten, Hans & Hinskens, Frans. 2005. Diversificatie van het Nederlands door taalcontact. *Nederlandse Taalkunde* 10(3/4): 283–309.

Dimmendaal, Gerrit. 1989. On language death in Eastern Africa. In *Investigating Obsolescence: Studies in Language Contraction and Death*, Nancy C. Dorian (ed.), 13–31. Cambridge: CUP.

Eersel, Hein. 1983. Varieteiten van het Creools in Suriname. In *De talen van Suriname: Achtergronden en ontwikkelingen*, Eddy Charry, Geert Koefoed & Pieter Muysken (eds), 163–169. Muiderberg: Coutinho.

Eersel, Hein. 2007. Niet in andermans kleren: Nederlands in Suriname. *Tijdschrift van de Surinaamse Vereniging van Neerlandici* 12: 11–15.

Eersel, Hein. 2012. De Surinaamse taalsituatie in 2011. *The Academic Journal of Suriname* 3: 227–234.

Essed-Fruin, Eva. 1983. De veranderende status van het Sranan. In *De Talen van Suriname: Achtergronden en ontwikkelingen*, Eddy Charry, Geert Koefoed & Pieter C. Muysken, (eds), 47–52. Muiderberg: Coutinho.

Ferguson, Charles A. 1959. Diglossia. *WORD* 15(2): 325–340.

Fišer, Darja & Lenardic, Jakob. 2018. Parliamentary corpora in the CLARIN infrastructure. In *Selected Papers from the CLARIN Annual Conference 2017, Budapest, 18–20 September 2017* (Linköping Electronic Conference Proceedings 147:7, s. 75–85). <https://ep.liu.se/ecp/147/007/ecp17147007.pdf> (5 February 2022).

Gast, Volker & Borges, Robert. 2023. Nouns, verbs and oher parts of speech in translation and interpreting: Evidence from English speeches made in the European parliament and their German translations and interpretations. *Languages* 8(1), 39. <https://www.mdpi.com/2226-471X/8/1/39> (19 June 2023).

Geerts, Guido (ed.). 1984. *Algemene Nederlandse Spraakkunst*. Groningen: Wolters-Noordhoff.

Gobardhan-Ramvocus, Lila. 2001. *Onderwijs als sleutel tot maatschappelijke vooruitgang: Een taal- en onderwijsgeschiedenis van Suriname, 1651–1975*. Zutphen: Walkburg.

Grondelaers, Stefan, Speelman, Dirk & Geeraerts, Dirk. 2008. National variation in the use of *er* 'there': Regional and diachronic constraints on cognitive explanations. In *Cognitive Sociolinguistics*, Gitte Kristiansen & René Dirven (eds), 153–204. Berlin: Mouton de Gruyter.

Hirst, Graeme, Feng, Vanessa Wei, Cochrane, Christopher & Naderi, Nona. 2014. Argumentation, ideology, and issue framing in parliamentary discourse. *ArgNLP*. <http://ceur-ws.org/Vol-1341/paper6.pdf> (14 February 2022).

Kotze, Haidee & van Rooy, Bertus. 2020. Democratisation in the South African parliamentary Hansard? A study of change in modal auxiliaries. Special issue of *Language Sciences. New Perspectives on Democratisation* 79: 101264.

Kroon, Sjaak & Yağmur, Kutlay. 2012. *Meertaligheid in het onderwijs in Suriname: Een onderzoek naar praktijken, ervaringen en opvattingen van leerlingen en leerkrachten als basis voor ontwikkeling van een taalbeleid voor het onderwijs in Suriname*. The Hague: Nederlandse Taalunie.

Kruger, Haidee & Smith, Adam. 2018. Colloquialization versus densification in Australian English: A multidimensional analysis of the Australian Diachronic Hansard Corpus (ADHC). *Australian Journal of Linguistics* 38(3): 293–328.

Kruger, Haidee, van Rooy, Bertus & Smith, Adam. 2019. Register change in the British and Australian Hansard (1901–2015). *Journal of English Linguistics* 47(3): 183–220.

Léglise, Isabelle & Migge, Bettina. 2015. Language practices and linguistic ideologies in Suriname: Results from a school survey. In *In and Out of Suriname: Language, Mobility and Identity*, Eithne B. Carlin, Isabelle Léglise, Bettina Migge & Paul B. Tjon Sie Fat (eds), 13–57. Leiden: Brill.

Migge, Bettina & Léglise, Isabelle. 2011. On the emergence of new language varieties: The case of the Eastern Maroon Creole in French Guiana. In *Variation in the Caribbean: From Creole Continua to Individual Agency* [Creole Language Library 37], Lars Hinrichs & Joseph Farquharson (eds), 207–229. Amsterdam: John Benjamins.

Migge, Bettina & Léglise, Isabelle. 2013. *Exploring Language in a Multilingual Context: Variation, Interaction and Ideology in Language Documentation*. Cambridge: CUP.

Muysken, Pieter C. 2013. Ethnolects of Dutch. In *Dutch*, Frans Hinskens & Johan Taeldeman (eds), 739–761. Berlin: De Gruyter Mouton.

Rheault, Ludovic, Beelen, Kaspar, Cochrane, Christopher & Hirst, Graeme. 2016. Measuring emotion in parliamentary debates with automated textual analysis. *PLOS ONE* 11(12): e0168843.

Rybka, Konrad. 2017. Contact-induced phenomena in Lokono (Arawakan). In *Boundaries and Bridges: Language Contact in Multilingual Ecologies*, Kofi Yakpo & Pieter Muysken (eds), 257–282. Berlin: De Gruyter Mouton.

Rys, Kathy, Heeringa, Wilbert, Sif Rutten, Janneke, Hinskens, Frans, de Caluwe, Johan, Belesar, Usha & Doerga, Sita. 2021. *Staat van het Nederlands: Onderzoeksrapport 2021*. The Hague: Nederlandse Taalunie.

Schoonhoven, Coen W. 1939. Het Nederlands in Suriname. *Nieuwe Taalgids* 32: 90–91, 155–169.

Sloetjes, Hans & Wittenburg, Peter. 2008. Annotation by category: ELAN and ISO DCR. In *Proceedings of the 6th International Conference on Language Resources and Evaluation (LREC 2008)*, Nicoletta Calzolari, Khalid Choukri, Bente Maegaard, Joseph Mariani, Jan Odijk, Stelios Piperidis & Daniel Tapias (eds). European Language Resources Association (ELRA). <http://www.lrec-conf.org/proceedings/lrec2008/> (14 February 2022).

Smith, Adam, Korhonen, Minna, Kotze, Haidee & van Rooy, Bertus. 2021. Modal and semi-modal verbs of obligation in the Australian, New Zealand and British Hansards: 1901–2015. In *Exploring the Ecologies of World Englishes: Language, Society and Culture*, Pam Peters & Kate Burridge (eds), 301–323. Edinburgh: EUP.

Tjon Sie Fat, Paul. 2015. They might as well be speaking Chinese: The changing Chinese linguistic situation in Suriname under new migration. In *In and Out of Suriname: Language, Mobility and Identity*, Eithne B. Carlin, Isabelle Léglise, Bettina Migge & Paul B. Tjon Sie Fat (eds), 196–228. Leiden: Brill.

van Bergen, Geertje & de Swart, Peter. 2010. Scrambling in spoken Dutch: Definiteness versus weight as determinants of word order variation. *Corpus Linguistics and Linguistic Theory* 6(2): 267–295.

van Craenenbroeck, Jeroen, van Koppen, Marjo & van den Bosch, Antal. 2019. A quantitative-theoretical analysis of syntactic microvariation: Word order in Dutch verb clusters. *Language* 95(2): 333–370.

van Dijk, Chantal & Coopmans, Peter. 2013. On the acquisition of *daar* and *er*. *Linguistics in the Netherlands* 30(1): 73–88.

Villerius, Sophie. 2018. *Development of Surinamese Javanese*. Utrecht: LOT.

Westmaas, A.Y. 1983. De taalkeuze als meter van de intimiteits-relatie tussen veeltaligen. In *De Talen van Suriname: Achtergronden en ontwikkelingen*, Eddy Charry, Geert Koefoed & Pieter Muysken (eds), 169–187. Muiderberg: Coutinho.

Winford, Donald. 1985. The concept of 'diglossia' in Caribbean Creole situations. *Language in Society* 14(3): 345–456.

Winford, Donald & Plag, Ingo. 2013. Sranan structure dataset. In *Atlas of Pidgin and Creole Language Structures Online*, Susanne Maria Michaelis, Philippe Maurer, Martin Haspelmath & Magnus Huber (eds). Leipzig: Max Planck Institute for Evolutionary Anthropology. <https://apics-online.info/contributions/2> (5 February 2022).

Yakpo, Kofi. 2017. Out of India: Language contact and change in Sarnami. In *Boundaries and Bridges: Language Contact in Multilingual Ecologies*, Kofi Yakpo & Pieter C. Muysken (eds), 129–150. Berlin: De Gruyter Mouton.

Yakpo, Kofi & Muysken, Pieter. 2014. Language change in a multiple contact setting: The case of Sarnami (Suriname). In *Pidgins and Creoles beyond Africa-Europe Encounters* [Creole Language Library 47], Isabelle Buchstaller, Anders Holmberg & Mohammad Almoaily (eds), 101–140. Amsterdam: John Benjamins.

CHAPTER 11

Morphosyntactic and pragmatic variation in conditional constructions in English and Spanish parliamentary discourse

Cristina Lastres-López
University of Seville

This chapter explores conditional constructions introduced by *if* and *si* in British English and European Spanish parliamentary discourse, with data drawn from the Hansard Corpus of the British parliament and the *Diario de Sesiones del Congreso de los Diputados* of the Spanish parliament. I propose a categorisation of conditionals according to the metafunctions set out by Halliday and Matthiessen (2014), in order to encompass prototypical and less prototypical uses of these constructions. Corpus findings indicate that in addition to their prototypical use in expressing cause–consequence relations, conditionals in parliamentary discourse also function, to a lesser extent, as interpersonal and textual devices, especially in Spanish. Results also suggest a correlation between pragmatic and morphosyntactic variation in some of these constructions.

Keywords: conditionals, Spanish, English, ideational, interpersonal, textual

1. Introduction

From a linguistic perspective, the study of parliamentary discourse has attracted increasing scholarly attention in recent years (Bayley 2004; Fuentes-Rodríguez & Álvarez-Benito 2016; Guitart-Escudero 2005; Ilie 2010; Ionescu-Ruxandoiu 2012; Steiner et al. 2004, among others). Parliament serves as a setting for debate and discussion and hence certain linguistic phenomena play an important role, functioning as "position-claiming, persuading, negotiating, agenda-setting, and opinion building" strategies (Ilie 2015: 3).

In this chapter, I explore the functions of conditional constructions in parliamentary discourse in British English and European Spanish. Building on prior research (Lastres-López 2019), I argue that constructions introduced by the prototypical markers of conditionality in the two languages examined – *if* in English

https://doi.org/10.1075/scl.111.11las
© 2023 John Benjamins Publishing Company

and *si* in Spanish – present variation in terms of their discourse-pragmatic functions in parliament, ranging from prototypical conditional meaning (cause–consequence relations), as in Examples (1) and (2), to interpersonal functions in discourse, as illustrated in Examples (3) and (4).

(1) If the Conservatives press the amendments to a vote, we shall oppose them.
(British Hansard Corpus, 23 January 2003, Mr Edward Davey)

(2) *Si el decreto no está aprobado esos pagos no pueden realizarse.*
'If the decree is not approved, those payments cannot be made.'
(*Diario de Sesiones del Congreso de los Diputados*, 21 July 2004, Mr Díaz Díaz)

(3) If I were impolite, I might point out that the Government – who are so keen to join the euro quickly – were running the risk of not getting them right.
(British Hansard Corpus, 1 February 2000, Mr Howard Flight)

(4) *Si he de ser sincero, señorías, no sé bien cómo interpretar el discurso de esta mañana.*
'If I must be honest, honourable members, I don't know very well how to interpret this morning's speech.'
(*Diario de Sesiones del Congreso de los Diputados*,
8 April 2008, Mr Rajoy Brey)

In considering the functions of these constructions in parliament, I will also seek to examine the extent to which such functions show cross-linguistic similarities and/or divergences. First, differences across languages are expected if we consider that the British and the Spanish parliament belong to two different types of parliaments, as pointed out by Gallagher, Laver and Mair (2011): debate and working parliaments. The British parliament is categorised as a debate parliament, whereas most European parliaments – including the Spanish one – are described as working parliaments. Ilie (2018:309) argues that the first category of parliaments "function largely as an arena for lively adversarial debate and display of rhetorical skills", whereas the latter have "less spectacular and less confrontational interactions or statements, placing the emphasis on legislative proceedings and committees, rather than on the political struggle with the government". This suggests, therefore, that persuasive strategies seem to be less important in working parliaments than in debate parliaments. By way of illustration, Weber (1994), who anticipated the distinction between these two types of parliaments, describes discourse at the German parliament – which would fit into the working parliament category – as follows:

> [s]peeches are not attempts to persuade an opponent to change his mind. Rather they are official declarations by the party which are being addressed to the country at large [...] Once the representatives of all the parties have had their turn in speaking once or twice the debate is closed. (Weber 1994:70–71)

These two different parliamentary contexts – debate and working parliaments – are, therefore, worth exploring from a linguistic point of view. In particular, this chapter seeks to explore the different functions that *if/si*-constructions may have in these two different parliamentary settings, the British parliament and the Spanish parliament.

Second, recent research suggests a trend towards colloquialisation in contemporary parliamentary discourse (Hiltunen & Loureiro-Porto 2020; Hiltunen, Raïkkönen & Tyrkkö 2020). According to Farrelly and Seoane (2012:393), colloquialisation is understood as a subtype of democratisation involving "a shift to a more speechlike style". As illustrated in Examples (1) to (4) above, conditionals can express both cause–consequence relations in discourse and interpersonal functions. In line with the aforementioned change related to colloquialisation in parliamentary discourse, this chapter also seeks to examine, from a synchronic perspective, whether current discourse in the British and Spanish parliaments shows a similar tendency towards the interpersonalisation of conditionals; that is, towards the use of these constructions for interpersonal functions. If parliamentary language is shifting towards a more conversational style, a high-frequency use of interpersonal conditionals may be expected. Indeed, prior research on *if*-conditionals has shown that these constructions are more frequently used in their interpersonal rather than in their ideational (i.e. cause–consequence) function in informal face-to-face conversation (Lastres-López 2020a). This chapter will examine if the findings reported for conversation can also be extended to parliamentary discourse, and if such a tendency is evident in both parliaments examined.

The methodology adopted is corpus-based. Data are drawn from the Hansard Corpus of the British parliament and from the *Diario de Sesiones del Congreso de los Diputados* 'Journal of Sittings of the Spanish Parliament', the official record of parliamentary sessions in the Spanish parliament. A sample of 500 *if/si*-tokens was retrieved for each language and manually examined according to a number of variables, namely: (1) the discourse-pragmatic function of the construction, (2) the degree of likelihood of the condition, (3) the markedness of the apodosis, and (4) the position of the *if/si*-clause in the conditional construction.

The chapter is structured as follows. Section 2 offers a brief overview of studies on conditionals, and proposes an analytical paradigm. Section 3 discusses parliamentary discourse and conditionals. Section 4 describes the corpora and methodology used. Section 5 presents and discusses the cross-linguistic corpus findings. Finally, Section 6 offers some conclusions.

2. The discourse-pragmatic functions of conditionals

Conditional constructions, as in Example (5), are formed by two clauses: the protasis, or subordinate clause, often introduced by *if* in English and *si* in Spanish (in bold type); and the apodosis, or main clause (in italics). Prototypical conditionals express a relation of contingency between the two clauses and exhibit a cause–consequence pattern, with the protasis indicating the cause, and the apodosis the consequence or effect.

(5) **If the current international uncertainties and volatility remain,** *I will not proceed with the change.*
(British Hansard Corpus, 9 April 2003, Mr Gordon Brown)

Many different taxonomies have classified conditionals depending on the degree of probability of the condition being realised, ranging from conditions which are likely to be fulfilled, to others which are hypothetical or impossible. Adopting the labelling proposed by Harris (1986a, 1986b), we can thus distinguish between real, potential and unreal conditions. Horsella and Sindermann (1992:138) describe the distinction between these three types as "a cline from conditionals that are sufficient and necessary to those that are merely probable, thus determining the degree of certainty of the conclusions reached". In particular, real conditions comprise those in which the speaker does not indicate an opinion about the likelihood of the state of affairs described in the apodosis being realised. Potential conditions include those in which the situation described in the apodosis can only hypothetically happen. Unreal conditions are those impossible to be fulfilled, since the state of affairs refers to a past time and is therefore impossible to be changed. Examples of the three types are discussed in Section 4.

Classifications of this type, however, focus solely on cause–consequence patterns and their degree of hypotheticality, and do not take into account the wide range of pragmatic variation that these constructions can display in discourse, since, as Traugott et al. (1986:1) note, "some sentences with the formal markers of conditionality are semantically and pragmatically only marginally conditional or not conditional at all".

Sweetser (1990) and Dancygier and Sweetser (2000, 2005) distinguish, in addition to cause–consequence patterns of conditionals (content conditionals in their terminology), two further types: epistemic conditionals, in which the speaker infers from the protasis a conclusion in the apodosis, and which can be paraphrased by "If *I know* [protasis], then *I conclude* [apodosis]" (Sweetser 1990:118), as in Example (6); and speech act conditionals, paraphrasable as "If [protasis], then let us consider that I perform this speech act (i.e., the one represented as the apodosis)" (Sweetser 1990:121), as illustrated in Example (7).

Similarly, Spanish grammars make a distinction between cause–consequence patterns of conditionality (*condicionales del enunciado*) and other constructions in which the conditional is related to the speech act of the utterance rather than to the propositional content of the apodosis (*condicionales de la enunciación*) (Real Academia Española & Asociación de Academias de la Lengua Española 2009: 3550–3551).

(6) If resolutions on Iraq are important, so are resolutions on Palestine.
  (British Hansard Corpus, 11 March 2003, Mr Mike O'Brien)

(7) However, may I remind the honorary gentleman that, if I recall correctly, the Select Committee suggested that it was reasonably impressed by the speed with which the Government acted on that front?
  (British Hansard Corpus, 6 November 2002, Mrs Margaret Jackson)

In the present study, I propose a taxonomy of conditionals according to the three metafunctions distinguished by Halliday and Matthiessen (2014) – ideational, interpersonal and textual – as a means of explaining the multifunctionality of these constructions in parliamentary interaction. The ideational metafunction is, broadly speaking, concerned with "language to talk about the world" (Thompson 2014: 30) and would thus include prototypical cause–consequence patterns of conditionals, such as those presented in Examples (1) and (2). The interpersonal metafunction, illustrated in Examples (3) and (4), by contrast, focuses on the exchange, and puts the emphasis on the interaction between the discourse participants. A broad conception of the interpersonal category would encompass the epistemic and speech act subtypes distinguished by Sweetser (1990) and by Dancygier and Sweetser (2000, 2005). It would also cover stance and engagement, involving two notions associated with how speakers express "personal feelings, attitudes, value judgments, or assessments" (Biber et al. 1999: 966) – the former – and how speakers involve addressees as discourse participants (Hyland 2005) – the latter.

Finally, textual conditionals are those which have a cohesive function in discourse and allow the speaker to navigate to and fro within their speech, as in Example (8).

(8) *Si vamos a lo que ustedes están planteando en estos momentos de cumplimiento del Plan 2002–2005, en este documento que ustedes editan, el Gobierno informa [...].*
  'If we go to what you are proposing at this moment on the compliance of the 2002–2005 Plan, in this document that you publish, the Government informs [...]'
  (*Diario de Sesiones del Congreso de los Diputados*, 14 October 2003, Mr Morlán Gracia)

3. Parliamentary discourse and conditionals

Parliamentary discourse is often described as a hybrid genre, mid-way between two spheres, treated by some authors as legal discourse (Lehto 2012) and by others as political discourse (Ädel 2010; Bayley 2004). Studies on conditionals in legal language in recent years have been numerous (Berezowski 2011; Facchinetti 2001; Garofalo 2006; Nivelle 2008; Nivelle & van Belle 2007; Mazzi 2010, 2013; Montolío-Durán 2000, 2010; Visconti 2000), although very few have adopted a contrastive perspective that examines more than one language.

However, legal discourse is far from being homogeneous. Bhatia's (1987) classification of legal genres includes a distinction between juridical and legislative language. Most of the materials analysed in the aforementioned studies can be encompassed in the juridical category. For instance, Facchinetti (2001) examines conditionals in statutes and law reports from the Helsinki Corpus of English Texts and the ARCHER Corpus; Nivelle's (2008) dataset includes conditionals in civil cases in Dutch-speaking Belgian courts of law; and Montolío-Durán (2010) analyses translations of conditionals in Babylonian legislation and compares them with the conditionals used in a law passed in Spain in 2008. In contrast with other legal genres, the uniqueness of parliamentary debates resides in

> a spirit of adversariality, which is manifested in position-claiming and opponent-challenging acts, and, on the other [hand], a spirit of cooperativeness, which is manifested in joint decision-making and cross-party problem-solving processes.
> (Ilie 2003:73)

With the exception of Mazzi (2010) – who compares parliamentary data from the House of Lords of the British parliament and from US Supreme Court judgments – conditionals in parliamentary discourse have been much less explored. The current chapter intends to fill this gap by analysing conditionals in English and Spanish parliamentary discourse, a genre in which, as Bayley (2004:13) notes, complex cases of subordination, such as conditional and concessive constructions, are among the distinctive grammatical features.

The research gap just mentioned is not exclusive to conditionals in particular, as, with a few recent exceptions (see Hou & Smith 2018, on passives; or Labat, Kotze & Szmrecsanyi, this volume, on relative clauses), the use of grammatical constructions in parliamentary language has not received sufficient scholarly attention. Instead, research on parliamentary discourse has focused mainly on legitimisation and delegitimisation strategies (Berrocal 2019; Cap 2010; Charaudeau 2005; van Dijk 2005), on politeness and impoliteness (Garrido-Ardila 2019; Guitart-Escudero 2005; Harris 2001; Ilie 2001, 2004; Nowak 2019), or has adopted a gender-based approach (Fuentes-Rodríguez 2018; Fuentes-Rodríguez

& Álvarez-Benito 2016; Ilie 2013). Parliament, however, as a prototypical setting for debate, discussion and argumentation, is also worth exploring from the point of view of the linguistic constructions used. This type of research can shed new light on, for example, the colloquialisation of parliamentary discourse alluded to in Section 1.

4. Corpora and methodology

To analyse conditionals in parliamentary discourse in English I have used the Hansard Corpus of the British parliament (Alexander & Davies 2015), considering only debates in the House of Commons. Although in earlier research I argued that there is no comparable source to the Hansard Corpus for Spanish parliamentary discourse (Lastres-López 2019: 58), work on this type of discourse in Spanish has often used the *Diario de Sesiones del Congreso de los Diputados* as a corpus (de Cock et al. 2018; Kern 2018; Soler-Bonafont 2018, 2019, 2020).[1] Although this resource is not designed for linguistic purposes, it can be – and indeed has been – employed as a data source for parliamentary language in the absence of a corpus of Spanish parliamentary discourse. As with the Hansard Reports, the *Diario de Sesiones del Congreso de los Diputados* is the official record for parliamentary sessions in the Spanish parliament and contains a (more or less) verbatim transcription of each parliamentary session.[2] The transcription of the speeches of members of parliament (MPs) in the record is preceded by a summary written by official parliamentary stenographers, which I have removed from my corpus when preparing the texts to be used for linguistic analysis, keeping only the original parliamentary speeches.

In line with prior research showing that *if* and *si* are the most frequent markers of conditionality in legal discourse (Lastres-López 2019: 60; Mazzi 2013: 31), I focus the analysis on constructions introduced by these conjunctions. A randomised sample of 500 *if/si*-tokens was retrieved from each language.[3] Given the large time span covered by the two corpora, the analysis focuses on present-day parliamentary discourse and the data selected for analysis cover the years 2000

---

1. I am grateful to Amparo Soler Bonafont for drawing my attention to the usefulness of this resource as a corpus of Spanish parliamentary discourse.

2. For differences between oral parliamentary discourse and its official written records, which are not fully verbatim, see Slembrouck (1992), Mollin (2007), Alexander (this volume), and Kotze et al. (this volume).

3. The English tokens from the Hansard Corpus were randomised automatically in the corpus interface, whereas the Spanish tokens were manually randomised.

to 2010. The data for English were extracted directly from the BYU web interface of the corpus (Alexander & Davies 2015), searching for *if*. For Spanish, I used the free concordance software AntConc (Anthony 2017) to retrieve tokens of *si* in each language. After the automatic extraction and the randomisation of the tokens, the data were manually analysed and annotated in a database according to a number of features: (1) the metafunction of the construction, (2) the degree of likelihood of the condition, (3) the markedness of the apodosis, and (4) the position of the *if/si*-clause in the conditional construction.

The aforementioned variables have often been discussed in prior research in connection with conditional constructions. First, the analysis of conditionals according to the three metafunctions (ideational, interpersonal and textual), as explained in Section 2, will allow us to determine the discourse-pragmatic functions of conditionals in parliamentary discourse.[4] Since recent research on conditionals in English conversation has shown that interpersonal conditionals outnumber their ideational counterparts in this register (Lastres-López 2020a), the analysis will also allow us to determine the extent to which parliamentary discourse reflects the style of informal conversation, as also expounded in Section 1. Second, with respect to the degree of likelihood of the condition, a distinction is made between real, potential and unreal conditions (see Section 2). The distinction between these three types is based on the verb tenses used in the constructions. While the protases of real conditions contain a verb in the present tense, potential and unreal conditions use a past tense in the protasis (simple past in the case of potential conditions and past perfect in unreal conditions). The focus is on the tenses of the protases, since the variety of possible tenses in conditional apodoses is much more diverse.[5] Third, the markedness of the apodosis by *then* and its Spanish equivalents is also considered to be a distinctive feature of conditionals which marks the construction as being more categorial in tone (Dancygier & Sweetser 1997). The analysis will examine whether parliamentary discourse favours this categorical feature. Fourth, regarding the position of the *if/si*-clause in the conditional construction, a distinction is made between initial (protasis-apodosis), final (apodosis-protasis) and middle position (when the protasis occurs in the middle of the apodosis). The unmarked or default order is the

---

4. In some cases, interpersonal and textual conditionals may be ambiguous since both types of constructions involve a certain degree of interpersonalisation (i.e. both may include an explicit allusion to the interlocutors). Conditionals are assigned to the interpersonal metafunction when this is their sole function, while they are categorised as textual when, in addition to this function, the conditional is used as a text-structuring device.

5. For an exhaustive analysis of different tense patterns in conditional protases and apodoses, see Declerck and Reed (2001).

initial one for the protasis (Greenberg 1963: 84; Haiman 1978). The analysis will uncover if this order is also the preferred one for conditionals in parliamentary discourse and which discursive contexts favour the protasis occurring in final or middle position in parliamentary speeches. A summary of the variables coded and their values is presented in Table 11.1.

Table 11.1 Variables analysed

Variable	Values
Metafunction	Ideational
	Interpersonal
	Textual
Degree of likelihood	Real condition
	Potential condition
	Unreal condition
Markedness of the apodosis	Marked
	Unmarked
Position	Initial
	Final
	Middle

5. Results and discussion

This section presents and discusses the corpus findings. It is structured as follows: Section 5.1 shows the frequency of conditionals in parliamentary discourse as compared to other constructions introduced by *if* and *si*; Section 5.2 explores the metafunctions of these constructions; Section 5.3 analyses conditionals in terms of the degree of likelihood of the condition; Section 5.4 examines the markedness of the apodosis; and Section 5.5 investigates the position of the *if/si*-clause with respect to the whole construction.

5.1 Frequency

After the automatic extraction of the data and the randomisation of the tokens, I manually examined all the tokens in the sample to determine whether they were cases of conditionals or other types of *if/si*-constructions. Table 11.2 sets out the multiple uses of *if/si*-constructions in the two languages examined.

Table 11.2 Frequency of *if* and *si* in parliamentary discourse

Type	English		Spanish	
	N	%	N	%
Conditional	470	94.00	360	72.00
Complement	3	0.60	109	21.80
Concessive	18	3.60	13	2.60
Manner	5	1.00	14	2.80
Insubordinate	4	0.80	4	0.80
Total	500	100	500	100

The conditional pattern – to be discussed in full in subsequent sections – is clearly dominant in both languages, but it should be noted that English shows a higher proportion of conditionals (94%) than Spanish (72%), where *si*-constructions can be employed with a greater diversity of uses.

Among the non-conditionals, we can find complement clauses, as in Example (9), which allow for the expression of indirect interrogatives. In terms of frequency, it is notable, however, that these constructions appear predominantly in Spanish, as compared to their low attestation in the English corpus. A separate study (Lastres-López 2020b) has compared these constructions in English and Spanish conversation, and finds, in line with the results presented here for parliamentary discourse, that the frequency of indirect interrogatives in Spanish is twice as high as in English, where the direct interrogative pattern is presumably employed more frequently.

(9) *Ha dicho algo que no sé si es verdad.*
'You have said something that I don't know if it is true.'
(*Diario de Sesiones del Congreso de los Diputados,*
20 September 2000, Mr Pérez Rubalcaba)

Other cases of *if* and *si* include concessive clauses, as in Example (10), introduced by *even if* in English and *si bien* and *incluso si* in Spanish, which are equally infrequent in both languages. Even less frequent in both languages are manner adjuncts introduced by *as if* in English and *como si* in Spanish, as in Example (11); and cases of *if/si*-insubordination,[6] as in Example (12). All these cases have been

---

6. Insubordinate clauses are those introduced by markers of subordination which appear in isolation in discourse, without the presence of a main clause, which cannot be retrieved from the context either (Evans 2007). For quantitative analyses of *if*-insubordination in English, see Kaltenböck (2016) and Lastres-López (2018).

discarded from the following analysis, which focuses exclusively on conditional constructions.

(10) *En cuanto a la cuarta enmienda, si bien hay una serie de competencias que están en manos de algunas comunidades autónomas – quiero recordar Euskadi y Cataluña – sobre el modelo, la normalización y los tipos de señales de tráfico, no es menos cierto que al Ministerio del Interior le corresponde el diseño y normalización de nuevas señales de tráfico.*

'As for the fourth amendment, although there is a series of competences that are in the hands of some autonomous communities – I want to recall Euskadi and Catalonia – about the model, normalisation and types of traffic signs, it isn't less certain that the design and normalisation of new traffic signs corresponds to the Interior Ministry.'

(*Diario de Sesiones del Congreso de los Diputados,*
16 May 2001, Mr Rejón Gieb)

(11) However, the problem is that the Americans seem to be moving towards that almost as if it were a target.

(British Hansard Corpus, 19 June 2002, Mr David Curry)

(12) If I could just have 30 seconds.

(British Hansard Corpus, 26 November 2001, Mr Tam Dalyell)

5.2 Metafunctions

In the classification of conditionals according to their metafunction, English and Spanish show a preference for ideational conditionals, showing that cause–consequence patterns of conditionals are dominant in parliamentary discourse.[7] However, in Spanish the frequency of ideational conditionals is statistically significantly lower (see Footnote 8) than in English (59.17% and 78.51% respectively). Consequently, in Spanish we observe a higher frequency of interpersonal conditionals (38.89%) than in English (20.64%). Textual conditionals are attested in low frequencies in both languages, but again the frequency of textual conditionals in Spanish is more than double than in English. A summary of absolute frequencies and percentages is provided in Table 11.3.

---

7. Studies on conditionals in other spoken genres, such as conversation, show the opposite trend, with interpersonal conditionals outnumbering their ideational counterparts (Lastres-López 2020a). Similarly, other studies also mention the relevance of interpersonal uses of conditionals in speech (Chodorowska-Pilch 2017; Ford 1997; Ford & Thompson 1986).

Morphosyntactic and pragmatic variation in conditionals   319

Table 11.3 Metafunction of conditionals

Metafunction	English		Spanish	
	N	%	N	%
Ideational	369	78.51	213	59.17
Interpersonal	97	20.64	140	38.89
Textual	4	0.85	7	1.94
Total	470	100	360	100

Figure 11.1 graphically illustrates the distribution of conditionals across the three metafunctions using 95% Wilson confidence intervals.[8] As we can see, English and Spanish show statistically significant differences in the use of ideational and interpersonal conditionals, whereas the difference in textual conditionals is not statistically significant.

Ideational conditionals allow MPs to convey conditions under which events are enabled, as in Example (13), and to hypothesise, as in Example (14). Results suggest that this function is more frequent in English parliamentary discourse, in which the majority of conditionals are used for this purpose. These constructions express a cause in the subordinate clause and its consequence or effect in the matrix clause, as illustrated in Examples (13) and (14).

(13)   Common owners are adopting the custom of charging residents for access to their homes if driveways pass over common ground.
               (British Hansard Corpus, 20 March 2000, Mr Andrew Hunter)

(14)   *Si no hay acuerdo entre los dos grandes partidos, nunca alcanzaremos la mayoría necesaria para llevar a cabo esas modificaciones.*
     'If there is no agreement between the two major parties, we will never reach the necessary majority to carry out those modifications.'
               (*Diario de Sesiones del Congreso de los Diputados*,
               16 April 2004, Mr Rivero Baute)

---

8. Here and hereafter, figures show 95% Wilson confidence intervals (see Wallis 2013, 2021), which is a way of expressing the accuracy of a given observation. Although confidence intervals are often employed in choice contexts (see, for example, Aarts, Close & Wallis (2013), on the choice between *will* and *shall*); they can also be employed in semasiological studies (see, for example, Levin (2013: 209), on the different meanings of the verb *think*), as is the case here. The use of confidence intervals allows us to go beyond the data analysed and make generalisations about the use of conditionals in parliamentary discourse at 0.05 error level. When the confidence intervals do not overlap, the results are statistically significant. In contrast, when any point of the confidence interval overlaps with another, the differences across the two languages are not statistically significant.

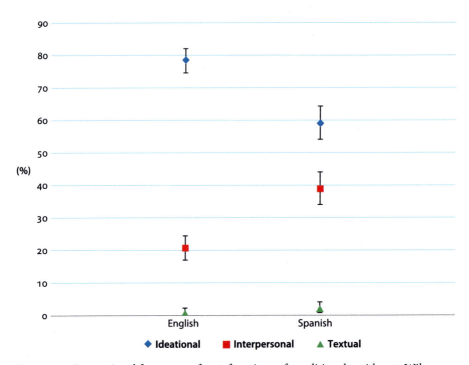

Figure 11.1 Proportional frequency of metafunctions of conditionals, with 95% Wilson confidence intervals

It is also frequently the case that ideational conditionals contain an interrogative apodosis, to ask other MPs about hypothetical situations, as in Example (15); or they may contain several protases for the same apodosis, that is, several conditions which must be satisfied, as noted by Montolío-Durán (2010) and illustrated in Example (16). Ideational conditionals also allow MPs to reformulate certain messages and render them more hypothetical. In Example (17) the speaker employs *cuando* 'when' and later reformulates the message through a conditional, as a means of making the message more hypothetical and less assertive.

(15) *Si es una acción humanitaria, ¿por qué sólo han fallecido hasta hoy miembros del servicio de inteligencia?*
'If it is a humanitarian action, why have only members of the intelligence service died up to now?'
(*Diario de Sesiones del Congreso de los Diputados*, 2 December 2003, Mr Anasagasti Olabeaga)

Morphosyntactic and pragmatic variation in conditionals   321

(16) If we and Spain can, after taking stock, reach agreement on the kind of frame-work that I have outlined, and if thereafter all parties can build on those principles to produce a comprehensive settlement, the whole package will be put to the people of Gibraltar in a referendum and they will decide.

(British Hansard Corpus, 12 July 2002, Mr Jack Straw)

(17) *El debate del referéndum, cuando se celebre, si llega a celebrarse, esperando que para entonces nadie haya querido asumir la responsabilidad de bloquear el proceso, será la ocasión para que expliquemos las distintas concepciones de Europa que unos podemos tener [...].*
'The referendum debate, when it is held, if it is held, hoping that by then nobody would have wanted to assume the responsibility of blocking the process, will be the occasion to explain the different conceptions of Europe that some of us can have [...]' [9]

(*Diario de Sesiones del Congreso de los Diputados*,
14 October 2003, Mr Borrell Fontelles)

As discussed in Section 2, interpersonal conditionals, by contrast, focus on establishing relations between speakers and addressees rather than on reflecting on premises. In this case, the *if/si*-construction no longer expresses a cause–consequence relation between two propositions, but rather allows speakers to convey stance, expressing their opinions and viewpoints, as in Example (18), or to engage with their addressees as a way of mitigating the force of the message, as in Example (19). Sometimes interpersonal conditionals also express an evidential meaning, indicating the source of information that the speaker follows in making the assertion in the main clause, as in Example (20). Also frequent within the interpersonal category are epistemic conditionals, which present claims or conclusions in the apodosis, based on given evidence presented in the protasis, as in Example (21).

(18) *Si es tan importante para todos ustedes, creo que también es importante que tenga un debate en toda su integridad, con toda la grandeza que tiene la Constitución.*
'If it's so important for all of you, I think it's also important that it has a debate in all its integrity, with all the grandeur that the Constitution has.'

(*Diario de Sesiones del Congreso de los Diputados*,
14 October 2003, Ms Lasagabaster Olazábal)

---

9. As an anonymous reviewer pointed out, occurrences similar to Example (17) are close to interpersonal epistemic conditionals. For a continuum between the different metafunctions, see my earlier work (Lastres-López 2020a).

(19) If I may, with respect, I would advise the Commissioner for Standards to get hold of the Provisional IRA's rule book, which is very similar to a company's articles of association.

(British Hansard Corpus, 26 March 2002, Mr David Burnside)

(20) *El propagandístico lema del pleno empleo como objetivo no atiende a unos mínimos de cobertura digna y se contenta con asumir la normalidad de un paro estructural de más de un millón y medio de personas, si nos atenemos a las cuentas del Partido Popular.*
'The propagandist slogan of full employment as objective doesn't attend to a certain minimum of decent coverage and it is happy to assume the normality of structural unemployment of more than a million and a half of people, if we stick to the numbers of the People's Party.'

(*Diario de Sesiones del Congreso de los Diputados,*
26 April 2000, Mr Rodríguez Sánchez)

(21) I hope that there will be a free vote for Conservative Members as well, although I doubt it. If she is nurturing the illusion that in some way there is a diminution of democracy in the proposals, she definitely has not read the report. (British Hansard Corpus, 6 July 2000, Mrs Margaret Jackson)

Finally, textual conditionals appear with low frequency in parliamentary discourse, but have been attested in both languages as a mechanism that allows MPs to move backwards and forwards in their speech, as in Example (22), or put the focus on a certain issue, as in Example (23). These uses of conditionals help MPs structure their discourse and make their speeches more cohesive. An illustration of a textual conditional in Spanish, in which they appear slightly more frequently, is given in Example (22). Here, the conditional allows the speaker to move cohesively from built dwellings to the next point in his argumentation, rental dwellings. A textual conditional in English is provided in Example (23). In this case, the conditional allows the speaker to put the focus on a certain issue, the problems involved in opening an account.

(22) *Por si alguno no lo sabe, lo quiero recordar: de las viviendas construidas, las que se destinan a VPO no llegan al 10 por ciento, y si vamos a las viviendas en alquiler, de todas esas viviendas protegidas, se destinan al alquiler entre el 1 y el 2 por ciento.*
'Just in case someone doesn't know, I want to remind them: out of the built dwellings, those allocated to the social housing system don't attain 10 per cent, and if we go to rental dwellings, of all the social housing, only between 1 and 2 per cent are intended for rental.'

(*Diario de Sesiones del Congreso de los Diputados,*
14 October 2003, Mr Morlán Gracia)

Morphosyntactic and pragmatic variation in conditionals **323**

(23) If we look at the problems involved in opening an account, we see that the complex system put in place by the Government, not the Post Office, has led to difficulties and confusion for hundreds of thousands of people.

(British Hansard Corpus, 11 June 2003, Mr Oliver Heald)

5.3 Degree of likelihood of the condition

As discussed in Section 2, conditionals may express different degrees of likelihood, distinguishing between real, potential and unreal conditions. Table 11.4 summarises the absolute frequencies and percentages found for each type in English and Spanish.

Table 11.4 Type of condition depending on the likelihood of the state of affairs being realised

Semantic type	English		Spanish	
	N	%	N	%
Real condition	333	70.85	294	81.67
Potential condition	120	25.53	49	13.61
Unreal condition	17	3.62	17	4.72
Total	470	100	360	100

Real conditions are the most frequent in parliamentary discourse in the two languages. As shown in Figure 11.2, Spanish presents a higher proportion of conditionals of this type and this difference is statistically significant as compared to English. Differences in potential conditions in the two languages are also statistically significant at 0.05 error level, with potential conditions having a higher use in the British parliament than in the Spanish one. Finally, unreal conditions are found at very low frequencies in parliamentary discourse in both languages, with no statistically significant differences.

Both languages show a clear preference for real conditions, as in Examples (24) and (25). These are the default types of conditions in parliamentary discourse in that they are helpful for the speaker, with no position having to be taken in terms of how likely it is that the condition might come to fruition. Spanish MPs show a preference for these constructions as opposed to their British counterparts.

(24) If we want to change the composition of those who enjoy the benefits of a university education, we must work extremely hard to raise standards, achievements and aspirations in all our schools.

(British Hansard Corpus, 13 March 2003, Mrs Margaret Hodge)

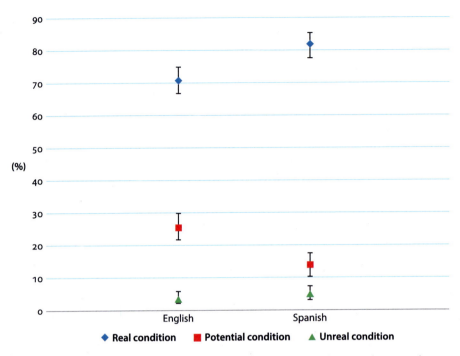

Figure 11.2 Proportional frequency of the degree of likelihood of the condition, with 95% Wilson confidence intervals

(25) *Van a invertir, porque si no invierten se quedarán sin negocio y sin clientes.*
'They are going to invest, because if they don't invest, they will find themselves out of business and with no clients.'
(*Diario de Sesiones del Congreso de los Diputados*, 20 September 2000, Mr Pérez Rubalcaba)

By contrast, in both potential and unreal conditions, the speaker expresses through the conditional construction a degree of likelihood which is not neutral. On the one hand, in potential conditions, as in Examples (26) and (27), the condition is presented as something which can potentially happen, as a hypothetical possibility. Thus, when MPs employ potential conditions instead of real ones, their messages are regarded as more tentative. British MPs employ potential conditions more frequently than Spanish MPs, probably resorting to the hypotheticality and tentativeness of these constructions as face-saving devices. On the other hand, unreal conditions refer to past situations which cannot be changed, and thus, as Alcaide-Lara, Carranza-Márquez and Fuentes-Rodríguez (2016: 154) note for Spanish, these constructions are used in parliament to express reproach, as in Examples (28) and (29).

(26) But if he had the opportunity some time to come to speak to farmers in Cumbria, they would welcome the opportunity to tell him what the problems are.
(British Hansard Corpus, 15 March 2001, Mr Eric Martlew)

(27) *Si usted permitiera un referéndum, o que lo convocara otra institución, nosotros respetaríamos el resultado.*
'If you allowed a referendum, or allowed that it was called by another institution, we would respect the result.'
(*Diario de Sesiones del Congreso de los Diputados,*
26 April 2000, Mr Lasagabaster Olazábal)

(28) However, if the honorary gentleman had phrased his question in a slightly more sensible way, I might have been willing to give him a rather more serious response.   (British Hansard Corpus, 30 October 2000, Mr Geoff Hoon)

(29) *Si las hubieran ganado no hubieran elegido repetirlas.*
'If you had won them, you wouldn't have chosen to repeat them.'
(*Diario de Sesiones del Congreso de los Diputados,*
14 October 2003, Mr Ruiz López)

5.4 Markedness of the apodosis

I employ here the term 'markedness of the apodosis' to refer to conditional apodoses that signal their beginning by means of *then* in English and *entonces* or *pues* in Spanish. As already mentioned, this is considered to be a distinctive feature of conditionals, which marks the conditional as being more categorial in tone (Carter-Thomas & Rowley-Jolivet 2008; Dancygier & Sweetser 1997). In addition, when the apodosis is optionally introduced by *then* in English or *entonces* or *pues* in Spanish, the conditional construction must follow the protasis-apodosis order. Puente-Castelo (2016: 170) argues that the presence of these markers to indicate the beginning of the apodosis may be useful "when the subordinate clause is particularly long or when the syntax of the conditional structure is especially complex". Lengthy sentences are particularly frequent in parliamentary discourse, with abundant cases of subordination, as Bayley (2004: 13) notes. However, and contrary to expectations, no single apodosis in parliamentary language is marked in the data sample examined for English. In Spanish only three conditionals contain a marked apodosis. They occur in particularly long sentences with several protases, as in Example (30).

(30) *Si Europa es una comunidad de valores y principios fundados en un legado cultural que denominamos la civilización europea, si decimos, además, que esa comunidad se traduce en el respeto a la dignidad humana, la libertad, la democracia, la igualdad, el Estado de derecho y el respeto de los derechos humanos, entonces requiere ser eficazmente protegida y promovida en su vivencia cotidiana por los ciudadanos.*

'If Europe is a community of values and principles founded on a cultural legacy that we call European civilisation, if we say, furthermore, that that community is translated into respect for human dignity, for freedom, for democracy, for equality, for the rule of law, and for the respect for human rights, then it is required to be effectively protected and promoted in its daily experience by the citizens.'

(*Diario de Sesiones del Congreso de los Diputados,*
11 January 2005, Mr Rajoy Brey)

The results on parliamentary discourse are surprising and show a clear difference with other legal genres in which marked apodoses in conditionals are attested in significant numbers. In particular, in courtroom discourse marked apodoses occur in 16% of the cases in English and in 28% in Spanish (Lastres-López 2019: 67). This shows a clear difference with the results found in parliamentary discourse. Their absence or very limited use in parliamentary language is probably motivated by the previously mentioned fact that *then* and its equivalents are regarded as categorial in tone, taking the conditional as "existing" rather than as a hypothetical possibility (Dancygier & Sweetser 1997: 109). This seems to be the reason for their infrequent use in parliament, where facts should not be presented as imposed realities, but rather as negotiable through argumentation.

5.5   Position

If/si-clauses can display three positions in the conditional construction: initial, as in Example (31), in which the protasis precedes the apodosis; final, as in Example (32), with the reverse order, the apodosis preceding the protasis; and middle, as in Example (33), in which the protasis interrupts the apodosis. Initial position for the protasis is the default for these constructions cross-linguistically (Greenberg 1963: 84; Haiman 1978). In final position, as in Example (32), it seems that the speaker affords greater importance to the result or the consequence, hence the final position for the cause or condition that must be satisfied.

(31)   If grain prices were down, people would get a better price for potatoes.

(British Hansard Corpus, 31 January 2002, Mr Henry Bellingham)

(32) In addition, we should never be asked to pool or share our sovereignty if the outcome is no greater than what could be achieved by our acting alone or even bilaterally with other countries.

(British Hansard Corpus, 10 July 2003, Mr Colin Challen)

(33) *Estos tres millones de euros que nos marca para el ejercicio de 2004 son, si tomamos el total de 409 millones, menos de un 1 por ciento de los daños habidos.* 'These three million euros that are marked for the year 2004 are, if we take the total of 409 million, less than one per cent of the damages that have arisen.'

(*Diario de Sesiones del Congreso de los Diputados,*
21 July 2004, Mr Grau i Buldú)

Table 11.5 sets out the absolute frequencies and percentages for the three positions across the two languages examined. In line with the general trend, the initial position is the default one in parliamentary discourse. As can be seen in Figure 11.3, statistically significant differences are found between English and Spanish for the frequency of the initial and final position, whereas the middle position is not used at significantly different frequencies between the two languages. Final position is twice as frequent in English parliamentary discourse as in Spanish. This suggests that, when using conditionals, British MPs put the emphasis on the result or consequence of the condition more often than Spanish MPs. Middle position, by contrast, is attested at low frequencies in both languages. It is remarkable, however, that in Spanish this position represents one third (31 out of 91) of all the non-initial position conditionals, as opposed to English, where the percentage is far lower, as can be seen in Table 11.5.

Table 11.5 Position of the *if/si*-clause in the conditional construction

Position of the *if/si*-clause	English		Spanish	
	N	%	N	%
Initial	300	63.83	269	74.72
Final	148	31.49	60	16.67
Middle	22	4.68	31	8.61
Total	470	100	360	100

Table 11.6 sets out the position of the protases in the conditional constructions with respect to their metafunctions, with the aim of finding out whether certain metafunctions favour specific positions. Leaving aside textual conditionals, which all occur in initial position in both languages, we observe variation between initial, final and middle position across the two other metafunctions. Although initial position shows no difference with respect to metafunction in Spanish, Eng-

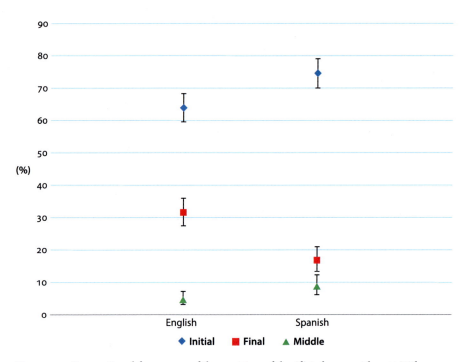

Figure 11.3 Proportional frequency of the position of the *if/si*-clause, with 95% Wilson confidence intervals

lish presents a different picture. Interpersonal conditionals in English occur in approximately half of the cases in non-initial position, with final and middle positions representing around 30% and 20% respectively. This also explains the overall higher frequency of the final position in English, graphically illustrated in Figure 11.3, as opposed to Spanish.

6. Conclusions

This chapter has examined morphosyntactic and pragmatic variation in conditional constructions in British English and European Spanish parliamentary discourse. The corpus findings have shown that these constructions can exhibit functions other than prototypical patterns of conditionality, in which the protasis conveys the cause and the apodosis the consequence. As also happens in conversation (Lastres-López 2020a), conditionals can express interpersonal functions in parliamentary discourse, allowing MPs to express stance and reinforce their opinions and viewpoints, and also to engage with other parliamentarians. This interpersonal function of conditionals is attested to a significantly higher

Morphosyntactic and pragmatic variation in conditionals **329**

Table 11.6 Relation between position and metafunction

Metafunction	Position	English		Spanish	
		N	%	N	%
Ideational	Initial	248	67.21	158	74.18
	Final	118	31.98	43	20.19
	Middle	3	0.81	12	5.63
	Total	369	100	213	100
Interpersonal	Initial	48	49.48	104	74.29
	Final	30	30.93	17	12.14
	Middle	19	19.59	19	13.57
	Total	97	100	140	100
Textual	Initial	4	100.00	7	100.00
	Final	0	0.00	0	0.00
	Middle	0	0.00	0	0.00
	Total	4	100	7	100

degree in Spanish parliamentary discourse than in British parliamentary discourse. However, the frequency of interpersonal conditionals in parliament in both languages is lower than in conversation (20% versus 53% in English, and 38% versus 51% in Spanish) (Lastres-López 2021). This lower frequency of interpersonal conditionals in parliamentary discourse as compared to conversation seems to suggest that, despite the general tendency towards the colloquialisation of parliamentary discourse (Hiltunen & Loureiro-Porto 2020; Hiltunen, Raïkkönen & Tyrkkö 2020), conditionals do not fully participate in this trend. It should be noted, however, that this tendency is not homogeneous in the two languages, since the use of these constructions in the Spanish parliament is closer to informal conversation than it is in the British parliament. Finally, at far lower frequencies, conditionals also serve textual functions in both languages, allowing MPs to use *if/si*-clauses as mechanisms of cohesion in their discourse.

In terms of the degrees of likelihood that these constructions can express, real conditions are the dominant ones in parliament, followed by potential and unreal conditions. Especially interesting here is the case of Spanish. Correlating with a higher proportion of interpersonal conditionals, as already mentioned, Spanish also presents a statistically significantly lower number of potential conditions than English. It seems, therefore, that the construction no longer needs to express a certain degree of probability or hypotheticality when it is fulfilling discourse-pragmatic functions that are no longer conditional but, rather, interpersonal.

Coexisting with this semantico-pragmatic variation of conditionals, the present chapter has also examined two morphosyntactic properties of conditionals: the markedness of the apodosis and the position of the protasis in the conditional construction. Corpus results have shown that marked apodoses are practically absent in parliamentary discourse (only three cases were found, all in the Spanish corpus), as opposed to what is found in other genres, such as courtroom discourse, where they appear in significantly higher proportions (Lastres-López 2019). The absence of marked apodoses in parliamentary discourse can probably be explained on the grounds that they are considered more 'authoritarian' than their unmarked counterparts, disfavouring their use in a genre where negotiation and argumentation typically prevail. The non-occurrence of this authoritarian feature in conditionals in parliamentary discourse seems to be in line with the results reported for other grammatical features also considered similarly authoritarian, which decrease in use in certain parliaments over time (see also Kotze & van Rooy 2020, on the decline of modal verbs of obligation in British and Australian parliamentary discourse). Regarding the position of the clause, as expected, we can observe a preference for the default position (protasis–apodosis) in both languages. However, English differs significantly from Spanish in that it shows a notably lower proportion of clauses in initial position and a higher proportion in final position. This suggests that the emphasis of British MPs when using a conditional is more often on the result or consequence than in the cause. Corpus findings have shown that this ordering correlates with the metafunction of the construction in English, with initial and non-initial position being equally distributed in interpersonal conditionals, as opposed to Spanish, which maintains the preference for initial position regardless of metafunction. A possible explanation for this may be that sometimes conditionals are produced as afterthoughts (Ford & Thompson 1986: 367). These afterthoughts are more likely to be interpersonal than ideational conditionals, which may explain the higher use of final position interpersonal conditionals. Differences between Spanish and English in this respect require further research.

The results of this study open avenues for further cross-linguistic and cross-varietal research on conditionals, to determine whether the findings reported here for British English and European Spanish can also be extrapolated to other parliamentary contexts.

Funding

For generous financial support, I am grateful to the Spanish Ministry of Science and Innovation (Grant PID2020-114604GB-100).

Acknowledgments

I would like to thank Teresa Fanego, the volume editors and two anonymous reviewers, for their valuable comments on an earlier version of this chapter.

References

Aarts, Bas, Close, Joanne & Wallis, Sean. 2013. Choices over time: Methodological issues in investigating current change. In *The Verb Phrase in English: Investigating Recent Language Change with Corpora*, Bas Aarts, Joanne Close, Geoffrey Leech & Sean Wallis (eds), 14–45. Cambridge: CUP.

Ädel, Annelie. 2010. How to use corpus linguistics in the study of political discourse. In *The Routledge Handbook of Corpus Linguistics*, Anne O'Keeffe & Michael McCarthy (eds), 591–604. London: Routledge.

Alcaide-Lara, Esperanza, Carranza-Márquez, Aurelia & Fuentes-Rodríguez, Catalina. 2016. Emotional argumentation in political discourse. In *A Gender-based Approach to Parliamentary Discourse: The Andalusian Parliament* [Discourse Approaches to Politics, Society and Culture 68], Catalina Fuentes-Rodríguez & Gloria Álvarez-Benito (eds), 129–160. Amsterdam: John Benjamins.

Alexander, Marc & Davies, Mark. 2015. The Hansard Corpus 1803–2005. <https://www.english-corpora.org/hansard/> (29 October 2019).

Anthony, Laurence. 2017. *AntConc* (Version 3.5.0) [Computer software]. Tokyo: Waseda University. <https://www.laurenceanthony.net/software> (29 October 2019).

Bayley, Paul (ed.). 2004. *Cross-Cultural Perspectives on Parliamentary Discourse* [Discourse Approaches to Politics, Society and Culture 10]. Amsterdam: John Benjamins.

Berezowski, Leszek. 2011. Curious legal conditionals. *Research in Language* 9(1): 187–197.

Berrocal, Martina. 2019. Delegitimization strategies in Czech parliamentary discourse. In *Political Discourse in Central, Eastern and Balkan Europe* [Discourse Approaches to Politics, Society and Culture 84], Martina Berrocal & Aleksandra Salamurović (eds), 119–146. Amsterdam: John Benjamins.

Bhatia, Vijay K. 1987. Language of the law. *Language Teaching* 20(4): 227–234.

Biber, Douglas, Johansson, Stig, Leech, Geoffrey, Conrad, Susan & Finegan, Edward. 1999. *Longman Grammar of Spoken and Written English*. Harlow: Longman.

Cap, Piotr. 2010. *Legitimisation in Political Discourse: A Cross-Disciplinary Perspective on the Modern US War Rhetoric*. Newcastle upon Tyne: Cambridge Scholars.

Carter-Thomas, Shirley & Rowley-Jolivet, Elizabeth. 2008. *If*-conditionals in medical discourse: From theory to disciplinary practice. *Journal of English for Academic Purposes* 7: 191–205.

Charaudeau, Patrick. 2005. *Le discours politique: Les masques du pouvoir*. Paris: Vuibert.

Chodorowska-Pilch, Marianna. 2017. Atenuación pragmática: El caso de las condicionales. *Normas* 7(1): 97–106.

Dancygier, Barbara & Sweetser, Eve. 1997. *Then* in conditional constructions. *Cognitive Linguistics* 8(2): 109–136.

Dancygier, Barbara & Sweetser, Eve. 2000. Constructions with 'if', 'since', and 'because': Causality, epistemic stance, and clause order. In *Cause, Condition, Concession, Contrast: Cognitive and Discourse Perspectives*, Elizabeth Couper-Kuhlen & Bernd Kortmann (eds), 111–142. Berlin: Mouton de Gruyter.

Dancygier, Barbara & Sweetser, Eve. 2005. *Mental Spaces in Grammar: Conditional Constructions*. Cambridge: CUP.

de Cock, Barbara, Marsily, Aurélie, Pizarro-Pedraza, Andrea & Rasson, Marie. 2018. ¿Quién atenúa y cuándo en español? La atenuación en función del género discursivo. *Spanish in Context* 15(2): 305–324.

Declerck, Renaat & Reed, Susan. 2001. *Conditionals: A Comprehensive Empirical Analysis*. Berlin: Mouton de Gruyter.

Evans, Nicholas. 2007. Insubordination and its uses. In *Finiteness: Theoretical and Empirical Foundations*, Irina Nikolaeva (ed.), 366–431. Oxford: OUP.

Facchinetti, Roberta. 2001. Conditional constructions in Modern English legal texts. In *Modality in Specialized Texts*, Maurizio Gotti & Marina Dossena (eds), 133–150. Bern: Peter Lang.

Farrelly, Michael & Seoane, Elena. 2012. Democratization. In *The Oxford Handbook of the History of English*, Terttu Nevalainen & Elizabeth Close Traugott (eds), 392–401. Oxford: OUP.

Ford, Cecilia. 1997. Speaking conditionally: Some contexts for *if*-clauses in conversation. In *On Conditionals Again*, Angeliki Athanasiadou & René Dirven (eds), 387–413. Amsterdam: John Benjamins.

Ford, Cecilia & Thompson, Sandra. 1986. Conditionals in discourse: A text-based study from English. In *On Conditionals*, Elizabeth Close Traugott, Alice ter Meulen, Judy Snitzer Reilly & Charles A. Ferguson (eds), 353–372. Cambridge: CUP.

Fuentes-Rodríguez, Catalina. 2018. *Mujer, discurso y parlamento*. Sevilla: Ediciones Alfar.

Fuentes-Rodríguez, Catalina & Álvarez-Benito, Gloria. 2016. *A Gender-based Approach to Parliamentary Discourse: The Andalusian Parliament* [Discourse Approaches to Politics, Society and Culture 68]. Amsterdam: John Benjamins.

Gallagher, Michael, Laver, Michael & Mair, Peter. 2011. *Representative Government in Modern Europe*. London: McGraw-Hill.

Garofalo, Giovanni. 2006. I connettivi condizionali complessi nei testi normativi spagnoli. *Rivista Internazionale di Tecnica della Traduzione* 9: 75–97.

Garrido-Ardila, Juan Antonio. 2019. Impoliteness as a rhetorical strategy in Spain's politics. *Journal of Pragmatics* 140: 160–170.

Greenberg, Joseph H. 1963. Some universals of grammar with particular reference to the order of meaningful elements. In *Universals of Human Language*, Joseph H. Greenberg (ed.), 73–113. Cambridge MA: The MIT Press.

Guitart-Escudero, M. Pilar. 2005. *Discurso parlamentario y lenguaje políticamente correcto*. Madrid: Congreso de los Diputados.

Haiman, John. 1978. Conditionals are topics. *Language* 54: 512–540.

Halliday, Michael A.K. & Matthiessen, Christian. 2014. *Halliday's Introduction to Functional Grammar*. London: Routledge.

Harris, Martin. 1986a. The historical development of conditional sentences in Romance. *Romance Philology* 39: 405–436.

Harris, Martin. 1986b. The historical development of *si*-clauses in Romance. In *On Conditionals*, Elizabeth Closs Traugott, Alice ter Meulen, Judy Snitzer Reilly & Charles A. Ferguson (eds), 265–284. Cambridge: CUP.

Harris, Sandra. 2001. Being politically impolite: Extending the politeness theory to adversarial political discourse. *Discourse and Society* 12(4): 451–472.

Hiltunen, Turo & Loureiro-Porto, Lucía. 2020. Democratization of Englishes: Synchronic and diachronic approaches. *Language Sciences* 79: 101275.

Hiltunen, Turo, Raïkkönen, Jenni & Tyrkkö, Jukka. 2020. Investigating colloquialization in the British parliamentary record in the late 19th and early 20th century. *Language Sciences* 79: 101270.

Horsella, Maria & Sindermann, Gerda. 1992. Aspects of scientific discourse: Conditional argumentation. *English for Specific Purposes* 11: 129–139.

Hou, Liwen & Smith, David. 2018. Modeling the decline in English passivization. *Proceedings of the Society for Computation in Linguistics* 1(5): 34–43.

Hyland, Ken. 2005. Stance and engagement: A model of interaction in academic discourse. *Discourse Studies* 7(2): 173–192.

Ilie, Cornelia. 2001. Unparliamentary language: Insults as cognitive forms of ideological confrontation. In *Language and Ideology, Vol. 2: Descriptive and Cognitive Approaches* [Current Issues in Linguistic Theory 205], René Dirven, Roslyn M. Frank & Cornelia Ilie (eds), 235–264. Amsterdam: John Benjamins.

Ilie, Cornelia. 2003. Discourse and metadiscourse in parliamentary debates. *Journal of Language and Politics* 2(1): 71–92.

Ilie, Cornelia. 2004. Insulting as (un)parliamentary practice in the British and Swedish parliaments: A rhetorical approach. In *Cross-cultural Perspectives on Parliamentary Discourse* [Discourse Approaches to Politics, Society and Culture 10]. Paul Bayley (ed.), 45–86. Amsterdam: John Benjamins.

Ilie, Cornelia. 2010. *European Parliaments under Scrutiny: Discourse Strategies and Interaction Practices* [Discourse Approaches to Politics, Society and Culture 38]. Amsterdam: John Benjamins.

Ilie, Cornelia. 2013. Gendering confrontational rhetoric: Discursive disorder in the British and Swedish parliaments. *Democratization* 20(3): 501–521.

Ilie, Cornelia. 2015. Parliamentary discourse. In *The International Encyclopedia of Language and Social Interaction*, Karen Tracy, Cornelia Ilie & Todd Sandel (eds), 1113–1127. Hoboken NJ: Wiley-Blackwell.

Ilie, Cornelia. 2018. Parliamentary debates. In *The Routledge Handbook of Language and Politics*, Ruth Wodak & Bernhard Forchtner (eds), 309–325. London: Routledge.

Ionescu-Ruxandoiu, Liliana. 2012. *Parliamentary Discourses Across Cultures: Interdisciplinary Approaches*. Newcastle upon Tyne: Cambridge Scholars.

Kaltenböck, Gunther. 2016. On the grammatical status of insubordinate *if*-clauses. In *Outside the Clause: Form and Function of Extra-clausal Constituents* [Studies in Language Companion Series 178], Gunther Kaltenböck, Evelien Keizer & Arne Lohmann (eds), 341–378. Amsterdam: John Benjamins.

Kern, Beate. 2018. La promesa atenuada en el discurso parlamentario español. *Spanish in Context* 15(2): 177–197.

Kotze, Haidee & van Rooy, Bertus. 2020. Democratisation in the South African parliamentary Hansard? A study of change in modal auxiliaries. *Language Sciences* 79: 101264.

Lastres-López, Cristina. 2018. *If*-insubordination in spoken British English: Syntactic and pragmatic properties. *Language Sciences* 66: 42–59.

Lastres-López, Cristina. 2019. Conditionals in spoken courtroom and parliamentary discourse in English, French and Spanish: A contrastive analysis. In *Corpus-based Research on Variation in English Legal Discourse* [Studies in Corpus Linguistics 91], Teresa Fanego & Paula Rodríguez-Puente (eds), 51–78. Amsterdam: John Benjamins.

Lastres-López, Cristina. 2020a. Beyond conditionality: On the pragmaticalization of interpersonal *if*-constructions in English conversation. *Journal of Pragmatics* 157: 68–83.

Lastres-López, Cristina. 2020b. On the variation between *if* and *whether* in English and their Spanish equivalents. In *Lingüística prospectiva: tendencias actuales en estudios de la lengua entre jóvenes investigadores*, Cristóbal J. Álvarez-López, María Carrillo-Rivas, Diego Jiménez-Palmero, María Méndez-Orense, Adriana Moratinos-Flórez, M. Soledad Padilla-Herrada, Víctor Pérez-Béjar, Marta Rodríguez-Manzano, Ana M. Romera-Manzanares & Natalia Silva-López (eds), 539–550. Sevilla: Editorial Universidad de Sevilla.

Lastres-López, Cristina. 2021. *From Subordination to Insubordination: A Functional-pragmatic Approach to if/si-constructions in English, French and Spanish Spoken Discourse*. Bern: Peter Lang.

Lehto, Anu. 2012. Development of subordination in Early Modern English legal discourse. In *Proceedings of the Corpus Linguistics 2011 Conference*. <https://www.birmingham.ac.uk/documents/college-artslaw/corpus/conference-archives/2011/Paper-176.pdf> (22 March 2021).

Levin, Magnus. 2013. The progressive verb in modern American English. In *The Verb Phrase in English: Investigating Recent Language Change with Corpora*, Bas Aarts, Joanne Close, Geoffrey Leech & Sean Wallis (eds), 187–216. Cambridge: CUP.

Mazzi, Davide. 2010. The centrality of counterfactual conditionals in House of Lords and US Supreme Court judgments. In *Legal Discourse across Languages and Cultures*, Maurizio Gotti & Christopher Williams (eds), 243–262. Bern: Peter Lang.

Mazzi, Davide. 2013. "If it be the case that the appellants are under such an obligation…": A comparative study of conditionals in English legal discourse. In *Realizzazioni testuali ibride in contesto europeo: Lingue dell'UE e lingue nazionali a confronto*, Stefano Ondelli (ed.), 27–40. Trieste: EUT Edizioni Università di Trieste.

Mollin, Sandra. 2007. The Hansard Hazard: Gauging the accuracy of British parliamentary transcripts. *Corpora* 2(2): 187–210.

Montolío-Durán, Estrella. 2000. Les estructures condicionals [si p, q] i la seva rellevància en les formulacions legislatives, administratives i jurídiques. *Revista de llengua i dret* 34: 67–91.

Montolío-Durán, Estrella. 2010. Discourse, grammar and professional discourse analysis: The function of conditional structures in legal writing. In *Researching Language and the Law: Textual Features and Translation Issues*, Davide Simone Giannoni & Celina Frade (eds), 19–48. Bern: Peter Lang.

Nivelle, Nele. 2008. Counterfactual conditionals in argumentative legal language in Dutch. *Pragmatics* 18(3): 469–490.

Nivelle, Nele & van Belle, William. 2007. The use of counterfactual conditionals expressing causation in legal discourse. In *Proceedings of the Sixth Conference of the International Society for the Study of Argumentation*, Frans H. van Eemeren, J. Anthony Blair, Charles A. Willard & Bart Garssen (eds), 989–996. Amsterdam: SicSat.

Nowak, Bartholomäus. 2019. Impoliteness in parliamentary questions. In *Political Discourse in Central, Eastern and Balkan Europe* [Discourse Approaches to Politics, Society and Culture 84], Martina Berrocal & Aleksandra Salamurović (eds), 147–178. Amsterdam: John Benjamins.

Puente-Castelo, Luis. 2016. Explaining the use of *if… then…* structures in CEPhiT. In *The Conditioned and the Unconditioned: Late Modern English Texts on Philosophy*, Isabel Moskowich, Gonzalo Camiña-Rioboo, Inés Lareo & Begoña Crespo (eds), 167–180. Amsterdam: John Benjamins.

Real Academia Española & Asociación de Academias de la Lengua Española. 2009. *Nueva gramática de la lengua Española. Vol. 2: Sintaxis II*. Madrid: Espasa.

Slembrouck, Stef. 1992. The parliamentary Hansard 'verbatim' report: The written construction of spoken discourse. *Language and Literature* 1(2): 101–119.

Soler-Bonafont, María Amparo. 2018. Sobre *creo (que)* subjetivo (e intensificador) en las sesiones de debate parlamentario. *Textos en proceso* 4(1): 61–92.

Soler-Bonafont, María Amparo. 2019. Semántica y pragmática de los verbos doxásticos en la interacción oral en español: Un estudio monográfico sobre la forma verbal creo. PhD dissertation, University of Valencia.

Soler-Bonafont, María Amparo. 2020. Usos discursivos de la forma verbal doxástica *creo* en la interacción oral en español. *Pragmática sociocultural / Sociocultural Pragmatics* 8(2): 204–231.

Steiner, Jürg, Bächtiger, André, Spörndli, Markus & Steenbergen, Marco R. 2004. *Deliberative Politics in Action: Analysing Parliamentary Discourse*. Cambridge: CUP.

Sweetser, Eve. 1990. *From Etymology to Pragmatics: Metaphorical and Cultural Aspects of Semantic Structure*. Cambridge: CUP.

Thompson, Geoff. 2014. *Introducing Functional Grammar*. London: Routledge.

Traugott, Elizabeth Closs, ter Meulen, Alice, Reilly, Judy Snitzer & Ferguson, Charles A. 1986. *On Conditionals*. Cambridge: CUP.

van Dijk, Teun. 2005. War rhetoric of a little ally: Political implicatures and Aznar's legitimatization of the war in Iraq. *Journal of Language and Politics* 4(1): 65–91.

Visconti, Jacqueline. 2000. A comparative glossary of conditionals in legal language: English, Italian, German, French. *Marie Curie Fellowships Annals* 1: 81–86.

Wallis, Sean. 2013. Binomial confidence intervals and contingency tests: Mathematical fundamentals and the evaluation of alternative methods. *Journal of Quantitative Linguistics* 20(3): 178–208.

Wallis, Sean. 2021. *Statistics in Corpus Linguistics Research: A New Approach*. London: Routledge.

Weber, Max. 1994. Parliament and government in Germany under a new political order. In *Weber: Political Writings*, Peter Lassman & Ronald Speirs (eds), 130–271. Cambridge: CUP.

CHAPTER 12

Colloquialisation, compression and democratisation in British parliamentary debates

Gerold Schneider & Maud Reveilhac
University of Zurich | University of Lausanne

We conduct an analysis of the link between colloquialisation and democratisation in debates in the British parliament. Our corpus is a sampler of the Hansard archive, covering the period 1803–2005 and containing 170 million words. We first investigate how the linguistic patterns of parliamentary debates have evolved, and second how the content of the debates has changed over time. Combining these two research questions allows us to step to a third question: are there direct relations between linguistic features, most notably colloquialisation and compression of language, and the topical content of parliamentary discourse, particularly its underpinnings in social and political democratisation processes? We also critically discuss strong correlations between features of language complexity and democracy indices. We adopt an interdisciplinary perspective embedded in both linguistics and political sciences.

Keywords: colloquialisation, compression, democratisation, topic modelling, language change, language and society, culturonomics, Digital Humanities

1. Introduction

Colloquialisation and democratisation are related in several ways. For instance, expressing complex topics in a simple, accessible, more speech-like style enables citizens to fulfil their democratic rights and obligations. Participatory democracy can only flourish if citizens are able to follow and comprehend the arguments of their representatives. In contrast, sophisticated and technocratic language can compromise the democratic decision-making process, by compromising successful communication across social hierarchies.

https://doi.org/10.1075/scl.111.12sch
© 2023 John Benjamins Publishing Company

This chapter aims to build a conceptual and empirical bridge from linguistic features to democratisation – a challenging endeavour. To shed light on this complex relation we have employed three operationalisable research questions. The first research question (RQ1) is: What changes are there in linguistic patterns of parliamentary debates, and are there differences in these patterns in the two parliamentary chambers? To answer this research question, we follow approaches in the recently established research field of democratisation of Englishes (Hiltunen & Loureiro-Porto 2020). The second research question (RQ2) is: What are the changes in the content of these debates? As the content features are even harder to establish than linguistic features, we follow a largely data-driven approach to extract them. In particular, we investigate the formation of new concepts by noun compounding and employ topic modelling (Blei 2012) to detect inherent topics. If the linguistic patterns and changes in content over time can be detected reasonably well by our data-driven methods, we also pose a third question (RQ3): Are indices of democratisation and our features, both related to form and content, correlated?

1.1 Colloquialisation and democratisation

To answer these research questions, we adopt an interdisciplinary perspective embedded in linguistics and political sciences. An overview of our conceptual framework is given in Figure 12.1.

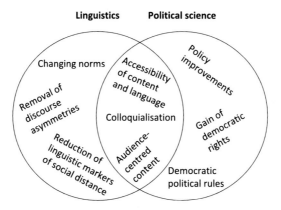

Figure 12.1 Conceptual framework: Differences and commonalities between the linguistic and political conception of democratisation

From the linguistic side, we envisage the change in linguistic patterns that tend to arise in the colloquialisation of language as a process of incorporating informal and speech-like features into written English. The closely related and partly overlapping concept of democratisation is subject to a slightly different focus in linguistics and political science. An element of the linguistic definition of democratisation is "the removal of inequalities and asymmetries in the discursive and linguistic rights, obligations and prestige of groups of people" (Fairclough 1992:201), which involves the "speakers' tendency to avoid unequal and face-threatening modes of interaction" (Farrelly & Seoane 2012:393). In this view, democratisation refers to the goal of reducing markers of social distance to increase social equality through language.

While linguistic aspects, such as treating opponents respectfully and equally, and avoiding face-threatening speech acts, is part of the picture, the political definition of democratisation involves on the one hand the introduction of a democratic system or democratic principles, and on the other hand the action of making something accessible to everyone. From the political side, we concentrate on the democratising aspect of language by looking at the content of the parliamentary debates. Accounting for the topics discussed in parliament is paramount to assess parliamentary accountability to public opinion (Rix 2014), notably by showing which topics become prevalent in the debates and are communicated to the public. The linguistic definition is an obvious element of the second part of the political definition: giving everyone due respect, endorsing the right and possibility to participate in discussions and education, ensuring freedom of speech, and removing social, ethnic and gender-based barriers, thus making important political discussions (at least partly) accessible to the population.

In addition to providing a lens through which to study changes in linguistic and topical patterns in parliamentary debates, the notion of colloquialisation also facilitates a number of other perspectives for studying democratisation processes. Scholars from a wide range of fields, including psychology, applied linguistics, computer science, sociology and cultural studies, conducting research on the relationship between new communication technologies and language, emphasise linguistic and social differences between online and offline interactions and the impact of global English on the non-English-speaking world (Cook 2004). Much recent scholarship is focused on the promise of new communication technologies to subvert social boundaries such as race, gender and ethnicity through text-based media that withhold certain identity markers (e.g. Herring 1993; Herring, Johnson & DiBenedetto 1995; Smith & Balka 1991). Others have considered the role of communication technologies in promoting social justice, economic equality, and democratisation (e.g., Baron 2002; Crystal 2001; Glowka, Melançon & Wyckoff 2003; Wilson & Peterson 2002). However, most of these studies conclude that computer-mediated communication reproduces the (often unequal) social, political and economic relations that exist in the real world (Cook 2004).

While most of this research focuses on the recent digitalisation of society, technology has undeniably had an important impact in all periods of our data.

Relying on a long period of transcripts of parliamentary debates, we are able to cover the vast scope of technological changes that may have impacted linguistic patterns but also the topics of the debates. For instance, industrialisation brought a large part of the population into factories in the cities and allowed more people to travel, both of which brought new perspectives and opportunities, but also desperation and hardship, reflected in discussions of poverty, starvation and inhumane working conditions (C.W. 2013; Schneider 2020). The eventually increasing levels of income and education associated with industrialisation arguably also paved the way for democratisation (Inglehart & Welzel 2009), which in turn links to our third research question. A further example of a breakthrough with a possible impact on colloquialisation is the fact that from the 1950s on, television brought news into the homes of all social classes, airing both critical perspectives and state propaganda (e.g. Müller 2014).

1.2   The use of records of parliamentary debates to study democratisation

Parliamentary records are a rich source to evaluate how linguistic patterns are closely associated with the surrounding society. As diachronic data, parliamentary records permit the analysis of language change (Hou & Smith 2018; Korhonen & Wiliams 2018; Kruger & Smith 2018; Kruger, van Rooy & Smith 2019; Macalister 2006), of societal shifts reflected in language (Alexander & Struan 2017; Hiltunen, Räikkönen & Tyrkkö 2020; Michel et al. 2010; Tyrkkö & Nevala 2018), as well as of important political and social concerns addressed by political representatives (e.g. Curran et al. 2018). While providing unparalleled opportunities for the empirical investigation of both language and content change, researchers should also consider that changes in the editorial practices may impact on the completeness or accuracy of records of what was spoken in parliament (Hiltunen, Räikkönen & Tyrkkö 2020; Kruger, van Rooy & Smith 2019; see also Kotze et al., this volume).

At the same time, profound changes took place in the practices of recording parliamentary proceedings, most importantly whether utterances of members of parliament (MPs) are reported as indirect or as direct speech (see Alexander, this volume). Further changes in the patterns due to deliberate changes in editorial practices are related to the move towards more verbatim reporting. Until 1909, the Hansard was based on journalists' notes rather than transcriptions of actual spoken language. Although these changes also reflect the social change of taking the spoken register more seriously, they nevertheless result in a text-typological shift in the primary data which complicates the analysis of frequency developments over time. Hiltunen, Räikkönen & Tyrkkö (2020:14) summarise this shift as follows:

it shows how an environmental, language-external change principally motivated by societal democratization – the aim to provide a fair, accurate and comprehensive report of parliamentary debates to the public – can bring about a clear stylistic shift in the texts. As a "substantially verbatim" account of the debates, the official report clearly marks a shift towards an increasingly colloquial parliamentary report.

Correlating the answers to our research questions allows us to assess direct relations between linguistic features, most notably colloquialisation and compression of language, and the topical content of parliamentary discourse, particularly its underpinnings in social and political democratisation processes.

1.3 Changes in linguistic patterns of parliamentary debates

With respect to our first research question, previous diachronic studies have established that written language has increasingly adopted features associated with spoken language, although genre and register differences are considerable (Biber & Gray 2013; Hundt & Mair 1999). This tendency towards greater informality and equality in language use and the fact that parliament has become more demographically representative of the population over time leads to the expectation that informal features in parliamentary language may also have increased, which has been supported by some previous studies (Hiltunen, Räikkönen & Tyrkkö 2020; Kruger & Smith 2018).

At the same time, differences between the two chambers of the British parliament are also likely. Whereas members of the House of Commons are publicly elected and debate big political issues of the day, the members of the House of Lords are appointed for life, forming an elite that complement the work of the first chamber. As the members of the House of the Lords are older and more remote from the daily details of implementation, we expect to find language use that is slightly less technical and scientific (thus more spoken-like in this sense) but possibly more formal (thus possibly also less colloquial and spoken-like).

Linguistic changes do not happen in isolation, but are embedded in social processes and historical changes that mutually influence each other (e.g. Bell 2013:131); there is a reciprocal motion in "languages constructing society and being constructed in society" (Nevalainen 2015:246). Yet, as Fairclough (1992:1) points out, a major problem "is the isolation of language studies from other social sciences, and the domination of linguistics by formalistic and cognitive domains". Fairclough believes that linguistic analysis requires social analysis, and vice versa. It is a truism that the level of lexis is directly related to social and historical change rather than linguistic change, as far as the principle of compositionality holds. It is

Colloquialisation, compression and democratisation **341**

therefore important to account for the coevolution of both linguistic patterns and topical content related to important social and political concerns.

An example of the entwinement of linguistic and societal changes is the increase in noun compounds (see Section 2.2.1, also Leech et al. 2009). This increase is partly related to the advent of ever more complex machines and technical tools that have fundamentally changed our daily lives. However, it also reflects diverse other social forces: medical and scientific advances, the development of a more individualised society, the increased prominence of names of companies and organisations, and increasingly complex legal systems.

Another example is the change in the frequency of modals, where "the increase of emergent modals is far from commensurate with the decline of core modals" (Leech 2013: 96) may also be due to changes in the ways in which people interact with each other; for example, in the use of hedging and face-saving strategies. Mandating others to do certain things may decrease in a more egalitarian society. Democratisation in its linguistic definition may directly entail a reduction in the use of modal verbs of obligation. However, ethical considerations can also impose new kinds of obligations possibly leading to a higher use of modal verbs of obligation.

Relying on the parliamentary debates from the British Hansard, Hiltunen, Räikkönen and Tyrkkö (2020) demonstrate how processes of linguistic colloquialisation and democratisation can be understood as tendencies towards greater informality and equality in language use. The authors' focus on democratisation is oriented towards the assessment of the tendency to incorporate features typical of speech into written language. This tendency to colloquialisation has also been supported by Kruger and Smith's (2018) study of the Australian Hansard. For instance, the authors identified a decrease in the use of passives and relative clauses, and an increase in the frequency of contractions and emphatics.

In line with previous findings, our results in this study demonstrate trends toward an increase of the Saxon genitive (Mair 2006; Röthlisberger & Schneider 2013), shorter sentence length (Rudnicka 2018), more contractions, more pronouns (Tyrkkö 2017), and a slight move towards more nominal style (Leech et al. 2009). Furthermore, to answer our third research question, we also correlate linguistic features to democracy indices.

1.4 Changes in the content of parliamentary debates

As far as our second research question, which focuses on changes in the content of parliamentary debates, is concerned, it is much harder to agree on an established set of features that express such changes. Rühlemann and Hilpert's (2017: 105) caution on the risk of missing relevant features is particularly acute here. We thus use a data-driven approach to answer our research questions. Such approaches are frequently used for automated analysis of media content to detect trends and shifting topics in society, but only rarely in historical linguistics (Hilpert & Gries 2016: 44–45).

Curran et al. (2018) showed how a topic modelling approach can be used to describe the political discourse in the New Zealand parliament using transcripts of parliamentary records since 2003. The authors linked MPs to the topics they discuss and demonstrated how topic popularity changes over time according to specific social, economic and legislative events. Another study, from Greene and Cross (2017), analysed how the political agenda of the European parliament plenary has evolved over time in the period 1999–2014. The authors also relied on topic modelling to detect latent themes in legislative speeches over time. They show the benefit of relying on an unsupervised classification approach to detect niche themes, and also demonstrate how the parliamentarians' discourse reacts to events such as EU Treaty referenda and the emergence of the Euro Crisis.

In our study, we cover a larger period of parliamentary debates than has been the case in previous papers, and we also assess how topics evolve in relation to real-world events. Substantively, we are able to account for several of our expectations, most notably timescales fitting historical developments (e.g. important events such as the World Wars leaving strong traces), and topics reflecting democratisation processes (e.g. education and gain of social protections). Furthermore, to address our third research question, we also correlate important topics to indicators of democratisation and gross domestic product (GDP).

In the next section, we present the data and methods of analysis in more detail. Then, we discuss our findings in three parts in Section 3: linguistic change, content change, and relationship between both types of change. In Section 4, we further discuss the limitations of our study and conclude with an outlook to future research.

2. Data and methods of analysis

2.1 Data

We conduct our analysis of the link between colloquialisation and democratisation in the context of parliamentary debates in the British parliament. Our corpus consists of a sample of the Hansard archive which covers the period 1803–2005 and contains 170 million words.[1] It includes the records of parliamentary *debates*

---

1. See <https://www.hansard-archive.parliament.uk>.

but not *speeches* (which are less spontaneous). We created a random sampler of approximately 10% of Hansard (files ending in *1P0.xml) including extracted utterances by MPs (XML tag <membercontribution>). Figure 12.2 shows the distribution of words per decade. The corpus constitutes the best available record of all debates held in the two houses of parliament.

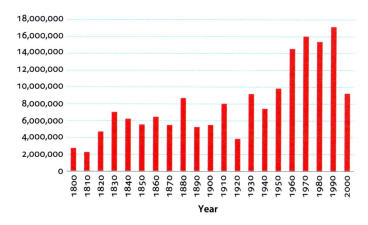

Figure 12.2 Word count per decade in our random sample of the Hansard

2.2 Methods

We conducted several pre-processing steps including tokenisation and POS-tagging, for which we used the *TreeTagger* (Schmid 1994). With respect to linguistic change, we relied on counting occurrences of individual linguistic features, including the Saxon genitive, contractions, pronouns, nouns, verbs, and noun compounds. Our selection of features is based, on the one hand, on described changes in English in the past 200 years, and, on the other hand, on features that are indicators of formal, written language versus informal, spoken language.

2.2.1 *Individual linguistic features*

Leech et al. (2009) demonstrate an increase in the frequency of nouns between 1960 and 1990, particularly for compound nouns. Schneider, El-Assady and Lehmann (2017) trace this change in the COHA corpus, for the entire period 1910–2000, and Schneider (forthcoming) shows that it is also one of the strongest data-driven features of Present-Day English compared to earlier periods. Röthlisberger and Schneider (2013) show an increase in the frequency of Saxon genitives between 1900 and 2000. Biber (1988, 2003) and Biber and Conrad (2009) find that noun frequency is an important factor distinguishing formal from informal writing; it is one of the most important features of the dimension of "oral vs. literate discourse" (Biber & Conrad 2009: 228).

Apart from analysing the frequency of nouns as such, we also investigate the frequency of noun compounds as two nouns in combination. We also investigate the frequency of the lexical pairing of the two nouns participating in the noun compound in a data-driven fashion. Our hypothesis is that new and particularly frequent pairs are indicative of societal and historical trends.

We rely on POS-tagging to detect noun compounds as sequences of two nouns. This method also reports some false positives (noun sequences that are not noun compounds). The biggest sources of error are, first, titles (e.g. *Captain Miller*), which we avoid by only including common nouns. A second source of error are two NPs in a sequence such as after a ditransitive verb (e.g. *gave the girl flowers*), which also lead to false positives. We filter them by using a high frequency filter, and by only considering those sequences which occur in an alternation with a prepositional counterpart, following the method of Röthlisberger and Schneider (2013) and Schneider, El-Assady and Lehmann (2017). For the longitudinal visualisation of noun compounds, we apply a motion chart using *GoogleVis* through the R language (Gesmann & de Castillo 2011).

In contrast to nouns, frequency of pronouns is a feature of informal discourse and spoken language. Pronouns, and in particular first-person pronouns, are also associated with greater focus on one's self or one's social world (Tausczik & Pennebaker 2010). Pennebaker et al. (2014) show that there is a significant correlation between use of pronouns and college grades, as high frequency of pronouns is a feature of involved instead of academic abstract style. Additionally, high pronoun frequency is also typical of populist language (Partington & Taylor 2018) and is often a feature of older speakers (Ronan & Schneider 2020). We might anticipate, then, a higher frequency of pronoun use by speakers in the House of Lords, who are typically older, compared to the House of Commons.

We measure further well-known linguistic features, for instance the frequency of passive forms. Using active instead of passive verbs can be seen as an effort to avoid hiding agents and using simpler, more easily accessible language; we thus expect a decrease in the use of passive forms over time. We also analyse sentence length as a simple measure of linguistic complexity. In line with Leech (2013), we moreover investigate the change in the frequency of modal verbs. Finally, following Kruger and Smith (2018) we analyse changes in the use of contractions and emphatics.

We show that there are systematic differences for each of the linguistic features investigated when comparing the two chambers of parliament, which are composed of the House of Commons with elected politicians and the House of Lords with nobility or upper class unelected individuals.

2.2.2 *Correlation with indices of democracy and economy*

We correlate each of the linguistic features investigated with a democracy index, including democracy and polity (e.g. Marshall & Elzinga-Marshall 2017), education rate (e.g. Dwyer 2010), as well as growth rate of GDP (e.g. Bolt et al. 2018), using Pearson correlations between the frequency of the features and the democracy index as they change over time. We test correlations on the basis of lists per decade, containing 21 data points. We also investigate differences between the two chambers of parliament.

The democracy index includes competitiveness of political participation, openness and competitiveness of executive recruitment, plus constraints on the chief executive. The polity index implies subtracting the autocratic score from the democracy score. It is based on annual cross-national data accounting for the democratic and autocratic patterns of authority.[2] The GDP index is measured per capita in 2011 in US dollars. It stems from the *Maddison Project Database*, which provides information on comparative economic growth and income levels over the very long run. The 2018 version of this database covers 169 countries and the period up to 2016.[3] The education index is based on enrolment rate and stems from Dwyer's *Growth and Finance* project. To calculate the enrolment rates for higher education, the author used total enrolments by year divided by the year population between the ages of 18–24. The data cover a very long period.[4]

2.2.3 *Topic modelling*

With respect to change in content, we rely on longitudinal topic modelling keeping only nouns and adjectives. Topic modelling is a data-driven method able to detect topics from a large text collection fully automatically. Like distributional semantic methods it exploits the Firthian hypothesis (Firth 1957) by learning from the context. In particular, it combines document classification with the strong semantic unity of the discourse of a topic and of a document. Church (2000) observed that the chance of a word occurring in a document radically changes if the same word has occurred before. While a given word w generally has probability p(w) the chance of seeing w a second time if it has occurred once is much closer to p(w)/2 than p(w)^2, which we would expect if the first and second appearance were independent. This shift in probability also applies to some degree at the

---

2. The link to the data and the codebooks can be found under the *Polity5 Project* <https://www.systemicpeace.org/inscrdata.html> and can be exported in several formats (data for years 1800–1945 are Polity IV values).

3. See <https://www.rug.nl/ggdc/historicaldevelopment/maddison/releases/maddison-project-database-2018>.

4. The data can be found at <http://www.jerrydwyer.com/growth/index.html>.

discourse level of topics, a fact that topic modelling exploits. Intuitively we know that specific topics are much more likely to generate specific words – this is also the reason why the classification of documents into known classes of topics performs reliably.

Topic models maximise p(*topic*|*document*) x p(*word*|*topic*) for all given documents in a collection. It thus combines document classification (p(*topic*|*document*)) and keyword generation (p(*word*|*topic*)). *Documents* and *words* are given; *topics* are fitted iteratively starting from a random configuration.

It can be argued that for well-studied domains, the mapping from words to concepts is available in the form of thesauri, which have been developed carefully and often inspired by painstaking corpus research. A tool mapping words to concepts is the rule-based system *WMatrix* (Rayson 2008).[5] While this approach performs well on general newspaper texts, specific genres and historical texts often end up with unsatisfactory analyses (see Moreton & Culy 2020), as many of the words have undergone strong semantic shifts, have domain-specific readings, or tend to be expressed indirectly. Addressing the problem of mapping words to concepts by using contexts in a purely data-driven fashion is a viable alternative, provided that sufficiently large amounts of domain data are available. Based on previous experience, about a million words is minimally needed.

We use *Mallet* (McCallum 2002), a popular implementation of the topic modelling algorithm of Latent Dirichlet Allocation. *Mallet* is implemented in Java, but it can also be used from the UNIX command line, Python or R. We used N = 100 topics. About 80 of them are easy to interpret. Among those which are harder to interpret we find topics that are dominated by terms of address (e.g. *Sir, Majesty, Lord*), by very general and frequent words (e.g. *pound, day, people, country*), or procedural issues (e.g. *bill, procedure, committee*). We also correlate relevant topics related to democratisation processes with the same indices of democracy, economy and education as set out in Section 2.2.2.

2.2.4 *Relationship between linguistic and content changes*

We finally assess direct relations between linguistic features and topics related to political and social democratisation processes relying on correlation between both the evolution of linguistic features and the longitudinal prevalence of topics. We again use the Pearson correlation measure for this comparison. We will show that some of the correlations are very high, but we will warn that great care must be taken in the interpretation of these figures: high correlations may be a side-effect of other correlated variables, or independent developments. Addition-

---

5. See <http://ucrel.lancs.ac.uk/wmatrix/>.

ally, correlations cannot be interpreted as expressing causality (see Partington & Taylor 2018: 89–92).

3. Results

3.1 Linguistic change across time

We find an increase in noun compounds, the Saxon genitive, and a slight move towards a more nominal style, and a more personal style (*I* and *we*). While these trends are well known from other domains, particularly press and scientific language (Biber 2003; Biber & Conrad 2009; Leech et al. 2009), they are also increasingly reaching parliamentary debates. Figure 12.3 displays the normalised frequencies of these features per 1,000 words by decade. For enhancing the interpretability of the graph, we also include technological innovations in the communication domain.

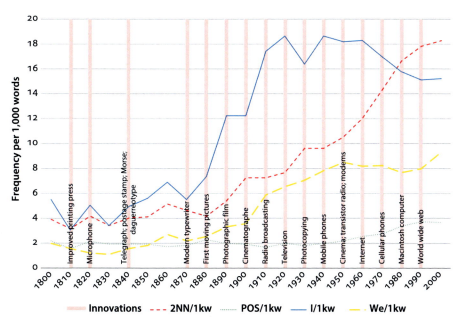

Figure 12.3 Evolution of frequency of features associated with nominal style (normalised frequency per 1,000 words), with major technological innovations indicated. 2NN = noun compounds, POS = Saxon genitives, I = pronoun *I*, we = pronoun *we*

Figure 12.3 shows a mild increase in the use of the Saxon genitive (POS), which is in line with other linguistic studies, for example Röthlisberger and Schneider (2013). There is a strong increase in frequency in the first-person pronouns *I* and *we*. This is partly evidence of colloquialisation: some more formal and abstract styles are replaced by personal, involved styles. In Biber (1988) first-person pronouns are a strong feature for the dimension which distinguishes between involved, personal style and informational, abstract style (see also the discussion in Section 2.2.1).

Another explanation for the steep increase is the change of editorial style of the Hansard. Utterances of MPs are reported as indirect speech until about 1880, and increasingly as direct speech afterwards (see Alexander, this volume). This text-typological shift in the primary data adds a substantial bias to our data. On the one hand, it complicates the analysis of frequency developments of first-person pronouns; on the other hand the conscious shift of the editorial conventions is itself an intended democratisation step, as the spoken register of the direct, authentic speech was considered increasingly more important.

Figure 12.3 also shows that the frequency of noun compounds (2NN) has increased dramatically. It starts at about 4 noun compounds per 1,000 words, reaches 7 in 1900, and peaks at 18 in the latest period. The increase is particularly steep from about 1880 onward. Noun compounds are non-compositional, which makes them difficult to understand for the uninitiated. The steep increase in frequency may therefore be surprising. Jespersen (1942) and Biber (2003) describe the difficulty as follows:

> Compounds express a relation between two objects or notions, but they say nothing of the way in which the relation is to be understood. That must be inferred from the context or otherwise. (Jespersen 1942:137)

> These increasingly compressed styles of expression are at the same time less explicit in meaning. For example, noun-noun sequences can represent a bewildering array of meaning relationships, with no overt signal of the intended meaning. (Biber 2003:179)

If noun compounds are difficult to understand, why should they increase so much in frequency? It has been observed that they are very frequent particularly in the genre of newspaper writing. On the one hand, the need to compress complex information into a few words, for example a headline, is particularly pressing in this genre. On the other hand, readers are typically aware of what happened yesterday, and a brief update on the latest situation is often all they need; yesterday's association will guide them to the correct interpretation:

> [...] news relies primarily on pre-modifying nouns from those semantic domains most commonly associated with current events such as government, business, education, the media and sports. These are areas where news writers can reasonably expect readers to have well-developed pragmatic knowledge, and so be able to decode noun + noun relationships without too much difficulty.
>
> (Biber 2003:180)

Noun compounds are a prime method for the creation of neologisms in English. According to Master (2003:2), "noun compound is a grammatical structure in which nouns are linked together to indicate a new concept". In Figure 12.3 we have added key inventions in on the temporal axis. New inventions lead to new concepts, which need new names. Some of the inventions lead to new concepts that can be traced directly. For example, the success of the printing press leads to an increased demand for paper. The noun compound *paper manufacturer* appears very early: the mean year of all its occurrences is 1860; for *paper trade* it is 1891. The success of printing also made newspapers and thus mass information possible. The compound noun *morning paper* appears on average in 1883. Further advances in printing also led to *paper money* (1857). There was obviously money to be made in this industry, which explains the average year of 1858 for *paper duty* – a tax levied on paper. The invention of posting stamps in the 1840 led to the establishment of a *mail service* (1896), via *mail steamer* (1884) or *mail train* (1888).

The invention of film took longer to be reflected in noun–noun compounds. We find *film hire* (1948) and *film production* (1962). *Radio broadcasting* has its first occurrence in Hansard in the 1950s, and peaks in 1972. *Radio station* appears first in Hansard in the 1920s, and peaks in 1976. The dangers to democracy are highlighted from early on; the first occurrence of *radio propaganda* in Hansard is in the 1920s. The impact of television is visible from later on. For example, we find *colour television* from the 1950s on, peaking in 1964. *Cable television* only peaks in 1982. *Phone call* appears first in the 1950s, and peaks in 1987. The first occurrence of *office computer* in Hansard is in the 1960s, and *home computer* in the 1980s.

After this data-based step of looking for expected words, we also conducted a data-driven experiment in which the recency of any noun was calculated and could then be compared, without risking overlooking salient compound nouns. We automatically extracted the average year of appearance of all compound nouns that appear at least ten times in any decade in Hansard and then manually analysed the 1,000 compound noun types that appear on average very early, and the 1,000 that on average appear very late. Strong differences can be observed. Among the earliest compound nouns, we find particularly many Latin terms (e.g. *viva voce* (mean of occurrence is 1843), agricultural terms (e.g. *herring brand* (1880), *corn market* (1845), *grazing farm* (1887), *barley malt* (1888), and also more religious terms (e.g. *church accommodation* (1847) and *parish priest* (1870)).

Among the latest compound nouns, there are particularly many medical and social terms. Most of the latest compound nouns peak in the latest decade, after 2000. From medicine, we find for example *cell research, NHS plan, smoking cessation* and *cancer plan*. Among the social concepts, we find for example *binge drinking, suicide bomber, homelessness strategy, child contact, gender gap* (1999) and *people trafficking* (1998). Among the early compound nouns, we find very few social concepts; these include for example *pauper asylum* (1877), *marriage ceremony* (1877), *burial service* (1863) and *prison dress* (1866).

We speculated in Section 1.3 that the increase is partly related to the advent of ever more complex machines and technical tools; medical progress; an increasingly individualised society; and a complex legal system. While the effects of medical progress and social factors are clearly visible, what about the other suggested factors?

Legal terms are relatively frequent among the early and late compound nouns. Among the early ones we find *crown lawyer* (1805), *summary punishment* (1859) and *wine duty* (1866); the latest terms include *(market) abuse regime, planning duty* and *landfill directive*. The last of these, *landfill directive*, is also an environmental term. Terms relating to environment and energy are indeed more frequent among the latest terms, including, for example, *fuel security, wind farm* (1999) and *emission trading* (1999). Among the rare early energy and environment terms we find *roadside waste* (1880) and *coal trade* (1914).

And what about technology? Basic technology, relating to factories, railway infrastructure, and so on, is in fact more frequent among the earliest terms, mirroring the industrial revolution. Here, we find *linen manufacture* (1821), *silk trade* (1838), *machine maker* (1847), and *railway scheme* (1882). Among the latest terms, we find more that are related to communication, such as *access authority, connexion service, call centre* (1998), *phone mast* (1998) and *junk mail* (1997). But overall, there are fewer technology-related compounds than the many we find from the domains of medicine and society. It almost seems as if either communication technology had less of an impact on the discussions in parliament (than on people's daily lives), or that the legal system is lagging behind technological progress.

Finally, we observed that many compound nouns, both early and late, are financial and military terms. Early legal terms include *crown lawyer* (1805) and *canon law* (1849). Early financial terms include *gold coin* (1860), *paper money* (1857) and *slave trade* (1852); late financial terms include, for example, *saving credit, consumer debt* and *risk management* (1999). Early military terms include *navy board* (1801), *war ship* (1893) and *cavalry regiment* (1897); late army terms are *weapon inspector, child soldier* (1998) and *missile defence* (1997).

We also investigated the creation of new compound nouns. Following Röthlisberger and Schneider (2013), and Schneider, El-Assady and Lehmann

(2017), we only considered those sequences which occur in an alternation with a prepositional counterpart. Figure 12.4 shows the most frequent compound nouns in Hansard and compares their realisation as noun compound or noun–PP combination. We show the situation in 1820, 1920, and 2000 in Figure 12.4.[6] Noun combinations in the top left corner are mostly realised as compound nouns. The alternating pair *officer of police* (noun–PP variant) and *police officer* (noun compound variant) is already mostly realised as noun compound, while most other noun–noun combinations, for example *rise in price*, are not, or rarely, realised as noun compounds. In 1920, we see a mixed situation, and in 2000 the noun compound variants are generally more frequent, except for, for example, *welfare of child*, which is only rarely realised as *child welfare*.

A further well-known change that we investigated are modal verbs. One could expect that democratisation in its linguistic definition may entail a reduction in the use of modal verbs of obligation (Leech 2013). But while the central modals of obligation (*must, should, shall, ought,*) reduce in frequency (by about 20% across the entire Hansard time span), the semi-modals of obligation (*need to* and *have to*) largely compensate for the lower frequency of the central modals.

Figure 12.5 shows a clear trend toward shorter sentence length by decade. Mean length reduces from 30 words in 1810 to 20 words in 2000. Shorter sentences are an indication of colloquialisation, but possibly also reflect the editing conventions. Indirect speech can easily combine several T-units into one sentence, while a transcription of direct speech typically stays closer to the T-units of the original utterance. Reduction of sentence length is a diachronic trend that has been observed in a large variety of corpora. For example, Rudnicka (2018) describes the development of sentence length in the COHA corpus. Two of the five coarse-grained genres in COHA behave very similar to Hansard: in magazine writing, sentence length reduces from an average of 27 words per sentence in 1810 to 17 words per sentence in 2000, and in non-fiction average sentence length drops from 28 words per sentence in 1810 to 20 words per sentence in 2000.

A further well-known feature of colloquial style is the use of contractions. In Biber and Conrad (2009) contractions are a strong predictor of the dimension which distinguishes oral vs. literate discourse. Contractions in spoken language have probably been used for a very long time; for example, the Old Bailey Corpus (Huber, Nissel & Puga 2016) contains some contracted forms right from its start in 1720. But as their use in written language has been stigmatised, the forms hardly appear in later decades, only to rise slightly in the last decade again (1900–1910).

---

6. The dynamic graph can be accessed at <https://uzh.mediaspace.cast.switch.ch/media/HANSARD_NN_NPN/0_c5ybxrjo>.

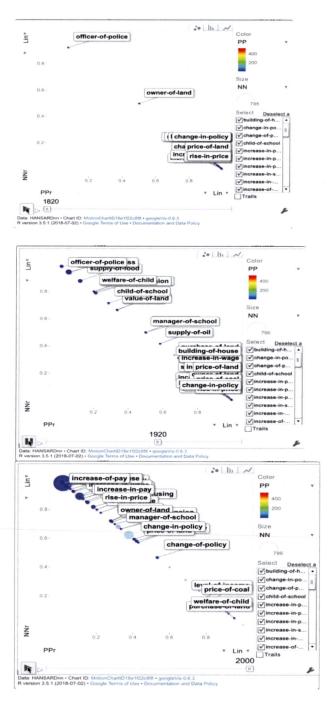

Figure 12.4 GoogleViz movie caption from 1820, 1920 and 2000. Bottom right noun combinations are with PP, top left are with noun compounds

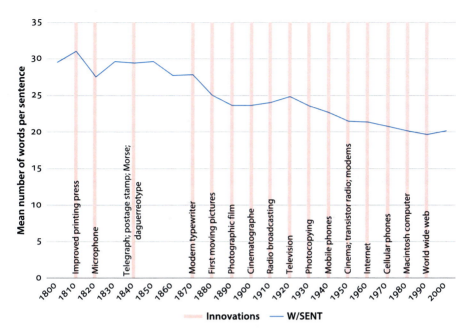

Figure 12.5 Evolution of the mean number of words per sentence (w/SENT) by decade, with major technological innovations indicated

Contractions are still stigmatised in formal registers, and there is considerable regional variation, for example in the ICE corpora.

Figure 12.6 shows contraction rates of *'ve* and *'m* per 1 million words (we have excluded some other frequent forms, notably *'s* and *'d* as they are ambiguous). In spoken language, the distinction between a full and a contracted form is often unclear. The conventions that are used by the transcriber are often as important as the actual pronunciation. In this light, Figure 12.6 is also a mirror of changing transcribing conventions, which themselves are changing due to social developments (see Section 1.2). In their analysis of the Australian Hansard, Kruger and Smith (2018) and Kruger, van Rooy and Smith (2019) show that there is a clear change in editorial policy in the 1960s leading to increased frequency of contracted forms, possibly also reflecting a changing social attitude of finding contractions less stigmatised.

3.2 Linguistic difference between the two chambers

Concerning the influence of the opposing powers of compression (Biber 2003; Biber & Conrad 2009) on the one hand, and colloquialisation and soundbite journalism (Hallin 1992) on the other hand, Figure 12.7 shows that there are

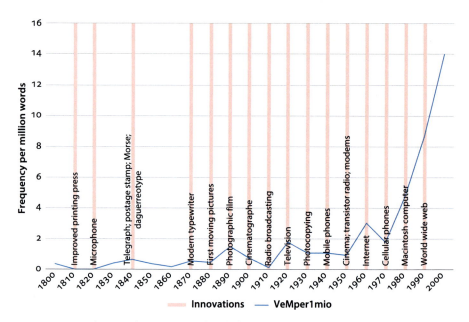

Figure 12.6 Evolution of contractions ('ve/'m): Normalised frequency per million words (VeMper1mio) per decade, with major technological innovations indicated

systematic differences when comparing the two chambers of parliament. Figure 12.7 shows on the one hand two diachronic changes: an increase of the noun/verb ratio, which can partly be explained by the increase in noun compounds discussed in Section 3.1, and partly by a general increase in technical language. Biber and Conrad (2009) explain why scientific, technical language and newspaper language contain more nouns, and why noun frequency is a strong feature on the dimension distinguishing between involved and informational language: "Informing readers about a specific topic requires precise noun phrases. The time allowed for production of the text enables writers to formulate the denser noun phrases" (Biber & Conrad 2009: 118).

The second diachronic trend evident in Figure 12.7 is a reduction in passive verb forms. This is on the one hand a general trend, and one that is a feature of democratisation: it reflects less complex, less abstract language; a more personal touch; and also an effort to avoid hiding agents. Hundt, Schneider and Seoane (2016: 56) write that

> [a] defining quality of the hard sciences discourse is impersonality, since research in this area is assumed to be objective. The passive is a good strategy for the writer who wants to step back and hide their personal involvement.

Biber et al. (2002: 40) point out that "engineering (and, to a lesser extent, natural science) is extremely marked for the dense use of passive constructions. This pattern fits the stereotypical characterization of technical and scientific prose."

In addition to the diachronic changes, we can observe strong and highly significant differences (chi-square contingency test, all $p < 0.0001$) between the two chambers. Speakers in the House of Lords use fewer nouns, a smaller noun/verb ratio (reflecting less technical language) and fewer passive forms (reflecting a more involved, less abstract style). It can also be said that the language of the Lords is more prototypically spoken-like, more spontaneous, and slightly less technical and scientific.

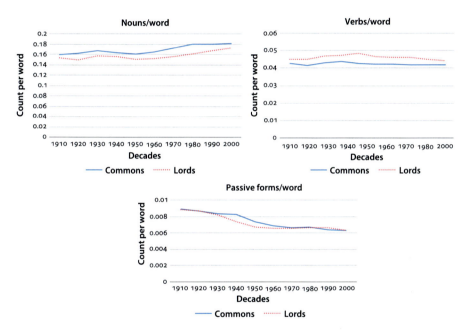

Figure 12.7 Evolution of the use of verbal versus nominal style and passive voice (normalised frequency per word) by decade for the House of Lords and the House of Commons

Figure 12.8 shows the frequency of noun compounds, average sentence length, and the frequency of the pronoun *I* in the House of Lords and House of Commons data. The frequency of noun compounds is lower in the House of Lords, which fits our expectations. Speakers in the House of Lords also use the pronoun *I* much more frequently, reflecting an involved, personal, narrative style. Pronouns, and in particular first-person pronouns, can be an indication of a self-centred perspective (Tausczik & Pennebaker 2010). An increased use of pronouns has also been described for older speakers (Ronan & Schneider 2020). Members of the House of the Lords are typically older than members of the House of Commons.

Sentence length, however, is a feature that is colloquial, and shorter sentence lengths are also more typical of older speakers (Kemper 2010). However, average sentence length remains consistently considerably longer in the House of the Lords, in contrast to the other observed differences. Statements of speakers in the House of Lords are obviously more verbose. What could be possible reasons? First, narrative style does not necessarily lead to shorter sentences. The difference between narrative and non-narrative style is typically more between hypotactic and paratactic style; in other words, subordinating versus coordinating style (e.g. Halliday & Matthiessen 2004). Second, although sentence complexity typically decreases for older speakers, it increases until about 50 years of age, and there are strong individual differences (Moscoso del Prado Martín 2016). Some politicians use very long, and others very short sentences (Ronan & Schneider 2020). The observation of decreasing sentence length applies to the average of the population. Older MPs are typically highly socially and mentally active, self-confident personalities, who are sure that they have something important to contribute. We get the impression of verbose, narrative style, delivered by very experienced and highly confident speakers, and a slightly more formal style, as in Example (1).

(1) I can assure you that we who live in almost daily intercourse with all classes of society in South Wales cannot look at this question dispassionately, nor contemplate without horror the harm that will inevitably ensue, and the utter disorganisation of all religious life in Wales that will be caused if this Bill is forced on the community. (House of Lords, 12 February 1913, Lord Kensington)

To summarise, members of the House of the Lords use a style that is slightly less technical and scientific (thus more spoken-like) in the sense that it contains more verbs, more pronouns and fewer passive forms and nouns; but also some features of more formal language (less colloquial and spoken-like), in particular long sentences and involved style.

3.3 Correlation of linguistic features with external indices

To account further for the link between language change and democratisation, Table 12.1 shows the correlation of the observed change in linguistic patterns to democratisation indices and education rate, as well as growth rate of GDP. We tested correlations on the basis of lists per decade (which contains 21 data points).[7]

---

7. We were surprised at how high some of the correlations are, so we suspected the influence of sparse data. Thus, we also analysed the correlations by year (thus lists containing 200 data points). The correlations remain similar, although slightly less strong. For example, the correlation between compound nouns and education rate reduces from 0.99 to 0.93. On the one hand,

Colloquialisation, compression and democratisation 357

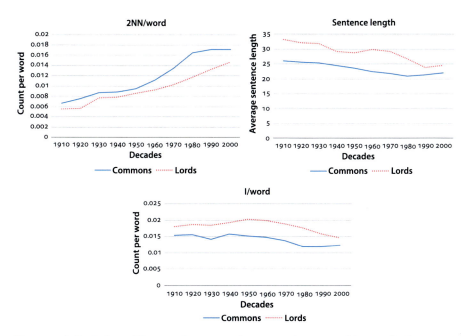

Figure 12.8 Evolution of the use of compound nouns and pronoun *I* (normalised frequency per word) and average sentence length by decade for the House of Lords and the House of Commons

The linguistic features that we have chosen are relative frequencies of nouns (NN/1kw), verbs (VB/1kw, sentence length (w/SENT), Saxon genitives (POS/1kw), contractions (VeM/1kw), compound nouns (2NN/1kw), the pronoun *I* (I/1kw), and passive verb forms (passive/1kw). From Table 12.1 it is evident that the correlation of the frequency of noun compounds to education rate, and also the correlation with the GDP and polity indices is extremely high.

While the strengths of these correlations invite the drawing of conclusions, we must point out several caveats. First, statistical correlations must not be understood as causal correlations. Second, indicators can develop into the same direction for independent reasons. Third, building political arguments on correlated trends is a dangerous undertaking as correlations can also be due to chance and no cause–effect claims can be made – a "slippery slope" as Partington and Taylor (2018: 89–92) put it, giving several examples from history. Fourth, values for the democracy index, GDP, and the frequency of compound nouns have all seen an

---

a correlation between more data points is more reliable; on the other hand, the counts per year are affected by sparse data: we frequently observe fluctuations by 10% or 20% from one year to the next.

Table 12.1 Correlations between selected linguistic features and political democratisation features

	NN/1kw	VB/1kw	w/SENT	POS/1kw	VeM/1kw	I/1kw	passive/1kw	2NN/1kw
GDP	−0.30	−0.30	−0.75	0.87	−0.38	0.51	0.64	0.90
Democracy	−0.11	−0.11	−0.87	0.49	−0.07	0.87	0.83	0.80
Polity	−0.13	−0.13	−0.87	0.43	0.07	0.85	0.71	0.69
Education	−0.26	−0.26	−0.83	0.84	−0.53	0.55	0.67	0.93

almost exponential increase in the past few decades, as Figure 12.9 shows (which plots compound nouns per 1 million words, GDP, and the democracy index value scaled times 1,000 to be of comparable size).

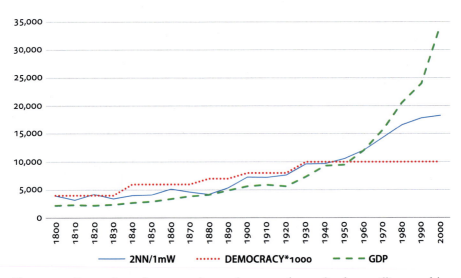

Figure 12.9 Comparison of compound noun frequency (normalised per million words), democracy index (times 1,000) and GDP

Despite these caveats, there are also other reasonable explanations for the correlations. High levels of education lead to more formal, more technical language, a sign of which is the frequency of noun compounds, and a high level of education is at the same time a cornerstone of a working democracy. This refers both to general linguistic and societal changes, but also to the British parliament, with the differences between the House of Commons and the House of the Lords (outlined in Section 3.2).

3.4 Change in content

Concerning changes in content, we conduct a diachronic analysis of the parliamentary debates by means of topic modelling (Blei 2012). From the approximately 80 identifiable topics, we manually selected those topics which are internally and externally coherent (Grimmer & Stewart 2013), relate to social and political processes of democratisation, and depict clear timescales which fit historical developments. We selected 11 topics which we display in four groups in Figures 12.10 to 12.13. To illustrate the output of topic modelling, we give a random section of the raw *Mallet* output. The detected keywords for the 30 topics and weights are shown in Table 12.2. As the topic-IDs are arbitrary, any selection (such as our first 30 here) is a random selection. The column 'Weight' indicates the proportion of the discourse which is covered by the given topic. These 30 topics include two of those that we will discuss in a longitudinal view: Topic 0 (for which we propose the label *University & Science*) and Topic 1 (*Ireland*). Several other topics also have a clear interpretation; for instance Topic 8 refers to *Nobility*, 12 to *Jurisdiction*, 20 to *the European Union*, 21 to *India*, 23 to *Scotland*, 25 to *Housing*, 27 to *Employment*, and for 30 the label *Air Defense* would fit. For other topics, for instance Topic 3 and Topic 17, a semantic core or an internal coherence of the topic is hard to discern. Topic 3 is one of the topics with the most weight (10.19%); it covers very general and unspecific subject areas, including the word *people* which is typically the most frequent content word.

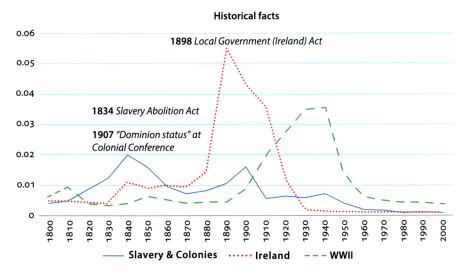

Figure 12.10 Longitudinal topic modelling of topics related to historical facts (*Slavery & Colonies*, *Ireland* and *World War II*)

Table 12.2 30 random topics out of the total 100 and their keywords and weights in the original *Mallet* output

Topic ID	Topic weight	Keywords
0	0.0214	university student college education art research science institution museum national high gallery oxford professor year cambridge work council scientific
1	0.0272	mr ireland secretary chief irish lord county dublin hon lieutenant gentleman member question cork general sir aware fact case
2	0.0355	land tenant landlord rent property case owner estate holding lease act farm improvement valuation bill compensation purchase agricultural acre
3	0.1019	people lb good country life thing money community day bad poor home man problem world job thousand family social
4	0.0759	government policy majesty proposal action present good responsibility position intention view matter office measure fact step clear minister responsible
5	0.0432	scheme fund grant money year aid lb contribution cost financial assistance purpose sum amount charity loan trustee trust payment
6	0.0272	election vote member constituency candidate representation franchise voter party majority borough reform elector system parliament bill ballot seat people
7	0.0644	house majesty petition subject opinion country lord duty motion conduct public present parliament occasion person great measure feeling respect
8	0.0655	lord noble lords friend baroness minister point lady government amendment lordship earl grateful aware honourable matter place viscount order
9	0.0751	lb issue service important community agency group work role support public programme problem area review minister level concern resource
10	0.0659	system change present great time plan country good year advantage reform result part effect improvement experiment principle proposal operation
11	0.0313	board president trade poor local rate relief law case district parish act power guardian union person workhouse inquiry guardians
12	0.0325	court case judge offence justice law jury magistrate punishment trial person criminal sentence penalty man crime imprisonment jurisdiction sheriff
13	0.0697	committee report commission recommendation select inquiry matter house evidence government royal chairman view subject advisory proposal point consideration decision
14	0.0357	mr order speaker hon point member deputy house chairman matter debate question chair madam sir time ruling standing motion
15	0.0207	government treaty country france french spain england russia war turkey europe british power foreign turkish part powers nation majesty

Table 12.2 *(continued)*

Topic ID	Topic weight	Keywords
16	0.0570	noble lord earl lordship friend lords viscount marquess duke chancellor word place opposite speech majesty salisbury thing moment opinion
17	0.0423	commissioner duty person great house subject present public expense objection object purpose commissioners opinion property respect commission man return
18	0.0714	power public control government interest body parliament authority case responsibility matter bill duty executive order question great point function
19	0.0484	minister prime statement ministers cabinet matter secretary meeting friend conference week state day official policy responsibility ministry view position
20	0.0319	european community lb europe country common union policy member treaty market state british britain council economic commission agreement negotiation
21	0.0429	secretary state india home government department indian office council governor parliamentary statement general matter present position power responsibility chief
22	0.0495	house motion day resolution order committee member business question debate time government discussion bill notice rule vote paper night
23	0.0421	scotland scottish wales england welsh glasgow member english people scotch edinburgh assembly state part advocate highland office north devolution
24	0.0148	licence beer public premise spirit licensing club alcohol drink sale person liquor licensed people whisky trade asylum registration certificate
25	0.0334	house housing building accommodation rent lb home authority property local private people problem site council subsidy owner dwelling repair
26	0.0302	society association organisation body national council voluntary member lb work people representative operative british meeting advice group institution operation
27	0.0400	man work employment labour wage unemployment worker job training unemployed employer young factory woman week industry number workman time
28	0.0497	authority local government lb area council service grant rate minister central housing community responsibility money expenditure ratepayer district provision
29	0.0277	hon mr member friend mrs lady miss gentleman minister point isle valley aware taylor castle ms dr vale sir
30	0.0230	defence air aircraft force lb ministry civil equipment machine royal service war production aviation gun supply minister operation services

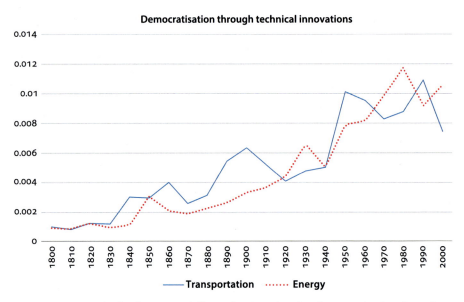

Figure 12.11 Longitudinal topic modelling of topics related to democratisation through technical innovations (*Transportation* and *Energy*)

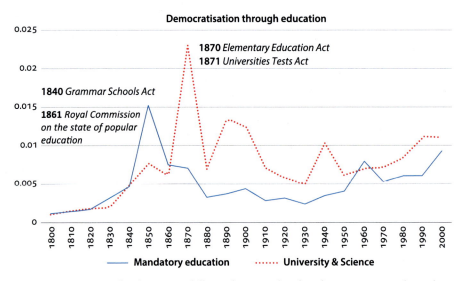

Figure 12.12 Longitudinal topic modelling of topics related to democratisation through education (*Mandatory Education* and *University & Science*)

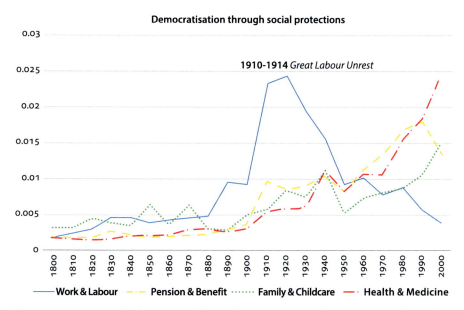

Figure 12.13 Longitudinal topic modelling of topics related to democratisation through social protections (*Work & Labour, Pension & Benefit, Family & Childcare* and *Health & Medicine*)

Figures 12.10 to 12.13 illustrate the longitudinal topic modelling of a selection of relevant topic areas across time. In these four figures, the vertical axis reflects the weight of the topic in the given decade. In Figure 12.10, the topics of *Slavery & Colonies, Ireland* and *World War II* reflect clear timescales fitting historical developments with peaks reflecting important policy acts and important political discussions. In Figure 12.11 we display topics related to democratisation through technical innovations and show that the topics *Transportation* and *Energy* have become more prevalent in parliamentary discourse across time. In Figure 12.12, reforms in the educational system are clearly reflected, both for *Mandatory Education* and *University & Science*, with peaks corresponding to important policy changes. Finally, Figure 12.13 shows that democratisation through social protection has also been prevalent in parliamentary debates, especially concerning *Work & Labour, Pension & Benefit, Family & Childcare* and *Health & Medicine*.

Some events are difficult for political representatives to ignore, such as historical events, education reforms and strikes, which influence the prevalence of certain topics over time. However, for other topics it remains difficult to assess whether the increased interest in some topics is a reflection of exogenous impacts on parliamentary debate or endogenous factors resulting from conscious decisions by parliamentarians to engage or not with certain topics.

As we have done for the linguistic features (see Section 3.3), we correlate topics with democracy, economy and education indices. Again, we display only a sample of topics that were found to exhibit interesting patterns. Table 12.3 shows particularly strong correlations between the *Health & Medicine* topic and democracy indices. On the one hand, both are highest in the latest period, pointing to independent development; on the other hand, health systems are a bigger concern in democracies. Access to medical help for everyone is a typical characteristic of democratisation. Concerning *Energy* and *Transportation*, the technological development allows citizens to spend more time on social duties and political discussions. Somewhat tongue-in-cheek our study gives a new meaning to the catchphrase "power to the people". The strong negative correlation to the *Slavery & Colonies* topic is expected, since in that political system large parts of the population were barred from any political rights, and society was deeply marked by inequality.

Table 12.3 Correlations between topics and indices of democracy, polity and GDP

	Ireland	Slavery & Colonies	WWII	Transportation	Energy	Mandatory Education	University & Science	Pension & Benefit	Family & Childcare	Health & Medicine
GDP	−0.13	−0.49	0.37	0.88	0.88	0.34	0.22	0.85	0.71	0.76
Democracy	0.05	−0.40	0.36	0.85	0.80	0.41	0.21	0.77	0.63	0.67
Polity	−0.31	−0.62	−0.11	0.73	0.88	0.27	0.32	0.85	0.85	0.98
Education	−0.42	−0.78	−0.07	0.80	0.93	−0.02	0.03	0.93	0.81	0.96

3.5 Linking linguistic and content change

Direct strong relations between linguistic features and topics related to political and social democratisation remain a matter of debate. Therefore, combining both of our research questions, we finally assess direct relations between linguistic features and topics related to political and social democratisation processes.

Table 12.4 shows that there is a strong correlation between the technical and recent debates on the topics *Pension & Benefit*, *Family & Childcare*, and *Health & Medicine*, and the technical and recent linguistic feature of noun compounds. The correlation of these topics to frequent use of the pronoun *I* is not entirely clear, but indicates that MPs often relate to their personal experience.

Again, these are not causal correlations, but possibly independent developments happening at the same time, thus resulting in secondary effect. This method, however, allows one to bridge linguistic changes and topical content variation.

Table 12.4 Correlations between topics and linguistic features

	Ireland	Slavery & Colonies	WWII	Transportation	Energy	Mandatory Education	University & Science	Pension & Benefit	Family & Childcare	Health & Medicine
NN/1kw	−0.44	−0.52	−0.19	0.31	0.53	−0.13	−0.03	0.55	0.53	0.65
VB/1kw	−0.22	−0.10	0.40	−0.36	−0.28	−0.37	−0.51	−0.14	0.00	−0.18
w/SENT	−0.22	−0.10	0.40	−0.36	−0.28	−0.37	−0.51	−0.14	0.00	−0.18
POS/1kw	0.04	0.60	−0.16	−0.91	−0.89	−0.34	−0.11	−0.87	−0.68	−0.81
VeM/1kw	−0.36	−0.58	−0.33	0.67	0.79	0.17	0.28	0.77	0.69	0.88
2NN/1kw	−0.25	−0.50	−0.19	0.56	0.70	0.26	0.35	0.68	0.80	0.91
I/1kw	−0.32	−0.67	0.04	0.86	0.97	0.24	0.26	0.95	0.83	0.95
passive/1kw	0.00	−0.53	0.53	0.79	0.76	0.20	0.01	0.80	0.63	0.63

4. Discussion and limitations of our study

In this section we discuss the implication of our findings, draw some conclusions, and consider limitations and best practices when relying on transcribed and heavily edited material to conduct linguistic analyses.

4.1 Main findings

Concerning linguistic change (RQ1), we have observed an increased use of the Saxon genitive and contractions, and shorter sentence lengths, which represent signs of colloquialisation. Furthermore, the increased frequency of the first-person pronoun *I* reflects a more subjective and personal style, while the slight increase in pronoun *we* reflects a more inclusive style. In addition, the decrease of passive constructions, a feature associated with abstract and agent-less style, is compensated by a slight move towards a more nominal style. As discussed in

Section 1.2, the observed trends are also partly explained by changes to editorial practices for the Hansard, potentially especially relevant for the increase in the first-person pronouns *I* and *we*. There is a strong increase in the frequency of compound nouns. This is, on the one hand, a linguistic change; however, on the other hand, it also reveals trends in history and society, as evident in our analysis of some individual compound nouns, namely the on-average earliest and latest ones. This investigation shows changes in content (RQ2) interacting with linguistic change (RQ1). Further, we have seen that in the latest decade, social developments are possibly more topical than technological ones.

While providing unparalleled opportunities for the empirical investigation of linguistic change (RQ1), we also showed that records of parliamentary debate are of interest for observing changes in the topical content (RQ2). First, the observed topics demonstrate timescales fitting historical developments. Second, the extracted topics also reflect political and social democratisation processes, be it through education, innovation or social protections. Third, addressing RQ3, the topics correlate with indicators of democratisation and GDP. A functioning health system is a bigger concern in individualised societies and democracies. Access to medical help for everyone is a typical feature of social democratisation. Concerning energy and transportation, technological developments have freed us to be able to have more time for self-fulfilment, social duties and activities, and for forming political opinions.

Correlating the answers to RQ1 and RQ2 allowed us to assess a further aspect of RQ3: the direct relations between linguistic features, most notably colloquialisation and compression of language, and the topical content of parliamentary discourse, particularly its underpinnings in social and political democratisation processes. We observed strong correlations, most notably between linguistic complexity in the form of compound nouns, and democracy and education indices. On the one hand, we must not forget that statistical correlations must not be understood as causal correlations, as indicators can develop in the same direction for independent reasons, and building political arguments on correlated trends is dangerous (Partington & Taylor 2018: 89–92). On the other hand, there are also other reasonable explanations for the correlations. High levels of education lead to more formal, more technical language, a sign of which is the frequency of noun compounds, and are at the same time a cornerstone of a working democracy.

4.2 Limitations

With respect to the limitations of our study, we underline several aspects. First, the material is transcribed and heavily edited (e.g. hesitation markers are consistently removed or not transcribed). This is likely to mainly influence the findings on linguistic changes. While researchers ought to be generally cautious in their use of transcriptions that have not been made for linguistic purposes, one could also argue that the changing editorial styles also reflect a global move towards colloquialisation and democratisation. Such issues have already been noted in the empirical work by Kruger and Smith (2018), Kruger, van Rooy and Smith (2019), and Kotze et al. (this volume), which show that the tension between colloquialisation and densification in political discourse is also partly accounted for by the possible influence of editorial practices on the language.

Second, the majority of topics delivered by topic modelling, but not all, are interpretable or relevant (e.g. some contain formulae of address and speakers' status, or everyday topics). Such issues could be partly overcome by comparing the results obtained from an automatic topic detection with the manual topical annotation of the transcripts, such as the one available in the SAMUELS project (Alexander et al. 2015).[8] However, the SAMUELS project merely relies on an ontology of the words and therefore does not well align with the underlying logic of topic modelling. Furthermore, including metadata on speakers, such as their political affiliations and backgrounds, could include the tagging of individual speakers, so as to enable the investigation of speaker effects on the debates. Relying on topic modelling allowed us to track changes in the content of parliamentary debates across time, which can be related to particular issues or events (Michel et al. 2010; Schneider 2020).

Third, the direct strong relations between linguistic features and topics related to political and social democratisation processes are debatable. We observed correlations, which are not to be taken as causalities, but may help us to interpret connections between social developments, technology, colloquialisation and democracy.

4.3 Outlook

Future studies could also look in more detail at the evolution of certain terms, for example by conducting document classification (e.g. *vagrant* has been increasingly replaced by *homeless*). Our investigation of individual noun compounds could also be extended further. Including more metadata will allow us to study speaker effects, and topics and stance of individual parties.

Our evidence of strong correlations between linguistic features, topics, and indices of democracy suggests broad scope for further research – an interdisciplinary extension to pragmatics, if not a new paradigm. On the one hand, linguistic changes do not happen in isolation; their social and democratic embedding

---

8. See <https://www.gla.ac.uk/schools/critical/research/fundedresearchprojects/samuels/>.

and underpinnings are an important part of the change. Merely classifying non-linguistic factors as external factors does not do justice to the complex reality. For example, the increase of noun compounds should be considered in the context of increasing complexity of technology, society and the legal system. Our investigation of the most recent and oldest noun compounds is only a beginning. As further example, moral and ethical discussions and involved personal stance typically involve modal verbs. De-contextualised linguistic studies on modal verbs risk reporting flawed results, even if the genre is considered. On the other hand, societal changes also have a strong effect on language. Higher levels of education often lead to more complex linguistic expressions, to writers and speakers who are more able and willing to express themselves in complex registers, be it for the expression of technical concepts or their political opinions when participating in deliberative democracy. Therefore, an additional contribution of our study, and a guiding light for future research, is to study societal and linguistic changes in combination – and both can be equally well detected in historical corpora.

References

Alexander, Marc, Dallachy, Fraser, Piao, Scott, Baron, Alistair & Rayson, Paul. 2015. Metaphor, popular science and semantic tagging: Distant reading with the Historical Thesaurus of English. *Digital Scholarship in the Humanities (DSH)* 30(Suppl. 1): i16–i27.

Alexander, Marc & Struan, Andrew. 2017. Digital Hansard: The politics of the uncivil. In *Digital Humanities 2017, Montréal, Conference Abstracts*, 378–380. <https://dh2017.adho.org/abstracts/DH2017-abstracts.pdf> (28 September 2021).

Baron, Naomi S. 2002. Who sets e-mail style? Prescriptivism, coping strategies, and democratising communication access. *The Information Society* 18(5): 403–413.

Bell, Allan. 2013. *The Guidebook to Sociolinguistics*. Chichester: Wiley-Blackwell.

Biber, Douglas. 1988. *Variation across Speech and Writing*. Cambridge: CUP.

Biber, Douglas. 2003. Compressed noun-phrase structures in newspaper discourse: The competing demands of popularization vs. economy. In *New Media Language*, Jean Aitchison & Diana Lewis (eds), 169–181. London: Routledge.

Biber, Douglas & Conrad, Susan. 2009. *Register, Genre, and Style*. Cambridge: CUP.

Biber, Douglas & Gray, Bethany. 2013. Being specific about historical change: The influence of sub-register. *Journal of English Linguistics* 41(2): 104–134.

Biber, Douglas, Conrad, Susan, Reppen, Randi, Byrd, Pat & Helt, Marie. 2002. Speaking and writing in the university: A multidimensional comparison. *TESOL Quarterly* 36(1): 9–48.

Blei, David M. 2012. Probabilistic topic models. *Communications of the ACM* 55(4): 77–84.

Bolt, Jutta, Inklaar, Robert, de Jong, Herman & van Zanden, Jongand L. 2018. *Maddison Project Database 2018*. <https://www.rug.nl/ggdc/historicaldevelopment/maddison/releases/maddison-project-database-2018> (31 March 2019).

C. W. 2013. Did living standards improve during the Industrial Revolution? *The Economist*, September 13. <https://www.economist.com/free-exchange/2013/09/13/did-living-standards-improve-during-the-industrial-revolution> (31 December 2020).

Church, Kenneth. 2000. Empirical estimates of adaptation: The chance of two Noriegas is closer to p/2 than p^2. *Proceedings of the 17th Conference on Computational Linguistics*, 180–186.

Cook, Susan E. 2004. New technologies and language change: Toward an anthropology of linguistic frontiers. *Annual Review of Anthropology* 33: 103–115.

Crystal, David. 2001. *Language and the Internet*. Cambridge: CUP.

Curran, Ben, Higham, Kyle, Ortiz, Elisenda & Vasques Filho, Demival. 2018. Look who's talking: Two-mode networks as representations of a topic model of New Zealand parliamentary speeches. *PLOS ONE* 13(6): e0199072.

Dwyer, Jerry. 2010. *Growth and Finance*. <http://www.jerrydwyer.com/growth/index.html> (31 March 2019).

Fairclough, Norman. 1992. *Discourse and Social Change*. Cambridge: Polity Press.

Farrelly, Michael & Seoane, Elena. 2012. Democratization. In *The Oxford Handbook of the History of English*, Terttu Nevalainen & Elizabeth Closs Traugott (eds), 392–401. Oxford: OUP.

Firth, John Rupert. 1957. *A Synopsis of Linguistic Theory 1930–1955* [Studies in Linguistic Analysis], 1–32. Oxford: Blackwell.

Gesmann, Markus & de Castillo, Diego. 2011. Using the Google Visualisation API with R. *The R Journal* 3(2): 40–44. <https://journal.r-project.org/archive/2011-2/RJournal_2011-2_Gesmann+de~Castillo.pdf> (31 July 2021).

Glowka, Wayne, Melançon, Megan & Wyckoff, Danielle. 2003. Among the new words. *American Speech* 78(2): 228–232.

Greene, Derek & Cross, James P. 2017. Exploring the political agenda of the European Parliament using a dynamic topic modeling approach. *Political Analysis* 25(1): 77–94.

Grimmer, Justin & Stewart, Brandon. 2013. Text as data: The promise and pitfalls of automatic content analysis methods for political texts. *Political Analysis* 21(3): 267–297.

Halliday, Michael A.K. & Matthiessen, Christian. 2004. *An Introduction to Functional Grammar*, 3rd edn. New York NY: Hodder.

Hallin, Daniel C. 1992. Sound bite news: Television coverage of elections. *Journal of Communication* 42(2): 5–24.

Herring, Susan C. 1993. Gender and democracy in computer-mediated communication. *The Electronic Journal of Communication* 3(2). <http://www.cios.org/EJCPUBLIC/003/2/00328.HTML> (31 July 2021).

Herring, Susan C., Johnson, Deborah & DiBenedetto, Tamra. 1995. "This discussion is going too far!": Male resistance to female participation on the Internet. In *Gender Articulated: Language and the Socially Constructed Self*, Kira Hall & Mary Bucholtz (eds), 67–96. New York NY: Routledge.

Hilpert, Martin & Gries, Stefan. 2016. Quantitative approaches to diachronic corpus linguistics. In *The Cambridge Handbook of English Historical Linguistics*, Merja Kytö & Paivi Pahta (eds), 36–53. Cambridge: CUP.

Hiltunen, Turo & Loureiro-Porto, Lucía. 2020. Democratization of Englishes: Synchronic and diachronic approaches. *Language Sciences* 79: 101275.

Hiltunen, Turo, Räikkönen, Jenni & Tyrkkö, Jukka. 2020. Investigating colloquialization in the British parliamentary record in the late 19th and early 20th century. *Language Sciences* 79: 101270.

Hou, Liwen & Smith, David. 2018. Modeling the decline in English passivization. *Proceedings of the Society for Computation in Linguistics*, vol. 1 article 5. <https://scholarworks.umass.edu/scil/vol1/iss1/5> (28 September 2021).

Huber, Magnus, Nissel, Magnus & Puga, Karin. 2016. *The Old Bailey Corpus 2.0, 1720–1913 Manual*. <https://fedora.clarin-d.uni-saarland.de/oldbailey/downloads/OBC_2.0_Manual%202016-07-13.pdf> (10 September 2018).

Hundt, Marianne & Mair, Christian. 1999. "Agile" and "uptight" genres: The corpus-based approach to language change in progress. *International Journal of Corpus Linguistics* 4(2): 221–242.

Hundt, Marianne, Schneider, Gerold & Seoane, Elena. 2016. The use of the BE-passive in academic Englishes: Local versus global usage in an international language. *Corpora* 11(1): 31–63.

Inglehart, Ronald & Welzel, Christian. 2009. How development leads to democracy: What we know about modernization today? *Foreign Affairs* 88(2): 33–48. <https://papers.ssrn.com/sol3/papers.cfm?abstract_id=2391678> (31 July 2021).

Jespersen, Otto. 1942. *A Modern English Grammar on Historical Principles*, Vol. VI. Copenhagen: Munksgaard.

Kemper, Susan. 2010. Language production in late life. In *Language Development: The Lifespan Perspective* [IMPACT: Studies in Language, Culture and Society 37], Annette Gerstenberg & Anja Voeste (eds), 59–75. Amsterdam: John Benjamins.

Korhonen, Minna & Williams, Cara Penry. 2018. Discursive *like* across apparent time in Australian English. In *Discourse-Pragmatic Variation and Change 4, Helsinki 28–30 May Conference Abstract Book*. <https://www2.helsinki.fi/sites/default/files/atoms/files/dipvac-abstractbook.pdf> (28 September 2021).

Kruger, Haidee & Smith, Adam. 2018. Colloquialization versus densification in Australian English: A multidimensional analysis of the Australian Diachronic Hansard Corpus (ADHC). *Australian Journal of Linguistics* 38(3): 293–328.

Kruger, Haidee, van Rooy, Bertus & Smith, Adam. 2019. Register change in the British and Australian Hansard (1901–2015). *Journal of English Linguistics* 47(3): 183–220.

Leech, Geoffrey. 2013. Where have all the modals gone? An essay on the declining frequency of core modal auxiliaries in recent standard English. In *English Modality: Core, Periphery and Evidentiality*, Juana I. Marín-Arrese, Marta Carretero, Jorge Arús Hita & Johan van der Auwera (eds), 95–118. Berlin: De Gruyter Mouton.

Leech, Geoffrey, Hundt, Marianne, Mair, Christian & Smith, Nicholas. 2009. *Change in Contemporary English. A Grammatical Study*. Cambridge: CUP.

Macalister, John. 2006. The Maori presence in the New Zealand English lexicon, 1850–2000: Evidence from a corpus-based study. *English World-Wide* 27(1): 1–24.

Mair, Christian. 2006. Inflected genitives are spreading in present-day English, but not necessarily to inanimate nouns. In *Corpora and the History of English*, Christian Mair & Reinhard Heuberger (eds), 235–248. Heidelberg: Winter.

Marshall, Monty G. & Elzinga-Marshall, Gabrielle. 2017. *Global Report 2017: Conflict, Governance and State Fragility*. Vienna VA: Center for Systemic Peace.

Master, Peter. 2003. Noun compounds and compressed definitions. *English Teaching Forum* 41(3): 2–25. <http://americanenglish.state.gov/files/ae/resource_files/03-41-3-b.pdf> (31 December 2020).

McCallum, Andrew Kachites. 2002. *MALLET: A Machine Learning for Language Toolkit. Ms.* <http://mallet.cs.umass.edu> (31 December 2021).

Michel, Jean-Baptiste, Shen, Yuan Kui, Aiden, Aviva P., Veres, Adrian, Gray, Matthew K., Pickett, Joseph P., Hoiberg, Dale, Clancy, Dan, Norvig, Peter, Orwant, Jon, Pinker, Steven, Nowak, Martin A. & Aiden, Erez Lieberman. 2010. Quantitative analysis of culture using millions of digitized books. *Science* 331(6014): 176–182.

Moreton, Emma & Culy, Chris. 2020. New methods, old data: Using digital technologies to explore nineteenth century letter writing practices. In *Message and Medium: English Language Practices across Old and New Media*, Carolin Tagg & Mel Evans (eds), 329–358. Berlin: De Gruyter Mouton.

Moscoso del Prado Martín, Fermín. 2016. Vocabulary, grammar, sex, and aging. *Cognitive Science* 41(4): 950–975.

Müller, Lisa. 2014. *Comparing Mass Media in Established Democracies: Patterns of Media Performance*. Basingstoke: Palgrave Macmillan.

Nevalainen, Terttu. 2015. What are historical sociolinguistics? *Journal of Historical Sociolinguistics* 1(2): 243–269.

Partington, Alan & Taylor, Charlotte. 2018. *The Language of Persuasion in Politics: An Introduction*, 2nd edn. Abingdon: Routledge.

Pennebaker, James W., Chung, Cindy K., Frazee, John, Lavergne, Gary M. & Beaver, David I. 2014. When small words foretell academic success: The case of college admissions essays. *PLoS ONE* 9(12): e115844.

Rayson, Paul. 2008. From key words to key semantic domains. *International Journal of Corpus Linguistics* 13(4): 519–549.

Rix, Kathryn. 2014. "Whatever passed in parliament ought to be communicated to the public": Reporting the proceedings of the reformed Commons, 1833–55. *Parliamentary History* 33(3): 453–474.

Ronan, Patricia & Schneider, Gerold. 2020. "A man who was just an incredible man, an incredible man": Age factors and coherence in Donald Trump's spontaneous speech. In *Linguistic Enquiries into Donald Trump's Language: From 'Fake News' to 'Tremendous Success'*, Ulrike Schneider & Matthias Eitelmann (eds), 62–84. London: Bloomsbury.

Röthlisberger, Melanie & Schneider, Gerold. 2013. *Of*-genitive versus *s*-genitive: A corpus-based analysis of possessive constructions in 20th century English. In *New Methods in Historical Corpora*, Paul Bennet, Martin Durrell, Silke Scheible & Richard J. Whitt (eds), 163–180. Stuttgart: Narr Francke Attempto.

Rudnicka, Karolina. 2018. Variation of sentence length across time and genre. In *Diachronic Corpora, Genre, and Language Change* [Studies in Corpus Linguistics 85], Richard Jason Whitt (ed.), 220–240. Amsterdam: John Benjamins.

Rühlemann, Christoph & Hilpert, Martin. 2017. Colloquialization in journalistic writing: Investigating inserts in TIME magazine with a focus on *well*. *Journal of Historical Pragmatics* 18(1): 104–135.

Schmid, Helmut. 1994. Probabilistic part-of-speech tagging using decision trees. *Proceedings of International Conference on New Methods in Language Processing, Manchester, UK, Vol. 12*, 44–49.

Schneider, Gerold. 2020. Changes in society and language: Charting poverty. In *Corpora and the Changing Society: Studies in the Evolution of English* [Studies in Corpus Linguistics 96], Paula Rautinaho, Arja Nurmi & Juhani Klemola (eds), 29–56. Amsterdam: John Benjamins.

Schneider, Gerold. (Forthcoming). Comparing data-driven to corpus-based approaches for diachronic variation: Document-classification and overuse metrics. In *Comparative Approaches to Methods in Corpus Linguistics*, Julia Schlüter & Ole Schützler (eds). Cambridge: CUP.

Schneider, Gerold, El-Assady, Menna & Lehmann, Hans Martin. 2017. Tools and methods for processing and visualizing large corpora. In *Big and Rich Data in English Corpus Linguistics: Methods and Explorations* [Studies in Variation, Contacts and Change in English 19], Turo Hiltunen, Joe McVeigh & Tanja Säily (eds). Helsinki: VARIENG. <https://varieng.helsinki.fi/series/volumes/19/schneider_el-assady_lehmann/> (31 December 2020).

Smith, Judy & Balka, Ellen. 1991. Chatting on a feminist computer network. In *Technology and Women's Voices*, Cheris Kramerae (ed.), 82–97. New York NY: Routledge & Kegan Paul.

Tausczik, Yla R. & Pennebaker, James W. 2010. The psychological meaning of words: LIWC and computerized text analysis methods. *Journal of Language and Social Psychology* 29(1): 24–54.

Tyrkkö, Jukka. 2017. Looking for rhetorical thresholds: Pronoun frequencies in political speeches. In *The Pragmatics and Stylistics of Identity Construction and Characterisation* [Studies in Variation, Contact and Change in English 17], Minna Nevala, Ursula Lutzky, Gabriella Mazzon & Carla Suhr (eds). Helsinki: VARIENG. <https://varieng.helsinki.fi/series/volumes/17/tyrkko/> (31 December 2020).

Tyrkkö, Jukka & Nevala, Minna. 2018. Lunatics, crackpots and maniacs: Mental illness and the democratisation of British public discourses. Conference presentation at ICEHL20, Edinburgh.

Wilson, Samuel M. & Peterson, Leignton C. 2002. The anthropology of online communities. *Annual Review of Anthropology* 31(1): 449–467.

Index

A

accessibility
    of data, 1–2
    of large datasets, 8
    of parliamentary discourse, 338
    of the Hansard Corpus, 24
accuracy of speeches in British Hansard, 33
adjectival modification patterns, 167–168
adjective-noun pairs, study of, 124–126
adjectives
    as important modifiers, 182
    as indicators of sentiment, 125–126, 128–130, 140
analysis of Australian Hansard data, 57
analysis of data, 264–265
analysis, multidimensional, 63
analysis, statistical
    of British Hansard, 97
    of transcripts vs. Australian Hansard, 64
analytical techniques, 18
    apodosis and *entonces* or *pues*, 325–326
    apodosis and *then*, 315, 325–326
assembly, lawful vs. unlawful, 102–103
attitude shift, indicators of, 62
audibility, effect on accuracy of Hansard, 33
Australian English, linguistic evolution of, 255–256, 273
Australian Hansard
    analysis of data from, 57
    comparison with transcripts, 60
    decontextualisation in, 58
    reduction of interpersonal elements, 58
    verbatim policy, 258

Australian parliament, 8
Australian parliamentary discourse, orthographic transcription of, 60 *see British Hansard 1889–1908*
automated data classification: pros and cons, 74, 78–79

B

background variables, 5
Barrow vs. Hansard rivalry, 35–36
big data
    perspective, 12
    pros and cons, 167–168
    techniques, 302–303
Brexit, 6, 9, 143–163
Britain vs. Europe, 138
British Empire, 9, 122–123
British English, 10
British Hansard
    accuracy of, 26, 33, 200
    as a complete dataset, 199–200
    as a verbatim transcript, 25–26
    considerations pre- and post-1909, 200
    contributors to, 50
    correction of, 33
    detail of vs. newspapers, 38
    digitisation of, 22, 90
    employment relationship in, 175–189
    fidelity of, 27, 91
    incompleteness of, 34, 46
    linguistic outline 1803–present, 49
    production of, 259
    reported speech in the early, 31
    size of by year and series, 22
    sources of, 36–37
    the series of, 23
    two major phases of, 22

British Hansard 1803–1888
    linguistic characteristics, 38–39
    overview, 29–40
British Hansard 1889–1908
    funding challenges, 40
    linguistic characteristics, 42
    overview, 40–43
British Hansard 1909–present
    full-length verbatim reporting, 43
    in-house reporting, 43
    overview, 43–48
British Hansard Corpus, history and language, 7
British Hansard in the 1800s, 21
British Hansard publishers, 23–24, 42
British Hansard's volumes, structure of, 21
British parliament, 11
British parliament as a debate parliament, 309
British vs. Australian Hansard: restrictive relative clause markers, 265–268, 271

C

close reading, 59, 61–62, 64–72, 120–121, 188
close reading vs. distant reading, 8, 56–57, 85–86, 120–121
Cobbett's Parliamentary Debates, 20, 23
codeswitching in parliaments, 7
collocation of
    lexical verbs, 158, 161
    lunatic, 218–221
collocation, computational, 98
colloquialisation
    and democratisation, 336–337, 366
    contractions in, 351–353
    effect on relativiser choice, 270

in Australian Hansard, 65
in parliamentary discourse, 310
of English, 11
of parliamentary language, 6
shorter sentences as indicators of, 351
colonial language, parliamentary discourse as a barometer of, 6, 127, 134–135
colonial policy: effect on language, 283–284
colonies, language of, 11
communication within parliament, 4, 262
compression of English, 11
concordance
corpora, 156
research, 98, 101, 108
searches, 287
concordance statistic (C-index), 269
conditional construction, position of *if/si*, 326–328
conditionals
analysis of, 315
degree of likelihood of, 323–325
discourse-pragmatic functions, 311–312
frequency in parliamentary discourse, 316–318
metafunctions of, 318–322
parliamentary discourse and, 313–314
conservatism, stylistic
see editorial decisions
contemporary corpora, comparison with Hansard Corpus, 119
contextualisation of *foreign immigrant*, 123–124
contractions in colloquialisation, 351–353
corpora
as indicators of changes in society, 9
design of, 2–3
to study social changes and events, 9
to track sociocultural changes and events, 10

corpus
characteristics of a, 2, 121
compilation of a, 2–3
corpus linguistics
in cultural studies, 134–139
keywords, 98
corpus-assisted discourse studies (CADS), 144
corpus-linguistic methods, value of, 12
corpus-pragmatic approach, 228, 234–236
correction of British Hansard, rules for, 92
critical discourse analysis (CDA), 143–145
cross-linguistic research, 308–330
cultural studies, corpus linguistics in, 134–139

D
data
accessibility of, 1–2, 90, 95–96
different forms of, 1–2
historical, 1–2
interpretation thereof from distant reading analyses, 75
reliability of, 12
searchable, 3, 90, 93, 95–96, 99, 102, 115
use of, 1–2, 91
visualisation of, 110–116
data analysis
inclusion vs. exclusion criteria, 147
validity of, 246
data collection
automated (online), 4, 279
systematic, 4
data selection for corpus construction, 285
data, parliamentary
different uses of, 11
nature of parameters studied, 6
dataset
Hansard as a complete, 199–200
House of Commons, 143, 163

datasets, large
accessibility of, 8
power and problems of, 3
usefulness of, 4
De Nationale Assemblée (DNA)
composition of, 284
rules of conduct, 285
usefulness of data, 284–285
democracy indices, correlation with, 345
democratisation, 9, 167–191
and colloquialisation, 336–337, 366
as a political concept, 170
definition of, 194
effect of Industrial Revolution on, 169
effect on language, 194
inclusive language in, 365
linguistic definition, 337–338
political definition, 337–338
topic modelling with, 359–364, 366–367
demographic composition of parliaments, 5
demonstratives: use of in Australian Hansard, 79, 82
Diario de Sesiones del Congreso de los Diputados (Journal of Sittings of the Spanish Parliament), 310–314, 316–318
digital collections, 3
usefulness of, 278
digital corpora, production of, 279
Digital Humanities, 3, 56, 121, 336
digitisation of British Hansard, 90, 100
dimension score analysis, 72–76
direct speech (DS), 28
discourse markers
function in parliamentary discourse, 70
in Australian Hansard, 69–71
discrimination, colour, of the 1970s, 137–138
discussion distribution, patterns of, 102–103
diglossia, 'leaky', as an indicator of language shift, 281

Index   375

distant reading, 63–64, 72–80,
120–121
distant reading analyses,
interpretation of, 76, 242
distant reading vs. close, 8, 56–57,
85–86, 120–121
distributional analysis of relative
markers, 265–268
DNA corpus
construction and analysis,
285–288
distribution of er in,
293–294
frequency of lexemes in,
296–297
Dutch, Netherlandic
Dutch, Netherlandic vs.
Surinamese, 289–301
Dutch, Surinamese, 277, 279,
281–284

E
editing of transcripts to produce
Hansard, 58
editorial decisions
consistency of, 70
effect on Australian
Hansard, 61, 65–69,
76–79, 82–83, 86
effect on Hansard Corpus,
27, 38, 91, 171–172
editorial policy
Australian Hansard, 55
British Hansard, 34
changes over time, 10, 58,
68–69, 71–72
effect on linguistic change,
348, 366
education and language, 358
Elan project, 286–287
emigration *see migration*
employment relationship in the
British Hansard, 175–189
er (there)
distribution in DNA corpus,
293–294
Dutch particle, 289–294
in Belgian Dutch, 290
uses in Netherlandic Dutch,
290–292
uses in Sranantongo,
292–293

European Union
British attitude towards, 138
inclusion of the UK, 144
study of pronouns to
indicate attitude of British
MPs towards, 9, 149–153
expert knowledge
definition of, 227, 233
in policymaking, 227–228
to support political claims,
228, 244
expert, rhetorical function of
terms, 243–246
expertise, types of, 232–233
experts
characteristics of, 229
communication strategies
of, 230
role in technical decision-
making, 230–231
extensible markup language
(XML) version of the Hansard
Corpus, 145, 201

F
first-person content, 31
first-person pronouns
as indicators of
colloquialisation, 344, 348
as indicators of rhetorical
strategy, 67
categories in the British
Hansard, 150
frequency in the Hansard
Corpus, 32, 41–42
first-person vs. third-person
pronouns, 66–69
first-person vs. third-person
reporting, 42–43
foreign immigrant,
contextualisation of, 123–124
formalisation of Hansard
content, 58
formality
changes in, 69, 78
indicators of, 66–69, 71–72,
82–83
free direct speech (FDS), 28, 30,
39, 48
free indirect speech (FIS), 28
full-length verbatim reporting, 43

H
Hansard
2017 definition of, 46
as a written representation
of spoken discourse, 55,
90, 121
purpose of, 49, 90–91
rivalry vs. Barrow, 35–36
use by other
Commonwealth
countries, 258
usefulness to linguists, 26,
50, 91
Hansard at Huddersfield
function of, 94
interpretation of data from,
101, 115
keyword plots, 113–114
minimising
misinterpretation, 115
searching the, 99, 102
tagging inaccuracies in, 94
to track historical events or
figures, 99–103
to track topics, 109–113
to track word usage,
104–109, 112
Hansard competitors:
Mirror/Barrow, 35
Hansard content, formalisation
of, 58
Hansard corpora, versions of, 25
Hansard Corpus
accessibility of, 24, 90
analysis of, 18
complexity of, 18
density of, 18
effect of editorial decisions
on, 27
extensible markup language
(XML) version, 145, 201
online, 171, 201
size of, 18, 202
understanding of, 18
Hansard language, features of, 17
Hansard Publishing Union,
40–41
Hansard's Parliamentary Debates,
23
Hansard's Parliamentary Debates
vs. *Official Report*, 31

Hansard's Parliamentary Debates,
accuracy of, 36–37
historical events
effect on language, 280
indicators of, 186–189
Historical Thesaurus of English,
use of, 9–10, 225–226, 235
House of Commons, 9, 19, 21, 33,
105, 143, 163
House of Commons vs. House of
Lords: linguistic patterns, 340,
354–356
House of Lords, 21, 33, 199
House of Lords verbosity, 356

I

immigration *see migration*
imperfect marking: Surinamese
vs. Netherlandic Dutch,
299–301
inclusion vs. exclusion criteria in
data analysis, 147
inclusive language in
democratisation, 365
India, colonial attitude towards,
134–136
indicators of activity, verbs as,
157, 160
indicators of attitude shift, 62
indicators of sentiment towards
master–servant relationship,
173
indicators of colloquialisation,
first-person pronouns as, 344,
348
indicators of cultural change, 235,
240
indicators of democratisation,
adjectival and prepositional
modifications as, 167–168
indicators of formality, 66–69,
71–72
indicators of narrative vs. non-
narrative reporting, 73
indicators of rhetorical strategy,
first-person pronouns as, 67
indicators of sentiment of Britain
towards the EU, 159, 162
indicators of sentiment towards
mental illness, 195, 197, 199,
213, 215, 220–222

indicators of sentiment,
adjectives as, 125–126, 128–130,
140
indirect speech (IS), 28, 30
Industrial Revolution
effect on democratisation,
169
effect on language, 339
ingroup inclusion
effect of 21st century EU
developments, 151–152
indicators of, 159–160
in-house reporting in British
Hansard 1909–present, 43
innovation, noun compounds as
indicators of, 349
in-person reporting, importance
of, 47
interface of spoken and written
language, 6–7
interpretation in parliaments, 7
IQ and race, 137
Irish
as a race, 134
discourse regarding mental
health, 218

K

key terms
democratisation, 9, 172–173,
180, 186, 189–190
employment, 175, 179
expert, 236–241
expert knowledge, 241–243
master, frequencies of
referents of, 182, 190
mental health, 195, 199,
201–205, 225–226
mental health patients,
206–211
migration, 124
personal pronouns, 9
psychiatric illnesses, 212–213
psychiatric institutions,
212–215
race in the Hansard Corpus,
119–120
servant, frequency of, 190
which, that, 10
keywords in corpus linguistics,
98, 113

L

labour legislation, changes in,
169–170
Lancaster-Oslo-Bergen (LOB)
Corpus, 22
language processing, 263–264
language transmission in
Suriname, 282
legal discourse, parliamentary
discourse as, 313
legislation, mental health:
influence on and by discourse,
198–199, 220–222
legislation: master–servant
relationship, 169
lemma search, 128
lexemes in the *DNA* corpus,
296–297
lexical shift, 216
lexical verbs
collocation of, 158, 161
study of, 156–157, 160
lingua franca, unofficial, in
Suriname, 284
linguistic changes and social
changes, relationship between,
340–341
linguistic changes over time,
347–353
linguistic corpora, 1–2
linguistic features and external
indices, correlation of, 356–358
linguistic norms, distant central,
6
linguistic outliers as indicators of
historical events, 186–189
linguistic patterning, 11
linguistic patterns
changes in parliamentary,
340–341
differences between House
of Lords and House of
Commons, 340, 354–356
subconscious, 174
linguistic trauma, definition of,
202
linguistic usefulness of Hansard,
26
linguistic variation, 11
linguistics, scope of, 1
local use (vs. distant central
linguistic norms), 6

lunatic, case study of the term, 217–220

M

Margaret Thatcher, 109
markers of conditionality, prototypical: in English and Spanish, 308–310
master–servant relationship
  indicators of changing sentiment towards, 173
  legislation governing, 169
mediation in parliaments, 7
megacorpus, characteristics of the ideal, 4
mental health discourse, highest frequency of, 205
mental health in Britain
  indicators of sentiment towards, 195, 207
  overview, 9–10
  pre-1800, 196
  stigma of, 195
mental health, emergence of new terms, 197
mental health, major shifts in lexis thereof, 220–222
metafunctions of conditionals in Spanish, 318
migration, 9, 122–126
  effect on language, 280
  indicators of sentiment towards, 139–140
  tracking of word usage, 124
  use of Hansard to establish historical discourse, 139–140
Mirror of Parliament
  accuracy of, 39
  competitor of British Hansard, 34–35
modal verbs, 351
modals
  as indicators of formality, 71–72
  in Australian Hansard, 71–72
modification patterns, adjectival and prepositional, 167–168
Multidimensional Analysis Tagger (MAT), 63–64
multilingualism in parliaments, 7

N

narrative report of speech acts (NRSA), 28, 30–31, 39, 42
narrative style, trend towards, 73
narrative vs. non-narrative reporting, indicators of, 73
narrator vs. reporter, difference between, 27
noun compounds as indicators, 131
noun compounds as indicators of innovation, 349
nouns and noun compounds, frequency of, 343–344, 348
NRSA sources, limitations of, 34

O

Official Report
  accuracy of, 45–46
  construction of, 46–47
  editorial policy, 44–45, 47–48
  inauguration of, 21
Official Report vs. *Hansard's Parliamentary Debates*, 31
Official Report vs. transcripts: discrepancies of pronouns, 174
Old Bailey Corpus, 173
one-third rule, 41–42
oral discourse vs. written, 8
orthographic transcription of Australian parliamentary discourse, 60
outgroup languages in Suriname, 281

P

parallel corpora, 8
parliamentary archives/records, 1–2
parliamentary corpora, comparison of spoken and written, 303
parliamentary data
  analysis of, 8
  rich potential of, 8
Parliamentary Debates (Official Report), 24
Parliamentary Debates
  changes in content of, 341–342

production after Hansard business was sold, 21
parliamentary discourse, 1
  accessibility of, 338
  as a barometer of colonial vs. post-colonial language, 6, 127–128
  as legal discourse, 313
  changes in recording techniques over time, 339
  colloquialisation in, 310
  complete dataset of, 199–200
  conditionals in, 313–314
  effect of time on, 5
Parliamentary Discourse project, 22
parliamentary language, 1
  colloquialisation of, 6
  corpora of, 279
  definition of, 4
  driver or inhibitor of change, 278
  history of, 119
parliamentary records, oral vs. official, 8
parliamentary reporting
  accuracy of, 19–20, 200
  increase before 1803, 20
  prohibition of in the UK, 19
parliamentary speeches
  interventions in, 127–128
  nuances of reporting of, 48
parliaments, demographic composition of, 5
passive forms, frequency of, 344
personal pronoun use in ingroup vs. outgroup separation, 162
personal pronoun we, 143–145
personal pronouns, 9
Peterloo Massacre, 99–103
political party differences: attitude towards EU, 153–155
polysemous terms in mental health discourse, 204
possessive constructions in employment-related terms in the British Hansard, 176, 178, 191
POS-tagging, 344

post-colonial language,
parliamentary discourse as a
barometer of, 6
pragmatism in parliamentary
discourse, 11
predictors of relative marker
variation, 253, 261–264
predictors of relativiser choice,
269–271
prepositional modification
patterns as indicators of
democratisation, 167–168
prescriptivism
effect on speech and
writing, 257–258
in restrictive relative clause
choice, 252, 256–258, 270
specific to Hansard, 262
prescriptivism and processing,
interplay of, 10
pronouns as indicators of
formality, 66–69
pronouns, discrepancies in
Official Report vs. transcripts,
174
pronoun-verb compounds, study
of, 148
protasis–apodosis position,
preferential, 330
publishers of British Hansard,
23–24

Q

quotations within the Hansard,
123

R

race, 9
18th and 19th century
definition of, 127
approaches to in linguistics,
121
change in usage, 127–128
colonial vs. contemporary
discourse, 127, 130–131
raciolinguistics, purpose of,
121–122
racism, 133, 136
recency of nouns, 349–350
referents
first-person pronouns in
British Hansard, 150

importance of, 107
register variation, 72
relative clauses, definition of
restrictive vs. non-restrictive,
254
relative marker variation,
predictors of, 253, 261–264
relative markers which, that, 10
relative markers which, that,
distributional analysis of,
265–268
relativiser choice, predictors of,
269–270
relativisers
formal, 251
informal, 251
wh-, 255
reliability of data, 12
reported speech in the early
Hansard, 31
reporter vs. narrator, difference
between, 27
research design
corpus pragmatic approach,
228, 234–236
mixed methods, 228,
234–236
quantitative vs. qualitative,
4, 120
research methodology
collocation, 146
concordance, 146
manual analysis/annotation,
315
mixed methods, 195
qualitative, 93
sampling, 259–260
variable clustering, 215–217
research potential: British
Hansard, 91–92
restrictive clauses, markers of, 10
restrictive relative clause markers
British vs. Australian
Hansard, 265–268, 271
differences in American
English, 255
prior research into, 251–252
rhetorical strategy, indicators of,
67

S

sampling techniques:
randomised tokens, 314,
342–343
search strings, use of, 122
search techniques
adjective-noun compound,
183
comparison of, 125
lemma search, 128, 130
lexical verbs, 156
search span, 146
selection criteria, 260
term selection, 195
searches, regex, 300–301
second-person pronouns in
parliamentary discourse, 68,
262
semantic shift: lunatic, 207–209
sentence length as an indicator of
colloquialisation, 351
shorthand records neglected by
newspapers, 36
social change, 11
social changes and linguistic
changes, relationship between,
340–341
sociocultural changes and events
effect on language, 10
indicators of, 9
sociocultural factors: impact on
language, 9
sociolinguistic variables, 5
Spanish grammar, conditionals
in, 312 *see Diario de Sesiones
del Congreso de los Diputados*
Spanish parliament, 11
Spanish parliament as a working
parliament, 309
speech report interference, 27
speech representation, factors
that influence, 7
speech to text: automated, 286
advantages of, 288
inaccuracy of, 287
speeches, uncorrected, in British
Hansard, 33
speech-to-text software, 11
spoken discourse, reduction of
features thereof in Australian
Hansard, 80–82
spoken English vs. written, 252

spoken language vs. written, 6–7
spoken language, variations in, 11
Sranantongo (Sranan), 277, 280–282, 284
Stanford Tagger, 260
statistical analysis
    of frequencies, 205, 252
    of quantitative results, 205–217, 252
sub-corpora, complementary, 60–61
sub-corpora, complementary: features for investigation, 61
supplementary contemporary material, British Hansard, 50
Suriname
    language transmission in, 282
    languages of, 278
    linguistic history of, 280–283
    parliamentary language of, 302

T
tagging of corpus text, 24
term frequency by genre, 350–351
term selection, 236–238, 241
    European Community, 146
    mental health, 201–204
    search strings, 122
    searching Hansard at Huddersfield, 107
    searching the Hansard Corpus, 172–173
terminology shifts as a result of World War II, 10
that as a restrictive relative clause marker, preference for, 254
that as an informal relativiser, 251
that-rule, 252, 256–257, 268
third-person vs. first-person pronouns, 66–69

Thomas Curson (T.C.) Hansard Jnr, 20
Thomas Curson (T.C.) Hansard Jnr, retirement of, 21, 40
Thomas Curson (T.C.) Hansard Snr, 20
Thomas Curson (T.C.) Hansard Snr, death of, 21
time (of year and during election cycle), effect on parliamentary discourse, 5
timeframe as a predictor of relative marker alternation, 271
topic modelling, 345–346, 359–364, 366–367
topics
    frequency and significance of, 39
    peaks of discussion, 123
tracking
    of democratisation, 167–168
    of historical discourse, 139–140
    of historical events or figures, 99–103, 186–189
    of topics, 109–113
    of word usage, 104–109, 112, 119–120, 124
transcription as the interface between spoken and written language, 6–7
transcription, orthographic: of Australian parliamentary discourse, 60
transcripts
    clarity in, 26
    different types of, 26
    fidelity of, 28
transcripts vs. Australian Hansard
    changes in frequency of selected markers, 65

convergence over time, 86–87
reduction of spoken discourse features, 80–82
use of demonstratives, 79, 82
transcripts vs. *Official Report*: discrepancies of pronouns, 174
translation in parliaments, 7
turnaround time of British Hansard, 90

V
variable clustering, 215–217
variation, register, 72
verbatim
    definition of, 26, 43
    elements most likely to be reported, 93
verbatim policy, Australian Hansard, 258
verbs as indicators
    of activity, 157, 160
    of sentiment, 159
video recordings of Surinamese parliament, 278

W
which as a formal relativiser, 251
which as a restrictive relative clause marker, preference for, 252
word clouds, 110–112
word order: Surinamese vs. Netherlandic Dutch, 295–299
World War II, effects on language, 10
written discourse vs. oral, 8
written English vs. spoken, 252
written language vs. spoken, 6–7